# STAFFORD CRIPPS' MISSION TO MOSCOW, 1940–42

Cripps in June 1941

# STAFFORD CRIPPS' MISSION TO MOSCOW, 1940–42

oꙩoooꙩo

GABRIEL GORODETSKY

*Senior Lecturer in History, Tel Aviv University*

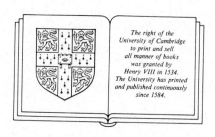

The right of the
University of Cambridge
to print and sell
all manner of books
was granted by
Henry VIII in 1534.
The University has printed
and published continuously
since 1584.

## CAMBRIDGE UNIVERSITY PRESS

*Cambridge*

*London   New York   New Rochelle*

*Melbourne   Sydney*

Published by the Press Syndicate of the University of Cambridge
The Pitt Building, Trumpington Street, Cambridge CB2 1RP
32 East 57th Street, New York, NY 10022, USA
296 Beaconsfield Parade, Middle Park, Melbourne 3206, Australia

First published 1984

Printed in Great Britain at the University Press, Cambridge

Library of Congress catalogue card number: 84-7613

*British Library cataloguing in publication data*
Gorodetsky, Gabriel
Stafford Cripps' mission to Moscow, 1940–42.
1.. Cripps, *Sir* Stafford   2. World War,
1939–1945 – Diplomatic history   3. Great
Britain – Foreign relations – Soviet Union
4. Soviet Union – Foreign relations –
Great Britain
I. Title
940.53′22′41   D750

ISBN 0 521 23866 8

# CONTENTS

# Contents

# ILLUSTRATIONS

## Illustrations

# PREFACE

In the study of the Soviet Union's relations with the West the prevalent historiographical tendency has been to distinguish between two periods: the inter-war years and 1941 onwards. The interest of most historians in the earlier period has focused on the question of whether the emergence of the Soviet Union as an expansionist super-power after the Second World War was the realization of a blueprint conceived by Stalin in the 1920s, and in which the Ribbentrop–Molotov pact was a landmark, or whether it was an *ad hoc* consequence of the closing stages of the war.[1] From the British point of view, it has often been debated whether the Soviet Union's superseding of Britain as the major power in Europe was a result of diplomatic and strategic blunders committed during the war or a reflection of Britain's gradual decline since the First World War. Relations between the two countries therefore assume utmost importance for the understanding of the post-war order. And yet, it is surprising that 1941 is chosen as the dividing line between the two periods. Although formally it was only then that both Russia and the United States became involved in the war, the clues to understanding the course of the war, the nature of the alliance and the seeds of subsequent conflict are all to be found in the crucial period of 1939–41. This is a blank page in not only Soviet but also western historiography.

The little that has been written is highly emotional and is influenced by either the atmosphere of the German–Soviet pact or anachronistic Cold War attitudes. An objective analysis of this period, based on the ample archival material and collections of private papers now available, is urgently called for. The records provide us with clear answers to the questions of how far the British were aware of the changing balance of power, what they were doing to redress it and how it all affected their relations with Russia at that time. The conduct of Anglo-Soviet relations sheds light on the British perception of war aims, which was the source

of most subsequent major conflicts. Moreover, the increasing involvement of the United States in the course of Anglo-Soviet relations, which can be traced back to summer 1940, further demonstrates the gradual dependence of British policy-making on the Americans.

In fact, it can be confidently asserted that 1939–41 was the most traumatic and dynamic period of the war, in which the illusions of peace created at Versailles were totally shattered and a completely new map of Europe was being drawn. The new geopolitical conditions and the demonstration by the Germans of their military might brought about a shift in attitudes and policies. For the Soviet Union, this period saw the erosion of the position of aloofness and manoeuvrability gained by the Ribbentrop–Molotov pact; she was forced to contend with continuously changing circumstances such as the Winter War, the annexation of the Baltic States, Bessarabia and Northern Bukovina and frequent reorientations in relations with Britain and Germany. Britain, having lost practically all her allies on the Continent, had to reckon with the least welcome alternative of an alliance with the Soviet Union. Thus the story of the dynamic changes in Anglo-Soviet relations during these years provides an insight into the formulation of new policies which were to be followed with little fluctuation from 1941 onwards.

Also instructive in this context is an examination of the sharp swings in public opinion and policies of the different political parties in keeping pace with events. In Britain, the Nazi–Soviet pact and policies in Finland and the Baltic countries inspired a wave of protest and indignation across the political spectrum, to be replaced after the German invasion of Russia by enthusiastic and uncritical support of the Soviet Union. Similar changes occurred in Russia, where the benevolent tenor of relations with Germany after the pact contrasts with the earlier vehement and consistent anti-Nazi stance and the later fierce and emotional anti-German sentiments and the spirit of amity discernible in relations with the West.

In view of the British government's slow adaptation to the altering circumstances and lack of a clear definition of war aims, the diplomatic service played a valuable role in policy-making. After the fall of France the embassy in Moscow became, with the sole exception of that at Washington, the most vital legation abroad. This post was assigned to

Sir Stafford Cripps, whose mission to Russia from early 1940 to 1942 thus assumes special significance.

The two decades prior to the opening of the archives saw the predominance of Churchill's voluminous personal history of the Second World War with its persuasive, but often misleading, interpretation of the war. Relations with Russia, in which Cripps took a prominent part in the crucial formative stages of the alliance, are a case in point. They were examined in the light of the Cold War, Cripps' major political challenge to Churchill in 1942 and their continued political rivalry after the war. Cripps emerges from Churchill's memoirs as an *enfant terrible*, an image he had projected throughout the 1930s. His refusal to transmit Churchill's famous warning to Stalin about the German invasion, for example, is blown up out of all proportion to expose his rebellious and erratic behaviour contrasted with Churchill's strategic wisdom and foresight. Unfortunately the occasional references to Cripps have established an erroneous version which has been uncritically repeated since. The documentary sources reveal a different figure, inspired by a vision and yet possessing a pragmatic and detached approach to pressing issues, which made his ambassadorship so impressive. The evaluation of Cripps has also suffered from the failure of his contemporaries to place him in a familiar political framework. His original political thinking, cutting across conventional party allegiances, his social origins and standing and his eccentricities provoked conflicting and confusing reminiscences from politicians of different convictions. The mission to Moscow and its aftermath are therefore fertile ground for myths.

The detraction of Cripps is perhaps understandable from another point of view. Cripps' mission, culminating in the challenge to Churchill at the end of 1941, symbolizes the closing chapters of Britain's unrivalled international leadership and Churchill's 'finest hour', and the dawn of a new period of social reforms at home and political decline abroad. Cripps' confrontation with Churchill, the undoubted leitmotif of the mission, was not merely a struggle for power but a clash between Cripps' search for revolutionary post-war reconstruction and Churchill's commitment to the war effort and defence of the British pre-war order.

The distortion might have been amended by the three biographies of Cripps.[2] However, there is much to be said for well-researched mono-

graphs focusing on crucial phases of a politician's public life as opposed to a full biography. The chapters in the biographies relating to Cripps' mission are based on scraps of information and hardly uncover the tip of the iceberg. Moreover Estorick's better-known biography was written during Cripps' lifetime under the auspices of the family and tends to gloss over controversial issues.

To some extent the deficiencies are remedied by H. Hanak's penetrating study of the mission.[3] Naturally the format of an article is too limiting for an adequate integration of the personal side of the mission into the larger scope of Anglo-Soviet relations and the general course of the war. Moreover the mission should be treated as a whole. The events after the German invasion of Russia can hardly be regarded as an anticlimax. The mission shows distinct continuity and progress, reaching its peak with Cripps' open antagonism with the government on the eve of his final return to London.

An exhaustive investigation of Cripps' activities within the swiftly changing framework of Anglo-Soviet relations at the outbreak of the war and the creation of the Grand Alliance is definitely called for. Cripps' mission provides the historian with a unique opportunity for scrutinizing the motives behind the formulation of British policy towards Russia. Cripps' unorthodox diplomacy, radical outlook, intervention in policy-making and presentation of alternative policies evoked ceaseless confrontations with the government and the civil servants, testing the British ability to adapt to the changing circumstances in 1939–41. Thus the study of the mission opens up a whole new dimension on vital related issues such as the British and Soviet appreciation of and reaction to intelligence on 'Barbarossa', the nature of the alliance which was taking shape, the origins of the controversy over assistance, the 'second front' and frontier issues – all indispensable for the understanding of the Grand Alliance and the ensuing Cold War. The historian must weigh the relative influence of the different personalities, preconceived ideas and dynamic reappraisals in the formulations of relations with Russia and grasp the underestimated role of the civil service in the policy-making process and the impact of political concepts on the perceptions of the armed forces.

The mission also provides an insight into Cripps' meteoric political rise from a dejected radical backbencher in the late 1930s to membership in the small War Cabinet in early 1942, posing an unprecedented

challenge to Churchill's almost unassailable position as warlord, and eventually to a prominent position in Labour's post-war government. Did the metamorphosis reflect an acute change, as is often suggested, in Cripps' political outlook – a process of maturation effected by an allegedly disappointing experience in Moscow, the bastion of world revolution? Or did the pendulum of British politics swing towards Cripps' steadfastly held opinions?

Largely owing to the influence of Churchill's account, the question of Cripps' standing with the Russians has overshadowed his ceaseless and substantial confrontation with the government. Most accounts echo Churchill's doubts as to the wisdom of sending to Russia a socialist rather than a 'rude duke'.[4] But this oversimplified view overlooks the fact that the Russians gave their consent to the appointment and that their relations with Cripps underwent several reversals during his stay in Moscow. It is arguable in fact that Cripps' political convictions were of more immediate concern to the Cabinet in London. Indeed, it is worth examining whether the fluctuating Soviet attitudes were not merely a reflection of their view of the British government and whether blaming Cripps for the failure to achieve rapprochement does not conceal the government's own negligence.

Cripps' confrontation is particularly noteworthy in view of the virtual disappearance of Labour's traditional moderating influence on the policies pursued towards the Soviet Union. The reader may be justifiably perplexed by the wavering of Labour's international and strategic policies. This process started with the embarrassment over the Ribbentrop–Molotov pact and the Winter War, when Labour tried to shake off any insinuation of association with Russia. Surprisingly its policies underwent little alteration despite the enthusiasm which the Russian resistance inspired in the British public after the German invasion.

The distinctive feature of this book in comparison with earlier studies of the mission is the combined use of official and private papers. The earlier biographies of Cripps, published before the records at the Public Record Office were made available for research, were based on a selection of private papers and interviews. This limitation inevitably resulted in a one-sided portrait. Moreover, the abundant records of the Foreign Office, Cabinet Committees and armed forces provide evidence on a variety of aspects of the mission which are otherwise

incomprehensible. On the other hand, private papers are equally indispensable as Cripps, by no means a conventional diplomat, laxly observed the Foreign Office's routine practice of reporting. There are, for instance, large gaps in the Foreign Office's records covering the period from June 1941, the invasion of Russia, to the end of Cripps' mission, which can only be bridged by Cripps' meticulously kept daily letter-diary.

A serious handicap in tracing Cripps' own correspondence is his political isolation; the great majority of his letters was addressed to members of his family and is deposited with his current biographer, Mr Maurice Shock. His otherwise occasional correspondence had to be dug out from a large number of archives which yielded infrequent though often significant results. The Cripps archives at Nuffield College, Oxford, are somewhat disappointing for this period since they contain mostly official and printed material. Because of the increasing American intervention in the war the National Archives in Washington and various collections of private papers, notably in the Library of Congress and at Hyde Park, New York, were also consulted.

It can only be regretted that the Soviet archives are inaccessible and are rarely quoted, even by Soviet historians. The period on the whole is the least studied in Soviet diplomatic history, but the relevant Soviet histories and memoirs have been consulted and referred to in the text. It was nonetheless possible to illuminate many aspects of Soviet foreign policy through western sources.

Information on all collections and their location can be found in the acknowledgements and bibliography. The bibliography does not purport to be a comprehensive list of books on the subject but rather contains the works which are either referred to in the text or are of immediate concern to the story.

Unfortunately, the latest volume in M. Gilbert's biography of Churchill, *Finest Hour: Winston S. Churchill 1939–1941* (London, 1983), dealing with the period examined here, reached me after the completion of this book.

# ACKNOWLEDGEMENTS

This book is the fruit of research carried out in 1979–80 when I was a visiting fellow at St Antony's College, Oxford. I am grateful to the Warden and Fellows of the College for the congenial atmosphere which I encountered there.

I am deeply indebted to Maurice Shock, Vice-Chancellor of the University of Leicester, who is writing a biography of Cripps, for his unstinted assistance throughout my work. He was kind enough to permit me unrestricted access to Sir Stafford Cripps' papers, including a voluminous and revealing diary, and gave me the benefit of several stimulating conversations. He also read the manuscript with close attention and made suggestions of great value. The responsibility for the opinions expressed in the final version, however, is mine alone.

I am most grateful to the late Lord Butler of Saffron Walden, Governor W. Averell Harriman, the late Professor Michael Postan, Lady Ricketts, Sir John Russell and Sir Geoffrey Wilson for sharing their recollections with me. Lady Ricketts kindly allowed me to consult those fragments of her diary bearing on political issues and to reproduce a number of photographs from the family album. Governor Harriman likewise made available to me rare photographs of his visit to Moscow in summer 1941. I am also indebted to Sir John Cripps for permitting me to reproduce an historic photograph from the collection in his possession. I should like to express my deep appreciation to Mrs Peggy Appiah, who painstakingly copied for me her father's letters from Moscow as well as conveying her own impressions, and to Sir Tobias Weaver, who placed at my disposal copies of letters from Cripps.

I owe a special debt to my editor at Cambridge University Press, Elizabeth Wetton, for her enthusiastic and cooperative treatment of the production of the book. I wish to thank Professor Shlomo Ben-Ami, Head of the School of History at Tel Aviv University, for providing

financial assistance in the final stages of the book's preparation. I also wish to thank my friend Professor Etan Kohlberg for his careful reading of the manuscript and for his advice on form and presentation.

The ultimate expression of gratitude belongs to my wife Sue for her invaluable criticisms, meticulous editorial help and above all tolerance of the inevitable burden which the writing of the book introduced into our lives.

I would like this work to be a tribute to the late E. H. Carr, who encouraged me to embark on the project when I was first considering it. I was fortunate to be able to draw on his unrivalled understanding of Soviet foreign policy in the inter-war period in a number of conversations up to his death in 1982.

# ORIGINS OF THE MISSION

### Early involvement

The outbreak of the Second World War marked a watershed in the political career of Stafford Cripps, who had just turned fifty. A decade of radical activity on the fringes of British politics was drawing to an end. In June 1939 Cripps' protracted campaign for a united front against fascism had provoked his expulsion from the Labour Party. Just as unsuccessful was his attempt to find a common cause with Tories opposed to Chamberlain, notably Churchill and Eden, during the negotiations with Russia in the summer of 1939.[1] Cripps' isolation was most conspicuous in the upsurge of national unity which followed Britain's declaration of war on Germany. As inactivity was foreign to his nature, Cripps' immediate impulse was to 'wipe out all discussions and get back and help in the Party'. Labour's condemnation of the Russian invasion of Poland on 16 September made him change his mind.[2]

Having clearly reached a dead end in domestic politics, Cripps decided to divert his energies and talents to the arena of international politics and toyed with the idea of embarking on an exploratory tour of Russia. The absence of a power base did not discourage him. A natural nonconformist, Cripps had often stood alone and the position of a lone warrior even seemed to appeal to him.[3] In order to contribute his utmost to the war effort Cripps now made a long-due decision to wind up his exceedingly lucrative practice at the Bar. Throughout the 1930s Cripps, whose health was fragile probably as a result of gas poisoning in a munitions factory in the First World War, had combined a strenuous career as the leading patent lawyer in England with an intensive and time-consuming involvement in politics, both in Parliament and as a leader of the left wing of the Labour Party.

Cripps' decision to seek an official post by no means signalled the abandonment of his revolutionary outlook but perhaps underlined his unique combination of idealistic vision and penetrating grip on reality. He certainly had a patriotic impulse to serve his country, especially in a war against fascism, but also believed that the war would prove a catalyst for change and an opportunity for implementing his own ideas. This may clearly be traced on the pages of *Tribune* and in letters written to his constituents. In a typical letter, which also explains his decision to offer his services to the government, Cripps expressed his belief that:

having been got into this intolerable mess by the Government we have got to help in some way or another, but this does not of course mean that I am relaxing one whit of my opposition to the Government or my attempts to turn it out of office. Indeed at the present time it is easier to work along these lines if one can get somewhere into the machine, as in war time it is difficult to break a machine of Government except from inside . . .

My own view is to Maximise the drive to get rid of the present Government in favour of anything that is better with the ultimate hope of breaking the power of capitalism before the war is ended.[4]

This dialectical approach is discernible in his attitude to international relations in general and Russia in particular, which displays the varied sources of influence on him. The choice of Russia was natural, since throughout the 1930s Cripps had been a staunch supporter of that country. In 1933, early in his political life, he defied popular feeling by defending the Soviet courts for their decision to convict British engineers employed in Russia by the Metro-Vickers company of spying and subversion. The Socialist League which he chaired, and *Tribune* which he founded, edited and largely financed, had been advocates of an alliance with Russia. This affinity with the Soviet Union was even more pronounced in the negotiations in 1939.[5] Cripps' advocacy of the Soviet Union stemmed from his socialist convictions; these however owed more to the Bible and an assortment of other humanitarian and egalitarian considerations than to *Das Kapital*, which he had not ever pretended to have read. Moreover, Cripps had never belonged to the grass roots of the British Labour movement and he had little interest in its traditions and history. His convictions, in his own words, were the application of 'elementary truth . . . the tenets of our religion . . . in the

complexities of our modern civilization'. The concepts of brotherhood, love, freedom, equality and the value of the human individual frequently appeared in his speeches, writings and private correspondence.[6]

On the ideological front Cripps could thus be heard defending the Soviet occupation of Poland as an assistance to the Polish peasants in the struggle against their landlords.[7] And yet his approach to international relations and to Russia could be exceedingly sober, closely resembling the views held by the Union of Democratic Control and the Fabians.[8] Despite his campaign in favour of a popular front and his extreme left-wing opinions, unlike other fellow-travellers of the 1930s he was by no means infatuated with the Soviet Union; this must have been recognized in Moscow too. In an open letter to a member of the British Communist Party, he fully supported Harry Pollitt's resignation from the Political Bureau of the party, over the Ribbentrop–Molotov pact, on the grounds that at such grave times the party should be 'controlled by the people in it and not by any ideas or actions of Foreign Government'. He even went on to admonish the party's leadership for being 'bad and confused'.[9] Cripps himself was one of the few politicians who were not swayed by the anti-Soviet sentiments which overwhelmed Britons of all political persuasions after the conclusion of the Ribbentrop–Molotov pact. This, however, was not a result of external pressure but rather a realistic appreciation that had Russia 'come in on the side of the Allies [she] would be doing all the fighting in the East, and France and Britain would no more be able to assist her than they had been able, or willing, to assist Poland'.[10]

The ambiguity was also a product of his singular personality. Cripps' entire political career had been propelled by the rather naive notion that universal understanding and socialism could only be achieved through persuasion and personal contact. His overwhelming confidence in his mental superiority, his ability to digest vast amounts of material and extract the gist, his administrative ability – all acquired at the Bar – often contributed to his political effectiveness. His background, a wealthy family with deep roots in the rural gentry, ensured his social acceptability, despite his radical views and eccentricities. Moreover, his meteoric rise within the Labour Party was due to some extent to his father, Lord Parmoor, who had served in MacDonald's first Labour government.[11]

However, Cripps lacked an overall view and tended to treat political

issues as if they were court cases. For the same reason he tended to become fully absorbed in one or two causes at a time. No less of an impediment, and unexpected in a shrewd and successful lawyer, was his basic and uncritical faith in people which made him a poor judge of character and contributed to his political naivety. His invincibility in private discussions, his self-righteousness, though never aggressive, aggravated by his ascetic and spartan image, prevented him from becoming widely popular. This image was somewhat mistaken. His abstemiousness was to a great extent a result of poor health. Those who came in direct contact with him often attested to his warm personality and even his robust sense of humour.

The cross-roads in Cripps' public life now curiously coincided with a transformation in his appearance. It was wittily described by an astute observer:

In the middle 'thirties he had been black-haired and rather chubby. He wore round spectacles with rims. It was possible to think of him as a precocious schoolboy who had turned into a clever but immature lawyer. At the age of about 48 . . . he thinned down and assumed a more ascetic and formidable visage. He also became converted to a system of conscious bodily control which . . . gave him a peculiarly erect and detached but dedicated carriage. And the spectacles became smaller and rimless. The Cripps of his Chancellorship had assumed bodily shape.[12]

Cripps' hopes of redressing relations with Russia were not far-fetched. Having failed to achieve their security aims, the Russians had chosen out of sheer realism the lesser evil of concluding a neutrality pact with Germany.[13] Their borders were momentarily secured but diplomatic manoeuvrability was lost. The Russians' miscalculation, however, was revealed by the crushing defeat of Poland without any British involvement in the fighting. It was seriously feared in Moscow that the war would turn against Russia after all. Hasty measures were taken to exploit the pact with Germany and achieve by military means what they had failed to do through diplomacy in the 1930s. The establishment of a buffer zone through the partition of Poland, and later the annexation of the Baltic States and the secession of Finnish territories to the Soviet Union, were defensive moves in keeping with the policy consistently executed between 1933 and 1939, and directed indiscriminately against any belligerent power.

1 Cripps strolling in Southport with his wife Isobel after being expelled from the Labour Party

Given the inherent suspicion of Russia prevailing in Britain and the indignation caused by the Ribbentrop–Molotov agreement, announced while the British and French military missions were still negotiating in Moscow, it is not surprising that the initial reaction in London was that Russia had thrown in her lot with Germany. The Russians therefore resorted to strenuous efforts to placate Britain and consolidate their own neutrality. This was reflected in numerous interviews conducted by Ivan Maisky,[14] as well as the presentation of the invasion of Poland as a defensive move against Germany. Moreover, Stalin personally persuaded Ribbentrop to modify a proposed speech on the course of German–Soviet negotiations which might lead the West to assume his complicity with German military schemes. Nor did Germany's efforts to enlist Russia's political support and exploit the friendship clauses of the pact meet with much success. Molotov and Stalin repeatedly declined German invitations to visit Berlin. Count Werner von

Schulenburg, the German ambassador to the USSR, informed his superiors in Berlin that Russia was 'determined to cling to neutrality and to avoid as much as possible anything which might involve it in a conflict with the Western Powers'.[15] The 'rapidity' of the German conquest, as confessed by Maisky, had come as 'a great surprise' to the Russians, who by no means wished for a German victory. Andrew Rothstein, head of the Tass Agency in London, informed an official in the Foreign Office that the Russians did not 'contemplate with pleasure a future in which a powerful and victorious Germany should be her next door neighbour'.[16]

Further, the Russians were concerned by the failure of the British Expeditionary Force to intervene in Poland and the stagnation of the ensuing 'phoney war'. They feared that this left the door open for Chamberlain, whom they regarded with 'profound mistrust', to come to terms with Germany, which would in turn isolate the Soviet Union. Maisky openly admitted that a Cabinet led by Churchill and Eden with Labour representatives 'would be trusted by the Kremlin in a way which Chamberlain's would not'. His unwearied activity was clearly aimed at demonstrating Russia's strict neutrality and keeping a vigilant eye on Chamberlain rather than achieving a rapprochement with Britain. It was, as Maisky explained to Halifax, 'an uncertain world and . . . no friendship was very secure'; Russia had to be 'prepared for any eventuality'.[17]

When the first wave of indignation over the German–Soviet pact had subsided and the realities of war sank in, a vacuum became apparent in British policy-making with regard to future relations with Russia. Britain was obviously at a loss when attempting to evaluate Soviet aims. The military, not yet on a war footing, were still under the spell of outmoded concepts. In a report submitted to Cabinet, their non-committal observation was that the Russians had a dual policy: 'to spread world revolution' and improve their strategic situation. The old threat to the East was disproportionately prominent and the Cabinet was called upon to protect those areas 'likely to be infected by the Virus of Bolshevik doctrine'. Soviet military power was belittled and the possibility of a clash with England was estimated as remote. Nor did Soviet encroachment in the Baltic area pose any 'immediate threat to British interests'. The report was rejected by Cabinet, not only for its superficiality but because it did not consider, for instance, the political aspects of an

improvement in Anglo-Soviet relations; this might sow dissent within the unstable Soviet–German alliance.[18]

The ambassador to Moscow was not much more forthcoming. Sir William Seeds, who had been recalled from his retirement to patch up the deteriorating relations with Russia after Munich, saw in the German–Soviet pact a personal blow; he was now a bitter man. The only evaluation he was prepared to make was that the chances of the Soviet Union joining forces with Germany against Britain were 'perhaps fifty-fifty'.[19] The advice of the Foreign Office was equally unhelpful. The abrupt end of the negotiations with Russia was received there with considerable relief. It ended a protracted internal debate on the advisability of alliance with Russia in which the proponents had been steadily losing ground. The almost unequivocal recommendation now was to 'sit tight and avoid friction as far as possible'. The so-called 'reserve' policy had been consistently pursued since the consolidation of the Soviet régime in the 1920s. A strong emotional undercurrent, hitherto somewhat subdued, flowed under the apparent indifference and was now given a vent. It thus seemed inconceivable to Robert Vansittart, who in the mid-1930s had favoured rapprochement with Russia, 'to go traipsing off to Moscow at Soviet beck and call – after a line of other supplicants had already trod the same humiliating course'.[20] The 'frigid but unprovocative' attitude[21] resulted in in-attention to the increasing weight of the Soviet Union in the European war. It had hampered the participation of the Soviet Union in an effec-tive arrangement of collective security and contributed to her emergence as the leading power in Europe during the course of the war.

In the absence of an overall view the Cabinet aimed at short-range targets, often purely economic in nature, which fell in line with its general strategy of winning the war through stringent economic pres-sure. It concluded, for instance, a 'bargain' – a barter agreement by which British boats stranded in Soviet ports were loaded with timber. Even such a minor arrangement was accompanied by serious reser-vations which demonstrate the suspicion with which the Soviet Union was regarded. It was feared that the Russians might direct German sub-marines to sink the boats after they had left port.[22]

The origins of Cripps' ambassadorship to Moscow go back to 16 September 1939. In a letter to Halifax, Cripps recalled his warning in

July 1939 of an impending German–Soviet understanding if negotiations with Russia were allowed to lapse. To forestall a Soviet move
into East Poland, which he believed was now imminent, he urged
Halifax to send to Moscow 'an all party delegation' to arrange a non-
aggression pact. Before the proposal reached the Foreign Secretary,
however, the entry of Soviet troops into Poland had made it obsolete.
Cripps, who continued to hold that Britain had 'grossly mishandled' the
negotiations with Russia, was not deterred from offering to go 'right
away' to Moscow. On the contrary, to prevent the consolidation of a
Soviet–German military understanding he urged the government to
'try and maintain Russia neutral'.[23]

Both Cripps' suggestions, to dispatch emissaries to Moscow and to
conclude a non-aggression pact with the Soviet Union, were greeted
with profound resentment in the Foreign Office. Sir Alexander
Cadogan, the Permanent Under-Secretary of State, was quick to point
out that the term non-aggression 'stinks somewhat'; an alliance with a
country which had committed 'even a more flagrant act of aggression
than Germany' was out of the question. The humiliation inflicted on
the military mission, which was present in Moscow when the pact with
Germany was signed, meant that nobody could go to Moscow 'without
appearing to go to Canossa'. A more substantial argument against any
initiative was raised by Sir Robert Vansittart, former Permanent Under-
Secretary and now nominally Chief Adviser to the Foreign Secretary,
and was shared by no less a figure than Chamberlain. They expected the
'alarm and discouragement' that such a policy was likely to cause in
Italy and Spain to outweigh its advantages. As for Cripps' proposed
mission, it was argued that notwithstanding his political affiliations he
would 'inevitably' be regarded 'as an Englishman' and mistrusted. The
sole consideration in favour of allowing him to go was that in view of
'his past record and well known sympathies' there was a mere
possibility of 'his gleaning something of interest' in Moscow.

Support for Cripps came from an unexpected quarter. Halifax, who
had declined a Soviet invitation to visit Moscow at a crucial stage of the
1939 negotiations and who had been singled out as responsible for their
failure, now instructed the Foreign Office 'to encourage' Cripps and
even proposed a personal discussion of such a mission with him.[24]
Arrangements for the journey, however, did not proceed any further.

The Russians, who throughout the 1939 negotiations had been handled by second-rank officials, were not enthusiastic. Maisky intimated on 20 September that a socialist delegation to Moscow at that moment was not propitious. A few days later, visiting his close friends the Webbs, he dismissed the 'frivolous and futile' plan of Cripps, who enjoyed 'no authority or personal standing' with the government and had 'very little knowledge of Soviet institutions'. Indeed, Cripps was soon forced to make the embarrassing admission to Halifax that he had been refused a visa.[25]

The significance of this frustrating episode is that it saw the emergence of Cripps' idea of a mission to Moscow and his faith in his ability to effect a change in a major political issue. Equally clearly demonstrated is the subtle though distinct shift in Halifax's outlook in defiance of the Foreign Office's increased reluctance to approach Russia; this eventually made Cripps' mission possible.

Halifax, who had accepted with misgivings the post of Foreign Secretary after Eden's resignation in 1938, exercised little influence on the formulation of British policy before the war. He had scant knowledge of and little interest in European affairs. In office he lacked the vigour and enthusiasm which characterized Eden. A conciliator, Halifax often took the longer route to make 'a detour round the swamps', rendering his decision-making notoriously slow. R. A. Butler, his Parliamentary Secretary, has eloquently described him as 'always open to the last comer'; faced with new ideas, he would 'commune with himself, with his Maker, and with Alec [Cadogan]. So plenty of time elapsed before he took a decision.'[26] Consequently, senior Foreign Office officials were given unprecedented latitude. However, owing to their criticism of appeasement, the officials exercised little influence on policy-making, which was handled directly by Chamberlain and his private advisers. Halifax was thus not even invited by Chamberlain to attend the conference with Hitler in Bad Godesberg and Munich. His tacit support of appeasement stemmed more from personal loyalty to the Prime Minister and his poor grasp of foreign affairs than from conviction.[27] Faced by mounting criticism in the wake of Munich, Halifax was in fact drifting away from appeasement, and even advised Chamberlain to invite Churchill and Eden as well as Labour representatives to join the Cabinet. By summer 1939 he was 'reluctantly' forced

to the conclusion that Germany could be stopped only if 'met by force', though he did not feel strongly enough to force a significant rift within the Cabinet.[28]

When war was declared the Foreign Secretary's authority in Cabinet was enhanced in relation to the disillusioned and ailing Prime Minister. The Cabinet, which was now absorbed with military affairs, once again entrusted the conduct of foreign policy to the Foreign Office. Halifax's vulnerability to varying influences from his senior officials encouraged the emergence of different and often contradictory policies. Relations with Russia, which gradually became of primary importance, are a case in point. Since taking office Halifax had maintained an attitude of suspicion bordering on hostility towards the Soviet Union. This did not originate in a class outlook, as is always suggested by Soviet historiography.[29] He followed the long Conservative tradition of seeing in Russia and later in the Soviet Union a threat to western civilization in general and the British empire in particular. In Stalin he saw a successor of Peter the Great rather than of Lenin. His experience as Viceroy of India in the 1920s must have contributed to this feeling. Halifax's early attraction to Hitler was based on the assumption that Nazi Germany could serve as a bulwark against Russia. 'An intelligent rabbit', he wrote in 1939, referring to the Polish refusal to accept Soviet help which torpedoed the tripartite negotiations, 'would hardly be expected to welcome the protection of an animal ten times its size, whom it credited with the habits of a boa-constrictor.'[30]

At the outbreak of war Halifax, unlike Chamberlain, who remained bitterly anti-Soviet, and in contrast to the Foreign Office's officials who belittled the advantage of collaboration with Russia, displayed a more even-handed policy. Although he continued to share the commonly held view that the Soviet Union was the 'query mark' in Europe and admitted to lack of understanding of the 'strange Bolshevik mind', a break with the past was apparent. He grimly observed that England was living in 'strange days' and condoned rapprochement with the Soviet Union to drive a wedge between that country and Germany.[31] In this he was supported even by the arch-appeaser John Simon, who recognized the Soviet potential for 'stopping the Drang-nach-Osten'. In Cabinet Halifax exercised a moderating influence. After Russia's invasion of Poland he rejected proposals to aid Poland by declaring war on Russia and even opposed Chamberlain's suggestion of a protest to Moscow.[32]

sations centred on India. Cripps, who was a close friend of Nehru, tried to interest the former Viceroy in his plans for the independence of India.[42] Russia, however, increasingly figured more prominently. Confused by the recent Soviet approaches, Halifax found in Cripps a source of valuable information and advice. On 13 October Cripps, who frequently met Maisky, conveyed to Halifax the Russians' wish to open trade negotiations. A day earlier Eden emerged from lunch with Maisky convinced that the recent Soviet moves were overtly directed against Germany. In his usual metaphorical style, Maisky had asserted that in a world 'where wild beasts were loose' Russia had to secure 'certain vital strategic points . . . for its own safety'.[43] Unlike Eden, however, Cripps was never really satisfied with either being an intermediary or playing second fiddle. His dealings with Halifax were a portent of the political traits which characterized his ambassadorship in Moscow. Having conveyed the Soviet hopes of embarking on negotiations, Cripps presented Halifax with an elaborate scheme which he thought the government should endorse. Once progress was made, he proposed that Oliver Stanley, the President of the Board of Trade, whom he had already sounded out,[44] should head the delegation. To himself he assigned the modest task of legal adviser to the delegation. The effect of this on Halifax was immediate. Early next morning Halifax, adopting many of Cripps' positions of the previous night, encouraged Stanley to accept the plan, to which he attached 'a good deal of political importance'. He appeared anxious to remedy 'the complete political deadlock and absence of political touch' with the Soviet Union.[45]

At Cripps' suggestion Halifax also consented to meet Maisky, who reassured him that Russia's policy in the Baltic was to improve her strategic position against Germany. Maisky was faithfully conveying appraisals made in Moscow. In presenting territorial demands to a visiting Finnish delegation, Stalin used the same words to explain that although relations with Germany were good 'anything [might] change'. The interview was marked at that early stage by a strong undercurrent which both Halifax and his mentor Cripps seem to have overlooked. Maisky was trying to ascertain, as a result of his meeting with Churchill, the possibility of British connivance at Soviet defensive measures. At the same time he was sounding out whether Britain would consider further peace proposals by Hitler. Halifax, however, confined himself to the

ostensible subject of the interview and, in conformity with Cripps' memorandum, proposed the improvement of political relations through the channel of trade.[46]

Within a week of his meeting with the Soviet ambassador Halifax circulated in Cabinet a memorandum, closely resembling Cripps' proposals, advocating the conclusion of a barter agreement. 'The considerable political value' of such an agreement, he pointed out, 'outweighed the public outcry it was likely to cause'. He further seconded Cripps' recommendation that Stanley should sign the agreement in Moscow. The thought of a ministerial visit to Moscow aroused considerable opposition in Cabinet. Once again Halifax won the day by quoting from a recent letter from Cripps in which he argued that the visit was indispensable to ensure a 'maximum political effect'.[47]

The Cabinet's endorsement of the proposal was received with disbelief by the Foreign Office, which was unaware of developments. Vansittart urged Halifax to put an end to Maisky's lobbying, which went 'beyond his functions'.[48] Halifax, however, disregarded those reservations and summoned Maisky once again to inform him of the Cabinet decision. The interview nonetheless exposed the differing expectations. Cripps, overconfident of his ability to convert politicians and governments to his point of view, convinced Halifax that it was still possible to drive a wedge between Russia and Germany. In initiating the talks Halifax therefore did not realize that the Russians were in fact seeking recognition of their neutrality and tacit support for their security arrangements in the Baltic. Halifax's insinuation that trade negotiations might lead to fostering political relations met a cool reception. The cautious Maisky professed satisfaction with the existing political relations; Halifax's appreciation of the bilateral relations, he thought, was 'too pessimistic'. Halifax, on his part, had feared a fully-fledged German–Soviet alliance. He was lulled by the general tone of the meeting and remained satisfied with the hope that the actual negotiations would forestall such a collaboration.[49]

That very evening the President of the Board of Trade received Maisky for a preparatory talk. The ubiquitous Cripps was also present, and could observe with pleasure the implementation of his policy. Stanley was now prepared to overrule the Cabinet's preference for separate barter deals and conclude in Moscow a general trade agreement.[50]

14

## A visit to Moscow

While attempts to improve relations with Russia were under way, negotiations between the Soviet Union and Finland had begun; their failure would soon lead to the Winter War. In the face of obdurate Finnish resistance to their terms, the Russians sought to achieve Britain's connivance at a forceful solution or at least to avoid a confrontation with her. However, since time was running out and a settlement with Finland was still remote, the attainment of this aim was becoming exceedingly difficult. Halifax had earlier warned Maisky that the success of the negotiations with Britain depended on an amicable settlement of the dispute with Finland.[51] The Chiefs of Staff (COS), however, had warned against military assistance to Finland, which was only 'likely to consolidate the alliance between Germany and Russia'. The warning to Maisky did not prevent Halifax from agreeing with the COS. In Cabinet he presented Soviet encroachment in the Baltic as a defensive measure; the Russians, he asserted, 'were not out for adventures'.[52]

The British attitude towards the Finnish–Soviet dispute seemed to be somewhat ambivalent. On the one hand some assent to the Russian position was apparent, and the preliminary negotiations revealed the unlikelihood of Britain's responding to the German peace initiative. The recurrent nightmare of Britain and Germany sinking their differences and combining their military efforts to crush communist Russia subsided. On the other hand Britain was overtly stiffening Finnish resistance to the Russians' claims while the Anglo-Soviet negotiations had not got off the ground.[53] Primarily concerned about the German threat, the Russians were forced to order their priorities. Security measures became uppermost in their strategy, while the negotiations were only a means of achieving them. They therefore resorted to delaying tactics, keeping up British expectations from the negotiations while exerting pressure on the British government to secure its acquiescence in a possible military conflict. An example of this was the sudden emergence in mid-November of the Soviet military attaché, who had been in London for three years but had not formed any personal contacts. Over lunch he proposed to Butler that 'some personality could enter into closer relations with their higher personalities in the Soviet Union'. The main message, however, was that if

15

England 'smiled upon the negotiations' with Finland a 'great improvement of relations' would follow.[54] Halifax's assurances to Cabinet that progress was being made in the negotiations and that he hoped shortly to lay the matter before the Cabinet was rather premature. Indeed, in the next Cabinet meeting Halifax explained that consultations with Cripps had convinced him that Britain's tacit support of Finland was likely to delay the Soviet reply until the dispute with Finland was resolved.[55]

The policy of encouraging the Finns came under direct attack from Churchill. In full agreement with Cripps, he believed British interests were 'to secure as much support as possible in this war from the U.S.S.R.'. The prevention of German control of the Baltic was of such significance to British strategy that Russia should even be allowed to increase its strength there.[56] Such views, particularly in the light of the changing trend of the negotiations, encountered bitter resentment in the Northern Department of the Foreign Office. Halifax, fluctuating as usual, was gradually succumbing to pressure to reconsider the recent rapprochement with the Soviet Union. Mutual distrust marred Halifax's conversations with Maisky a few days before the outbreak of war in Finland, exposing the gulf which separated them. While Maisky finally disclosed Russia's determination to acquire naval bases in Finland, Halifax made it clear that Britain could not countenance such a move. The Soviet expectations from the talks were therefore shattered. Halifax, on his part, realized that the incentive of a trade arrangement was not attractive enough to influence Soviet military and political considerations. He came out of the meeting in agreement with Cadogan's view that it was 'quite useless talking to Maisky'. The Russians, he now minuted, were simply 'impossible people' to deal with. He brushed aside Churchill's arguments for allowing the Russians, who only wished 'to play up their nuisance value as high as possible on both sides', a free hand in the Baltic.[57] Even Butler preferred to lunch with Maisky at his Parliamentary Secretary's home so as not 'to be seen with him in public'. The host, upon his return, did not forget to 'check up on the snuff boxes . . . but did not notice anything missing'.[58]

The outbreak of hostilities in Finland could hardly have come as a surprise. The Russians had frequently defined their limited and defensive objectives in the area. Indeed, when news of the fighting came through, the Cabinet admitted that it would have 'no direct effects' on

16

Britain. It was even anticipated that the conflict would introduce tension into German–Soviet relations. However, in response to public indignation both at home and in America the Cabinet expressed alarm that the war might be a 'prelude to further Russian expansionist schemes', which would force Britain 'to declare war upon her'.[59] Privately Halifax still intimated that he was 'frightened of going to war with Russia', and in Cabinet he confessed he was not 'sure how the matter should be handled'. Nevertheless, he joined his colleagues in fully approving the assistance to Finland. The Foreign Office shared none of Halifax's reservations. It endorsed the opinion unanimously held by foreign diplomats in Moscow, and bluntly expressed by Seeds, that Russia had 'settled down definitely into an undeclared war' against Britain and therefore stood with Germany 'as partners in crime'.[60]

In adopting a rigid attitude towards Russia, the government was also under pressure from its French allies. In the midst of an acute domestic crisis, the French were no less eager for a spectacular victory preferably away from their own borders. Their communications with Russia had become outspokenly aggressive and the Soviet ambassador was declared *persona non grata*.[61] It was a French initiative which brought about the expulsion of the Soviet Union from the League of Nations on 14 December, an event which increased the prospects of an armed conflict between Russia and the Allies.[62] A resolute and moralistic speech by the British delegate in Geneva, defending 'the standards of international decency', equating Soviet aggression with that of Germany and promising full support to Finland, skilfully concealed the fact that the British government 'was not clear as to its attitude to Russia'. Neither the Cabinet nor the Foreign Office had seriously explored the implications of such a move on Anglo-Soviet relations. Halifax's sole worry was that the expulsion 'might awaken disagreeable echoes' in Mussolini.[63] However, senior officials in the Foreign Office hoped the expulsion might induce the Russians to 'take the initiative' and sever relations.[64] Determined to avoid the pitfall, Maisky expressed his intention to remain at his post although Seeds had been recalled for consultations and was not in fact returned to Moscow.[65]

Willy-nilly Halifax came round to the conclusion that it was worth 'taking a certain risk'. The Cabinet followed suit, endorsing uncritically the view that Russia was acting in collusion with Germany in the North. At a low ebb of the war, the prospect of opening a new front in the

North was attractive.[66] The Cabinet was also affected by the disappearance of the traditional obstacle to military measures against Russia. The Labour Party and particularly the trade unions were firm in their support of Finland. Sir Walter Citrine, General Secretary of the TUC, and Noel Baker 'evinced the strongest hostility against the Soviet Union' in their meeting with Halifax after their return from Finland. On the whole the Labour movement, while reluctant to go to war with Russia, was determined nonetheless 'to help stop the crime against Finland'. 'Finnish resistance', declared Citrine, 'did not increase, but diminished the risk of war between Russia and the West.'[67]

The probable repercussions of hostilities with Russia on the grand strategy of the war received perfunctory consideration. Assuming the German–Soviet policies were 'definitely co-ordinated', the Foreign Office prevailed on the COS to resort to force. 'The two robbers', it concluded, were bound to 'continue to hang together until they both hang separately.'[68] The role of executioners did not, however, appeal to the COS, who considered the issue to be 'mainly a political' one. They objected to the 'additional commitments' involved in war with Russia and were not moved by the Foreign Office's insistence that from the political point of view it was advisable 'to bring about the complete downfall of the Russian military power'. Their final conclusion was that war with Russia was acceptable only if it hastened the defeat of Germany, which did not seem to be the case.[69]

The Cabinet had adopted a fatalistic outlook, allowing events to determine its policies. At the end of January Chamberlain had said that 'events seemed to be leading . . . towards open hostilities with Russia'. Similarly on the eve of the expedition to Finland he still preferred to 'wait and see' what would be the effects of the expedition on Russia.[70] The equanimity with which the government regarded war with Russia cannot be satisfactorily explained by Halifax's weakness, pressure from France or inherent hostility towards the Soviet Union. Chamberlain's government was severely handicapped by a 'Munich complex'. It was fettered by an obsessive need to atone for past mistakes. Acting on the assumption that Russia was fully allied with Germany, the Cabinet seized the opportunity of compensating for appeasement towards Germany by showing stiff resistance to Russia in Finland. Thus, when Butler reacted favourably towards the Soviet request for mediation in the conflict, he was reproached by Cadogan for attempting 'another

appeasement'. Likewise Chamberlain thought that the Russians' 'usual treacherous and cowardly way' of enlisting Britain to mediate was 'copied from the Hitler technique in Poland and Czechoslovakia only more clumsily done'.[71]

Meanwhile Cripps had paid his first visit to the Soviet Union. The deceptive political calm which characterized the 'phoney war', the stalemate in relations with Russia and the seemingly stable position of the government reduced his ability to influence politics at home. Without official sanction Cripps embarked on a fact-finding tour around the world accompanied by Geoffrey Wilson, a young lawyer and a close friend of the family. Indian independence and the situation in China were Cripps' main concern. His departure on 30 November, however, coincided with the outbreak of war in Finland and relations with Russia regained his attention. While a guest of Chiang Kai-shek in Chunking he met the Soviet ambassador, who had been briefed by Maisky about Cripps' major contribution to defusing hostility towards Russia in recent months. In the course of a 'frank conversation' Cripps' restless mind enquired into Soviet motives in Finland and sought solutions for the looming conflict with Britain. He strongly advised the Russians to emphasize their neutrality and the defensive nature of their war and to deny any intention of annexing Finland. Personally he appeared anxious to explore the situation with 'one of those in authority' in Moscow.[72]

The advice of Cripps could not be treated lightly in Moscow. Not only had he been the driving force in the recent negotiations, but it was also wrongly assumed that he had been assigned his present mission by the British government. Moreover, widespread rumours of an impending British–French operation against Russia had aroused much concern in Moscow. Maisky, who could boast as late as November 1939 that he was 'like a rich bride with many suitors', now faced universal ostracism and feared he might be expelled from England 'any day'.[73] The Russians' alarm was further enhanced by the ill-timed visit of the American Under-Secretary of State, Sumner Welles, to Berlin and London; it revived their constant nightmare of an early peace and the diversion of the war to eastern Europe.

To forestall those developments the Russians went 'out of their way . . . to placate' the American and other major legations in Moscow.[74] As Cripps had advised, Maisky approached Halifax, whom he had not seen

19

since the outbreak of war with Finland. He reiterated that there was 'nothing sentimental' in German–Soviet relations, repeating his habitual message: 'In the jungle the strangest animals got together if they felt their joint interests made this advisable.'[75] To back up their diplomatic efforts in London Cripps was rushed to Moscow from China by special plane. The brief and hasty mission had little chance of success. Cripps, away from England for almost two months, was unaware that relations had deteriorated so rapidly that an outbreak of hostilities seemed imminent.

Cripps' experience in Moscow is nonetheless enlightening in that it foreshadows many aspects of his later ambassadorship. Despite his public image as an uncompromising radical and his staunch support of the Soviet Union, Cripps' encounter with Russia differs from the pilgrimages undertaken by fellow-travellers of the 1930s. Rather than a pursuit of a new Jerusalem, his journey emerges from his diary mainly as an adventure, while its political aspects were less prominent. Neither Moscow nor revolutionary Russia seem to have left a strong impact on Cripps. He and Wilson reached Moscow after a tedious flight on 15 February. Having shed the Chinese trousers, fur coats and warm boats with which they had been supplied by Mme. Chiang Kai-shek, and back into 'respectable western clothes', they had 'a glimpse at a good many things' in a freezing −30°C Moscow. After trivial amusing incidents in the hotel, the next morning was spent shopping or rather 'cadging', as the two had no Russian money with them; Cripps noted that they were 'accomplishing the fact of travelling 5,500 miles in Russia without the expenditure of a single kopek!' Following a stroll in the streets and a short visit to an art exhibition, Cripps was finally summoned to the Kremlin in the afternoon for a meeting with Molotov.[76]

Although Cripps was favourably disposed towards the Soviet Union, his conversations in Moscow manifested his businesslike and rational approach to the Soviet leadership. In a speech on the international situation delivered earlier in Chunking and now submitted for Molotov's consideration, Cripps preached his credo that Soviet foreign policy 'had turned from the idea of international revolution' to one of 'pure realpolitik in which the safety and peace of Russia was the overriding factor'. He regarded the invasion of Finland as defensive and a direct result of the 'ignominious neglect and distrust' of Britain and France towards Russia since Munich.[77] The preliminary conversation at the Moscow

2 Cripps and Geoffrey Wilson set off for Moscow, February 1940

airport with M. Tikhomirov, a senior official of the Soviet Foreign Office, revealed to Cripps the Soviet expectations from the visit. Tikhomirov appeared 'most anxious' to resume the suspended negotiations 'as soon as possible', laying stress on the 'deep ideological cleavage . . . which could not be bridged' between Germany and Russia.[78] The meeting with Molotov at the 'beautifully furnished and decorated' offices of Narkomindel at the Kremlin confirmed Cripps' early impression. Although Molotov appeared to be an 'extremely careful man', the sense of urgency was overriding. Characteristically Cripps dominated the meeting from the start. He reproached the Russians for having missed an opportunity of improving relations in the negotiations which he had initiated. Molotov suggested that Cripps should pick up the threads. Cripps, however, was not due back in London before the end of April, which Molotov disappointedly conceded was 'too long to wait'. To goad Cripps into action he warned that in the absence of an early rapprochement Russia might have 'to commit herself elsewhere'. In conclusion Cripps promised to communicate Molotov's message but was personally doubtful whether any progress could be made until the war with Finland was over.

Since he was unfamiliar with the complex circumstances which had led the Russians to seek his services, Cripps emerged satisfied from the interview. It had enabled him to establish cordial relations with Molotov which he hoped to utilize later. Throughout his stay in Moscow Cripps typically conducted the negotiations on his own, avoiding any contact with the British embassy, which had been informed of his arrival.[79] It was not until his return to China on 3 March that he was able to dispatch his impressions to Halifax. After transmitting the gist of his talk with Molotov, he concluded that German–Soviet relations appeared so strained that 'their gradual separation . . . might be brought about'. Halifax was urged to 'prevent Russia from committing herself too far to Germany in the immediate future'.[80]

From the outset the Cabinet had regarded Cripps' proposed visit to Moscow as 'most untimely'. The COS's objections to an expedition to Finland had just been overruled and preparations were proceeding at full steam. It was rightly believed that Cripps' active participation in the previous negotiations 'might give rise to misunderstandings'.[81]

Both the Foreign Office and the Intelligence, which were now invited to comment on Cripps' report, had a better insight into the

motives behind the Russian approach. It was unanimously held that it reflected 'an intense desire to avoid war' with Britain. Giving vent to their hostile feelings towards Cripps, discernible already in the earlier stages of the negotiations, the officials of both departments dismissed him as a 'willing tool' of the Russians. Vansittart expressed more openly the prevalent feeling in the Foreign Office that Britain ought 'to nibble no more at any Russian bait of any kind'. Once Germany was defeated, he suggested, it would be possible to 'deal with Stalin & his pseudo-Communism', which it was 'just as necessary to destroy as Nazism'.

The sole voice of reason was once again that of Butler. He observed that by outright rejection of any Russian initiative the government would tend 'to increase rather than to decrease German Russian amity'. However, he concluded wryly, the British were 'a proud people' and seemed 'to enjoy the "world at arms" ' against them. Halifax was carried along by the consensus though significantly he did not share the attitude to Cripps.[82] In Cabinet, however, he displayed a more moderate view. Sceptical about the outcome of the expedition to Finland and as always willing to defer a major decision, he recommended ignoring the Soviet offer until the cessation of hostilities in Finland. He did not exclude the possibility of then exploring the chances of detaching Russia from Germany.[83] Cripps had proposed to break off his tour and return to London. A pattern was now established in dealings with Cripps when it was recognized that he was better kept away from home. The troops were fully mobilized for dispatch to Finland, and it was feared that Cripps might jeopardize the campaign through the disclosure of the Soviet proposition. A telegram personally redrafted and softened by Halifax awaited Cripps in Tokyo, politely but firmly declining his services.[84]

Once the Russians realized that Cripps could be of no avail to counter the British buildup they resorted to a last-ditch diplomatic effort. The day after Cripps' preliminary talk in Moscow, Maisky lunched with Butler. He discussed with him *inter alia* the Russians' wish to end hostilities in Finland. Following more specific instructions from Moscow, on 22 February he reaffirmed to Butler Russia's neutrality *vis à vis* the main belligerents and denied any 'intention of entering into a military alliance with Germany'. He then dropped a bombshell. Britain was officially asked to mediate a peace agreement with Finland. Incidentally the Germans, when they learned of the Soviet approach, were

seriously annoyed. In an attempt to pacify Britain the Russians abandoned earlier demands for installation of a puppet Finnish government and refrained from following up their successful breakthrough of the Mannerheim Line.[85] The off-hand rejection of the initiative irritated Butler, who had come to regard the improvement of relations as unlikely under a 'British Government of the present type'.[86]

Throughout the Winter War the Cabinet was aware that it was being dragged into action. When news of the Finno-Soviet agreement reached London on 13 March, prominent ministers led by Halifax could not 'resist some feeling of thankfulness at not having got an Expedition bogged'. However, the significance of having narrowly avoided war with Russia escaped those responsible for British policy. Once again under French instigation, they were now occupied with final operational plans for bombing Soviet oilfields in Baku.[87]

### Appointment as ambassador

The detention of Soviet ships in the Far East by the Allies, Sumner Welles' mission and rumours of an impending action in the Caucasus and Scandinavia aroused Soviet fears that armed confrontation had only temporarily been averted. Maisky therefore hastened to confide to Butler that Russia had no military alliance with Germany; nor did she wish 'to come under her heel' and be 'dragged into further complications'.[88] Although the COS evaluated that Germany had been 'seriously weakened by Russia's increased strength', the Foreign Office insisted that to all intents and purposes Russia was already acting as Britain's enemy. Maisky's soothing words were again dismissed as an attempt to divide British domestic opinion and impair the preparations for action in the Caucasus.[89]

Cadogan refused to give up the opportunity of solving the 'Russian problem' provided by the war in Finland. Now that the Finnish motive no longer existed it was necessary 'to pick a quarrel' with the Russians. He was even prepared to risk bombing Baku, although he was aware that such an action might lead to 'a definite alliance' between Germany and Russia. Such an alliance, he hoped, would encourage Mussolini to turn to the Allies. It would also enable Britain to 'dispose . . . once and for all' of the Soviet menace in the Middle East.[90] Butler once again regretfully noticed that there was 'a certain noble purity' about British

policy, which tended 'to add one enemy after another' to those opposed to her. He believed it was worth while to make Germany feel that there was '*something* uncertain in the East and not a completely sub-servient ally'.[91]

In the meantime Maisky had unofficially sounded out Hugh Dalton, the Minister of Economic Warfare, about the possibility of resuming the trade negotiations disrupted by the war in Finland.[92] It was followed up by a formal approach on 27 March. These negotiations, devised by Cripps in the first place, would now pave his way to Moscow as an ambassador.

The British evaluation of Soviet relations with Germany, which formed the basis for their approach to the negotiations, was wide of the mark. The Soviet Union was genuinely determined, as observed by none other than Schulenburg, 'to cling to neutrality . . . and avoid as much as possible anything that might involve it in a conflict with the Western Powers'. He did not foresee an immediate improvement in German–Soviet relations.[93] The conditions, therefore, were favourable to the conclusion of a trade agreement. The British government, however, working on mistaken assumptions, made an agreement con-ditional on effective contraband control of goods destined for Germany. Moreover, Paul Reynaud, the French Prime Minister, per-suaded Chamberlain in a meeting of the Supreme War Council to employ delaying tactics in any negotiations until a general policy was adopted.[94]

From the outset it was plain to economic experts that the meagre volume of trade between the countries did not justify a *quid pro quo* agreement. The advisability of responding to the Soviet initiative depended on 'considerations of a pure political character'.[95] Those con-siderations were discussed by the heads of all British missions in south-east Europe and the Soviet Union, who were summoned to Whitehall on 8 April. The participants were united in doubting the sincerity of the Soviet approach. However, two arguments were decisive in favour of resuming negotiations. On the home front it was essential to avoid accusations of having missed an opportunity of detaching Russia from Germany, and from the point of view of the war effort it was important to restrict even partially Soviet–German economic collaboration.[96]

These early deliberations coincided with a deepening crisis within Chamberlain's government, which was tottering towards collapse. On

8 April mines were laid at the entrance to Narvik in Norwegian territorial waters. This action was overshadowed on the next day when the Germans invaded Norway and Denmark, shattering all hopes of diverting the war to Scandinavia. The helplessness of the government was patent. The crisis prompted a reappraisal by some circles in the Labour Party, whose criticism of Russia had so far been as vehement as that of the government. Shortly after the German invasion of Scandinavia, Maisky noticed with satisfaction that Attlee and Greenwood had suddenly approached him 'to resume diplomatic relations'.[97] The *carte blanche* given to the government by Labour in relations with Russia during the Finnish war was withdrawn. Moreover, the subject once again figured prominently in the House of Commons,[98] and the government's vulnerability to increasing domestic pressure compelled it to moderate its attitude to Russia. Reynaud's insistence on bombing Baku 'as soon as possible' in a desperate attempt to divert the war away from France was overruled. Chamberlain agreed only that rumours of such plans could be useful as 'a weapon with which to persuade the Russians to adopt a more favourable attitude towards the Allies'.[99] Halifax therefore impressed on Cabinet that it was 'desirable for political reasons . . . to show their willingness' to embark on negotiations, although he remained sceptical about the outcome.[100] While Chamberlain realized the necessity of responding to the Russian offer, he warned that Britain's 'credit would be damaged' if the Russians were 'allowed to follow their habitual practice of spinning out the negotiations'. He intended to put the Russians to a severe test. They were virtually expected to return to the 1939 negotiations as if nothing had subsequently occurred on the international scene. To illustrate his attitude to the negotiations, he quoted to the Supreme War Council the saying 'He who sups with the Devil needs a long spoon.'[101] Nor were the negotiations furthered by the traditional Russophobia and fear of communism in influential circles. General Ismay, the head of the War Cabinet's secretariat, advised his close friend Orme Sargent, the Deputy Under-Secretary at the Foreign Office, to consult the relevant verses from Kipling's 'The Truce of the Bear' before embarking on negotiations:

[The Old Blind Beggar Speaks]
But (pay, and I put back the bandage) this is the time to fear,

When he stands up like a tired man, tottering near and near;
When he stands up as pleading, in wavering, man-brute guise,
When he veils the hate and cunning of the little, swinish eyes;
When he shows as seeking quarter, with paws like hands in prayer,
*That* is the time of peril – the time of the Truce of the Bear!

Over and over the story, ending as he began:
'There is no truce with Adam-zad, the Bear that looks like a man!' [102]

The British reply was handed to Maisky only on 19 April, three weeks after the approach had been made. It amounted to an ultimatum. The Russians were indirectly required to display benevolent neutrality towards Britain and discontinue their economic collaboration with Germany, which Halifax appreciated was 'just like . . . taking up arms' against Britain. He admitted that it was 'difficult to see' the Russians responding favourably. A few days later he told the American ambassador Joseph Kennedy that it was 'extremely unlikely' that anything would come of the talks. [103]

Halifax's pessimistic outlook was widely shared. The conditions for the start of negotiations were not only politically unacceptable but also economically unsound. Professor Michael Postan, the Russian émigré and renowned medievalist then serving as head of the East European section at the Ministry of Economic Warfare (MEW), warned that a war trade agreement was a 'chimera'. Britain had to 'cut [her] war trade agreement according to [her] cloth'. Even if Russia were willing to sacrifice her partnership with Germany, Britain could not offer an inadequate compensation. [104]

Once again the British procrastination in formulating policy had ended in a setback. The rapid German campaign in the North increased, at least outwardly, Soviet complicity in German policies. On the other hand it revived Soviet fears of war with the Allies if the Finnish question were to be reopened. [105] Not surprisingly in the new circumstances, the Russians were quick to reject the British memorandum. Maisky reiterated Russia's position 'as a neutral Power' and referred to the British proposal for a barter agreement in October 1939. [106]

The government departments concerned were divided in their reaction to the Soviet reply. The Foreign Office saw in it a proof that Russia was supporting Germany against Britain 'by every means short of going to war'. The MEW was deeply concerned about the question

of contraband. The Board of Trade, however, on purely economic grounds now appeared to be satisfied with an ordinary barter arrangement, arguing that 'half a loaf was better than no bread'.[107]

A long and deliberately vague reply, drafted so as not to appear 'a red rag' to the Russians, was handed to Maisky on 8 May. Scanning through it, he was quick to note that it 'simply repeated in a more elaborate form' early arguments. The conversation with Halifax, conducted in a chilly atmosphere, ended in deadlock. Maisky admitted he 'did not feel hopeful of any results'.[108] Two days later, however, the war assumed an altogether new dimension. Churchill's appointment as Prime Minister coincided with the German invasion of Holland and Belgium. The dramatic events did not precipitate an immediate improvement in Anglo-Soviet relations. The circumstances resembled very much those of 31 March 1939 when, by guaranteeing Poland's borders, Chamberlain in fact forced Hitler to become involved in war with the West, thereby unintentionally ensuring Russia's aloofness in the forthcoming conflict. However, the strict neutrality which the Russians regarded as the crowning success of their diplomacy remained precarious. It was threatened by the Ribbentrop–Molotov agreement, reluctantly signed by the Russians, by contemplated Allied action against Russia and by the gnawing fear of an impending reconciliation between Germany and England.

The news that the German army had engaged the British Expeditionary Force was, therefore, genuinely received in Moscow 'in an understanding spirit'. Molotov even went so far as to tell Schulenburg that he realized that Germany had to 'protect herself against British–French attacks'.[109] The anticipated long war in the West, it was hoped, would favour Russian neutrality and provide a long enough breathing space to enable her to arm. An improvement of relations was further hampered by Churchill's inclusion in the War Cabinet of prominent former appeasers. Maisky, in an indignant mood, explained to the Webbs that while Churchill would become a warlord the actual conduct of foreign affairs would remain in the hands of Halifax, 'the pious old fool'. Echoing Stalin's famous warning of March 1939 that the Russians did not intend 'to pull somebody else's chestnuts out of the fire', Maisky concluded that although they did not want Germany to win 'they were not going to fight her on [Britain's] behalf'.[110]

The soundness of Russian policy was quickly put to the test. Events,

to quote Maisky, 'advanced at breathtaking speed'. The decisive German breakthrough at Sedan on 14 May and the rush to Paris and the Channel meant that the collapse of both the British Expeditionary Force and the French government 'became ever certain'. Old apprehensions surfaced. The presence of the 'Men of Munich' in the British government might tip the scale towards a peace with Germany, which would then be able to direct its war machine eastwards. Soviet policy had become, as observed by the American chargé d'affaires in Moscow, 'largely defensive and based upon the fear of possible aggression by Allied or associated powers . . . and possibly upon uneasiness over the prospects of a victorious Germany'.[111]

The stalemate had become undesirable also from the British point of view. The indifference with which Halifax had received the collapse of the talks on 8 May must be partly attributed to the complacency of the Labour Party. By a majority of 13 to 2 its National Executive voted at the end of April against the resumption of negotiations.[112] For some time, however, Butler had been hard pressed in Parliament by Labour backbenchers on the advisability of returning an ambassador to Moscow.[113] Now that the fate of France hung in the balance similar pressure was exercised in the War Cabinet by the new Labour ministers. On 15 May Attlee proposed that Cabinet send 'an important figure in public life' to the USSR. A day earlier Halifax had waived his previous conditions for negotiations and even agreed to consider 'a purely barter agreement'. He was now prepared to contemplate a mission once the Russians had replied to his earlier communication.[114]

While these minor shifts in relations with Russia were taking place the gravity of the situation was quickly becoming apparent. On 16 May the still hopeful Churchill flew to Paris to appraise the battle picture personally. He returned in a despondent mood. Although orders had been given to defend Paris 'at all costs', he had witnessed the archives of Quai d'Orsay 'already burning in the garden'. The collapse of Holland added to the gloomy prospect and measures were contemplated for evacuating the British Expeditionary Force and organizing the defence of the British Isles.[115] The possibility of Britain's losing her ally and Italy's growing determination to enter the war on Germany's side meant that relations with Russia, which only a week earlier had been treated casually, assumed prime significance.

While Cabinet was digesting Churchill's cheerless cables from Paris,

Maisky approached Butler on 16 May with a proposal to conduct negotiations 'by word of mouth and not by notes'. Considering the anti-German implications of such negotiations, the Russians' wish for a confidential exchange certainly reflected their alarm at German successes. Fully aware of this, Butler urged that Halifax should 'really move a little more quickly'. He specifically proposed the appointment without delay of Sir Maurice Peterson, who had just been recalled from Madrid to make room for Samuel Hoare, as ambassador in Moscow. Meanwhile negotiations between Maisky and Dalton could be opened in London.[116] Such recommendations had been repeatedly opposed by the Foreign Office. Early in April Sargent had doubted the expediency of sending an ambassador, whom he suspected would be 'simply boycotted and humiliated' and could be 'no more than a journalist, picking up scraps of information'. He was equally doubtful now whether an ambassador 'would be able to do anything'.[117] However, in the struggle to shape Halifax's point of view Butler was clearly winning the upper hand. Maisky's proposal and Butler's recommendation coincided with a long conversation in the same vein between Halifax and Cripps on that very evening. Cripps proposed to go to Moscow as a special envoy. In an earlier meeting between the two, before the change of government, Cripps had tried unsuccessfully to persuade Halifax that Russia wanted 'to play the game in more friendly fashion'.[118]

Cripps had returned to England on 23 April. Beatrice Webb shrewdly discerned the turning point in her nephew's career: Cripps was likely either to 'bring about better relations' with the Soviet Union or to 'lead the after-war revolution'. The die was cast in less than a month after his arrival in Britain and was to hasten his transformation into a mature politician. His commitment to radical ideals and relationships with former political colleagues seem to have suffered from his determination to contribute to the war effort in Britain. Pacifist solutions for ending the war which might well have appealed to him earlier were now rejected outright. He refused such a collaboration with George Lansbury, his mentor in the Socialist League. Everyone, he wrote, should follow 'his own feelings'; he believed his 'contribution might be for the present in Eastern Affairs'.[119] His idea of creating a 'real opposition' in Parliament did not proceed very far. To D. N. Pritt, Hewlett Johnson, the 'Red Dean' of Canterbury, R. Strauss and other militants whom he summoned to discuss such a possibility he announced instead that he was

considering the government's proposal of sending him to Moscow.[120]

On the other hand his position as a lone warrior and his incessant assaults on the government were an obstacle to his assuming any official function. Shortly after his return he precluded in Parliament and in writing any possible collaboration with the 'Munich Men', who could 'never rally the people . . . to the supreme effort necessary to avoid defeat'. His refusal to consider readmission to the Labour Party, which had been granted to the rest of the 1939 rebels, prevented his inclusion in Churchill's government. In any case he had criticized the War Cabinet for comprising 'the leaders of various power groups in the House, irrespective of their qualifications'.[121]

The solution to his frustration on the home front seemed to lie in personal diplomacy. His already abundant confidence was further augmented by the contacts he had established with an impressive list of leaders throughout the world. Indeed he had hardly settled in Britain when he was already planning a journey to Paris to confer with Premier Reynaud.[122] As in autumn 1939, the opportunity to assume an official role occurred in connection with Russia. Early in the morning of 17 May Halifax sought Butler's reaction, before Cabinet met, to a mission headed by Cripps to Moscow. Butler had consistently protected Cripps from the Foreign Office's wrath and had maintained there was 'a lot' in what he had to say on the international situation.[123] He shared Cripps' forecast of the social change which Britain would inevitably undergo as a result of the war. Such 'a swing back towards the left', he wrote to Cripps in Moscow, necessitated a revision of imperial policy. Cripps for his part had learned from his experience that Butler was perhaps a 'dreamer' but could be 'galvanised into action in the right entourage'.[124] Butler now enthusiastically recommended Cripps, whose strength lay in 'mastering and presenting a brief and in assessing a position'. He would even allow him 'latitude to discuss over a reasonably wide field with the Soviet authorities'.[125] The increasing susceptibility of progressive Conservatives to ideas advocated by Cripps, once the extent of the world crisis had become apparent, was to prove as crucial to Cripps' meteoric political rise as the wide popularity he gained after the German invasion of Russia.

In view of subsequent interpretations of the decision to send Cripps to Moscow, it should be stressed that Churchill's part in the decision was minimal. It is true that in October 1939, when he was still at the

Admiralty, Churchill had responded favourably to vague proposals that Cripps be appointed as ambassador in Moscow. Now, however, engrossed in the deteriorating military situation in France and the reorganization of the Cabinet, he only exchanged a few words with Halifax in the garden of 10 Downing Street before the subject was raised in Cabinet. Later on Churchill could not even spare the time to discuss the mission with Cripps before his departure.[126] Relations with Russia remained entirely in Halifax's domain.

The actual appointment resembles Cripps' involvement in the first leg of the negotiations. It is a tribute to his political stature that despite the lack of any power base, his irrevocable criticism of the previous government and disapproval of the current one, his analysis of the situation and proposal for action were once again adopted word for word as a Cabinet resolution. There was no thorough discussion either of the course of relations with Russia or of Cripps' suitability for the post. Dalton's and Attlee's reservations stemmed from their close acquaintance with Cripps, and especially because of their 'very unsatisfactory experience' with him in the Labour Party. Dalton even warned Churchill privately but the Prime Minister 'with a friendly grin' brushed aside his misgivings: 'You're on velvet.' On Dalton's insistence the limits of Cripps' authority were defined as 'to explore . . . and to report' but 'not to attempt to make an agreement'. The Cabinet, however, failed to elucidate its policy towards Russia. By entrusting Cripps, renowned for his independent mind and unyielding character, with the amorphous task 'to create better relations', the Cabinet granted him the very manoeuvrability which Dalton was trying to deny him.[127] Dalton decided at that very early stage that 'to protect Economic Warfare positions from being compromised' Postan should be attached to Cripps. Postan eventually went with Cripps as far as Sofia but was refused a visa on account of his past record.[128] The Foreign Office followed suit in appointing a watchdog; Dan Lascelles was rushed from Norway to Moscow to join Cripps. The Office, he was instructed, had 'no illusions as to the prospects of the mission producing positive results'. The mission was 'only exploratory' and ought not to 'involve' the government 'in any commitment' towards Russia.[129]

Later controversies have overshadowed the events surrounding the decision to dispatch Cripps to Moscow. On 20 May Cripps was formally approached by Halifax and Dalton. Although Dalton continued

to stress the exploratory nature of the mission, it was generally understood that negotiations might 'flow over from trade into politics'. Dalton's insistence on introducing war trade elements into an agreement, despite Russian intransigence in the past and determination not to provoke Germany at present, reduced the likelihood of trade negotiations proceeding very far. Cripps, on the other hand, emphasized the political aspects of the mission. His acceptance was conditional on the government's affirmation that its attitude towards Russia had now become friendly. [130]

In the absence of a clearly formulated policy towards Russia, no further progress was made before Cripps' departure to define the aims of his mission. The President of the Board of Trade and a senior representative of the MEW even failed, while briefing Cripps, to agree on whether a barter or contraband agreement was desirable, the nature of the trade goods, or the means of payment. [131] Within a week Dalton himself softened his reservations. On the day of Cripps' flight, he frankly admitted to Maisky that the mission was designed mainly to remove 'mistrust on both sides' and 'indicate good will'. Trade negotiations, he reiterated, were 'apt to flow over to politics'. Privately he gradually came to appreciate the advantages of Cripps' absence in Moscow. [132] Cripps left for Russia without any feeling of restraint. He had, he told Butler, 'a "flexible brief" from M.E.W. and encouragement from B^d of Trade & Supply'. Halifax was already convinced that the Russians would indeed 'wish to talk a bit wider' than trade. [133]

The Russian policy too had been undergoing a process of reevaluation. On 20 May Maisky had ascertained through a series of interviews with Eden, Lloyd George and the Webbs that in the event of the collapse of France England would remain at war. [134] As he had not seen Halifax since their meeting of 8 May, he was surprised to be summoned to Whitehall late on that evening, which was unusual. He was 'delighted' to learn from Halifax, who was highly agitated, of the government's decision to send Cripps to Moscow; Cripps, he was further told, would 'enjoy full liberty to explore any other question' than trade. This confirmed Maisky's earlier assessment of the new Cabinet's determination to fight on. [135]

The Russians, however, could not act in haste. The decision on Cripps' mission had originated in the Soviet intimation that they would prefer personal and discreet negotiations to an exchange of notes. The

astonishing success of the German army obliged them to walk a tightrope. Apprehensive as they were of the threat of a powerful and victorious Germany in Europe, any improvement of relations with Britain had to be implemented without 'unduly incensing Germany'.[136] Considering the lack of a British ambassador in Moscow, the arrival of Cripps as a special emissary could only be interpreted by the Germans as a *volte-face*.

The ingenious solution to the dilemma was to play down the significance of the mission by making it conditional on Cripps' posting as ambassador. This would ensure the immediate appointment of a British ambassador, and moreover an acceptable one to the Russians. In a move which ran counter to their recent statement, the Russians suddenly produced a reply to the conditions set by the British on 8 May for the resumption of trade negotiations. Halifax, impervious to subtleties in foreign policy, assumed that the reply had 'crossed' the fresh British proposal to send Cripps. It is more likely, however, that the note was in fact tuned to German ears. An assiduous attempt was made to present the negotiations as a continuation of those conducted in the autumn of 1939. Both the note and a Tass communiqué falsely suggested that the talks had been initiated by the British in March. As far as the now obsolete British proposal was concerned, there could be no 'direct or indirect subordination of the trade negotiations to the war aims'; this would be in 'contradiction to the policy of neutrality' pursued by the USSR. Trade with Germany was 'exclusively in the competence of the Soviet Government'. The last paragraph, however, left the door open for compromise on the basis of 'equality and reciprocal obligations'.[137]

Having overlooked the connection between the Russian note and the proposed mission, the Cabinet failed to appreciate the far-reaching implications that the new Russian position was to have on the negotiations. The Russians had time on their side. As the Allies' military situation deteriorated the British were more likely to respond to their demands. There was also a tactical advantage in carefully timing Russian conditions for the mission. Apparently the idea of installing Cripps as ambassador in Moscow was already stirring in the Soviet embassy on 24 May, two days before it was presented to Halifax.[138] Maisky had gathered from Butler that Cripps was being flown to Athens the next day, to await the Soviet reply before air routes to France were cut off. The Russians must have correctly surmised that

they could tie the government's hands if the mission received full publicity once Cripps had already set out. Indeed, as early as 22 May Butler had warned Halifax that the 'strong urge . . . both on right and left' of the government for better relations with Russia meant that he would 'be pressed' if the mission did not materialize.[139] Moreover, the Russians hoped that well-timed publicity of their conditions would soften the German reaction. From Bournemouth, waiting to embark on his seaplane to Athens, Cripps grudgingly noted that the press had 'got it all' on the morning of 25 May.[140]

The Russian ploy had the desired effect. On 29 May Schulenburg could inform the German government that there was 'no reason for apprehension concerning Cripps' mission'. The selection, he believed, was 'unfortunate' for Britain, as the Soviet government preferred to 'negotiate important matters with a prominent representative of the Government'. The Germans eventually dropped the idea of sending a trade delegation to compete with Cripps.[141]

Assuming that Cripps had left England, Maisky broke to Halifax on 26 May the news of his government's decision to negotiate with Cripps, 'or any one else' in whom the Cabinet 'had confidence', only if he held the rank of a regular ambassador. Halifax's protest that 'he hardly supposed the Soviet Government claimed to choose' an ambassador for Britain could not disguise the fact that this was taking place. Halifax was particularly incensed as the War Cabinet had waived its objection to the appointment of an ambassador to Moscow, and had agreed to Peterson for the post, only two days earlier.[142] All efforts to persuade the Russians to receive Cripps as ambassador 'on a special mission', to be subsequently replaced by a regular ambassador, were abortive.[143]

There was a surprise in store for Maisky as well. On returning home he received a telephone call from Cripps explaining that mechanical problems had delayed his departure. After hearing about the new Soviet demands, Cripps got through to Halifax, who 'did not seem quite to have understood' the changed circumstances. On the spot Cripps secured from Halifax a promise to do 'whatever was necessary' to obtain for him ambassadorial status.[144] Thus, contrary to what is commonly believed, Cripps consented to become ambassador and was not faced by a *fait accompli* once far away from England. Similarly the government allowed him to proceed with the mission fully aware of the turn of events.

The mission, indeed, had gained its own momentum. The Russians now exerted the last pressure. A Tass communiqué, again directed towards Berlin, released the final Soviet demand for ambassadorial status before receiving the British reply. The Cabinet conceded without a murmur on 31 May.[145] Thus the Russians had gained the unprecedented achievement of not only forcing the British to return an ambassador to Moscow but also securing the appointment of their own candidate. After the bitter experience with British emissaries in 1939, Molotov could now feel assured that Cripps was 'entirely in confidence of His Majesty's Government'. This was undoubtedly more important than Cripps' political inclinations.[146]

Cripps' appointment sealed the debate raging in the Foreign Office through the 1930s on the advisability of improving relations with Russia, and hastened the consolidation of a new and unanimous concept. The response to Soviet overtures in the 1930s was dictated not by a wish to draw closer and erase past differences but rather by apprehension of a possible Soviet rapprochement with Germany in the spirit of the Rapallo treaty. Since 1935 Sargent, then at the Central Department, was the arch-enemy of such an orientation. He gradually succeeded in shifting the Office to his point of view, thereby negating Eden's policy as manifested in his visit to Moscow in 1935. A proponent of continuity in foreign policy, Sargent advocated the return to the traditional reserve attitude. The main challenge came from Laurence Collier, Head of the Northern Department, who had obvious liberal inclinations. His influence in support of collaboration dwindled, however, with the appointment of Cadogan as Permanent Under-Secretary in 1938. Cadogan, whether from ideological reasons or the customary tendency to overlook events in eastern Europe, attached little significance to recruiting Russia.[147]

With the sole exception of Butler, the Foreign Office now opposed the mission. Its views were clearly expressed by Collier, who had recanted his earlier stand; it was 'hopeless', he minuted, 'to expect to use the Soviet Union as a real counter weight to Germany'.[148] A briefing on British policy towards Russia prepared at Cripps' request and approved by Sargent was modified by Butler. In its original form it stated that Britain could not compete with Germany, which was 'able to play both on M. Stalin's fears and his greed', whereas from Britain Russia had 'nothing to fear, and nothing to hope for'. In other words the govern-

ment was advised at that juncture 'not to place too much confidence in the ability, or indeed in the readiness, of the Soviet Union to come to [Britain's] rescue'.[149]

The anticipated results of the mission were depicted by Sargent in sombre colours shortly after its announcement. Once in Moscow Cripps was likely to assume full authority to negotiate a settlement and the government would have to 'trust to luck' that he would not commit Britain beyond a 'harmless barter agreement'. Cripps was expected to manoeuvre the government into recognizing Soviet annexations on the grounds that these were required for her security.[150] Cadogan, the civil servant incarnate, deplored the appointment of an outsider. When a political appointment had been considered, the Northern Department had favoured installing 'rather a rude duke' in Moscow. Cripps, Cadogan argued, was 'an excellent lawyer & a very nimble debator' but he had 'not yet won his spurs in diplomacy'. This, of course, was directed at Butler as well. He mocked Cripps' confidence in his personal ability to ' "swing" a country'. His overall view, however, which attached 'no importance whatever to Russia', demonstrates that the Foreign Office was drifting away from the government. The last word belonged to Butler. He ironically admitted that diplomacy was 'a skilled art' and that he was 'learning by degrees'. Cripps, he believed, was 'under few illusions' about his ability to 'swing' the Soviet Union, but could employ his 'active brain' to find 'useful contacts'. One could not possibly ignore Russia, which had 'always counted in the history of Europe', even though she had 'always been difficult to gauge or to understand'.[151] On the whole the Foreign Office held a detached and sceptical outlook. 'It will be interesting to see', it was minuted once news of Cripps' arrival in Moscow came through, 'what, if anything, happens now.'[152]

There were other contestants for the job among left-wing proponents of closer relations with Russia such as Charles Trevelyan and Josiah Wedgwood. Wedgwood approached Churchill but claimed to have been told: 'My dear Jos, you are not *really* rich enough. It is the most expensive Embassy we have. Cripps is the one suitable left wing man we have who is rolling in money.'[153]

The implications of Cripps' appointment should now be considered in the light of the increasing significance assumed by Russia after the exit of France as a prospective ally in the war. They stand in sharp con-

3  The leading figures at the Foreign Office, l. to r.: Sir Alexander Cadogan,
R. A. Butler and Lord Halifax, April 1940

trast to the accepted view that Cripps' ideological convictions were a
handicap in Moscow. Such an interpretation follows Churchill's argument in his war memoirs that he did not 'realize sufficiently that Soviet
Communists hate extreme left wing politicians even more than they do
Tories or Liberals'.[154] His exposition, marred by the rivalry which
characterized his subsequent relations with Cripps, is mostly based on a
tendentious selection of Nazi documents on Soviet–German relations
released by the American State Department at the height of the Cold
War. The appointment, as has been shown, had been literally forced by
the Russians on an indifferent Cabinet immersed in the conduct of a
critical stage of the war in France. In fact, since the outbreak of war the
British government had failed to perceive the aims of Soviet policy, of
which they remained highly apprehensive. The Foreign Office had
naturally lost ground since the outbreak of war. Halifax's susceptibility
to diverse pressures further undermined the formulation of a consistent

policy. On the whole, however, the Foreign Office retained its traditional suspicion and hostility towards Russia. There was a particular aversion to the appointment of a politician and a left-winger as ambassador. Other government departments, concerned with the economic side of negotiations, had likewise failed to agree on a common policy.

The vacuum thus created allowed Cripps exceptional manoeuvrability. The various restrictions which were imposed on him did not make sufficient allowances for his personality. This was not crucial so long as an exploratory mission was contemplated. However, the appointment of Cripps as ambassador in unique circumstances was an altogether different story and would inevitably lead to friction. Cripps, who had asked to retain his seat in Parliament, regarded the ambassadorship as a temporary and essentially political appointment and was not therefore inclined to abide by the rules governing the civil service. The post itself seemed to him a forced masquerade: the obligatory 'full dress diplomatic performance' was 'an awful undertaking'. 'I have', he observed, 'no more ideas than the man in the moon as to how I shall run the embassy which is I imagine a large establishment with many servants etc. etc.!!!'[155]

Moreover, in contrast to the government, Cripps had embarked on the mission with a clear evaluation of Soviet aims and attitudes. It was almost axiomatic with him that Germany and Russia were 'fundamentally antagonistic'. The German successes and the threat of Allied action, he held, had made the Russians 'extremely nervous', and they were therefore 'anxious' to come to some sort of an agreement. His expectations were modest and realistic; he hoped to secure their 'more or less neutral position'.[156]

The imminent fall of France only increased his optimism about the mission. Before setting out on his last stage to Moscow, he described to the American minister in Sofia the 'tremendous change' in recent Soviet attitudes, which had become 'very constructive'. He believed Russia had finally realized that Germany would not stop until Russia was 'crushed'.[157] In long discussions with his host Sir George Rendel, British ambassador in Sofia, he explained the reasons for his optimism. It had little to do with his ideological leanings but stemmed from a 'remarkably objective' evaluation sustained by a 'broad Christian point of view'. The Russian government he believed to be 'sound at heart'

and the people fundamentally religious. Fully confident in his own magnetism, and somewhat naively convinced of the power of universal values as a uniting factor in international affairs, he was certain he could convert the Russians to his point of view if he 'treated them frankly and showed confidence in them'.[158]

# THE MISSION LAUNCHED

*Fruitless efforts*

Cripps was obliged to make a long detour now that the Germans had cut the direct northern route to Russia. With the exception of a hair-raising experience, when his plane was struck by lightning and turned upside down, the journey was uneventful. While waiting for Soviet *agrément* and for his credentials to be arranged he was entertained by the British ambassadors in Athens and Sofia. He thoroughly enjoyed the classical sites in Greece, the scenery, the flora and a much-needed rest. Idleness, however, was foreign to his temperament. Eager to reach Moscow, particularly in view of the alarming reports from France, Cripps grew increasingly impatient with Halifax's 'haggling with the Russians' as to his title, wasting valuable time over 'stupid formalities'. He finally even wired Halifax 'a sort of polite ultimatum' either to bestow him with 'necessary powers' or to 'send out someone else' with proper authority.[1] On 2 June he was finally informed of his appointment as ambassador; since Cripps continued to view himself as a politician rather than a career diplomat, he was even more gratified to learn that he had been granted the almost unique privilege of retaining his seat in Parliament.[2]

Precious time was likewise wasted on the preparation and transfer of Cripps' credentials. The Russians, as part of their reassessment after the stunning German victory, were scrutinizing British attitudes. At the beginning of June Molotov had requested that Cripps should proceed 'at once' to Moscow.[3] Halifax had however in the meantime accepted the Foreign Office's estimation that Russia was not likely to assist Britain actively in stemming the German advance.[4] In addition there had been no precedent for the telegraphing of credentials and particularly the King's signature. A solution which would not injure British

41

diplomatic traditions and at the same time would relieve Russian suspicions about the nature of the appointment took time to arrive at.[5] When eventually Cripps was formally accredited as ambassador the French had just capitulated, the British were isolated and the European balance of power seemed, at least temporarily, irrevocably altered.

Cripps assumed charge of the embassy upon his arrival in Moscow on 12 June even before receiving his credentials. The political indifference towards Russia was reflected in the delapidated state of the delegation and the resources allocated to it. The embassy, an imposing building on the Moscow River Embankment immediately opposite the Kremlin, had been the residence of a rich sugar merchant. For a while it accommodated the library of the English Church and later served as the residence of the Litvinovs. Cripps found the embassy 'in the most appalling oppressive state'. No attempt had been made by the Foreign Office or his predecessors to make the place more attractive. The drawing room in which he was expected to meet other diplomats was vividly described by Cripps:

The gilt and ormolu furniture is covered with a flowered silk brocade in a sort of pale beige which is most sickly, and the pink & blue flowers are pale & colourless. There is a particularly ugly screen in a brilliant light blue which swears at everything else . . . and a long plain stiff sofa with no cushions at all which would spoil any room.

His own room, overlooking a garden, was so furnished 'as to make it barrack like ugly'. The staff were mostly Russians and Volga Germans and the spoken language, rather embarrassingly, was German. It was impossible to entertain as the embassy had no butler or maid. The British ambassador's tableware consisted of 'all bits and pieces of odd China sets – no dishes, no proper glass or silver!' The renovation of the embassy achieved through the arrival of 120 cases of furniture and effects of closed-down embassies in the Baltic and occasional shopping expeditions had high priority in an attempt to make the place look 'a bit more lived in'. Cripps also improved the quality of life and changed the routine at the embassy, conscious of the need 'to keep people cheerful and normal as the isolation makes everyone so retrospective and heavy'.[6]

Far more serious was the fact that the embassy was severely understaffed; on busy days the staff could 'hardly keep pace with the

cyphering . . . working late into the night as well as all day'. Cripps' unceasing harassment of the Foreign Office for administrative reorganization had little result and the embassy was consequently ill prepared to cope with the burden that fell on it after the German invasion.[7]

On the personal level, despite the common belief to the contrary, Cripps did not share the prevalent abhorrence of service in Moscow, a place described by the *Times'* correspondent as 'appallingly dull and drab'. Cripps certainly would not have subscribed to his view that anybody who consented to 'be exiled here for a year or two does his newspaper an extraordinary favour'.[8] His occasional depressions had little to do with disillusion or resentment of life in Moscow. As a family man loneliness and homesickness, combined with idleness, to which he was not accustomed, made the protracted separation an ordeal. In fact criticisms about the realities of Soviet life and the exigencies of serving in Moscow are conspicuous for their absence. Instead Moscow had a distinct appeal to him as is illustrated in an untypical literary entry in his diary after his arrival:

I sat out & walked & lay on a garden seat after dinner last night smoking a cigar for an hour in the garden and it was a perfect warm soft starlight night. Searchlight beams were playing and dancing in the incredibly soft velvet of the sky, and on the other side of the embassy the Kremlin was looking its really beautiful best. There is some quality of romanticness about it, set on its hill above the river, with the most beautiful wall in the world surrounding it, that makes it a perpetual mystery and gives it at the same time a calm solidity!

A year later in the turbulent month preceding the German invasion, when the future of the mission was precarious, Isobel expressed very similar sentiments after a night walk across the Kremlin: 'I realised how the charm of it had grown with me & what a comfort it had been all these months to live opposite to it . . . for the rest of my life I shall feel a harmony with Moscow.'[9]

It is loneliness which accounts for one of the better remembered aspects of the mission. Immediately upon his arrival Cripps acquired an Airedale which he named Joe. Their attachment or perhaps the unfortunate name evoked comments from all observers. Cripps' decision to get the dog was a natural solution to his desperate need for com-

4 A view of the Kremlin from the British embassy with the steamer *Kalinin* in the foreground

panionship. 'It will be', he wrote home, 'a comfort to have something to talk to!! and also to have about with me always . . . it enables one to talk aloud without feeling one is going dotty talking to oneself.'[10]

Cripps had flown to Moscow with M. Labonne, the newly appointed French ambassador, who in view of the imminent fall of Paris had been authorized 'to compel the Soviet Union to decide once and for all' whether she was prepared to join the Allies. Cripps was convinced that the success of his own mission in the new conditions depended on a radical reappraisal of the British attitude to Russia and support of the French initiative. The British government, however, had failed to arrive at a policy towards Russia since the outbreak of war and was unlikely to do so at such short notice. In these circumstances Cripps was allowed greater latitude than that of a regular ambassador from the outset of his mission. He was given vague instructions 'to broach the question from the general standpoint of European equilibrium' as he was the 'best judge of how far he could successfully go' in his first interview with Molotov.[11]

Cripps prepared the ground for Labonne to make his urgent appeal when he paid a courtesy call on Molotov two days after his arrival in the

5 A Sunday walk in the company of the Yugoslav ambassador Milovan Gavrilovic with Cripps' Airedale Joe

Russian capital. The conversation first touched on the prospects of trade negotiations, which had been the ostensible reason for Cripps' appointment. Molotov proposed an early start for such talks. Cripps, however, soon reverted to politics. He suggested that relations might be best improved not through trade but by means of Soviet assistance in creating a Balkan bloc to stop German aggression. This idea, which had first occurred to Cripps on a brief stopover in Bucharest *en route* to Moscow, was no longer applicable. Somewhat insensitive to the complexity of the situation, Cripps had openly disclosed the major role he assigned to Russia in the formation of such a bloc. King Carol of Romania, however, had been pressing Britain to extend her guarantee to include Russian aggression. Alarmed by the German victories and the implications of Cripps' visit, he swiftly replaced Grigore Gafencu, the pro-western Foreign Minister.[12]

Molotov, presumably already engaged in preparations for the annexation of Bessarabia, confined himself to an ambiguous statement on the Soviet 'special interest' in Romania. He was also unwilling to admit common ground for collaboration in the Far East, where the American attitude was 'unsympathetic and unlikely to be in accordance with that of Russia'. Molotov seemed more concerned with the effect of the battles in France on Allied diplomacy. Cripps unequivocally excluded the possibility of France's suing for peace. As for the British, he concluded in Churchillian style, they 'possessed stubbornness and they would display that quality till they were victorious whatever the hardships through which the country might have to pass'.[13]

Within a short time, the surrender in Compiègne would raise serious doubts in Soviet minds as to the reliability of Cripps' forecasts. In fact, while Cripps was denying the possibility of a separate peace the Wehrmacht was marching unopposed into Paris. Labonne, encouraged by Cripps, now made a desperate call to Molotov for 'effective support' with a concealed warning that an Allied defeat would threaten the balance of power and might well end in Germany's turning eastwards. Playing on Soviet apprehensions of a separate peace, Labonne finally produced his trump: the attitude of the Soviet Union might have 'a decisive influence on French military and diplomatic decisions'. Molotov's reply implied that the approach had come too late. The 'very sudden' change in the French attitude, he stressed, stood in sharp contrast to persistent rumours that peace talks were under way. Moreover,

Labonne's casual allusions to Soviet 'legitimate interests' required 'elucidation'. Soviet policy, he reasserted, 'was based on neutrality'.[14]

It was thus self-evident that, as Cripps cabled the Cabinet on 17 June: 'with every hour that passes it is becoming more unlikely that Soviet Government will abandon their present attitude of reluctance to acquiesce in a German hegemony in Europe'. On the other hand, the desirability of persuading the Russians to cooperate with Britain was 'clearly greater than ever'. Cripps, however, had abandoned hope of speedily recruiting the Russians through economic inducements or vague declarations. The only door left open, he suggested, was for an 'authoritative assurance of American collaboration and support' to Russia.[15]

In view of the haphazard treatment of relations with Russia, it is not surprising that the Americans had not been informed of the recent approaches. At such a late hour, the Foreign Office was not enthusiastic about putting 'half baked ideas' to Roosevelt. It was indeed difficult to visualize the Americans pledging support to Russia. After all, Roosevelt had just produced a cautious and disappointing response to the personal appeals made by Churchill and Reynaud for direct assistance to France. Cripps' call for vigorous American intervention presupposed not only a close Anglo-American collaboration but also a more receptive mood in the United States. Soviet–American relations had been severely strained as a result of the Ribbentrop–Molotov pact, the Soviet occupation of eastern Poland and above all the Soviet incursion into Finland. The Americans had even imposed a 'moral embargo' on industrial goods destined for Russia.[16]

Cripps stood little chance of recruiting support from the American embassy in Moscow. Despite his extremely forthcoming attitude and almost blind trust of people, he took an immediate dislike to Laurence Steinhardt, his American counterpart in Moscow, as emerges from a letter to his daughter: 'I didn't care for the American Ambassador a typical bumptious U.S.A. business-lawyer type. I wouldnt trust him either very much. But still there he is & Moscow is a small place so we shall have to put up with him.'[17] Unlike Cripps, Steinhardt was motivated by powerful personal ambition. The nephew of S. Untermeyer, a well-known lawyer and activist in the New York Democratic reform movement, Steinhardt found his way into Roosevelt's pre-convention group and served on the Democratic National Finance Committee, to which he

contributed heavily. As a result he was appointed minister to Sweden in 1934 after Roosevelt's election. He later served in Peru and in 1939 was promoted to Moscow. 'There was little in Steinhardt's background', admits his biographer, 'to fit him for work in Russia'; he was far from being an expert on the Soviet Union, was suspicious of the Russians and abhorred life in Moscow.[18]

He did, however, exercise a strong influence on both the President and the Secretary of State. When Cripps suggested an approach to the Americans, Steinhardt happened to be on leave in the United States. He had persuaded Roosevelt to dismiss Soviet feelers for improved relations, similar to those made in London. An interview between Cordell Hull, the American Secretary of State, and Constantin Oumansky, Soviet ambassador in Washington, left no doubt as to the low ebb which relations had reached. The Russians, complained Hull, were getting 'tougher and tougher'; Steinhardt was 'under strict surveillance . . . even followed into the public toilets'.[19] This open hostility was to have a significant and lasting impact on Cripps' mission. It provided the British government with a vindication of its policies in view of Britain's increasing dependence on the United States.

There was, however, an undercurrent in the State Department which the Foreign Office preferred to overlook. The Americans were quicker to grasp the changing international scene. Loy Henderson, the head of the Eastern Europe Division at the State Department and by no means a proponent of the Soviet Union, admitted in a private letter referring to the Soviet annexation of the Baltic states: 'We can now talk over realism and realistic approaches with aplomb, while a relatively short time ago we were full of criticizms [sic] for nations which openly avowed that they were not interested in international morality.'[20]

Thus, when Lord Lothian, British ambassador to the United States, discussed Cripps' telegram informally with the President at the White House on 16 June and with Sumner Welles two days later, he found the Americans prepared to lift restrictions on the sale of machine tools and aviation petrol to Russia, although they were doubtful whether it would have the 'desired effect'. The embarrassing fact, however, was that the restrictions had been introduced to conform with British demands for strict contraband control. Moreover, the machines, as Halifax told Cabinet, were desperately needed by England; he therefore proposed not to press the Americans any further.[21]

Molotov's frequent if guarded contacts with Cripps and Labonne demonstrate Soviet anxiety over France's fate. By mid-June attention was focused on Britain. The Russians took steps not only to ascertain but also to encourage Britain's continued resistance though fear of German criticism imposed caution. Rothstein informed the Foreign Office of the Russians' wish for Churchill to have a 'frank discussion' on the situation with Maisky. The Russians still erroneously held Halifax responsible for the hostility they encountered in London, while equally unjustifiably attributing the recent thaw in relations to Churchill. In an extremely frank commentary on Soviet diplomacy, Rothstein confessed that Germany's progress in France was 'something of a surprise, even to the Moscow realists'. He intimated that neither the developments in the Baltic nor the recent deployment of Soviet troops on the Polish border would be 'popular in Berlin'. He finally noted the 'zeal with which Sir Stafford Cripps had commenced his duties' in Moscow and indicated that the time was propitious for improvement of Anglo-Soviet relations. Rothstein, however, was dismissed in the Office as an *agent provocateur* and the content of his message did not proceed beyond the head of the Northern Department.[22]

The Russians' diplomatic efforts to bolster Allied resistance were followed up, once French capitulation had become inevitable, by the hasty reinforcement of their own defences. It was patently obvious that the assumption of control of the Baltic States on 15 and 16 June was connected with events in France. The headlong transfer of troops to the western front, the overnight conversion of public institutions into military establishments and the transfer of the command of the Baltic fleet to the forward naval bases in Tallin could not be concealed.[23] The Russians therefore attempted to mollify the Germans to forestall any move eastwards. Molotov's congratulations to Schulenburg on the 'splendid success of the German Wehrmacht', which figure so prominently in Churchill's history of the war, were only a prelude for the flimsy explanation of the annexation of the Baltic States as a move to counter French and British 'intrigues'. The compliments were also intended to soften in advance German suspicions with regard to the Russians' 'extremely urgent' demand for a solution of the Bessarabian question, which was made to Schulenburg the next morning.[24]

The Russians abandoned their acrobatic efforts to maintain balanced

relations with both Germany and the Allies on the day France surrendered. As late as 21 June Maisky, who had constantly been on his toes to follow innuendoes in the policy of his superiors in Moscow, openly conceded to Butler that the ' "Drang nach Osten" remained a fixed point' in Germany's policy. The 'winter of discontent' in Anglo-Soviet relations he believed to be over, and he 'commented affably on the impression created by [Cripps] in Moscow'. However, the next morning great efforts were made in Moscow to disclaim a shift in Soviet policy as a result of the activities of Cripps and Labonne. A Tass communiqué denied the existence of any tension in Soviet–German relations. Molotov hastily divulged to Augusto Rosso, the Italian ambassador, the gist of his earlier talks with Cripps, fully aware that it would be passed on.[25]

The British government was slow in coming to terms with the altering international situation. Ironically, only on 22 June was a satisfactory solution devised for the transfer of Cripps' credentials. He was instructed to present them to Molotov to 'remove any doubts' which he might still entertain. This amusing but trifling episode is blown up out of all proportion in Maisky's memoirs as a proof of Britain's inherent hostility. It is in fact more of a cover-up for the obvious shift in Soviet foreign policy, paralysed by both the failure to accommodate with the western powers prior to the German *Blitzkrieg* and the crushing defeat of the Allies on the Continent.[26]

Cripps, on the other hand, was quick to discern the change. Since 18 June he had attempted in vain to see either Molotov or Anasthasias Mikoyan, the Minister of Trade. His deduction was that the Soviet government had reached 'the expected decision . . . to maintain its present show of benevolent neutrality towards Germany for the time being'. However, Cripps had not despaired of picking up the threads through an arrangement in the Balkans. Ignoring the original aim of his mission, he intended on next seeing Molotov to make further trade negotiations conditional on a Soviet definition of their 'future political intentions'. As if oblivious to the grave implications of the novel situation, the Foreign Office openly rejoiced in Cripps' discomfiture. Cripps, noted Sargent, was now entering the 'humiliating phase' which had befallen all previous negotiators. Stalin, who had never genuinely considered rapprochement, simply wished to counter German nagging by 'pointing to Sir S. Cripps on the doormat, and by threatening to have

him in and start talking'. Cripps, he concluded, ought 'to cultivate the virtues of patience and long-suffering . . . & to stay at his post!' Butler alone showed some sympathy, commenting on ambassadors 'who with complete disregard to their own private convenience undertake duties such as this which must at times be odious'.

Sargent, however, correctly evaluated that with France out of the picture and Britain facing an imminent invasion, Stalin could hardly be expected to respond to Cripps who 'as a suppliant on his doormat' was holding 'his pathetic little peace offerings of tin in one hand and rubber in the other'. Typically, however, Halifax continued to prescribe treatment which could no longer be effective. Butler had convinced Halifax that the only chance of securing a change in Soviet policy was through a personal approach to Stalin himself. Since the negotiations in 1939 Moscow had been seeking direct and authoritative involvement of the British Prime Minister in the conduct of relations. In the absence of any indication to the contrary, the Russians continued to act after the fateful events of May on the assumption that foreign affairs remained in Halifax's hands. In his history of the war Churchill gives the misleading impression that he was the instigator of the approach to Stalin. According to all available evidence it seems clear that even now Churchill continued to overlook the significance of the Soviet Union as a potential ally. The letter to Stalin, despite its unmistakable Churchillian idiom, was contemplated and drafted in the Foreign Office and merely signed by Churchill. In the Office it was hoped that the message would secure for Cripps an audience with Stalin and enable him to discover 'once and for all' the views and intentions of the Soviet government in the face of the sudden overthrow of the European equilibrium.[27]

Europe of July 1940, however, no longer resembled that of the previous year. Considering the dismal political and military position of Britain at the time, it is difficult to comprehend how, besides exploring Soviet policies, the message was expected to eradicate overnight the long history of mutual suspicion and effect a coup in Soviet policy. On the face of it the dramatic tenor of the message conformed with the occasion. However, on closer scrutiny it is clear that it conceded very little to the Russians. The admission that 'harmonious and mutually beneficial' relations should not be hampered by the fact that the two countries stood for 'widely differing systems of political thought' did not gloss over their substantially diverging interests. Germany and

Russia had shared a community of interests based on revisionism since the peace of Versailles. The outstanding feature of Churchill's message, which on the whole was shallow in substance, was its attachment to the *status quo ante bellum*. The Cabinet had on several occasions deferred discussion on war aims or post-war arrangements. Churchill, in his speeches and now in the message to Stalin, had vowed only to 'save England and free all the rest of Europe from the domination' of Germany. The message ended with support of Cripps' authority and explicitly expressed readiness to discuss fully with the Soviet government 'any of the vast problems created by Germany's hegemony in Europe'.[28]

When considering the draft telegram the Cabinet had in fact ruled out Cripps' proposed concessions to the Russians in the Balkans and the Far East. Before the meeting Dalton had urged Halifax to be 'a little more forthcoming' to the Russians over Bessarabia. He was even of the opinion that it might be 'the least unsatisfactory of various alternatives' that the Russians should 'occupy the Roumanian oil fields'. Ever suspicious of Soviet intentions, Halifax replied that the move into Bessarabia had little to do with Germany but was 'a push southwards in order to threaten the straits'. The correctness of Halifax's analysis was questioned the next morning, when the Russians in addition to annexing Bessarabia assumed control of Bukovina, which incidentally was not specified in the Ribbentrop–Molotov pact. This could only be interpreted as the bolstering of a vulnerable flank against a possible German attack.[29]

Cripps handed the message to Stalin on the evening of 1 July. A 'severely frank discussion', lasting from 6.30 to 9.15, left Cripps in no doubt that the evasive message would not achieve a major shift in Soviet foreign policy. In many ways the communication had the opposite effect. It seems to have enhanced Stalin's confidence in the correctness of his policies. 'If the Prime Minister wishes to restore the old equilibrium', Stalin grudgingly commented on the essence of Churchill's note, 'we cannot agree with him.' The weakness of the British approach was even recognized by General Ernst Köstring, the German military attaché in Moscow. Together with Schulenburg he was provided by Molotov with a precise résumé of the meeting. England, he noted in his diary, had failed to appreciate 'Stalin's refusal to restore former equi-

librium' in Europe. The approach was, therefore, unlikely to 'shake Stalin's loyalty' to Germany.[30]

It is interesting to note at this point Stalin's growing self-deception and acquiescence at German expansion as a result of the failure to reach accommodation with the Allies. Germany, Stalin told Cripps, was 'unable to establish a hegemony without the control of the seas'. He had encountered 'no signs of any wish to attain such hegemony' in his meetings with German representatives and was 'persuaded of the physical impossibility of such a thing'. This impression was strengthened a few days later when the French fleet was annihilated by the British at Oran. The invasion of Britain became more remote although Russian fears of renewed appeasement increased accordingly. Stalin, having just antagonized the Germans over the annexations in Romania, showed little interest in taking the lead to stabilize the situation in the Balkans. This role he assigned to Turkey. The only concession was his permission for Britain to bring about an improvement in Turkish–Soviet relations, which however had to be explicitly confined to a revision of the Montreux Convention. When the issue of trade was raised by Cripps, Stalin made it clear that he would abide by his agreement with Germany and would continue to supply non-ferrous metals in exchange for goods manufactured in Germany; if this proved to be an impediment to an agreement 'he was sorry, but it could not be helped'. Cripps emerged from the meeting with an unequivocal opinion which he would continue to maintain despite changing circumstances over the next two years:

It is, I think, perfectly clear that if we are to develop a closer political contact with the Union of Soviet Socialist Republics we must make up our minds about the nature of 'equilibrium' for which we are working. Presumably it must be one in which this country plays an important part and it is on this point above all that the Soviet Government will require reassuring.[31]

His recommendations provoked little reaction. Only A. V. Alexander, the Labour First Sea Lord of the Admiralty, was much impressed with the emphasis which the Russians had laid on their aim of a 'new equilibrium' in search of 'security of *European* Russia'. He did not force a debate in Cabinet, assuming that the Foreign Office was 'no doubt . . . already examining the implications of such views'.[32] The discussion in

Cabinet was first postponed and later confined to the side-issue of mediation between Turkey and Russia, the prospects of which did not seem to Halifax to be 'very sanguine'.[33] The attainment of even this aim was jeopardized by the German release of Allied plans, seized in Paris, for bombing the Russian oilfields at Baku. The Russians were given sufficient evidence to believe that the Turks were to be 'full and conscious partners' in the project.[34] The revelation, well timed by the Germans, certainly undermined Cripps' approaches. The British attempts to exonerate themselves only added fuel to the fire. The plans were justified by Russia's responsibility for the breakdown of the 1939 negotiations and their subsequent 'unfriendly attitude'. The negotiations conducted by Cripps, it was hoped in most uncomplimentary fashion, might 'remove the danger' of the Soviet government working either economically or militarily against Great Britain, a danger which Britain had 'naturally had to guard against when making their military plans'.[35]

Alexander's reliance on the Foreign Office, however, had little foundation. The Foreign Office maintained its fossilized outlook despite Britain's precarious position after the fall of France and the near certainty of an imminent German invasion. An astute but partisan observer, H. Channon, Butler's private secretary, witnessed in his diary: 'I call the FO "Bourbon House" since they have learnt nothing and forgotten nothing: in fact they are still asleep, dreaming in a pre-dictator world, foolish, carping, finicky, inefficient and futile.'[36] Entrenched in its position, the Foreign Office refused to revise its view of relations with Russia and even urged Cabinet to bring negotiations to an end. Upon receiving Cripps' report of his interview with Stalin, the Northern Department congratulated itself 'on having at last obtained an authoritative statement of Soviet policy'. They believed Stalin to be intransigent and committed to collaboration with Germany and gaining control of the Bosphorus straits.[37]

In mid-July Sargent submitted to Halifax an important memorandum on Soviet–German collaboration. He started by admitting that Russia was deterred from actively intervening on Britain's behalf 'by fear of German military might'. He went on to argue, however, that it was premature to assume from the obvious mutual suspicion and dissatisfaction that Germany and Russia would inevitably collide head-on. In accordance with the position held at the Foreign Office since the

outbreak of war, Sargent continued to regard both countries with equal rancour and distrust. 'Neither dictator', he wrote, '*dare* turn away lest the other stab him in the back'; neither was, however, prepared to 'face the other and fight it out'. As both leaders considered the British empire 'the ultimate enemy' it could be presumed that 'their appetites [would] grow with eating'. Once Stalin realized, therefore, that he could not keep his territorial gains in Europe 'without German permission' he would likewise decide that the collapse of the British empire would offer him 'considerable opportunities for expansion in Asia'. The inescapable conclusion was therefore that Stalin was simply 'strengthening his bargaining position with Hitler by starting a flirtation' with England.

The memorandum was met with serious reservations at the MEW, most directly involved in the negotiations, where Soviet–German relations were regarded as a 'cat-and-mouse game' rather than a full-blooded alliance. Although the Ministry would not go so far as to advocate the basing of a long-term policy on a belief in the 'permanence of Anglo-Soviet cooperation', they joined Cripps in expecting the Russians to assist Britain once she proved able to 'withstand the German onslaught'. On the whole, summed up Dalton, the Foreign Office's memorandum seemed 'very speculative', considering the fact that Soviet policy was 'difficult to make sense of'. Halifax evidently thought otherwise, attracting Churchill's attention to the 'very good examination of the problem'. Although the implicit line of the memorandum was never formally approved by Cabinet, in the absence of a clearly defined policy it gradually emerged as the ruling concept in the conduct of relations with Russia.[38]

As a result of his reevaluation of relations with Russia after the crucial events of June and his conversation with Stalin, Cripps found himself increasingly identifying with the Soviet point of view and at variance with his own government. In a confession made to Labonne, Cripps used a typical blend of liberal, Marxist and religious terminology to describe the war as a 'revolutionary one'. It was a revolution, he explained, because those who 'sat so long and so heavily upon the safety valve of progress' were the cause of exploitation and violence. The hope that the war would inevitably end in 'reconstruction' was the reason for the importance he attached 'to the resistance to Hitler by every means'.[39] The revolution, according to Cripps, was not confined

to the domestic scene. 'The old European balance had been destroyed', he claimed in apparent agreement with Stalin. The post-war arena was likely to be dominated by 'large scale groupings of powers' in which Britain would cease to occupy a key position. In view of the 'shifting of the centre of political gravity to the American continent', he concluded, Britain would have to accommodate herself as the United States' outpost in Europe.[40]

The England of those gloomy days of May and June was more faithfully represented by Churchill. The source of Churchill's rising prestige was his uncompromising determination to fight on. Churchill, as most aptly described by A. J. P. Taylor, 'expressed the spirit of the hour'.[41] He was driven not by visions of a new world to emerge out of the war but by a yearning to restore the old order. Churchill assumed the role of the saviour of western civilization as embodied in the British empire. The people were carried with him by his speeches and his colleagues by his magnetism, while thorough discussion in Cabinet of war aims or post-war reconstruction was neglected.

The growing alienation between the government and its representative in Moscow can be best illustrated by their diverging reactions to Hitler's triumphant speech to the Reichstag on 17 July, in which he announced his terms of peace with Britain. In a broadcast on 22 July, Halifax brushed aside the offer. He made clear that war would end only when 'Freedom' was secured. A directive to diplomatic representatives abroad, which was a *de facto* declaration of war aims, clearly stated that no peace could be achieved unless it ensured the 'restoration of the free and independent life' of those countries overrun by the belligerents during the war, as well as the 'effectual security of Great Britain and the British Empire in a general peace'.[42]

When Cripps heard of Hitler's initiative over the radio his instant reaction was that it was bound to 'cause much heart searching' in Cabinet, where 'two could not be found who would agree on the definition of war aims'.[43] Cut off from England, he was as yet unaware of the authority and unanimous support which Churchill enjoyed in Cabinet. Churchill's message to Stalin, closely followed by Halifax's reply to Hitler's speech, convinced him as it did the Russians, that the shifts in Cabinet had not altered the government's outlook. Halifax's voice seemed to Cripps to be that of 'Victorian Church-of-Englandism crying in the wilderness! No realisation that there were any problems

except keeping British predominance in the world and a conviction that it must be God's purpose for the British Ruling Class to rule the world.' It revealed the fact that Britain was 'fighting for the bad old world' whereas Hitler was fighting 'for a new one perhaps worse but *new*'. People, he stated in adherence to his personal credo, 'do *not want* to go back they want to go forward'. In contrast to what was surmised in the Foreign Office and often repeated by historians, it was this thorough disagreement with British policy rather than disappointment with the Russians or his mission which evoked in Cripps an impulse to return home. 'I felt like resigning on the spot', confided Cripps after listening to Halifax, 'as it is impossible really to say to other ambassadors & ministers that that sort of stuff is what I believe in and yet I cant disown it!!' He felt, moreover, that the Russians would be fully justified in assuming 'the futility of trying to agree anything with [Britain] in a political way'.[44]

Soviet hopes of improved relations were further clouded by the continued reserved attitude of the British. The surrender of France had intensified Soviet apprehensions of a British–German understanding allowing Germany a free hand in the East. On several occasions Maisky, elaborating on a favourite Soviet theme that the fiasco in France was a result of activities 'of about 200 families with great interests who feared French Communism more than they feared Hitler', sought to establish whether there existed 'a danger of something similar happening in England'.[45]

His repeated requests to see Churchill were presumably aimed at sounding out the new government and finding an answer to this question. The reluctant Cabinet finally responded when it was learnt that Stalin had consented to see Cripps. The idea never received Churchill's blessing. To sweeten the pill he was advised by the Foreign Office to regard the meeting 'merely in the nature of a gesture'. Maisky, it was wrongly assumed, was 'not in the confidence of his own Government', and therefore was 'useless for the purpose of discussing big political issues'. The interview, in Churchill's own words, 'resolved itself into a talk about the war . . . Russian affairs were not discussed'. Maisky saw in the purely 'social conversation' proof that a Cabinet led by Churchill did not necessarily mean an 'immense change of outlook' towards Russia.[46] Indeed, when entertained by the Webbs shortly after the interview, Maisky complained about the inclusion of 'Chamberlain and

Co.' in the government; they had 'prevented an understanding with the U.S.S.R. and had shown a muddle headed indecision'. He could no longer discount a defeat of Britain brought about through the 'betrayal by the ruling class, somewhat similar to that of Pétain and his group'.[47]

A week later Halifax invited Maisky for 'a general talk to keep relations warm'. When the host avoided raising the burning issues, Maisky significantly had recourse to a long lecture on the interrelations between land ownership and political power. Maisky, as witnessed by Halifax, 'was quite interesting from his beastly Bolshevik point of view about the Russian land system'. He failed to grasp that the Russians had come to regard the influence of English aristocrats like himself as the main deterrent to improved relations.[48] The overt conclusion, as Maisky told Dalton, was that even under Churchill there was 'still much inclination to appeasement'.[49]

A few words should be devoted to the German reactions to Cripps' mission, the significance of which the British could not appreciate at the time. The telegrams from Schulenburg and Köstring reassuring Berlin of Soviet loyalty are very often used to illustrate the stability of the Nazi–Soviet collaboration. Both men, however, were thorough proponents of rapprochement and perhaps as anxious as the Russians to avert a military confrontation. Cripps' active diplomatic efforts upon his arrival in Moscow, coinciding with frenzied Soviet attempts to improve their position *vis à vis* Germany, did not pass unnoticed in Berlin. The Foreign Ministry had learnt of Cripps' 'good relations with the official personages of the Soviet Government' through intercepted telegrams of his confidant, Milovan Gavrilovic, the Yugoslav ambassador in Moscow. The Germans were particularly irritated because doors were opened to Cripps in the Kremlin while Schulenburg had been denied access to Molotov on the feeble pretext that he was on vacation. They had also learned from the intercepts that the Russians were counting on the alignment of Yugoslavia with the Soviet Union 'if the occasion should arise'. In the Foreign Ministry and Wehrmacht circles in Berlin this reflected the 'real mood' of Russia.[50] The Americans, too, had been informed by reliable sources in Berlin of the great significance attached to Cripps' mission and the fact that he was 'credited with greatly influencing Soviet policy'. Only in the German Foreign Ministry was 'the fiction maintained that relations were normal and friendly'.[51]

The wide coverage of Cripps' achievement in the British and American press undoubtedly contributed to this impression.[52]

The clue to the Russians' surprising and belated leakage of Stalin's conversations with Cripps must be their realization of the ominous implications of the spreading rumours in Berlin[53] of a shift in their policy. Before seeing Stalin, Cripps had 'pledged himself to secrecy'. On 18 July, listening, as was his daily habit, to the late-night BBC news bulletin, Cripps was 'furious' to hear about his interview. He wrongly suspected 'sabotage somewhere' or 'leakage of information through drink in Cabinet!!'[54] Cripps was despondent, unaware that his mere presence in Moscow had put in play a series of events which would culminate in the German attack on Russia. It is now known that such early attempts by Stalin to placate the Germans were futile. Hitler had been surprised by British intransigence and determination to continue the war in the conditions in which they found themselves after the collapse of France. His somewhat simplistic answer was to pin the blame on the reported Anglo-Soviet rapprochement. Shortly after he had learnt of Stalin's meeting with Cripps, Hitler instructed Generals Keitel and Jodl to start plans for the invasion of Russia. During a decisive conference with the generals on 31 July, he explained at length his motives for striking in the East; the gist of which was: 'Our action must be directed to eliminate all factors that let England hope for a change in the situation . . . Russia is the factor on which Britain is relying the most . . . with Russia smashed, Britain's last hope will be shattered.'[55]

Once Cripps' attempts to exploit the unusual circumstances of his arrival in Moscow to cut corners and secure a political understanding had failed, the original target of a trade agreement was brought up again. While Cripps was still roving in south-east Europe, the MEW had suddenly expressed the opinion that he was not 'competent to purchase timber or any other commodities', nor had he the 'authority to engage in negotiations', which they wanted to see entrusted to an expert delegation. A draft telegram of instructions to Cripps prepared by the Ministry made it clear that a barter deal of timber against rubber and tin was no longer considered advantageous unless Russia agreed to divert oil and similar commodities which she had pledged to supply to Germany. Moreover, the import of timber from Russia was liable to

congest western ports and could prove a hazard in case of air bombardment. The Timber Controller had indeed in the meantime increased imports from Canada. Surprisingly the Cabinet, fully aware that timber topped Cripps' shopping list, had diverted trade in this commodity to private commercial channels. As for tin and rubber, it seemed advisable to sell these to the United States, a 'potential ally', rather than to the Soviet Union, a 'potential enemy'. The fact that in these circumstances the mission was doomed to failure was recognized with relief by Sargent, who felt: 'Sorry for poor Sir Stafford Cripps, who has been deprived of almost all his last wisp from the small supply of straw out of which he is expected to make an Anglo-Soviet brick.' Thus, even before Cripps had set foot on Russian soil, the Head of the Northern Department felt 'strongly' that 'it would be better for Sir S. Cripps to come away from Moscow' rather than conclude a barter agreement.[56]

In view of the confusion an interdepartmental meeting had to be arranged. A memorandum submitted by C. H. Gifford of the MEW, who was soon to join Cripps in Moscow, presented a more forthcoming attitude. It was finally adopted as the basis for the trade negotiations. Although 'sceptical of the sincerity' with which the Russians were professing their willingness to embark on negotiations, he conceded that a limited barter agreement could be of 'considerable economic benefit to England'. If the government wished to start negotiations in earnest, concessions had to be made regarding the sale of tin, rubber and nickel to Russia. Such a sacrifice of British war trading principles was justified if Cripps was able to make 'the fullest use' of the 'essential bargaining counters'.[57]

Stalin's *sine qua non* for pursuing the talks was, as he told Cripps on 1 July, the waiving of all restrictions on the final destination of goods he obtained in England. This, according to Cripps, formed no serious obstacle as the Russians, suffering from a chronic shortage of non-ferrous metals, were likely to reexport such metals only for the manufacture of goods destined for Russia.[58] The MEW on the other hand, convinced that substantial quantities of raw materials were bound to remain in Germany and opposed to the relaxation of the war trade elements in an agreement with Russia, came around to the opinion held by the Foreign Office. A draft telegram to Cripps in this vein was already on its way when Dalton intervened. To forestall opposition from his own party, ensure the continuation of Cripps' mission and yet

secure the principles of the Ministry, Dalton instructed Cripps to embark on negotiations provided the quantities of rubber and tin involved were small.[59]

By mid-July conditions were no longer promising for an agreement. Until his meeting with Stalin, Cripps had been optimistic and would not even leave the embassy 'for more than an hour or so in case anything urgent should turn up'. Shortly after meeting Stalin he grasped that there was 'a very difficult past history to be got over and it was going to be slow work at best'. He did not anticipate that negotiations would get 'much further' for quite some time. Indeed, his repeated requests to discuss the proposed barter agreement with Molotov were turned down. Cripps had little doubt as to who was at fault. 'We were too late', he wrote home, 'to do any good in this phase and can now only stand by in the hope that in the next phase, when it comes, things may alter.' The inescapable personal conclusion was that his stay in Russia was going to be much longer than he had anticipated. Being at odds with his own government, prevented by his office from admitting it, and confined to a kind of political exile irritated him. Hardly a month had therefore passed since his arrival when doubts concerning his mission began to occur: 'Just every now and then I turn around and look at myself and say "What odd chance has brought you here as an ambassador?" and it all seems so very odd, artificial, and out of place altogether.' However, he philosophically remarked that though things had turned out differently from his expectations it was 'no good worrying about them'.[60]

### At loggerheads with London

If he were a professional diplomat Cripps might well have abided by his own observation that all he could do was to be 'patient and just wait'.[61] However, since he abhorred inactivity he did not abandon his attempts to break through the *impasse*. In a rather desperate move, Cripps pressed Halifax at the end of July to point out to Maisky that the government was dubious about the usefulness of keeping him in Moscow. He even suggested that Maisky should be led to believe that the British response to Hitler's peace overtures depended on the progress made in the trade negotiations.[62]

Molotov's major survey of the international situation on 1 August raised doubts in Cripps' mind about the wisdom of harsh measures. In a

well-balanced speech Molotov reiterated Russia's adherence to neutrality despite Germany's victory on the Continent. Germany, he explained, had failed to 'solve her fundamental problem – to terminate the war on favourable terms'. While conceding that Cripps' appointment might 'indicate a desire on the part of Great Britain to improve her relations with the Soviet Union', Molotov brought to an end speculations of a substantial improvement in Anglo-Soviet relations. The malicious suggestions in the British media of friction in Soviet–German relations overlooked the fact that these were not founded on 'temporary and fragile considerations but on intrinsic mutual interests'. However, in a reference to the annexation of the Baltic states, Molotov warned against complacency and advocated a state of 'mobilized preparedness' to meet unexpected moves by Russia's 'foreign enemies'.

Cripps attended the meeting of the Supreme Soviet to hear Molotov, and it did not escape his notice that the speech 'appeared to lean towards Germany'. Earlier in the day he had learnt from various sources that Moscow was expecting an immediate invasion of England. On balance he was therefore 'not otherwise than content', as he wrote in his diary, noting the references to Britain which were 'less unfriendly than they might have been'.[63] Disregarding his earlier recommendations to Halifax, Cripps now produced a thorough analysis of Soviet policy, which he believed had undergone a change 'once the French *débâcle* developed'. He was convinced that the Soviet haste to assume defensive positions aimed at 'strengthening their position vis à vis Germany'. And yet the Russians, realizing that Britain was no longer in a position to render them any effective assistance and being militarily unprepared to counter a German offensive, were likely to do 'their utmost to ward it off'. Cripps did not exclude, however, a continued benevolent attitude to Britain as 'an insurance against future possibilities'. On balance Cripps had 'no doubt whatever' that if compelled to choose between Germany and England the Russians would opt for the former. The outright conclusion was that no 'useful action' was likely to 'alter the course of Anglo-Soviet relations until a meaningful turn in the war occurred'.[64]

The memorandum, sent by diplomatic bag, reached London only in mid-August. Meanwhile the Northern Department, erroneously assuming that Cripps had become so despondent as a result of his failure that he was now eager to return home, dismissed his earlier recommen-

dations for rigorous action. Dalton's ambivalent appreciation that Cripps' wish to be recalled was 'both amusing and troublesome' was commonly shared. 'Decided to tell him he must stay in Moscow nevertheless', summed up Cadogan in his diary, 'and damned good for him.'[65] The new memorandum was likewise set aside, despite its different conclusions. The general consensus in Whitehall, earlier moulded by Sargent, remained that Russia was willingly increasing its collaboration with Germany. The rejection of Cripps' alternating proposals drew only Butler's criticism that: 'whether we win or lose we cannot improve our relations'.[66]

Dissatisfaction with Cripps, however, became considerably more vehement when the Soviet annexation of the Baltic states came to dominate the course of Anglo-Soviet relations. Britain's indecisive attitude to the annexation demonstrates that in the absence of an overall policy relations with Russia continued to attract scant attention even after Churchill's ascendance and the drastic upheaval of the European balance of power. At first Cripps was authorized in early July to inform Stalin that he might 'affect to believe' that the British government consented to an action in the Baltic by the Russians in view of the 'imminence and magnitude of the German danger'. The instructions specified that the Russians might 'well have been justified in taking in self-defence such measures as might in other circumstances have been open to criticism'. Similarly, Halifax expressed in Cabinet 'little doubt' that the measures had been undertaken by Russia to 'strengthen her position against Germany, whose military successes were not to her liking'.[67]

A debate in Cabinet a month later on the recognition of the pro-Soviet régimes imposed on the Baltic countries coincided with Cripps' misguided telegram recommending harsh measures against the Russians. Halifax's briefing to Cabinet, ignoring his earlier statements, was again imbued with his fear of returning to appeasement. Recalling Germany's overrunning of Austria and Czechoslovakia, he was left in no doubt that 'from the moral point of view' there was 'everything to be said for refusing recognition'. Although he was fully aware of the historical lesson that refusal to recognize a *fait accompli* did 'no good in the long run', there seemed sufficient practical arguments against it. The precedent of recognition was bound to impair relations with Poland as well as with small and neutral countries, notably Sweden and Finland,

and undermine the contemplated Turco-Soviet rapprochement. From a different point of view, the embargo imposed on Baltic gold deposited in British banks counterbalanced the loss of nationalized British property in the Baltic. However, the most powerful argument against recognition was connected to the government's new evident orientation towards the United States in the formulation of policy towards Russia. The Americans' 'scathing denunciation' of the annexation was thought by Halifax sufficient reason to defer recognition. The possible repercussions on relations with Russia were scarcely referred to. Cripps' interview with Stalin was wrongly interpreted to mean that the British stand on recognition would not sour relations. 'Expediency', the Cabinet manoeuvred itself to the logical and convenient conclusion, 'recommends the same course of morality.' After proceeding to confirm the status of the exiled Baltic ministers in London, the Cabinet informed Cripps as a matter of course of its decision.[68]

The decision contravened Cripps' recent recommendation of caution. Nor did it conform with his view, expressed in private, that although the annexation might be 'hard and difficult for the ordinary people', it was certainly better than being 'nazified', which was the only possible alternative.[69] He therefore hastened to reprimand the government for its attitude, which was bound to have a 'disastrous effect' on the chances of improving relations. To start with, he foresaw difficulties in withholding recognition, considering that the Russians had 'certainly observed legal formalities' in the conduct of the elections, and warned that the continued acceptance of the Baltic ministers in London was tantamount to 'an advertisement of non-recognition'. He further argued that blocking Baltic assets, in itself an illegal measure, as a bargaining counter to achieve compensation in return for recognition of any kind was certain to 'cause grave prejudice to Anglo-Soviet relations'. He found the argument of the effect of recognition on relations with Polish representatives and the future of Finland unconvincing.

On the other hand Cripps, who was rapidly perceiving the increasing British dependence on the Americans, concurred that the reaction in the United States should 'no doubt be weighed in the scale against the inevitable effect on Anglo-Soviet relations'. Yet, the United States could 'still no doubt afford to antagonise the Soviet Government by adopting a moral attitude'. Britain, on the other hand, could not incur 'a risk of driving the Soviet Government into closer relations with

Germany'. If *de facto* recognition were refused, he emphasized, all hope should be abandoned of any improvement of Anglo-Soviet relations and a 'considerable degree of worsening' should be anticipated. The Cabinet could not but agree with Cripps that withholding recognition 'might alienate Russia'. However, in view of prevalent fears of Soviet expansionism it was now suggested that recognition might embolden Russia to complete the occupation of Finland. The decision was deferred pending preliminary discussion in the appropriate ministries.[70]

The Foreign Office rejected Cripps' recommendations out of hand. Referring to his demands for the lifting of the embargo, Collier argued emotionally that Britain could not be expected to 'swallow injury as well as insult with no retaliation at all'.[71] The MEW, partly under the influence of Maisky's hints that the embargo was hindering progress in the Moscow negotiations, complained that the Foreign Office 'had got into a fog' and considered its stand on the issue to be 'rather silly'. Their unequivocal recommendation was that 'the sooner [Britain] accepted the position in the Baltic States the better'.[72]

While interdepartmental talks were in progress the ball set rolling by Cripps' harsh cable earlier in the month was affecting the debate on the Baltic issue. Late in July Dalton complained to Maisky that Cripps was prevented from seeing Molotov, who 'appeared to spend most of his time with the German Ambassador'. Some days later, upon the receipt of Cripps' cable and long before his revised evaluation of Soviet policy reached London, Maisky was summoned to Halifax and warned not only that the fate of the Moscow negotiations now hung in the air but also that his own position in London had become precarious.[73]

The Russians had learned to live with the exigencies of maintaining correct relations with Britain without provoking the Germans. Maisky's reports prompted Molotov to see Cripps on 7 August, shortly before the discussion of the Baltic issue in Cabinet. The interview added little information to Cripps' earlier talk with Stalin and sustained his impression, gained a week earlier, that Soviet–German relations were 'undoubtedly too firm to be shaken *for the present!*'. Molotov did not deny the 'inequality' in relations, but explained that Russia had failed to obtain in England the political, economic and strategic benefits which she gained from Germany. He spared no effort, however, to stress Russia's eagerness to maintain normal relations with Britain. Although Cripps admitted in private that the interview had been not 'very

enlivening' and a 'rather negative one', it confirmed his feeling that 'an ultimate change' could occur only when Britain showed herself capable of resisting a German attack. He justified his continued stay in Moscow by the need for the ground to be 'prepared in advance'. His fatalistic evaluation derived no less from his government's 'semi hostile attitude'; its 'weak and compromising' foreign policy 'put obstacles' in the way of achievement in Moscow.[74]

However, like many observers in Moscow, Cripps had come to regard the invasion of England as imminent and found it extremely difficult to take his own advice to abstain from any major initiative. As the British attitude to the Soviet annexation of the Baltic states was frequently used by Molotov to explain the deteriorating relations, Cripps saw an opening here. The government, he suggested, should decide whether to 'go all out' for improved relations with the object of 'gradually divorcing Russia from Germany' or 'to get along as best' as they could. A middle course, he warned, might 'only embarrass British policy in other spheres'. Considering the Russians' scepticism about British intentions, Cripps felt justified in demanding 'some sacrifice and a thoroughness equal to that of Germany'. His proposal was to offer to the Russians the resumption of the trade talks and the opening of negotiations for a non-aggression pact. In return the Russians were expected to acknowledge these steps as 'inaugurating a new era in Anglo-Soviet relations' and to conduct further dealings with Britain 'in as friendly a spirit of neutrality as that governing their relations with Germany'.[75]

The reaction to Cripps' advice once again underlines the rigid attitude of the Foreign Office. Like the Cabinet, it was mesmerized by analogies to events preceding the war. Determined to preserve the Office's clean record of opposition to appeasement, Maclean thought it 'folly . . . to make any sacrifice in the vain hope of winning Soviet goodwill'. In an explicit parallel he claimed that Britain stood to gain nothing 'by pursuing a policy of appeasement'. The analogy conveniently dovetailed with prejudices and mistrust stemming, as admitted by the Head of the Northern Department, from 'long and unusually painful experience' of dealing with the Russians. Passing judgment on Cripps, it seemed to Collier 'odd' that those who blamed Chamberlain for pursuing appeasement towards Hitler should urge the government to adopt such a policy towards Stalin, who after all was 'quite as hard-boiled a

dictator'. It is no wonder therefore that it proved virtually impossible to uproot the belief that German–Soviet collaboration was natural and unshakable.

On the surface Cripps' assumptions resembled those of the Office. Both agreed that 'diplomacy "in the air" ', as it was termed by Butler, was elusive and that therefore it was advisable to wait until Britain became stronger. However, while the Office was concerned not to repeat the mistakes of the past and favoured inactivity, Cripps looked ahead, laying the foundations for the inevitable future collaboration.[76]

The Cabinet reexamined the Baltic issue on 9 August, soon after Cripps' interview with Molotov, and reluctantly agreed that *de facto* recognition must be conceded, while discussion of *de jure* recognition should be postponed pending a peace settlement. Halifax's proposal to allow Cripps 'a measure of discretion' on the issue of compensation was opposed, while the need for 'coordination' with the Americans was generally acknowledged. Cripps, when informed of these decisions on 13 August, was also told that the government doubted the value of concessions at that stage and that 'in any circumstances' Britain would continue to retain the Baltic gold and ships.[77]

The Cabinet had in fact adopted a short-range policy, the very middle course which Cripps had warned against. Disappointed, Cripps reverted to his earlier appreciation that the situation had been 'too crystallized' when he reached Moscow and that therefore it was 'too late' to expect any dramatic *volte face*. As he wrote home, this was particularly true because:

The Russian policy is still basically hostile to the present British Government and highly suspicious! nothing much can be done while the present British Government continues with its present type of Foreign Policy. The change is only on the very surface and all the distrust and hatred of the Russian Government is clearly discerned underneath. One cannot blame the Russians for their attitude – its the one I should adopt myself were I in their circumstances.

He attempted to practise self-control; one needed 'patience all the time and more patience' as it was 'no good getting hot and bothered at this job'.[78]

As might be anticipated, Cripps opposed the Cabinet's modified proposals. His own recommendations, forming part of a long-range policy, had been based on the assumption that it was 'by no means too

early to prepare the ground'. Their implementation, moreover, was likely to secure Soviet 'good-will . . . when other factors in international situation might be conducive' to collaboration. The retention of the gold as a bargaining counter represented in his opinion 'an illegal act and hence a "gesture of defiance" '. The Foreign Office, however, had become overtly impatient with Cripps' incessant attempts to introduce a major change in policy towards Russia. Cadogan's entry in his diary on the subject is a case in point:

Meeting with H. [Halifax] on Russia. Cripps argues that we must give everything – recognition, gold, ships and trust to the Russians loving us. This is simply silly. Agreed to tell him to sit tight. We will see what we can do here with Maisky. Exactly nil, I should say. Extraordinary how we go on kidding ourselves. Russian policy will change when and if they think it will suit them. And if they *do* think that, it won't matter whether we've kicked Maisky in the stomach. Contrariwise, we could give Maisky the Garter and it wouldn't make a penn'orth of difference.[79]

The consultations with the Americans on the Baltic issue illuminate the perfunctory treatment of relations with Russia. They were initiated, one suspects, so as to invite defiance which would put the onus on the Americans and absolve the Cabinet from committing itself either way. The MEW, immediately concerned with the practical repercussions of the measures taken by the government in reaction to the Soviet annexation of the Baltic, persevered in its opposition to the free hand which the Foreign Office enjoyed in conducting relations with Russia. The clash occurred over the draft telegram to Washington.

Professor Postan, who was thoroughly acquainted with Russian policy, had just returned from Sofia after being refused a Soviet visa to accompany Cripps. He induced the Ministry to challenge Sargent's memorandum on Soviet–German collaboration, which had become the guideline for the conduct of relations with Russia. The concepts of 'imperialist tradition' or 'communist ideology', used by Sargent to explain Soviet foreign policy, seemed to Postan to be 'ill-defined'. Soviet policy was motivated by a 'fear of Germany's future designs, tempered by a conflicting fear of German power at the present time'. Like Cripps, Postan was convinced that a policy based on expectations of immediate returns was therefore 'bound to fail'. Reliance on the inevitability of *entente* with the Soviet Union once Britain became

stronger and Germany weaker 'must form the basis of a policy, and not a justification for the absence of policy'. Postan further agreed with Cripps on the desirability of 'keeping the road clear for the future'. This could be best achieved through such concessions as would not 'impair British military, strategic or political position *vis à vis* Germany'. Soviet activity, he estimated, affected 'the position in the Baltic very little and British military position not at all'. Moreover, British investments in the Baltic amounted to the insignificant sum of £2 million. Was the price, he asked, 'too high for the chances of Soviet understanding?' Cripps, he reminded, proposed the concessions as part of a general bargain involving a reciprocal Soviet undertaking. The Foreign Office had conceded *de facto* recognition without demanding anything in return. 'On general commonsense grounds', he concluded, 'a partial, belated and forced concession without *quid pro quo* . . . is a more obvious illustration of weakness than a whole readjustment of policy as part of a two-sided deal.'[80]

In an interdepartmental meeting held on 14 August, representatives of the MEW headed by Postan persuaded the participants that the proposed telegram to Washington was 'completely inadequate and possibly dangerous' from the financial point of view, while politically it did not state the issues 'fully and clearly'. The draft, for instance, did not clearly indicate that the bargain proposed was inspired by political considerations. It was finally agreed that a revised telegram presenting 'the *whole* question' would be submitted for further deliberation. Halifax, however, pressed by his senior advisers at the Foreign Office, closed the debate; he was 'rather peeved' and agreed the telegram must 'go off at once'.[81] Halifax recited the opinion prevalent at the Office that Russia was 'determined to keep in' with Germany and to 'cold-shoulder' Britain. He was doubtful, as he wrote to the First Lord of the Admiralty, that England was in a position to 'change that determination'.[82] The Cabinet, overlooking the implications on Russia, was converted to the Foreign Office's point of view that *de jure* recognition was likely to have 'severe repercussions in Poland, Finland and Sweden – to say nothing of the USA'. The anti-Soviet bias in the Office had become so pronounced that even the suggestion of collaboration in the future was dismissed as likely to 'simply complicate the task of reconstructing eastern Europe'.[83]

This attitude was evident during an acrimonious meeting between

Maisky and Halifax on 15 August, in which Halifax insisted on defining the Soviet measures in the Baltic as 'aggression'. Although Maisky was now receptive to Britain's earlier proposal of releasing the Baltic assets against compensation, Halifax, having made the decision conditional on American consent, appeared evasive.[84]

Meanwhile prospects of progress in the trade negotiations in Moscow were fading. On 22 August, Cripps subjected Mikoyan, who happened to be 'chatty and humorous', to a tedious cross-examination. He had, as he confessed to his host, an 'advocate's mentality' and wished therefore 'to get to the bottom of things'. The results confirmed Cripps' impression that the British attitude over the Baltic issue increased Soviet mistrust. This he thought to be unfortunate, as the Russians were not yet 'sufficiently convinced' of the chance of a British victory 'to face the German reaction' if a far-reaching trade agreement with England were concluded. The Russians seemed anxious therefore to revert to the limited original aim of concluding a barter agreement. Cripps believed the government ought to show 'a certain coolness and detachment, refusing to deal with trade questions piece meal'.[85]

The ground was rapidly shifting under Cripps. On 28 August Lothian conveyed his impression that an agreement on the lines proposed by Cripps was likely to cause 'considerable embarrassment' in Washington. Lothian recalled that it was at Britain's request that the Americans had agreed to freeze the assets of territories occupied by Germany and Russia. His assessment lent force to the Foreign Office's conviction that a 'Baltic bargain' was undesirable 'altogether, or at least until the end of the war'. To ensure the Office's direct control of the trade negotiations it was decided to conduct them in London. The decision appeared 'incomprehensible' to the MEW. Maisky had been rejected in the past as a reliable negotiator. Moreover, Cripps had proposed a *quid pro quo* arrangement, while the Foreign Office was inclined to make concessions. The only explanation was that the talks in Moscow were likely to develop further than the Office would have preferred them to proceed. However, as recent experience had taught, little could be done to prevent the Foreign Office from making decisions in conformity with American policy, even if the two countries had in fact no common interest.[86]

Once again dependence on the Americans' attitude merely served as

an excuse to bring negotiations to a standstill. Cripps, as Steinhardt was told by a rather perplexed Secretary of State, must have been 'misinformed' by his superiors. The State Department had 'made it clear' that since the British situation was different from that of the United States, each country should feel free to adopt such policies 'as it may deem most likely to serve its interests'.[87]

By the beginning of September it was finally realized in the MEW that relations had reached bedrock. Cripps' authority was seriously curtailed, while his recommendations were consistently overruled in the Foreign Office. Halifax had become fully converted to the prevailing assessment in the Office that it was futile to make any concessions in return for 'illusory political advantages'. In full accord with Sargent's concept of Soviet–German collaboration, Halifax rejected Cripps' arguments that an understanding with Russia would take the form of 'refusing and even diminishing' the help which Russia was giving Germany 'on an increasing scale'.[88] On 9 September he secured agreement from an indifferent Cabinet that American benevolence was of 'far more value' than the 'somewhat illusory benefits of the goodwill of the U.S.S.R'. It was agreed that both Soviet and British claims in the Baltic 'should be put into cold storage'.[89] When Maisky was informed of the decision by Halifax the next morning, he wryly pointed out that British policy seemed to have been 'modelled' on that of the Americans. The decision, he warned, was certain to hamper negotiations under way in Moscow.[90]

The Russians, however, were not in a position to take offence. They were seriously concerned about Britain's rigid condemnation of their action in the Baltic and lapse of the negotiations, not to mention the fluid state of the Battle of Britain. Moreover, they had been increasingly alarmed throughout August and September by the German incursion into the Danube basin. To his dismay Molotov first learnt of this from the radio and the press; only on 31 August was he officially informed by Schulenburg that without prior consultations, as required by the Ribbentrop–Molotov pact, Germany had guaranteed the integrity of Romania only after she had ceded a 'considerable portion of Romanian territory' to Hungary. Despite German attempts to gloss over the move, Molotov maintained that it had been made 'not entirely in good faith'. Bilateral relations now deteriorated; on 12 September

Soviet–German negotiations on a trade agreement broke down, as the German delegation had not 'sufficient authority to reply to the Soviet proposals'.[91]

Reported British successes in the Battle of Britain were naturally followed with keen interest in Moscow. Maisky lunched with Max Beaverbrook, the powerful newspaper magnate now serving in Churchill's Cabinet as Minister of Air Production, and attempted to find out the number of planes supplied by the Americans and American pilots serving in the RAF – in short any clue which might indicate Britain's ability to resist.[92] Maisky's impression was that the danger of invasion had receded, but he was still doubtful about Britain's capacity to conduct a long-drawn-out war. Fears of a political settlement with Germany therefore surfaced once again.[93] Were it not for Cripps, he believed, relations would have been severed long before. He confirmed Cripps' call for 'spade work' as an essential condition for a change in policy.[94]

The Russians found it difficult, however, to break through the stalemate in the negotiations. Cripps, who had been denied access to Molotov for some time, had put the Russians in a delicate position by demanding to see only senior officials. While eager to play down their contacts with Britain, they were equally determined to avoid a breach. The ingenious solution of appointing Andrei Vyshinsky as Deputy Foreign Minister, one may surmise, provided a convenient channel for dealing with Cripps and relieved pressure on Molotov. Vyshinsky's earlier career as chief prosecutor during the purge trials and major role in engineering the take-over of the Baltic did not prove a deterrent. His first conversation with Cripps opened with 'mutual compliments on each other's careers as lawyers'. Although their views were dia-metrically opposed, Cripps wrote home that he would: 'Try and keep a close and continuous contact with him as, at present at any rate, he talks and discusses matters in a much freer way than Molotov and there is much more a feeling of friendly contact with some realities.'[95] Hopeful of reviving the mission, Cripps emerged from the meeting with a sug-gestion that the Russians be informed that a solution of the Baltic issue might be postponed until after the defeat of the German offensive on England. Halifax, however, having been persuaded by the Foreign Office to regard negotiations as fruitless, discouraged Cripps, instructing

him to restate that the British pressed their claim in respect to the Baltic property.[96]

The growing difficulties induced Cripps by the end of September to evaluate his mission so far. Six months of abortive efforts in Moscow had hardly, as can be easily seen from his private correspondence and diary, mellowed his militancy nor brought him any closer to the government. Paradoxically his detached and businesslike handling of contacts with Russia combined with his ideological outlook on the war. Cripps' discontent has often been wrongly interpreted as disillusionment with the Soviet system and frustration at his thwarted efforts. Writing to his intimate friend Sir Walter Monckton, Director of the Ministry of Information, Cripps expressed the opinion that the British government's policy was 'perfectly plain sailing for the moment – to win the war and subordinate all effort to that accomplishment'. However, he argued, attitudes taken, forces encouraged or weakened, propaganda made, were all bound to contribute to the 'formation of the world to be born after the war'. He regretted that the government was still in the 'pre-1914 era and trying desperately hard to keep there!', falsely assuming that it was possible to look behind and 'take a permanent position on the safety valve!!'

Ironically Cripps' attitude did not improve his standing amongst his previous left-wing associates, who regarded with suspicion his continued presence in Moscow in an official capacity. The avenue for reconciliation with Labour's formal leadership remained barred. Consequently, through Monckton's mediation, Cripps found himself by the beginning of 1941 drawn closer to the group of progressive Conservatives whose more prominent members were Butler, Viscount Cranborne, the Secretary of State for the Dominions, Richard Law, who later replaced Butler at the Foreign Office, Eden and to some extent Halifax. Although the group never adopted a common platform, created a formal organization or presented an open challenge, it had a wide following, as became apparent at the beginning of 1942 when Churchill's fortunes were low. At the end of 1940, however, the group was frustrated by the 'astonishingly unassailable' position of Churchill, which meant, as Monckton informed Cripps, that there was 'literally no one else in the same street'. Cripps' advocacy of post-war reconstruction seemed to provide a basis for joint efforts towards what Monckton defined as the

'revolutionary changes we both want – profit, private property, privilege'. Monckton clearly fuelled Cripps' confrontation with Churchill, which paved the way for his open association with the progressive Conservatives after his return from Moscow, by advising him that from the political point of view:

I fear that too long a stay in such an unsatisfactory position might injure your prospects of leading us all a little later on. The fact is that there is no satisfactory successor or alternative to Winston. I am pretty clear now that Ernie Bevin will not fill the part. Anthony is too conventional a thinker to make a great leader, and one looks in vain among the rest for the right quality of mind and character. I feel that if your stay in Russia is not very much longer, you will have gained by the experience both because, if I may say so, you will have increased your store of patience, and because other people will have seen your patience exhibited in very trying circumstances and will know you for a responsible person. I have discussed you as a leader with the most diverse people, from Nancy Astor up and down. I find them all attracted by the possibility.

Cripps was also quickly coming to grips with Soviet realities. Even the burden of loneliness which had marred his early months in Moscow was being lifted with the arrival of his family. Russia, as he confessed to Monckton, suffered from social inequality, economic and industrial inefficiencies and ruthless methods of government. However, he was convinced that despite these 'immense failures and drawbacks' she was determined to replace the 'effete civilisation' which Britain was trying 'desperately hard to cling to'. Stalin had stimulated and invigorated activity and progress, despite the high costs. Russia's slow and painful growth in strength and organization was bound in the long run to redound more 'to the advantage of the masses of the people than in the case of possibly more successful regimes in other countries'. 'One thing', he finally admitted, 'has been proved here – so far – and that is that you cannot leap into Utopia in one bound.' Stalin's achievement was neither the rosy picture painted by communists abroad nor the positive image he himself projected, but rather those small leaps forward in the right direction.

Cripps had come to regard his stay in Moscow in many ways as a self-imposed political exile. So long as Chamberlain and the 'bunch' were in Cabinet, Cripps believed he stood no chance of exercising any

influence at home. He felt therefore 'cheerful & happy about the future, and thoroughly reconciled to the present!!'[97]

As far as Anglo-Soviet relations were concerned, it was 'clear beyond all doubt' that Britain had not the 'slightest desire to work with Russia'. It was only too obvious, as he put it in a letter to his daughter, that the British government wished merely 'to play with' Russia.[98] Such attitudes and policies, according to Cripps, rendered the Russians excessively cautious. It was difficult to establish whether Vyshinsky's 'obvious keenness' to further negotiations should be interpreted as a Soviet attempt to keep Britain 'in suspense', a sincere desire to 'move closer', or a wish for 'certain particular commodities'. The explanation of the Russians' 'enigmatic' policy seemed to Cripps to be that 'we can't help them *now* very much even if we wanted to or if they wanted us'.[99] A change in Soviet policy could be expected only when the military power of Germany had been sufficiently impaired to obviate the possibility of a German invasion of Russia. Cripps' conclusion was therefore that something more valuable than a barter agreement might be achieved by 'waiting a little longer'.[100] As for the fate of his own mission, even if he appeared to Steinhardt to be 'extremely gloomy and disappointed as a result of his efforts in Moscow', he was fast learning, as he wrote home, that: 'A diplomat needs infinite patience he may have to wait 10 years and then in 5 minutes be able to do a real service to his country which makes all the ten years preparation worth while.' If a chance occurred of 'doing something useful' he believed himself to be the person best qualified to accomplish it.[101]

Events, however, were taking a new turn. In September Japan joined in a tripartite pact with Germany and Italy. Perhaps more significant was the increasing German intervention in central and south-east Europe, which overshadowed the Baltic issue. A series of arbitration agreements forced on Romania at the end of August culminated in large areas being ceded to Hungary and Bulgaria. King Carol consequently abdicated in favour of his son while real power was entrusted to the pro-Axis General Antonescu.

Cripps was informed that agreement had been reached during Hitler's meeting with Mussolini at the Brenner Pass on 4 October, providing an outlet for German expansion in Romania and Turkey. The Foreign Office deemed it necessary to guarantee the continued

benevolent neutrality of Turkey. A successful approach to Turkey, it was held, depended on the extent to which the Russians were willing to oppose the German plans. Cripps was therefore to alert the Russians with the aid of freshly obtained intelligence about the belligerent aims of Germany. German military attachés in European capitals had been informed by Hitler in Berlin, it was learnt, that the invasion of Britain had been temporarily abandoned. On the other hand, now that Germany's fear of a war on two fronts had subsided, Hitler, assisted by the triple alliance, planned to attack Russia in the following spring.[102]

The evidence gave force to Cripps' earlier assumption that, despite appearances to the contrary, Soviet relations with Germany were precarious. In sharp contrast to the Foreign Office, Cripps believed Russia's immediate concern was to 'build up her forces to protect herself *against* Germany'. Britain's denial of raw material and machine tools forced Russia paradoxically to increase her imports '*from* Germany in order to be able to gain strength should the clash come'. It was 'all so *mad*', he observed, seeing Russia being 'literally pushed into the arms of Germany'.[103] He could not therefore discount the possibility that Schulenburg, on his way back from consultations in Berlin, would carry 'attractive offers for Russia for her hostile neutrality to Great Britain'. Cripps was concerned that Russia, realizing that Britain and Turkey were unwilling to give her anything in return, might be tempted to forestall the German threat by joining the Axis until Russia was strong enough to 'meet and defeat it'. Britain, on the other hand, was urging the Russians to risk a war on two fronts by antagonizing the Axis without a serious offer in return. Cripps therefore believed it was 'almost the last opportunity' of moving Russian policy towards Britain. He thought it was 'completely idle' to divulge to Molotov the danger posed to Russia by Germany unless the government was prepared to discuss with the Russians their post-war plans. The time had arrived, he asserted, to do 'something really bold and imaginative' to alleviate Soviet fears. Cripps asked to be authorized to promise the Russians consultations with the victorious nations on post-war arrangements in return for a friendly attitude towards Britain and benevolent neutrality towards Turkey and Iran. In addition, he recommended that Britain should undertake not to form any anti-Soviet alliances after the war, to recognize Soviet *de facto* sovereignty over all territories occupied by her

hitherto, to provide her with essential war supplies, to resist Germany and to guarantee her against an attack from Turkey or Iran. Such an undertaking, he hoped, would ultimately result in a non-aggression pact modelled on the Ribbentrop–Molotov pact. The offer was to be accompanied by a veiled threat that if Russia was not willing to enter into such an arrangement she would be excluded from participation in a post-war settlement. [104]

Cripps' proposals focused on post-war reconstruction which, as we have seen, was cardinal to his political philosophy. In the hope of ensuring favourable consideration, Cripps addressed a long private letter to Halifax in which he complained that the most serious impediment to the accomplishment of his mission was the 'past and present *general* attitude of the British Government'. Twenty years' experience, he urged, had taught the Russians to look upon the present government 'as fundamentally hostile to the Soviet Union'; they were amply justified in assuming that the government was 'not prepared to acknowledge the importance or influence of the Soviet Union'. Since the outbreak of war the Russians had equal 'historical justifications' to suspect that the British were inclined to make allies only when they 'felt the shoe pinching very hard'. Repeated last-minute efforts to embroil Russia in the war only confirmed the Soviet suspicion that British policy, rather than forming 'a part of any general or fundamental attitude', aimed at separating Russia from the Axis. Any advance, concluded Cripps, was made excessively difficult particularly in view of the growing Soviet anxiety that the recent German moves were a prelude to an attack which they could not possibly repel for the time being. However, on the assumption that the Russians were aware that Britian was fighting their war and therefore 'most anxious not to antagonise H.M.G. in any irreparable way', Cripps had 'not by any means given up hope'. The reason they did not 'dare appear too friendly' was not only their fear of provoking the Germans but their doubts of the 'discretion' of the government. Cripps was here referring to recurrent leaks in London of information concerning his recent approaches to the Russians. The only way of avoiding all the pitfalls was to strive to achieve an agreement: 'On the basis of recognising a continuing friendship and a partnership in post-war reconstruction and not merely upon the basis of getting them to help us out of our awkward hole after which we might desert them and even join the enemies who now surround them.' [105]

Cripps' proposals presupposed a genuine change of attitude towards Russia based on an explicit definition of war aims. Halifax, acknowledging the force of Cripps' arguments but perhaps even more concerned with opposition at home, responded favourably. It was, as he told Cabinet, simply a matter of having it 'on record' that an approach was made. However, he acquiesced with his Foreign Office advisers that it was 'imprudent to build any hopes on the outcome'. Halifax entirely dismissed Cripps' premise that the inherent hostility of Britain had pushed the reluctant Russia into Germany's arms. The government, he argued, had to avoid implying *de jure* recognition of the Russian 'aggressions' in eastern Europe. Meanwhile she could do little to alter, 'at any rate until the end of the war', Soviet *de facto* control of the Baltic.[106]

The instructions to Cripps left little doubt that his appeal had had a limited impact. To prevent Cripps from committing the government too far, as well as to put the Russians to the test, Halifax made any British overture conditional on 'some practical proof of benevolent neutrality towards Turkey'. Cripps was informed that post-war consultations would not imply 'readiness' to accept Soviet views on the future of Europe. Moreover, the old bogey of 'Soviet revolutionary agitation', an impediment to normal relations since the Curzon Ultimatum of 1923, through the Zinoviev Letter in 1924 and the Arcos Raid of 1927, was now resurrected in order to avoid making an undertaking not to form anti-Soviet alliances after the war. Finally, Halifax dismissed Cripps' appreciation of the Russians' belief that by postponing a German attack they would be strong enough to defeat it. As the Russians were only concerned with the 'immediate consequences' of opposition to Germany, he summed up, Britain could 'not hope at present to remove their fear'.[107]

In view of widespread rumours of American involvement in Cripps' approach, the British took great pains to belittle its significance. The State Department was provided with a verbatim copy of Cripps' telegram and perhaps more significantly with Halifax's reserved approval. The Americans were reassured that, although it was obviously 'necessary to spare no effort to try to persuade the Soviet Government to draw nearer', the government subscribed neither to Cripps' views nor to his anticipation of positive results.[108]

Cripps was not to be so easily dissuaded. As in the past, the Foreign

Office's indifference to the negotiations, evident in their failure to provide him with lucid detailed instructions, allowed Cripps excessive latitude. He promptly prepared a draft agreement embodying his original proposals only slightly modified in the light of Halifax's reservations. It was nonetheless immediately observed in the Office that Cripps' proposals did not really accord with the government's directives. While the Cabinet consented to '*de facto* control' of the Soviet-occupied territories, Cripps went further in suggesting a recognition of Soviet '*de facto* sovereignty'. More significant, however, was a preamble which displayed the distinctive Cripps touch. It implied that benevolent neutrality might be nearly as valuable to Britain 'as armed assistance in shortening the war'. The British government, 'firm in their conviction of ultimate victory', wished to ascertain the degree of benevolence or hostility with which Russia intended to treat her so that she might recognize at the end of the war those who had furthered her cause and ask them to 'share actively in the task of reconstruction'.[109]

Cripps' efforts were made with an acute sense of urgency. Everybody in Moscow was attempting, as Cripps wrote to his daughter, a 'forecast of the Russian attitude'. It was therefore essential 'to try and influence [Soviet] uncertainty in the right direction'.[110] He found it difficult to make up his own mind. Once again Molotov was inaccessible and Cripps was fobbed off on Vyshinsky on 23 October. This, of course, might be attributed to pro-German sympathies on the part of Molotov, as he explained in a revealing letter to Sir Hugh Knatchbull-Hugessen, the British ambassador to Turkey, but it was more likely that the Russians had 'their ears very close to the ground' following the disposition of German forces. Stalin was probably 'trying to play both games . . . leaving one to Molotov and the other to Vyshinsky!' He found it extremely difficult to judge whether the Russians were 'playing' with Britain or were 'seriously trying to get on a better basis'.[111]

Cripps' urgent call to his government to act was fully justified. He was not to know that a policy which perhaps stood some chance of success in September in view of the deteriorating Soviet–German relations was quite outdated in October. Once again Britain's move was too late and not enthusiastic enough. Exactly when Cripps was engaged in formulating his views and debating with the Foreign Office, the Germans had come to the conclusion that the prolonged deterioration of relations with Russia was detrimental to their interests. On 7 October the

Russians were notified of a competent German delegation arriving in Moscow to resume the disrupted trade talks. Schulenburg returned from Berlin bearing a long personal letter to Stalin from Ribbentrop. The letter, a bizarre tirade against Britain and full of ingratiation, aimed to smooth the ailing relations by undermining and establishing a new platform for cooperation. In an unequivocal way Stalin was warned that the British 'slandered their erstwhile allies'. Dunkirk, Oran and Dakar were names which 'could sufficiently enlighten the world on the value of England's friendship'. Dwelling on the only too obvious Soviet apprehensions, Ribbentrop described Britain as a warmonger trying to embroil Russia in the war. It was 'superfluous to emphasize' therefore that the British presentation of the German defensive move in the Balkans as aimed against Russia was 'entirely unfounded and dictated solely by the intention to disrupt relations between the Axis and the Soviet Union'. The bait appeared at the very end. Molotov was invited to discuss with Hitler in Berlin: 'The historical mission of the Four Powers – the Soviet Union, Italy, Japan, and Germany – to adopt a long-range policy and to direct the future development of their peoples into the right channels by delimitation of their interests on a world-wide scale.'

The letter was handed to Stalin on 17 October and in a matter-of-fact manner he accepted the invitation on Molotov's behalf on 21 October.[112] The results of the forthcoming Berlin conference were still very uncertain. The Russians could not treat Cripps' offer lightly and yet could not possibly afford to conduct an open dual policy on the eve of Molotov's departure. Cripps was therefore informed by Vyshinsky on the night of 26 October that the draft was regarded as of 'very greatest importance and needed more serious consideration', and again on 2 November that the Soviet government were 'still studying the subject'.[113] Reporting to Steinhardt on the conversations, Cripps was uncertain whether the request for clarification 'was a device to gain time, or whether it indicated a favourable attitude'. He felt, however, that the offer was receiving 'real consideration'.[114]

# INTERREGNUM

### *The consolidation of Whitehall's concept*

Churchill, reflecting in his war memoirs on the Molotov–Hitler summit, expresses in retrospect a concern for:

what might have happened as the result of an armed alliance between the two great empires of the Continent, with their millions of soldiers, to share the spoil in the Balkans, Turkey, Persia and the Middle East, with India always in the background and with Japan as an eager partner in the 'Great East Asian Scheme'.[1]

At the time the meeting caused little alarm in the Cabinet; indeed, it evoked some disguised satisfaction at seeing Russia and Germany as partners on the other side of the barricade.

Molotov's negotiations in Berlin were an anti-climax to the pomp and circumstance which surrounded his departure from the Bieloruskaya station on 11 November, accompanied by a large Soviet delegation. Hitler had hoped to carry out his 'peripheral' strategy in the western Mediterranean by tempting Russia to join the Axis with a division of spheres of influence; this would create favourable conditions for an ultimate invasion of Britain. Molotov, rather than participate in the dismembering of the British empire, stubbornly insisted on the Soviet short-term strategic aim of a buffer zone in the Baltic and the Balkans. The negotiations therefore reached deadlock at an early stage over Germany's declared interest in Finland, Romania and Bulgaria. Soviet attempts to renew the talks after Molotov's return to Moscow were ignored. Hitler's decision on the need to crush the Soviet Union by force was made on 18 December with the issue of Directive 21 – the plans for 'Operation Barbarossa'.[2]

The news of Molotov's departure came in while Cripps was watching a film at the American embassy. The claim that Cripps exploded in a

denunciation of the Soviet government and officials, who were in his eyes 'the personification of evil', is not borne out by other evidence. He certainly was, as reported by Steinhardt, 'not only surprised but shocked by the news'. Cripps' immediate fear, however, was that influential circles in Britain might 'press for peace with Germany on an anti-Soviet basis'.[3] Cripps wrongly assumed that Molotov had embarked on his mission only after weighing the British and German proposals and deciding on a temporary alliance with Germany. He could not have known that the decision to send Molotov to Berlin had been made before his own proposals had been submitted. The most effective measure he could suggest, which was adopted by the Cabinet, was for the Air Force to pay 'special attention' to Berlin which might have a 'beneficial effect' on Molotov's attitude.[4]

Cripps' fear that he was in for a 'bad & dull time . . . a long spell of negative action' was shortly dispersed by the filtering of information on what had actually taken place in Berlin. In the meantime, convinced that Soviet–German animosity could not be eradicated, he interpreted the visit as reflecting a 'temporary attitude of expediency' unlikely to cause any 'irreclaimable damage'.[5] In an acrimonious meeting with Vyshinsky, coinciding with Molotov's encounter with Hitler, Cripps complained of Russia's 'unneutral behaviour', warning that the recent British offer would not remain open indefinitely and that friendly neutrality at a later stage would be of lesser value. He inquired whether he could inform the British government that the visit indicated the Russians' 'unwillingness to improve relations'. Vyshinsky, who appeared shaken, promised a prompt answer. The little he said indicated that the Russians had scant expectations from the conference except for the gaining of time. He vehemently objected to Cripps' interpretation of Molotov's 'unneutrality', referring obliquely to Russia's opposition to Germany's expansionism in the Balkans.[6]

Cripps' interpretation was written off by the Foreign Office. Analogies were instantly drawn to the negotiations in 1939, when the Russians were said to have exploited the British proposals to extract a pact from Germany. As the Russians were believed to understand only the language of force, retaliatory measures were called for. A minority view favoured a temporary extension of the reserve attitude. Halifax, vacillating as usual, allowed policy to form itself. The prevailing mood is summed up by Cadogan's recommendation: 'If there is a chance of

fighting them I sh^d take it.' This was not merely wishful thinking. The COS were indeed instructed by Cabinet to consider possible military measures against Russia.[7]

Meanwhile Vansittart emerged from oblivion, demanding 'sufficient publicity' for the British proposals and their treatment by Molotov. At Halifax's request his minute, which had at first been overlooked, received special attention. The demand coincided with growing interest by the press in the Berlin negotiations and their effect on Cripps' ambassadorship; rumours of his recall were in the air.[8]

The Foreign Office's News Department seems to have sensed a propitious moment for acquitting the Office from the charge of obstructing negotiations. It released to correspondents, who had received only crumbs of information, details of Cripps' proposals to Vyshinsky, including the former's pledge of secrecy. The failure of the Russians to respond was naturally emphasized.[9] The press almost unanimously assumed that the leak was a calculated move in the wake of Molotov's Berlin visit, putting a seal on further negotiations.[10]

On 16 November Cripps tuned in to the BBC news after breakfast, as was his daily habit. He was astounded to hear of his proposals. This, rather than the news of the Berlin conference, made it, as he wrote to his daughter 'quite the worst day I have had since I came here!' The telegram from London a few hours later explaining that the information emanated from Maisky seemed to him 'unsatisfactory'. Furiously Cripps warned Halifax in a personal telegram that in the circumstances created by the publicity, his continued stay in Moscow 'wasnt any good'. He was convinced that the leak had 'killed the very slender chances that remained of doing something effective'. Besides the blow to his personal reputation, he believed the government was responsible for playing straight into the hands of the Germans by making Russia 'definitely committed & hostile to Great Britain'. In one of his rare interventions in Anglo-Soviet relations at the time, Churchill rebuked Halifax for the leak. The Cabinet was satisfied, however, by the Foreign Office's suggestion that it was 'just as well' that left-wing elements in Britain should know how baseless was the charge that Britain had made no effort to cultivate relations with Russia. They also assented that it was not 'worth while' to make further advances to Russia.[11]

The inconclusive results of Molotov's visit led the Russians to play down the incident. In London Maisky hinted that, despite the 'Mexico-

like insults'[12] administered by Whitehall, Russia was still anxious to improve relations with Britain. In Moscow Cripps, who had anticipated a strong reaction, found Vyshinsky 'surprisingly pleasant and subdued'.[13] However, the leak permitted the Russians, who were now more vulnerable to German pressures, to ignore the British offer.

As winter set in Cripps once again faced the prospect of inactivity; with it came a gloomy evaluation of his work which was, as he wrote home, 'a bit anxious at times & for long periods seems ineffective & looks at present like a complete flop & failure!'[14] After exploring all avenues to reach an agreement, Cripps was being driven to the conclusion that only by maintaining 'pressure upon the Soviet Government in all directions' would it be possible to resume negotiations. The recommendation, on the surface, bore a resemblance to the Foreign Office's policy, though the latter was the result of a determination to remain aloof. Cripps wished to exert pressure only as a means of dragging the Russians to the negotiation table. However, his resolve to effect a change in relations at all costs was misinterpreted by the Russians. It increased their suspicion of British diplomacy and contributed to their disastrous appreciation of the international scene on the eve of the German invasion. Cripps now asked for authority to withdraw the proposals for an economic agreement, which incidentally had been the ostensible reason for his arrival in Moscow, whenever he felt it 'wise to do so'.[15]

Once again the Foreign Office rejoiced at Cripps' apparent change of heart. It seemed that irritation at recent events had got 'the better of his judgement'. The only drawback was Cripps' obvious failure to grasp that, since the Russians had not wished for an agreement in the first place, a threat would be counter-productive. Their main objection concerned the integrity of the Foreign Office itself: they anticipated that the Russians would take advantage of the threat and present it as further evidence of the 'insincerity' of Whitehall in its approaches to Russia. A draft telegram to Cripps denied him the authority he sought in blunt terms.[16] It was, however, unacceptable to the MEW, which had been in charge of the negotiations since their beginning. They had not gained the impression from Cripps' telegrams that he was either 'chagrined or personally hurt'. Moreover, they could not subscribe to the reigning concept that Soviet–German economic collaboration was bound to lead to a political one. From what could be gathered about the Berlin con-

ference it appeared that German hopes were shattered. In their opinion, therefore, a threat was a legitimate tactical move. It was conceivable that Cripps might be compelled in certain circumstances 'to tell Mikoyan that we can snap our fingers at them and can do without their trade'. The Foreign Office, however, would not give way. The Berlin conference confirmed the policy they had 'always' understood Russia to be pursuing. The MEW kept up the pressure until they became aware that the decision was essentially a political one and therefore in the realm of the Foreign Office. The most they could do was to modify the draft instructions.[17] Cripps was informed that the Foreign Office did not believe it was possible to instil in Russia a fear of Britain. The reserved attitude was reconfirmed in its traditional sense of leaving it to the Russians to 'make the next move', assuming this would never be made.[18]

The refusal of Cripps' request fed on the prevailing hostility towards Russia after Molotov's journey to Berlin. In the meantime the British military attaché in Moscow had been assured that the meeting was only a return of Ribbentrop's visit and that 'nothing special would come out of it'. This tallied with Maisky's insinuations to Butler that Molotov had been instructed to conduct negotiations in Berlin so as to 'preserve intact' Soviet neutrality.[19] Information from various sources compelled even Halifax to conclude in Cabinet that 'not very much' had been achieved in Berlin. However, the axiom that the foundations of German–Soviet collaboration were immovable remained intact.[20] Paradoxically, the new evaluation was used in order to justify the continued reserved attitude. If the Russians were 'genuinely anxious' to avoid committing themselves too deeply to the Axis powers, they would certainly make the next move. In short Cripps was advised again to 'abstain from any action which might suggest impatience, suspicion or irritation'.[21]

The wish to refrain from any initiative was also evident in Halifax's overdue reply to Cripps' personal letter. It was written shortly before his appointment as ambassador to Washington and epitomized the lack of guidance during his tenure of office. Halifax was anxious to accommodate the views of the Foreign Office with those of the ambassador in Moscow. His underlying assumption was that the Russians, being 'extreme realists', were only concerned with the security of the Soviet Union. On the other hand, he attributed their policy to an ideological

desire for the 'collapse of both Germany and Great Britain', when they would be able to impose their will on a 'Europe ripe for revolution'. The political concept which had been cultivated under his auspices was used to bridge the apparent contradiction. The Russians did not expect Germany ultimately to 'constitute a serious menace', but in the foreseeable future their policy was determined by 'fear of Germany's fighting machine' and a 'desire to appease' her. Cripps was therefore informed that it would be a mistake to suppose that Soviet sympathies were on the side of Britain, which the Russians felt they could 'ignore and rebuff with impunity'. An attempt was made to placate Cripps with the grudging admission that if the Berlin conference turned out to be 'mere window-dressing', relations with Russia could 'remain undisturbed or even take a turn for the better'. He was urged to remain at his post because if a turn did occur the Russians were bound to listen to him; his sincerity in wishing for an improvement in relations was undoubted.[22] It is revealing that when the Germans invaded Russia, Halifax confessed to his old Oxonian friend, Geoffrey Dawson, the editor of *The Times*: 'I never believed it would happen, and was greatly surprised. Nor have I yet succeeded in finding any explanation of it that satisfies my intellect.'[23]

Cripps was not moved by these communications and his prompt reply was to insist on the withdrawal of the offer. He entertained no illusions that the withdrawal in itself was a sufficient incentive to bring about an agreement. However, the Russians would understand that Britain could not be 'trifled with' and be compelled to adopt a 'more reasonable attitude'. On 8 December Cripps produced for Whitehall's comments the draft letter of withdrawal he intended to hand to Mikoyan. A week later he pressed for an answer. Some officials in the Foreign Office, ostensible proponents of a 'policy of uniform amiability' towards the Russians, proposed a corrected draft which would ensure that Cripps did not break off negotiations in an 'unduly abrupt and aggressive manner'. More sincere was their concern that, although Cripps was in the best position to judge how to approach the Soviet government, he did not consider the opportunity created by such a letter for the Russians to make trouble in England by inciting 'certain sections of public opinion'. If a 'carefully worded' letter were sent to Moscow it would leave the initiative to the Russians; once negotiations

broke down, the Foreign Office could conveniently 'saddle the Russians with the blame'.[24]

Both the MEW and the Board of Trade were still inclined to allow Cripps to react 'in his own way'. However, Cadogan, who had a tight grip on Halifax, would not sanction even the modified draft. As anticipated by the MEW, Cripps 'dug his toes in' and towards the end of December the Foreign Office gave way, leaving the draft letter almost unaltered. The procrastination of the Foreign Office caused a delay of six weeks and severely reduced the effectiveness of the act, which was intended as a reaction to Molotov's visit to Berlin.[25] However, the move and the reassessment of policy towards Russia were interrupted by Eden's return to the Foreign Office on 23 December.

Halifax's casual attitude to foreign affairs and lack of determination made the formulation of policy susceptible to varying pressures and influences. Eden's career, on the other hand, had been almost exclusively dominated by preoccupation with international relations. The appointment, therefore, seemed to herald firmer direction of the Foreign Office.[26] Churchill's often quoted observation that Eden was 'like a man going home' conceals the fact that he was reluctant to leave the War Office, although with the Foreign Office came a seat in the War Cabinet.[27] Relations between Eden and Churchill were characterized by mutual affection which, however, did not preclude disagreements. Eden preferred to bear his grudges in silence and reconcile Churchill with his characteristic charm. Churchill glossed over differences either by exerting his fatherly authority or by skilfully creating a diversion to nip in the bud the source of tension. This was obvious in the conduct of relations with Russia following the German invasion. Eden's promotion to the Foreign Office was another case in point. Eden had just scored a major success when his mission to the Middle East culminated in General Archibald Wavell's desert offensive on 9 December and the dazzling defeat of the entire Italian army in North Africa. Earlier Eden had often found himself at odds with Churchill over strategy in the Middle East, the deployment of forces and appreciations of the commanders-in-chief. Relations 'clearly *were* choppy' during that period.[28] Eden's increasing interference in the conduct of the war could not possibly appeal to Churchill, who as Defence Minister saw himself in the role of a warlord. Lord Lothian's sudden

death provided Churchill with the opportunity of assigning Halifax, manifestly against his will, to Washington and transferring Eden to the Foreign Office. Eden, a 'rebel of a sort', as aptly described by A. J. P. Taylor, submitted with hardly a murmur. He consoled himself with the rationalization that in wartime diplomacy was 'strategy's twin', although in fact diplomacy lagged behind military progress and Eden was bound to find his activities severely curtailed.[29] At the end of 1941 he was still complaining about the inactivity of the Foreign Office and longing for the War Office; he did not even exclude the possibility of a commission in the army. In the Cabinet crisis of 1942 Eden preferred the role of Defence Minister to the premiership.[30] For a while, however, he continued during his extensive Middle Eastern tour to deal with both strategy and diplomacy and left affairs in the Office unattended. For Russia this had serious repercussions.

Eden's sense of purpose was unpopular both with the senior officials in the Foreign Office and with Cripps. It was thanks to Eden that Cadogan had replaced Vansittart as Permanent Under-Secretary shortly before Eden's resignation in 1938. Nonetheless he was politically and personally closer to Chamberlain and exercised immense influence on Halifax who, it was observed, did 'all his work through A. Cadogan'. He must have been familiar with Eden's contempt for Halifax's handling of the Office. Immediately on assumption of office Eden appeared 'horrified at deadness of F.O. and its woolliness'.[31] Indeed John Harvey, Eden's political secretary and confidant, admitted regretfully a few months later that Eden did not seem to have changed the 'anti-liberal attitude of the F.O. officials'. As late as May 1941 Eden continued to be worried about the Office and complained that he found Cadogan 'very unhelpful'.[32] It is not surprising that Cadogan thought Churchill was making a 'grave mistake'; he found the change 'rather a gloomy prospect altogether'. In reality, when Eden became Leader of the House in November 1942, he was tied down in the Commons like Cripps before him, and Cadogan regained much of his earlier influence.[33]

As far as politics were concerned, Cripps had little in common with either Halifax or Eden. Nonetheless, there was no doubt where his preference lay; Cripps had openly advocated Halifax as Prime Minister in the 1940 crisis. In spite of occasional criticism or outbursts, Cripps wrongly saw in Halifax's conciliation and inclination to yield to intellectual superiority a positive response to his own general views.

Moreover Cripps owed his post in Moscow entirely to Halifax. Eden, on the other hand, although he may have occasionally entertained vague ideas on the reorganization of post-war Europe, was associated with Churchill and like him was primarily committed to an all-out war with Nazism.[34] Cripps had never moved in the same social circles as Eden. When rumours of a Cabinet reshuffle in which Eden was to replace Halifax first reached Moscow, Cripps' immediate reaction was: '*Absit omen*! though I think a change would be good not that one I hope.'[35]

Cripps was not likely to be impressed by Eden's pro-Soviet aura, gained from his dramatic meeting with Stalin in 1935 and his support of the tripartite negotiations in 1939, when he offered to go to Moscow. This reputation naturally caused commentators to assume on Eden's taking office that the policy pursued by Cripps was 'fully endorsed' by him.[36] Eden, however, like Churchill, had adopted a more balanced attitude to Russia only after she converted to collective security which he championed. In private, his biographer assures us, his sentiments were similar to those of his 'supposedly more anti-Communist colleagues'.[37] Eden's sentiments, however, unlike Halifax's, were based on the traditional anti-Russian bias rather than on ideological grounds. This is reflected *inter alia* in a typical minute he wrote upon resuming office: Stalin had struck him in 1939 as 'the true lineal descendant of Chingiz Khan, and therefore quite at home in Russia, most of it anyway'.[38]

There was therefore a marked change in nuance and style but the political concept underlying relations with Russia remained unaltered, at least until the German invasion. Cadogan noted in his diary: 'Glad to find A. [Anthony Eden] not "ideological" and quite alive to uselessness of expecting anything from these cynical, blood-stained murderers.' Although in the Office Eden became 'as jumpy as ever' and displayed 'the usual itch to do something', the change from Halifax's period was less drastic than expected.[39] After all, as has been noted,[40] Eden had excelled as a negotiator and as such his record, like Halifax's, was not marked by 'resolute action'; he was in fact the 'conciliator in chief'.

The reshuffle, however, did end the consideration of various retaliations against Russia in the aftermath of Molotov's visit. Cadogan, probably in an attempt to forestall new gestures towards Russia, sud-

denly supported Cripps' 'just arguments' for withdrawing the offer. He pressed for a continuation of policy, implying that Halifax 'would have accepted this'. Eden's concern for the appearance of firm handling of the Office, without however giving offence to the ambassador in Moscow, was discernible in his carefully worded instructions to Cripps. Eden reminded Cripps that he was held in esteem by the Russians, who now expected him to make special efforts to improve relations. In such circumstances a withdrawal was likely to be taken by them as a 'much sharper rebuff'. If Cripps, notwithstanding these considerations, still wished to proceed with his note he was given a free hand.[41]

Eden was under no real pressure to re-examine relations with Russia. He seems to have expected that the mere announcement of his appointment would alter the course of British war diplomacy. Circumstances, however, could not have been less propitious for rapprochement with Russia. The Russians, though hopeful about the change, were resolute not to make a false move which might compromise their standing with Germany. Eden himself continued to be absorbed in Mediterranean strategy even in his new post. Indeed on 12 February he and General John Dill, the Chief of the Imperial General Staff, left for two months in the Middle East in an attempt to establish a defensive line in the Balkans by recruiting Yugoslavia, Greece and above all Turkey.[42] The Foreign Office, under the damaging impression of Molotov's visit to Berlin, adopted an overtly hostile attitude towards Russia while Cripps, offended by the Russians' apparent disregard of his overtures, was outwardly drawing closer to Whitehall by advocating aloofness.

The Kremlin, which at the best of times was notorious for withholding information, became stifling in the delicate situation prevailing at the beginning of 1941. It was difficult to 'guess even vaguely', as Cripps complained, the course of Soviet policy. The only activity in Moscow, 'seething with rumours', was the 'eternal rounds of conversation and speculation' in the diplomatic colony. An observer noticed that diplomatic life in Moscow was 'about as close to prison as anything out of bars . . . it appears an intolerable existence for anyone with an active mind'.[43] It certainly was unsuited to Cripps' mentality and his taste for frank personal contacts. The distortion of information is described in Cripps' diary:

Last night the Turkish & American Ambassadors were here and before dinner I told the Turkish A [Ambassador] one or two of the latest items of news or of

6 A picnic in the woods outside Moscow, May 1941, standing left: Isobel Cripps and Cripps; Cripps' daughter Peggy is wearing a headscarf

gossip. After dinner the Turk & American had a long talk and later still I had a talk with the American in which he related to me most of what I had told the Turk!!

The misleading lull put Cripps off guard. He suddenly indulged in intensive social activities from which he had hitherto abstained. He mastered the skills of ice-skating on the improvised rink of the frozen tennis court at the embassy and cross-country skiing near the embassy's picturesque dacha, shadowed by the 'Y.M.C.A. boys' – his NKVD guards. When sport was off, once temperatures dropped below −20° C, he was taken by Isobel for his 'very first' sightseeing tour of Moscow. Another morning was spent at the opening of a Soviet art exhibition 'rather like a Royal Academy with a great deal in the way of pictures that was very bad'. The evenings likewise were a round of dinner parties ending in dancing, gossiping or card-playing well into the early hours of the morning. There were the occasional fabulous ballet performances at the Bolshoi theatre or the latest Hollywood movies at the luxurious premises of the American embassy.[44]

91

To overcome the tedium Cripps resorted to the unconventional diplomatic device of setting up an unofficial pro-allied 'club' of his 'special cronies'. These were the Greek Minister, Christophe Diamantopoulos, the Turkish ambassador, Haidar Aktay, and the Yugoslav minister, Milovan Gavrilovic, with whom Cripps enjoyed a 'special kind of contact & freedom'. The GETS (Greek, English, Turkish and Serb), so dubbed by the foreign correspondents, met daily, usually in Cripps' sunlit sitting room, exchanging information and interpretations over coffee.[45] Coincidentally, the combination mirrored Eden's abortive attempts at that time to form a Balkan understanding. In view of the isolation of Moscow and the growing antagonism at home, the club provided Cripps with a convenient forum for expounding his views. However, it also proved to be a source of disinformation and misinterpretations. Moreover, the inevitable deep personal attachments affected Cripps' judgment when Gavrilovic and Diamantopoulos were expelled from Russia after Germany had overrun their countries and Aktay became a hostile neutral after the German invasion of Russia.

The temporary evaluation of German intentions which Cripps made at this time was the result not of preconceived ideas but rather of the lack of background information which he had been pressing Whitehall to provide.[46] Putting himself in the Germans' shoes, he expected an imminent invasion of Britain before it could be foiled by massive American aid. Compared with the grave test lying ahead for Britain, all seemed 'completely quiet' in Moscow. No prospect of change could be detected unless Hitler proved 'so stupid as to go into the Balkans'. The 'political stagnation' proved particularly frustrating for Cripps, whose weakness in diplomacy was impulsiveness. In his worst moments he even feared that he would be forced to remain idle and then 'retire & write "Another mission failed!"' To Monckton he confessed that it was 'very trying sitting here waiting for things to happen!'; he even disclosed a hidden longing for a place where 'one could talk frankly and freely about political questions'.[47] Nevertheless, despite tempting appeals from old friends on the left to return and become a 'centre and leader', he was resolved to see his mission through; 'the more hopeless it looks', he wrote to his foster-son, 'the more I feel I must stick on and try to do something'.[48]

The opinion held in London was that Cripps had become 'dis-

7 The 'Club', l. to r.: Diamantopoulos, Cripps, Gavrilovic and Aktay

illusioned' with the Russians. Dalton acted on this assumption, publicizing Cripps' call for the tightening of the economic blockade in unison with the United States. The revelation provided the Germans with an opportunity to undermine Anglo-Soviet relations by spreading rumours in Moscow that Cripps was about to be recalled.[49] Steinhardt, whom Cripps found increasingly exasperating, made similar observations; though erroneous, these reflect Cripps' low spirits.[50]

Cripps' dejection and shift in tactics in no way mellowed his criticism of the government. He periodically returned to his old hobby-horse, producing an elaborate statement on war aims which he urged Halifax to move in Cabinet. A rejection, he informed Monckton, would mean that the government had 'no ideas as to the future at all, in which case they ought not to be where they are!' He consistently maintained that the poor relations with Russia were a legacy of the past.[51]

Now that Cripps' recommendations coincided with their own, the officials at the Foreign Office had no difficulty in dissuading Eden from

reconsidering relations with Russia. They ingeniously concealed the fact that Cripps' aloofness was a device to draw out the Russians. Consequently the Foreign Office were able to explain the German deployment of troops in eastern Europe and the spectacular events in the Balkans on the basis of the established but unwarranted concept that Germany and Russia shared a community of interests.

Cripps was the first to dampen Eden's confidence that his mere reputation would suffice to introduce a drastic change in the Soviet attitude. He pointed out the futility of responding to Maisky's keen attempt to revive relations in the wake of the Berlin conference unless the Cabinet was prepared to acknowledge the 'de facto sovereignty' of the Russians over the Baltic. Eden, in what would become his characteristic style, was unwilling to raise any contentious issue in Cabinet. Instead he proposed to revive the memories of his friendly visit to Moscow in 1935 by addressing Stalin personally, thereby disproving the notion that the Foreign Office was sabotaging relations.[52] Cripps strongly disagreed. A friendly message unaccompanied by concrete suggestions was likely to be interpreted as a sign of weakness and would compromise his present attitude of 'reserve and non-helpfulness'. Eden was advised to 'await [the] turn of events' before making a further approach. If in the past Cripps' suggestions had been rejected out of hand, they were now welcomed as being 'valuable and interesting'; after all, it was minuted, no one could accuse Cripps of 'being unsympathetic' to the Russians.[53] This accidental harmony was exploited to the utmost. The BBC and the press, which showed an inclination to 'indulge in optimistic speculations', were directed to play down their reports on Russia. Likewise stories in the vein of the *News Chronicle*'s 'Russia scotched German March through Bulgaria' were deplored in the Office as examples of what they 'and Sir Stafford Cripps' were anxious to avoid.[54] Geoffrey Dawson, editor of *The Times*, was reproached for a favourable account of a conversation between Eden and Maisky which raised expectations of the dawning of a 'new era' for which there was 'little or no warrant'.[55]

A new German–Soviet trade agreement concluded on 10 January after prolonged negotiations obscured even further Cripps' fundamental difference in outlook from that of Whitehall. The agreement enabled the Foreign Office to suppress any suggestion of serious friction between Russia and Germany in the Balkans. Cripps had anticipated an

agreement. The announcement of the news late at night after yet another dull day was nonetheless 'rather depressing', as the terms appeared to be loaded with political meaning.[56] On the face of it Cripps' recommendation to counter the agreement by 'rigorous' control of trade with Russia conformed with Whitehall's. So did his admission that relations with Britain continued to be subordinate to those with Germany. In reaching this conclusion he was to a large extent misled by the German exposition of the agreement as an outcome of the Berlin conference. The deliberate disinformation was an early attempt to conceal the offensive deployment of German forces in the East.[57] However, Cripps was still convinced of Russia's 'fundamental hostility' to Germany and 'desire to prepare to meet [the] German menace'. He believed Russia's signature was motivated by a need to bolster up the military industries and acquire machine tools which could not be obtained elsewhere. His overall advice was therefore for a 'flexible' policy to 'take advantage of all possibilities as and when they appear'.[58]

The Cripps' unyielding belief in an eventual shift in Soviet policy and dismay at the government's failure to appreciate it is well reflected in Isobel's diary:

This great country sits Sphinx like! hiding its fears &, no doubt, waiting for us to be 'worth while', as far as She is concerned. Germany, they must fear, but at the moment it is She who can help [Russia] most. *We* do feel strongly that if only our home powers that be could see their way to being a little more pliable over *secondary* things, & avoid such devastatingly curious psychological errors at critical moments, it might help a lot! Still I do believe *no one* could understand the atmosphere unless they came here, but we can pray for them to grow in imagination! 'To give or to go that little bit beyond half-way' at the right moment. If only people could realize, that, *that* is a sign of statesmanship & greatness, not *weakness*.[59]

Cripps' evaluation was read selectively. His operative recommendations, in line with the 'general attitude of reserve', were adopted. The commentary was dismissed, as it was taken for granted that far-reaching political *entente* was now taking shape between Germany and Russia. Cripps was therefore doomed to 'labour in vain in Moscow'. The only faint dissent registered was Butler's prophecy that Cripps would 'one day be rewarded'.[60] Cadogan next set out to discourage Cripps from

cherishing any hopes of converting Eden. On his own initiative he prepared for Eden a seemingly straightforward complimentary letter to Cripps. Its wording was masterly, giving prominence to the elements of Cripps' truce with the Foreign Office while pledging Eden to the reigning political concepts. Eden consoled Cripps that he too had a 'share of disappointment' in his endeavours to bring about rapprochement with Russia. He was most appreciative of the 'daily difficulties' which Cripps faced. His conviction that Cripps was the best man to effect an improvement in relations was practically contradicted by the declaration: 'Russian suspicions lie so deep and Russian fears of German military might are so vivid and real that our task must be a formidable one.' He further noted that Russian connivance at German advances in the Balkans seemed to point to the existence of secret agreements on spheres of influence. Eden thus endorsed the policy of aloofness, now attributed to Cripps, as he did not expect to gain much by making fresh proposals. The conclusion therefore was that Cripps should refrain from any action until British military might could 'inspire in the Soviet Government some of the fear and respect' which they felt for Germany. It was tantamount to a rejection of Cripps' demands for an examination of outstanding questions.[61]

A personal attempt by Churchill to improve Cripps' standing in Moscow by lunching with Maisky was similarly checked. In view of the 'recent demonstration of Soviet–German solidarity' in Berlin, it seemed to the Northern Department inconceivable that the government should be 'running after Maisky'. Eden followed suit, explaining to Churchill that it would be doing Maisky 'too much honour' and arranging for him to dine with Beneš instead.[62]

The consolidation of a political concept, despite evidence which foretold the spread of the war to the East, is best illustrated by the Foreign Office's weekly intelligence summary. It simply dismissed reports of German deployment in the Balkans, rumours of Soviet counter-preparations and Stalin's 'mythical' New Year's address on the Red Army's state of mobilization.[63] The consolidation of the concept was perhaps of little immediate significance but had far-reaching consequences in the months preceding the German invasion of Russia.

The Russians were momentarily beguiled by the false calm at the dawn of 1941. The breathing space seemed to have been extended now the Germans had been held back. They could not possibly know the

fateful implications of the discords in Berlin. In Britain the departure from the scene of Halifax, associated with the policy of Munich, held a promise for a brighter future. It was with a genuine sense of relief that Maisky hastily congratulated Eden on his new post. Soviet foreign policy, he revealed to Eden with unprecedented frankness, was based on the promotion of 'national interests'. The military actions carried out by Russia and the maintenance of neutrality were neither 'ideological' nor 'expansionist' but precautionary measures 'to ensure a hold upon essential strategic defensive positions'. He reflected the Kremlin's confidence, which was also affecting Cripps' evaluations, that Hitler was 'too cautious in military undertakings' to advance into the Balkans in the face of determined Soviet opposition. Like Cripps, he believed a solution of the Baltic controversy would considerably improve Anglo-Soviet relations.[64]

This complacency was short-lived. The Russians soon found out that the Germans showed no interest in continuing the political dialogue while openly trespassing on Soviet defensive assets. There had been a gradual build-up in Romania of German forces destined to cross into Bulgaria and forestall British deployment in Greece. In a *démarche* presented to the Germans by Molotov and Vladimir Dekanozov, the newly appointed Soviet ambassador to Berlin, they were reminded that Bulgaria fell within the Soviet 'security zone'. The Germans' prompt reassurances were belied by Schulenburg's disclosures to Molotov on 27 February and 1 March of Bulgaria's adherence to the Tripartite Pact and the entry of German troops into that country. In response Molotov, in a highly agitated mood, warned Schulenburg that the Germans could no longer 'count on support from the U.S.S.R. for their acts in Bulgaria'.[65]

The cultivation of the western alternative naturally now became a pressing need but had to be pursued discreetly so as not to antagonize the Germans, virtually on Russia's threshold. Already on 15 January Maisky intimated to Butler that it 'was not in the Soviet interest that German influence should spread in the Balkans' and that no policy was 'perpetual or eternal'. Very similar admissions were made to Victor Mallet and Fredrik Sterling, British and American ambassadors to Sweden, by Alexandra Kollontay, the Soviet ambassador there.[66] Such statements were not forceful enough to eradicate British suspicion and the steadfast attitude of 'reserve'. The Russians now faced a dilemma

which would become more acute as the German preparations for invasion intensified. A more outspoken overture was certain to spark off a German retaliation. On the other hand it was unthinkable to sacrifice the laboriously maintained western alternative. Of most immediate concern were the increasingly ominous signs of Cripps' despondency and rumours of his recall.

Maisky hoped to soothe the tension over lunch with Eden. The Northern Department believed the invitation should be refused as a protest against Cripps' disagreeable position in Moscow. Collier took the opportunity to acquaint Eden with the opinion held in diplomatic circles that 'if any other ambassador conducted himself like Maisky, he would be *persona non grata*'. This was a prelude to mounting demands in the Office to 'put his Excellency on the mat'.[67] In spite of the urgent overtones of Maisky's request, Eden accepted the invitation but postponed it to a much later date and resolved to deal exclusively with the maltreatment of Cripps in Moscow.[68] In the meantime Maisky attempted to draw out Monckton, whom he knew to be the person most in Cripps' confidence. Monckton unusually found the ambassador on his own, which indicated that he had 'a good deal he wished to say'. His message to Cripps was that Molotov's failure to confer with him had no bearing on him personally or on Anglo-Soviet relations in general. He ended with the rather feeble ploy of comparing Churchill's inaccessibility to Molotov's, who was also acting as the Chairman of the Council of the People's Commissars. Naturally Monckton could not divulge to Maisky Cripps' grievances against Whitehall and the Cabinet. Unaware of the reasons which had prompted Maisky's approach, he unintentionally confirmed his apprehension by hinting at Cripps' wish to resume his political activities in London. Maisky's advice to Cripps 'not to make too much of these things and be patient' convinced Monckton that his friend was not 'on such a bad wicket out there as someone might have thought'.[69] Two days later Maisky forced his way in to Eden, who was suffering from a 'most unpleasant headache' after a particularly busy day. Eden rather impatiently chose to lecture Maisky on the intolerable position of Cripps, 'whose desire to improve Anglo-Soviet relations was perfectly well-known'.[70]

The reaction was swift. On the evening of 1 February Cripps was summoned to the Kremlin. Throughout the interview Molotov stressed the 'considerable hopes' the Russians had entertained of Cripps'

appointment, which had been dispelled by the policy of his government. Oblivious of the circumstances which had brought about the
interview, Cripps assumed that Molotov wished 'somewhat stupidly' to
arouse in him a sense of 'personal failure' to goad him into settling
outstanding issues. It emerged nonetheless that Molotov was 'at pains'
to excuse his unavailability. Cripps was diverted to Vyshinsky who,
according to Molotov, had full authority to pursue negotiations. When
Cripps tried to raise the controversial issue of post-war reconstruction
to ensure that collaboration would not be based 'merely on the temporary expediencies of the war situation', he found Molotov ostentatiously 'bored and impatient'. Molotov's gesture, severely handicapped
by fears of German reprisal, was lost on Cripps, who was deprived of
the relevant background information. Cripps mistakenly attributed the
approach to the pressure he was applying. Consequently he even
renewed his suggestion to withdraw the economic proposals. His
recommendations, however, were made with the qualification that the
pressure should not inflict 'injury to the Soviet Government' but rather
induce her 'to come to some useful trade or barter agreement'. Nor did
he modify his basic tenet that a breakthrough in relations would only
take place after the Cabinet's revision of the Baltic issue.[71] Eden was
inclined to respond favourably. He retracted, however, when faced by
overwhelming opposition in the Office to Cripps' 'illogical deviation'
from the attitude of 'strict reserve' which he had allegedly been
advocating. While 'appeasement' with regard to the Baltic was thus
ruled out Cripps' other recommendations were enthusiastically
implemented. The Office paid no heed to the experts of the MEW,
who argued that conditions were propitious for a mutually satisfactory
solution of the Baltic problem.[72]

Cripps had been independently seeking American collaboration in
exerting economic pressure on the Russians. The State Department,
however, would not subscribe to Whitehall's concept. Hull feared they
might 'pin prick' Russia into a distinctly pro-German policy. Russia's
attitude, Cripps was told by Steinhardt, might 'tip the scales either way'
at a crucial stage of the war.[73] Although the MEW had made it clear that
an effective blockade was dependent on the Americans' 'whole hearted
support', the Foreign Office decided to proceed; the State Department
eventually concurred on the eve of the German invasion. It also
transpired that Dalton, in contrast to his experts at the Ministry, was no

longer 'oversanguine' about a trade agreement with Russia.[74] Accordingly Cripps informed Mikoyan on 21 February that the trade offer, the ostensible reason for his mission in Moscow, was 'out of date'.[75]

Lacking contact with Cripps, who refused to be diverted to secondary figures, the Russians formed a wrong impression of his outlook which in addition was deliberately misrepresented in London. They proceeded with conciliatory gestures. There was a marked relaxation of the ban against Russians mixing with foreigners. Barkov, head of the Protocol Department of Narkomindel, admittedly a minor figure, was nonetheless the first Soviet offical to pay Cripps a visit at the British embassy. There were other feelers such as an obviously prearranged approach by Korj, the First Secretary of the Soviet embassy, to a representative of British Military Intelligence during a party given by the Soviet military attaché. He clearly wished to convey that a division of labour had been worked out in the Kremlin: Vyshinsky had been assigned to communicate with Cripps, who was held in high esteem.[76]

The gloomy Russian assessment at the beginning of March was expressed in earnest by Maisky while visiting his close friends, the aging Webbs. He feared their nephew was 'not doing well at Moscow . . . Though Eden was friendly, the British Foreign Office was obdurate and Churchill supported the Foreign Office. Stafford had *apparently* agreed with his government's policy.' That regaining Cripps' confidence was now top priority was clear from his conclusion that 'it would be a disaster if the Embassies at Moscow and in London were bereft of Ambassadors'.[77]

### Encounter in Turkey

The withdrawal of the proposals for a trade agreement was the incarnation of the policy of reserve bordering on hostility. The landslide in relations enhanced mutual suspicion: it further consolidated the concept dominating British policy towards Russia while diverting the Russians from a sober appraisal of the danger lying ahead. Eden's visit to the Middle East alerted Cripps to the danger signals.

The strenuous efforts made by the Northern Department to preserve the temporary harmony with Cripps were to a large extent dictated by considerations of domestic politics. A suggestion made in the course of

a Parliamentary debate that Cripps should return home and review Anglo-Soviet relations in a secret session of the House was enthusiastically taken up in the Foreign Office. They mistakenly attributed the 'minor' differences of opinion with Cripps to his protracted stay in Moscow, which would lead to a 'distorted view of any problem'; 'a few hours of discussion around the table', they felt confident, would clear up these difficulties. Cripps' statement would then persuade 'certain sections' in Parliament to take a 'more reasonable view' of the government's policy.

Cripps' encounter with Eden, however, was to take place elsewhere and only augment the discord. He urged Eden to use the opportunity of his Middle Eastern tour to visit Moscow. Such a visit was likely to 'flatter' the Russians, eradicate suspicions and encourage British friends in south-east Europe. For Cripps, whose undoubted forte was personal persuasion, the visit held other 'inestimable advantages' if he were to confer with Eden in advance.[78] The reaction to Cripps' proposal was influenced by the generally overlooked changes in the conduct of the Foreign Office during Eden's absence in February and March. Churchill now took charge with his characteristic zeal and authority. Cadogan and Butler thus found themselves constituting a 'happy little Duumvirate' under the 'all-seeing eye of the Most High'.[79] When passing on Cripps' telegram to Eden, Churchill did not conceal his disapproval, stating that he did not trust the Russians as regards Eden's 'personal safety or liberty'. In conformity with the concept held at the Office, he advised Eden that the Russians could only be won over by a 'good show in the Balkans'.[80] Rarely in his career did Eden stand up openly to Churchill. Moreover, considering the discontent in Cabinet over his Balkan policy, he was unwilling to make the side-issue of relations with Russia another bone of contention. Eden therefore discreetly turned down the proposition, muting controversial overtones by emphasizing the physical constraints such as the 'exceedingly heavy programme of visits', his prolonged absence from London and the technical difficulties involved in a flight to Russia. His own commitment to the political concept is reflected in his rephrasing of Churchill's argument that it was senseless at the present state of Russo-German relations to 'run after the Russians'. On the other hand he was prepared to meet Stalin or Molotov in the Crimea, bearing in mind the beneficial effect it might have on Turkey, which clearly ranked high in his order of priorities.

Finally, much as he welcomed the idea of conferring with Cripps, a tight timetable and poor communications made him 'hardly hope' that it could be arranged.[81]

Cripps was not so easily dissuaded. His venture into diplomacy had been partly an outcome of his 1939 world tour and encounter with heads of state which, besides being a novelty, gave him a false sense of his political influence. The reality in Moscow in 1940 was an utterly different experience of frustration. A short sally to Ankara promised at least 'some appearance of movement!' His need to do '*something* to help' points to an acute guilt complex, emanating from his Christian and moral ethics, for 'leading a most comfortable & luxurious life which seems all wrong in view of what is being suffered in England'.[82] Prompt action was called for. Eden's discouraging telegram reached Moscow in the early afternoon of 25 February, and Cripps arranged to see Vyshinsky directly. Swift consultations with the Soviet government followed, after which Cripps was encouraged to proceed to Turkey as circumstances were '*not yet*' ripe for high-level talks. In London too Maisky confided to Butler that it was important for Cripps to 'acquaint' Eden with the fundamental principles of Soviet foreign policy.[83] By 7 p.m. of that day a Soviet Air Force Douglas was put at Cripps' disposal, by no means as a matter of course as this would be a pioneering direct flight from Moscow to Turkey across the Black Sea.[84] The Russians' extraordinary efforts bore a striking resemblance to their flying Cripps over from China a year earlier at a tense moment during the war with Finland. Yet another indication of growing Soviet 'complications', as Cripps noted, was the failure of Molotov to deliver the customary opening speech at the meeting of the Supreme Soviet on that very day.

Another precious day was wasted in obtaining Turkish clearance until Cripps finally left Moscow in the early hours of 27 February. The journey indeed satisfied Cripps' desire for a break. His diary, almost the sole source for this obscure episode, depicts with almost juvenile excitement the numerous adventures which such a flight then involved, the strong impressions of exotic Istanbul, encounters with 'all sorts of people from refugees & secret service agents to members of the staff and journalists', and his acquaintance with Hugh Knatchbull-Hugessen, the British ambassador to Turkey, who was the 'very charming and original person' he had expected him to be.

This enthusiasm contrasts with the fact that the political talks with

Eden were neither constructive as far as relations with Russia were concerned nor conducive to establishing close personal relations.[85] Upon
landing in Istanbul Cripps made a dash to catch the night train to
Ankara so that he could confer with Eden on his last day in Ankara.
Eden, however, slept late, having been entertained at a cabaret till 5
a.m., and arranged to see Cripps at 10 a.m. He eventually turned up
only towards lunchtime and was entirely preoccupied by his Balkan
project. Considering the disappointing results of his mission so far he
might have been expected to show keen interest in Russia. On 17
February, after Hitler had personally assured Turkey of his peaceful
intentions, Bulgaria and Turkey issued a non-aggression declaration
which paved the way for Bulgaria's adherence to the Tripartite Pact.
With their left flank secured, German troops crossed the Danube and
poured into Bulgaria. These developments were a serious blow to Eden
who gave precedence to recruiting Turkey for aid to Greece. On 27
February, the day after his arrival in Ankara, Eden's hopes were further
shattered when Prince Paul of Yugoslavia cold-shouldered British proposals for coordinating Yugoslav–Turkish resistance.[86] When Cripps
finally got in a word about Russia he found Eden was not familiar with
his recent communications; he could therefore only 'broach the Baltic
question, but there was not time to do more'. Lunch at the embassy with
other guests intervened, and Eden's schedule was full for the rest
of the day.

Cripps was directed to Dill, who could at least provide him with
authoritative briefing on British military capabilities and the COS's
evaluation of the German aims. Dill, like Eden, was committed to the
Balkan bloc. As Director of Military Intelligence in 1935 he had questioned Russia's military value as an ally and even suggested that
Germany ought to 'expand eastwards at Russia's expense'. In 1941 he
naturally identified with the political concept that Russia was bound to
Germany and therefore excluded the possibility of cooperating with
her. His concluding point, which supported Cripps' appraisal, was that
the invasion of Britain, still at the head of Hitler's priorities, 'would be
attempted, and its success was not a contingency to be lightly discounted'.[87]
Cripps' advocacy of a stern attitude, which later affected Russia's
appreciation of the intricate international scene, was based on Dill's
analysis and was justified as a last resort to relieve the pressure on
Britain.

Further fragmentary conversations with Eden were conducted on board the 'most luxurious train well stocked with food and drinks' which took the Foreign Secretary to Istanbul on his way to Athens. Cripps, who did most of the talking, emphasized the importance of removing the Baltic obstacle through *de facto* recognition of Soviet rule, and title to the gold and ships confiscated by the British government. He was critical of the Cabinet's rigidity, absence of foresight and tendency to regard the seizure of the Baltic as a *casus belli*; he advised them to be alert to the 'fluid' situation and ready to take 'immediate advantage' if circumstances changed. All he could extract from Eden, however, was a vague promise to raise the issue on his return.[88]

While Cripps found Eden indifferent to Anglo-Soviet relations, the regulation of Turco-Soviet relations held better prospects. Turkey's relations with Russia were closely linked to those with Britain. During the negotiations for an Anglo-French-Turkish treaty in 1939, Sukru Saracoglü, the Turkish Foreign Minister, insisted that Turkey be exempt from taking any action which might embroil her in war with Russia. He even went to Moscow to seek Soviet acquiescence with the treaty. The Russians blamed the British for the failure of these negotiations and for the attempt in the spring of 1940 to involve Turkey in the abortive plans to bomb the Baku oilfields. In their very first meeting Stalin had responded favourably to Cripps' proposal to act as an intermediary in Russia's claim for the revision of the Montreux Convention which gave Turkey virtual control of the straits. The Turks, however, were reluctant and the Foreign Office was unwilling to risk British standing in Turkey in favour of improving Turco-Soviet relations. Up to the collapse of France the Russians' main fear had been of Allied manipulation of Turkey, though this changed owing to the interest in Turkey displayed by Germany during the Berlin conversations and the subsequent incursion into the Balkans. Before leaving for the Middle East Eden had sought through Maisky a Soviet 'non-intervention policy' in favour of Turkey were she to be attacked by Germany. Prior to his departure Cripps possessed ample evidence that the Russians no longer viewed with equanimity the events in the Balkans and were anxious that a German presence in the Balkans should be opposed by Turkey. Aktay had told him of the relief with which Vyshinsky accepted assurances that the Turco-Bulgarian treaty would not introduce coolness into Anglo-Turkish relations. Vyshinsky even admitted that the

entry of German troops to Bulgaria was 'grave and very complicated', bearing in mind that 'appetite comes with eating'.[89]

In the hope of concluding an agreement Cripps rushed back to Ankara where together with Knatchbull-Hugessen he met the Soviet ambassador, Sergei Vinogradov. The Russians appeared more anxious than they had been to renew their contacts with the Turks. They were even prepared to consider the delivery of munitions to Turkey if an attack took place. Having secured Vinogradov's consent, Cripps handed Saracoglü the record of the conversations and received his promise to bring the negotiations to a speedy conclusion. After an informal press conference with British journalists Cripps caught the train to Istanbul, 'the fourth successive night to be spent on that line!!'

His reception by Vyshinsky on his return showed that the facilities granted him were not a mere courtesy. Vyshinsky, exceptionally cordial, pressed for information and promised a swift decision on Cripps' mediatory proposals. He made passing reference to their 'common work' in improving Anglo-Soviet relations, thwarted by 'others', and promised to see Cripps 'often'. Aktay duly informed the Russians of his government's wish to secure a mutual declaration of 'full understanding and neutrality' in the event of the invasion of one of their countries. On 10 March Cripps was summoned by Vyshinsky to a '*most* successful interview . . . the most useful' since his arrival in Moscow. Vyshinsky produced the text of the declaration submitted to the Turks and acknowledged the British contribution.[90] The Turks, however, had had second thoughts and hesitated in their response. Cripps was indignant about Whitehall's refusal to intervene and indifference to the obvious change in the Soviet attitude. The delay, he warned, might prompt the Russians to suspect that Turkey was contemplating joining the Axis and throwing in her lot with Germany. While the Southern Department recognized the force of Cripps' arguments, the senior officials continued to 'expect nothing'. The crux of the matter was Cripps' demand that Russia be treated on an equal footing with Turkey. The Foreign Office, which had not been consulted on Cripps' initiative, had throughout been sceptical about his reports which did not tally with their outlook. Sargent, the mind behind the concept, even suspected that Stalin had struck a bargain with Hitler whereby Russia was to annex the straits in return for conceding Soviet interests in Bulgaria.[91] On the eve of Cripps' visit to Ankara the weekly political intelligence sum-

mary, drawing on all available sources, had concluded that Russia, far from taking any steps of its own to prevent a German invasion of the Balkans, was engaged in a 'tortuous effort to discourage Turkish help to Bulgaria'.[92]

Although it was admitted in the Office in reviewing Cripps' telegrams that Turkey would not show 'any particular zeal' to cooperate with Russia unless encouraged, Churchill was won over by Sargent's arguments that Cripps had exaggerated the importance of the Soviet declaration and the negative effects which might ensue if Turkey were not sufficiently enthusiastic. The declaration, according to Sargent, was merely a gesture by which the Russians promised not to 'seize the opportunity of stabbing [Turkey] in the back'. Cripps was told that it was inadvisable to exert any pressure on Turkey owing to her 'extreme sensitiveness'; no such consideration was shown for Russia's vulnerability. When Churchill finally proposed to talk to the Turkish ambassador in London as a result of Cripps' perseverance, he was discouraged by Sargent. Knatchbull-Hugessen was instead instructed to advise the Turkish government that they 'would be wise' to express in general terms their satisfaction with the Soviet declaration. He was specifically warned not to follow Cripps' suggestion of seeking a precise definition, which might prove counter-productive. To forestall further rebukes from Cripps, who customarily bypassed the Foreign Office, Churchill consented to address him personally. Churchill's polite but firm telegram left Cripps in no doubt that he was acting in full conformity with the Office. The government, Cripps was told, had been influencing the Turks to the best of their ability, but they were understandably 'unresponsive through fear'.[93] The Turkish government of its own accord finally gave Russia the desired assurances on 17 March. The episode is less significant for its immediate repercussions than for its bearing on the Foreign Office's overwhelming influence in the shaping of relations with Russia, which continued to be subordinated to relations with other countries.

Worries over the German encroachment in the Balkans were also reflected in Russia's relations with Yugoslavia, of which the British were well informed. Diplomatic relations between Yugoslavia and Russia were established after the fall of France. At the time of Cripps' appointment the pro-British Gavrilovic, leader of the Serb Peasant Party, was cordially received in Moscow. While German pressure was building

up in the Balkans in the wake of the Italian declaration of war on
Greece, Britain could offer little to stiffen Yugoslavia's resistance
beyond the expression of moral support and faith in Britain's ultimate
victory, sustained by exceptionally warm letters from King Georve VI
to the regent Prince Paul. Molotov's visit to Berlin was followed up by
negotiations on possible Soviet material assistance to Yugoslavia,
which, however, came to nothing owing to a mutual fear of provoking
Germany. When in early 1941 reliable British sources disclosed that the
Germans contemplated launching their attack on Greece through
Yugoslavia, no faith was placed in Paul's verbal promise that he would
not join the Axis. An attempt was made to scare him into abandoning
neutrality by spreading rumours in Belgrade that the British sabotage
organization (the SOE) had been inciting pro-British political minority
elements. As a bait the Foreign Office followed Cripps' advice in offering
Yugoslavia what it had adamantly denied Russia: that it would 'disregard' the rule of not recognizing territorial changes during the war
and support the revision of the Italian–Yugoslav border. Prince Paul,
feeling the Germans breathing down his neck, vacillated and was finally
compelled to join the Tripartite Pact on 25 March to keep intact the
fragile national unity.[94]

The Foreign Office was little moved by the dramatic events, expecting
the reserve policy to hold ground for 'a good time longer'. Cripps was
increasingly doubtful. Although relations were 'negative on the surface', he explained to Monckton, there was a 'considerable advance forward'; it was 'as with a sailing boat which sails away from the starting
buoy to get a position to make a good start!'[95] He still attributed
Vyshinsky's statements on the need to 'prepare the ground' for
rapprochement to the policy of aloofness, which Cripps insisted should
be confined to economic measures. However, he alerted Eden in Cairo
to the fact that the Soviet declaration to Turkey and stance over
Yugoslavia and Bulgaria exposed Russia to the German menace, which
might 'any moment become intense'. He appealed to him to refute the
Soviet conviction that Britain was conducting a 'hopelessly hostile'
policy towards Russia through a political settlement of the Baltic issue.
Sargent was visibly concerned that the change in emphasis of Cripps'
thinking might assume significance as a result of the promise made by
Eden in Ankara to review relations with Russia. Although he would not
'grudge Sir S. Cripps the solace of hope', he adhered to his basic

assumption, partly a result of his obsessive desire to prevent the Foreign Office from repeating past mistakes, that Russia was set on 'appeasing Hitler'.[96]

Sargent's fears were partly justified. In desperation Eden was prepared to overlook the Foreign Office's objections and secure Soviet help, but confined himself to the specific topics which concerned him rather than a solution of outstanding issues. After learning of Prince Paul's decision, he determined on 22 March to back the SOE's attempts to effect a *coup d'état*.[97] On that evening Cripps, who had just seen Vyshinsky, received urgent instructions to encourage the Russians to support Yugoslav resistance. This request was backed up by Gavrilovic. The Russians, 'obviously anxious and sympathetic', were concerned at the news. Although further clarifications conducted by the Kremlin revealed that Prince Paul could not be deterred from the course he had chosen, they left the door ajar for a review of the situation in the next few days.[98] The news of Yugoslavia's 'betrayal by her leaders' seriously upset Gavrilovic, who had become not only Cripps' confidant but also a close friend of the family. He resigned on the spot and prepared to return home. The 'weight & sadness' of the events were deeply felt in the British embassy.

On 27 March, however, the news of a bloodless *coup* in Belgrade was received with tremendous relief by Cripps, as is vividly recorded by Isobel:

We are 'all over the place', & the joy-noises next door where are Vuka & Peg [the ambassadors' daughters] do ones heart good! . . . All these happenings are what we hoped for but did not *dare* expect . . . So is history made . . . If things came about as we think they did, it should be a lesson to all of us who know, of what quiet fortitude & right judgement can achieve, when almost all seems lost. We are all of us in a turmoil of emotions and now what will our 'friends' HERE say & do??? for they can not remain untouched & unmoved by it all.[99]

In the new circumstances Cripps sent another telegram to Eden to request an early discussion of the Baltic issue. Eden, anxious to secure Soviet help, could hardly be expected to remain silent. He was, however, absorbed by Yugoslavia, where the insurgents showed no enthusiasm for repudiating the pact or assisting Greece. In the mean-

time he reiterated his decision to postpone a discussion until his return to England.[100] Recognizing that Russia was at a crossroads, Cripps again appealed directly to the Cabinet, warning that it would be 'disastrous to lose an opportunity here through the lack of instructions'. It was necessary, he reproached the Foreign Office, to overcome prejudices and not allow 'the dead weight of the past lines of policy to prevent [the Cabinet] from reviewing their position in the light of to-day's fact'.[101] For months the Cabinet had not even referred to relations with Russia. On 31 March Attlee brought up Cripps' telegram. By then Churchill, to judge from his own account of his famous warning to Stalin,[102] had come to realize the significance Russia was to assume in the next phase of the war. His alleged foresight is not borne out by the records of the discussion in Cabinet. Butler, representing the Foreign Office in Eden's absence, encountered no difficulty in retaining the issue within the jurisdiction of the Foreign Office, although he left those present in no doubt that in the Office it was thought 'ill-advised' to modify either the blockade or the attitude on the Baltic issue. All he could say was that a contingency plan would be drawn up in case there were to be 'a marked improvement' in the Soviet attitude.[103] In fact the Foreign Office, again on a war footing with Cripps, wasted little time on deliberations. On 2 April Eden was privately advised by Cadogan to reject Cripps' 'imprudent and useless' initiative and return to the policy of reserve.[104] The recommendation was pressed home in a further telegram, repeated to Moscow, expressing scepticism about Stalin's intentions to 'edge away from Hitler', from 'subservience' to strict neutrality. Cripps' proposals, Eden was further enlightened, ran counter to the government's definition of war aims and the United State's declared policy. Moreover, it was arguable whether the proposed concessions were advantageous even if Britain's demands were fulfilled. Finally Eden was advised to refrain from action until Stalin had actually 'taken the plunge'. This proposition, however, was purely theoretical as the Office did not anticipate an armed clash in the foreseeable future. Postan, who protested that he had not even been consulted on a matter which directly involved the MEW, referred to it as the 'swan song of the dying Northern Department'. The Ministry had always made the distinction between Germany and Russia and been ready to relax the economic pressure on Russia. At Dalton's insistence a 'chaser' was sent

to Eden; it modified, however, only those paragraphs strictly relating to economic measures and the general tenor was preserved, much to the dismay of the MEW.[105]

Meanwhile events were proceeding at breathtaking pace. On the night of 4–5 April, the Yugoslavs and the Russians plucked up the courage to conclude a non-aggression pact which could only be interpreted as directed against Germany.[106] Infuriated by Whitehall's indifference, Cripps would not take no for an answer. Although he could not guarantee that fresh proposals would sway the Russians, he complained to Eden that 'the chance may come tomorrow and as it is admitted that I must judge the moment of its arrival, I am increasingly anxious to know exactly what I may offer'. He then repeated his own proposal for *de facto* recognition of Russian control of the Baltic, deferring a final solution to the peace negotiations. Cadogan would not hear of this, expecting the Russians to regard any concession as a sign of weakness.[107] While this exchange was taking place Eden finally returned to London. In his memoirs he competes with Churchill for the distinction of having been the first to lay the foundations of the Grand Alliance. The evidence of German intentions and Russia's varied activities to stem German aggression proved that 'the time had come for a smoothing out of relations' with Russia which, he assures us, ranked 'high on his list of priorities'. This, however, was not the case. A draft telegram to Cripps had been hastily prepared on the lines of Cadogan's minutes. Cadogan, it may be presumed, had hoped to forestall Eden's intervention. However, the Easter vacation and legal haggling over subtleties in defining *de jure* and *de facto* recognition delayed its dispatch.[108] Any alteration in the policy, the draft stated, must be initiated by the Russians in the absence of 'definite evidence' to show that they had abandoned the policy of cooperation with Germany. The recent Soviet gestures referred to in Eden's memoirs were specifically not considered as constituting such a sign. On the contrary, it was explicitly stated that Eden 'still' suspected that Stalin preferred to yield to Hitler's threats rather than risk an open breach. In short, a solution of the Baltic issue must be a 'seal to an Anglo-Soviet rapprochement and in no sense an attempt to buy such a rapprochement'. As could be deduced from the departmental discussion, Cripps' role was reduced to watching closely and discerning the turning point, which it was clearly insinuated was unlikely to come. The major part of the telegram, discussing the degree

of recognition to be accorded to the Soviet control of the Baltic, was of academic interest in view of the *modus operandi* adopted.[109]

It was clear that up to now, in the eventful period which had lapsed since his meeting with Cripps, Eden had not really come to grips with the Russian problem. He certainly was in no position to impose his will on the Foreign Office, where his trip was regarded as 'nothing but disaster'. His appearance in Parliament was 'rattled, even pathetic' and the press extremely critical.[110] Indeed, by the time the reply to Cripps was discussed all his attempts to coordinate the Yugoslav and Greek defences had been shattered. This was manifested in the astonishingly rapid advance made by the Germans in both countries since 6 April. By 13 April the swastika was flying in Belgrade and Yugoslavia's resistance had been crushed. A similar fate was hanging over Greece and the British Expeditionary Force there was already in full retreat when Eden for the first time considered relations with Russia. Eden must now have been fully aware that delays in formulating a policy had reduced the chances of coming to an agreement; he minuted that as the course of the war was expected to 'go hardly' for Britain in the Balkans, Russia's fears would increase. Although he recognized the need to modify Russia's 'unjustifiably' suspicious posture, he was reluctant to 'indulge in useless gestures'. It was, he confessed, a 'difficult hand to play' but the telegram to Cripps seemed the 'right move'.[111] The more forthcoming tone of his appeal to Maisky the next day to clear the 'ground of the débris of past differences' was in the best tradition of the British attitude to Russia – at the worst possible moment and as a last resort. The point of departure from the telegram was his consent to consider concessions in the Baltic in return for a 'comparable contribution' from the Russians. This was not followed up, despite Maisky's interest, as he was believed not to enjoy the confidence of his government.[112]

# 4

# THE TURN OF THE TIDE

### *Churchill's warning to Stalin*

The political background described in the previous chapters is indispensable for understanding Cripps' independent interpretation of the mounting intelligence reports on German intentions, culminating in his famous clash with Churchill over the warning to Stalin. Military Intelligence, partly supplied by and in close touch with the Foreign Office, had since the outbreak of war adopted a corresponding appreciation of Soviet–German relations. The newly formed Future Operations (Enemy) Section agreed with Military Intelligence in the first interdepartmental meeting held on 9 January 1941 that the German encroachment in the Balkans was a defensive move against Russia. They believed that the main German thrust was still directed against Britain. This appraisal was due neither to the absence of conflicting reports nor to the success of German disinformation.[1]

The inflexible posture of the Foreign Office, best represented by Sargent's entrenched concept, hindered a balanced review. This failure was particularly pronounced in view of the Cabinet's meagre interest in Russia and the absence of political guidance at the ministerial level. Cadogan, representing the Foreign Office in Cabinet, was in direct touch with the chiefs of the military services and the Office's weekly summaries were circulated among the different Intelligence branches and frequently discussed. Ample evidence dealing with Hitler's issue of the 'Barbarossa' directive was pouring in; this challenged the concept of the Foreign Office and was dismissed. Early reports from varied sources pointed to the construction of a second German defence line in Poland behind the demarcation line, increased troop movements to Romania, the deployment of German troops on the Carpathian border and the transfer eastwards of war material from the Maginot Line. In the

Foreign Office the forecast of an armed clash was held to be based on 'misleading rumours' and therefore 'extremely unlikely', serving the interests of 'wishful thinkers'. The explanation arrived at in harmony with the political concept was that the Russians' collaboration was in fact so close that they were 'ready to yield to the mere threat of force'.[2] This explanation would later be more persuasive than the Germans' attempts at deception. By mid-January, therefore, the unusual disposition of German troops in the East was dismissed as being 'nothing but normal'. Military Intelligence reached strikingly similar conclusions on purely military grounds.[3] Further information in February was interpreted on the basis of this appreciation. When the Military Attaché in Moscow reported that an exercise by the Soviet General Staff was based on the assumption of a German attack on Russia, this was discounted. The Germans, it was confidently stated, were not expected to invade Russia 'until either the issue of their conflict with [England] had been decided or else their position had become desperate'.[4] Similar information came from Swedish sources through Victor Mallet, the British ambassador in Stockholm. His contribution was the introduction of the explanation that the reports were merely a new phase of the 'war of nerves'. This explanation was immediately seized upon and incorporated in the established concept.[5]

More pronounced rumours of an impending German invasion of Russia came in March from several capitals, notably Washington, Budapest and Stockholm, and could no longer be dismissed out of hand. For the first time it was suggested in the Office that a German turn eastwards was 'within the bounds of possibility'. Such heresies, however, were immediately condemned by the upper echelon. The 'doubtful ... just anonymous talk', explained Cadogan, was disseminated by the Germans to 'intimidate' the Russians and therefore should not serve as a 'very sure guide' for reevaluation.[6] The casualness with which such reports were processed is reflected in the weekly collation of the political and intelligence summaries. After weighing the various sources, the possibility of an outbreak of hostilities in the East was replaced by the more convenient appreciation that the Germans were 'waging a war of nerves' against the Russians to deter them from stiffening Yugoslav and Turkish opposition or alternatively to make them 'more compliant' to future demands. Doubt was expressed whether 'Red Riding Hood [would] now pluck up courage to face these

113

dangers or [would] endeavour to appease the big bad wolf by a policy of further accommodation'.[7] This sheds light from a different angle on the reaction to Cripps' urgent call for a review of relations with Russia. Rather than attempting to enlist Russia's help through enlightening her of the approaching dangers, the real diplomatic effort, not unlike 1939, was invested in Eden's personal attempt to secure a Mediterranean and Balkan *entente* to thwart German aggression.

Cripps' waverings were not affected by the preconceived concept so much as by the misleading briefings from London, confirmed by the authoritative military exposé of Dill in Ankara. The trip to Turkey, however, had refreshed Cripps and familiarized him with the profound change that had occurred in south-east Europe. Although he still displayed unusual restraint, cautioning Eden that 'a fine day in late winter is often heralded as the beginning of spring when in reality spring is far off', it was obvious, as he wrote home, that: 'We are back in an atmosphere of possibility and not of impossibility so that now there is at any moment the *chance* of something turning up which makes life more interesting and less depressing!!'[8] He regained his confidence that German–Soviet collaboration was by no means eternal. Harold Elvin, the son of a trade union leader and friend of Cripps, who had been evacuated from Norway to Moscow and was employed at the embassy, describes in his diary Cripps' differing appreciation as early as summer 1940:

[Cripps] took me to the tremendous map on the wall. He said: 'Germany will flood through Europe this way,' and he detailed what, alarmingly, Germany has since achieved. He then said: 'They will next amass their forces here,' and he described a build-up against the Russian border. 'They will then attack here and here and here: of course they will send out a feeler towards Moscow and Leningrad, but more serious will be hundreds-of-miles encircling movements which will surround both in pincers' . . . I was worried. Here was a man, Sir Stafford Cripps, whom I had spent a decade admiring; now at last I faced him. In my first minutes he had a little petrified me with an electric-penetrating intelligence then, by his going to the map, he had bla-ed out the biggest load of craziness I had heard from any worthy.[9]

Cripps had returned from Ankara with the 'firm conviction', as he told fellow ambassadors, that Russia and Germany would be at war 'before summer'. He had come to expect that Hitler would overcome his fear of a war on two fronts and attack Russia before England became

too strong to form another front. In an off-the-record press conference he cast doubts on Dill's perceptions and predicted that Hitler would attack Russia 'not later than the end of June', certainly one of the earliest estimates to that effect.[10] Gafencu, highly cultivated and widely read in history, lent Cripps Paléologue's *Life of Alexander*; Cripps was so struck by the similarity of the strategy towards Russia adopted by Hitler and Napoleon that he recommended that Eden read it, remarking that it looked at times 'as if history would repeat itself'.[11] Consequently his apparent association with the policy pursued in London was drawing to an end. He could no longer discount the possibility, as he indiscreetly told Steinhardt, of his government's connivance at a German invasion of Russia in return for a separate peace. He was not swayed by Steinhardt's response that such a course did not suit 'an individual of Churchill's temperament'.[12]

Cripps' first explicit report to the Foreign Office about the German intentions was transmitted on 24 March, at a time of growing tension over Yugoslavia. This information was both prophetic and accurate, considering the early date of its origins, and was obtained from a source in Berlin through Vilhelm Assarasson, the well-informed Swedish minister in Moscow. The gist of the report confirmed Cripps' impression that the invasion of Britain had been abandoned and the struggle against her would be confined to submarine and air attacks. Consequently the Germans were determined to 'attack Russia by a blitz and to get hold of all Russia up to the Urals'. More striking was the detailed exposition of the plan to employ three spearheads under the command of Field Marshals von Bock, von Rundstedt and von List.[13] Cripps hoped that the information would be used to influence the Russians to reopen discussions. To prevent them from suspecting that this was merely a device to embroil the Soviet Union in war, he suggested an indirect approach to Maisky. Any attempt to give serious consideration to the proposal in the Central Department was brushed aside by senior officials who, as expected, regarded the information as 'part of the "war of nerves" against Russia, designed to force her into a closer partnership with Germany'. The War Office followed suit, again refuting the evidence as an attempt to 'intimidate' the Soviet government and 'mislead' Britain. This was a sufficiently convincing argument for Sargent, Cadogan and Butler that by passing on the information to the Russians the British government would be 'playing the German

game'.[14] There was perhaps a more even-handed appreciation of German intentions by the different branches of Military Intelligence but in view of the prevalent atmosphere, as in the Foreign Office, the ultimate conclusion as late as 27 March was that the information was 'not convincing'.[15] It can, therefore, be confidently concluded that up to that point Cripps' appraisal was considered inadmissible. The orthodox analysis was based to a large extent on an unsubstantiated prejudice rife since the outbreak of the war and rooted in the attitude to Russia throughout the 1930s.

By providing a version of the events leading to the German invasion of Russia which is highly censored and often out of context, Churchill passes judgment on Stalin and his commissars as the 'most completely outwitted bunglers of the Second World War' so far as 'strategy, policy, foresight [and] competence' are concerned. He glosses over Eden's disastrous attempts to organize a Balkan bloc and the mismanagement of the defence of Greece. Nor does he mention the neglect of Russia and the failure to grasp her significance as a potential ally. He further ignores the increasingly overt hostility towards Russia which in turn affected her perception of alternatives at that stage and clouded the alliance at its birth. By blowing up out of proportion his own warning to Stalin at the beginning of April as the major event leading to the surprise attack, Churchill directs the reader to the inescapable conclusion that he personally, against the 'collective wisdom' of the different branches of Military Intelligence, had remarkable foresight. The need to examine this episode in some detail derives not so much from its immediate significance but rather from Churchill's condemnation of Cripps in his memoirs, which has become the best-known aspect of his mission.

According to Churchill, it was with 'relief and excitement' that he came across a report from one of Britain's 'most trusted sources' that 'illuminated the whole Eastern scene like a lightning flash'. The source, as we now know, was the German air force Enigma intercepts, which indicated that three armoured divisions and other key forces had been ordered to move from the Balkans to the Cracow area a day after the signing of the Tripartite Pact of Yugoslavia. On the day of the *coup* this order was cancelled. This, according to Churchill, could only mean that Hitler was bent on invading Russia in May.[16] But was this really a stroke of genius? What prompted Churchill to decide on May as a likely date and was this particular report the only reason for his change of mind

about the German intentions and his decision to send a personal warning to Stalin?

Churchill's account is vague about dates, but it is clear that on 28 March he was already in possession of the Enigma reports, which do not seem to have left any marked impact on him. On the contrary, in a long and important telegram to Eden, dealing with overall strategy and drafted later that day,[17] only the final item made a casual reference to the possibility of a German–Soviet clash: 'Is it not possible that if a united front were formed in the Balkan peninsula Germany might think it better business to take it out of Russia?' Churchill did not, therefore, in spite of his claims, send the 'momentous news at once' to Eden.[18] He needed time and outside influence to enable him to digest the full significance of the intelligence. It must be remembered that Churchill was at the time replacing Eden at the Foreign Office and was therefore shown all important communications. It was when he drafted the telegram on strategy to Eden that his attention was drawn by Cadogan to information corroborating the Enigma reports which had been accumulating in the Office.[19] It is almost certain that Cripps' most detailed telegram on the subject was shown to him as well, because both the projected date of the invasion and the course later taken by him correspond to that telegram. A definite shift of policy occurred no earlier than 30 March, when in a second telegram to Eden, now in Athens, the possibility of a German invasion of Russia figured more prominently. However, this was only after both Air Intelligence and the Government Code and Cypher School had analysed the Enigma report and reached a similar conclusion. Even then Churchill refrained from giving positive direction to Cabinet in the long-delayed discussion on Anglo-Soviet relations which took place on 31 March.[20]

The decision to adopt Cripps' proposal and enlighten the Russians took even longer to materialize. Churchill was probably influenced by further reports received from Belgrade on 30 March and from Sumner Welles on 2 April; these were confirmed by news from Athens, where Prince Paul had sought refuge after the *coup*, that Hitler had revealed to him during their meeting at the Berghof on 4 March his intention to take military action against Russia. The information threatened to undermine the entrenched concept that Soviet–German relations were bound to improve and that reserve should remain the order of the day. It called for immediate cooperation. Both Collier and Cadogan,

however, desperately clung to the concept, repeating the familiar argument that as the Germans were raising the pressure to extract further concessions from the Russians, the transmission of the reports would be useless until the Russians were 'strong enough to react in the right way to it'.[21] An interesting feature which now came to light is that the political concept had infiltrated the Intelligence and come to dominate their thinking. Since they attached little significance to the Enigma reports, their conclusions were uncritical in similar fashion to the Foreign Office. Thus, on 1 April Military Intelligence concluded that the object of the movement of German armoured and motorized forces was 'undoubtedly to exert military pressure on Russia to prevent Russian interference in German Balkan plans'. Discounting the possibility of a clash, the Foreign Office weekly summary concluded a day later that the Russians showed no signs of giving way to the 'war of nerves' waged against her 'in the shape of rumours of impending German attack'. 'Everybody', noted Nicolson in his diary, regarded the idea of war as 'fantastic'.[22]

Six weeks earlier Churchill had held the view that there was no point in approaching the Russians 'while odds seem heavily against Britain in Greece'. Half-measures, he had warned, would be futile.[23] These views were in tune with the opinion held at the Foreign Office that, if viewed logically, the current situation in south-east Europe did not warrant a fresh approach. The point of departure, however, was Churchill's conviction that Germany had altered her overall strategy. He then resorted to alerting Stalin to the change. The message to Stalin, which was finally drafted only on 3 April, ran as follows:

I have sure information from a trusted agent that when the Germans thought they had got Yugoslavia in the net – that is to say, after March 20 – they began to move three out of the five Panzer divisions from Roumania to Southern Poland. The moment they heard of the Serbian revolution this movement was countermanded. Your Excellency will readily appreciate the significance of these facts.

It was, as aptly described by Churchill, 'short and cryptic'; its 'brevity and exceptional character', he first explained to Beaverbrook in late 1941 and then repeated word for word in his memoirs, was intended to 'give it special significance and arrest Stalin's attention'.[24] Sargent and Cadogan, obviously anxious that Cripps might commit himself further

than desired if allowed unhindered access to Stalin, hastened to provide him with a 'line on which to speak'. It so happened that Cadogan's telegram cancelled the effect which Churchill had intended for his message. As Cripps was not acquainted with the source of the evidence, the follow-up could only detract from its significance. The instructions embodied two schools of thought: Churchill's own and the sceptical position of the Foreign Office. Cadogan first explained the changes in the German dispositions as meaning that Hitler had postponed his previous plans of merely 'threatening the Soviet government'. By mounting tangible pressure he hoped to extract further concessions, but did not really intend to attack her. The draft thus far was so unsatisfactory that Churchill himself inserted a second paragraph stressing the military significance of the information. Two further points are of particular interest. The instructions did not reflect Churchill's sense of urgency or interpretation of the fresh intelligence. There was no emphasis on the inevitability of an imminent German attack resulting from an abandonment of the plans for 'Sea-Lion'. Moreover, although Churchill agreed with Cripps' suggestion not to imply an appeal to relieve Britain from her distress in south-east Europe, the instructions clearly did. Cripps was to impress on Stalin that as Hitler intended to 'attack them sooner or later', it was in Russia's own interest to grant material supplies to Greece and Yugoslavia and join in a 'united front'.[25]

When considering Cripps' reaction, the confusion resulting from the dispatch of the brief, personal and urgent warning and the contrasting instructions should be borne in mind. It should also be remembered that Churchill had hitherto displayed an almost complete lack of interest in Russian affairs. His sudden entry into the arena was somewhat capricious and did not take account of the political framework into which his message was to fit. Indeed, Churchill's subsequent argument that had Cripps followed his instructions 'some kind of relationship would have been constructed between [him] and Stalin' was contested by Eden; 'At the time', he reminded Churchill as early as October 1941, 'the Russians were most reluctant to receive messages of any kind . . . The same attitude was adopted towards the later messages which I gave to Maisky.'[26]

Churchill, surprisingly, tells us that he did not hear from Cripps until 12 April,[27] and makes no reference to the striking developments which were taking place in Yugoslavia when the telegram reached Moscow.

On 5 April Cripps informed the Prime Minister that to deliver a message personally to Stalin was 'out of the question'. On 7 April, the day after Greece and Yugoslavia had been invaded by Germany, Churchill agreed that the message could be handed to Molotov.[28] Churchill's telegram, however, crossed another one sent by Cripps on the eventful day of 6 April expressing second thoughts.

In the early hours of 6 April the Russians concluded a friendship and non-aggression treaty with Yugoslavia. Cripps of course was kept well in the picture by his intimate friend in the 'Club', Gavrilovic. It appeared that the Russians had been most forthcoming in accepting a more binding Yugoslav version to replace the Russian proposal for a neutrality pact. The signature took place ostentatiously in the Kremlin with Stalin, 'cheerful throughout', participating in a lively discussion which went on until 7 a.m. The significant factor was that Stalin appeared conscious of the looming German threat, stating confidently: 'Let them come.' Moreover, the Russians agreed to send assistance to Yugoslavia which, as Collier commented, meant that the Russians were 'burning their boats'.[29] However, at the end of the banquet the Russians had to face reality when news came in of the ferocious bombardment of Belgrade and the invasion of both Yugoslavia and Greece. The distribution of *Pravda* and *Izvestiya* had been withheld to allow full coverage of the signature. It was still possible to keep the news under wraps, but eventually the papers appeared at midday with large photographs of Stalin, Molotov and Gavrilovic signing the agreement. It proved to Cripps that the establishment of an effective buffer zone had been and remained the essence of Soviet foreign policy even at the cost of friction in relations with Germany. It was brought out in the commentary that the Yugoslav efforts in defending their interests could not but 'evoke sympathy in the Soviet Union'. The events also showed that the Russians were fully aware of the dangers ahead.[30]

In the light of these developments Cripps was convinced that through communications from the Greek and Yugoslav ambassadors and himself, the Russians were sufficiently aware of the essence of the information included in Churchill's message and were already acting on it. It seemed to him 'wiser' not to interfere at a moment when all was going 'as well as possible in [Britain's] direction'.[31] In the context of Cripps' direct political challenge to Churchill at the end of 1941 Churchill expressed himself outspokenly against Cripps, whose

'effrontery' in delaying the message demonstrated his 'lack of sense of proportion'. 'Cripps,' he summed up, 'has a great responsibility for his obstinate, obstructive handling of this matter.'[32] The responsibility should, however, be laid no less at the door of the Foreign Office, whose senior officials were in close touch with Churchill and were acquainted with the significance of the intelligence reports. Eden too was directly involved, though he preferred in retrospect to belittle his involvement in this contentious issue while exaggerating the importance of his later warnings to Maisky.

Cripps' alternative suggestion to communicate the reports to Maisky was refused. In the days following Churchill's message to Stalin the Office came across corroborating information. It was suggested that a compilation of reports and their appreciation in collaboration with the MEW and the armed forces might be invaluable for Cripps if the Russians were to respond favourably. The Head of the Northern Department stood out categorically against such a move. Since he was not informed of the source of Churchill's information, he thought there was only scanty evidence confined to '*preparations*, as distinct from intentions'. Victor Cavendish-Bentinck, the Foreign Office's representative and Chairman of the Joint Intelligence Committee (JIC), struggled with the drafting and finally agreed that there was no point in sending a 'hotch-potch of pretty unconfirmed and probably untrue information'. The political concept, which rejected evidence of a German–Soviet clash but readily clung to unconfirmed fragments pointing to increased collaboration, was evident in Collier's final comment. He dismissed the growing rumours while seizing upon a report of an agreement on Soviet oil delivery to Germany as 'a serious argument against the hope, which Sir S. Cripps still cherishes, that the Soviet Government might be induced to come down on our side of the fence by concessions over the Baltic States, etc'.[33] The antagonism to Cripps was outspoken. When he now suggested that Maisky might not be in tune with the decisions of his government, Collier commented that he hoped the Russians too realized 'the limitations of Sir S. Cripps!'[34]

Churchill had never shown an interest in following up the implementation of decisions relating to Russia. Although the instructions had come from him, the Foreign Office, when it suited them, proved only too eager to leave the matter to Cripps' 'judgement . . . and to his saying nothing, at least for the moment'.[35] On 8 April, in response to a

suggestion that he should approach Molotov, Cripps reiterated his previous argument, adding that Molotov and Stalin had been briefed about the content of Prince Paul's interview with Hitler, 'which they obviously believed and of which they took great notice'. If Cripps were to seek a special interview with Stalin, he would be bound to relate it to events in Yugoslavia and assume that Britain was 'trying to make trouble with Germany'.[36] A few days later evidence indeed came in from the military attachés in Moscow and Ankara that a partial mobilization had been carried out in the Red Army.[37] As Cripps had been left without definite instructions in reply to his first communication, Cadogan was now inclined to countermand the delivery of the warning altogether. Unexpectedly, however, Churchill intervened; ignoring Cripps' arguments, he stated that it was his 'duty' to convey the facts to Stalin. It was irrelevant to the importance of the facts if they or their channel were 'unwelcomed'. Instructions on these lines were accordingly sent to Cripps, stressing the military significance of the breathing space which Russia had gained while Hitler was tied up in the Balkans. Although Churchill's instructions were mandatory, Eden, on his first day in the Office after the Middle East tour, went through the file and in a last-minute alteration left the act still open to Cripps' discretion. The opening paragraph now read: 'Prime Minister still thinks message should be delivered [and Eden inserted:] and I hope you will now find this possible.'[38] Curiously these exchanges are missing in Churchill's account.

To understand the motives for Cripps' handling of the affair the political developments described earlier should be borne in mind. Cripps' advice to alert the Russians to the German threat had been given throughout March. Events, however, had been gaining momentum and the obvious need was to urge the Russians into action. Since his meeting with Eden at the end of February Cripps had been pressing the government to define its policy towards Russia in case a change occurred. Churchill, and for that matter Eden too, had decided that it was best to await favourable results in the Balkans. In the fateful weeks of March and April Cripps was therefore left to his own devices. When no response came to his earlier proposals Cripps sought in vain to see Molotov or Vyshinsky in connection with the Yugoslav *coup*.[39] Having failed to do so, he set out his grievances about the Soviet attitude in a personal letter to Vyshinsky. His main criticism, one not expressed

before which suggests that in the present circumstances it derived from the 'Club', was that rather than securing the neutrality of the Balkans as a bloc Russia had been busy providing security zones for her own frontiers. The new turn of the war meant, and here Cripps was in fact driving home the essence of Churchill's message, that it was 'perhaps the last opportunity for the Soviet Government to take action to prevent a direct attack upon its frontiers by the German armies' which would thereafter be 'freed from the embarrassment of fighting on other land fronts'. So far Germany had skilfully avoided war on several fronts; the opening of a third front in the Balkans 'might prove a decisive end to the German menace'.[40] The letter, which was sent by bag, reached London only at the end of the month.

It was only then that Cripps received Eden's telegram proposing that Churchill's message should nonetheless be passed on. Having just transmitted information on very similar lines, and with Vyshinsky's announcement that the attitude of the British government precluded discussions of a political nature still ringing in his ears, Cripps argued that Churchill's 'shorter and less emphatic' message would be not 'merely ineffectual but a serious tactical mistake'. The Russians, he reiterated, were well aware of the facts included in the message and would be suspicious about its purpose. In the Foreign Office Cripps' behaviour in first arguing against the delivery of the message and then 'off his own bat' raising the whole political issue with Vyshinsky was described as 'incalculable'. They nonetheless concurred that Churchill's 'short and fragmentary' message was inappropriate and were only too happy to sanction its withdrawal. To a large extent the mishandling of the affair is due to Eden who, in conformity with Cripps and his officials, had not abandoned his criticism of Churchill's message. Presumably apprehensive that Cripps' independent move might enrage Churchill, he decided to gain the Prime Minister's approval for withdrawal. Despite the image he had acquired in the 1930s, Eden was neither outspoken nor courageous and was bent on avoiding confrontations. Disregarding the fact that he himself had given Cripps room for manoeuvre, he first exonerated himself by giving a completely inaccurate paraphrase of his instructions to Cripps, purporting to have told him that 'notwithstanding his misgivings' he 'should' communicate the message to Molotov. Eden then presented Cripps' reservations as his own.[41]

Churchill's reply was prompt, sharply complaining of the delay and again stressing the military significance of the report. It is amazing that Churchill took no account whatsoever of Cripps' reasoning if we recall that news of Yugoslavia's capitulation had already reached London while the fate of the battle in Greece had virtually been decided.[42] On 19 April the message was sent to Vyshinsky and by 22 April it found its way to Stalin who, according to available evidence, regarded it with extreme suspicion.[43] Thereafter, until the very eve of the German invasion of Russia, Churchill displayed only a remote interest in Anglo-Soviet relations. Churchill's sudden obsession with Russia may well have been dictated by domestic considerations. The brevity and cryptic drafting of the message had been explained by Churchill as a means of arresting Stalin's attention and establishing confidential contact with him. After 10 April, when the battle took a turn for the worse, he no longer seems to have attached much significance to this argument. On that day Eden returned empty-handed from the Middle East and a gloomy Cabinet learnt that 2,000 prisoners, among them three generals, had been taken captive in Libya. There was a noticeable feeling of despair, reinforced by the renewed bombing of London. The prospects of a sudden dramatic event on the eastern front provided the only ray of hope. Bearing this in mind, and disregarding the effect on the Russians of a public declaration of supposedly secret information, Churchill suddenly divulged in Parliament during a debate on the course of the war his belief that Hitler might suddenly divert his campaign in the Balkans to seize 'the granary of the Ukraine and the oilfields of the Caucasus'.[44] The effectiveness of the message in its original form was further reduced when three days after its delivery Eden warned Maisky of German intentions, specifically quoting the content of Prince Paul's conversation with Hitler. This information had been transmitted to Oumansky by Hull at least a month earlier. Thus, the timing of both warnings after Yugoslavia's crushing defeat and the disaster in Greece could not but enhance the already deep Soviet suspicion.[45]

As rightly judged by both Eden and Cripps, the circumstances in mid April were not conducive to a personal approach which was only bound to inflame suspicion. Cripps alluded to this episode in summer 1941, complaining that no consideration was shown in London for the fact that 'not only Stalin, but even Molotov avoided me like grim death.

Stalin ... did not *want* to have anything to do with Churchill, so alarmed was he lest the Germans find out.'[46] Finally it is interesting to compare Cripps' dilemma with that of his American counterpart in Moscow, who was placed in a similar situation in early March. The still neutral Americans had better intelligence sources in Berlin and throughout south-east Europe. By the beginning of March they had sufficient indications of an offensive German deployment to warrant an approach to the Soviet government. Weighing the pros and cons, Steinhardt dissuaded Hull from taking this course, arguing that the question would be regarded by the Russians as 'neither sincere nor independent', leaked to the Germans and perhaps become the subject of a Tass communiqué.[47]

### A separate peace: Hess' mission

The sense of having lost an opportunity through the government's vacillation during the vicissitudes of March and April affected Cripps badly. 'It really is rather maddening', he wrote to Monckton, 'how slowly our machine works when we are up against people with no scruples and who can do work with great rapidity.' Employing the metaphor used by Eden in his meeting with Maisky, Cripps complained that since the collapse of France he had been provided with 'few cards to play here, but most of the possible ones [had] been taken away by H.M.G.'; he often found himself 'without a hand at all and in these circumstances – even if we wanted to – we cannot even bluff!!' Letters dating from this period convey the uneasy atmosphere in Moscow and a revival of pessimism that the 'grave happenings' might result in the failure of his mission and his recall. He was, as noted by Isobel, 'longing & "aching" for closer contact with those at home in authority ... I wish D. [Daddie] could have an hour or two's talk with the P.M.' Placed in compulsory isolation, Cripps intended, as he informed Monckton, to 'do my best on my own initiative if I can get this people to listen to me'.[48]

On 17 April Cripps bitterly complained to Eden that a perilous situation had arisen, due to a large extent to the government's failure to make up its mind whether it was prepared 'to make any or what bid for closer relations'. Consequently Russia had become more susceptible to pressure from the Axis. Schulenburg's sudden departure for consultations with Hitler seemed particularly alarming, as Cripps expected

him to return with a new offer on a large scale in exchange for Russia's 'whole hearted economic co-operation and with an alternative veiled threat'. It was quite possible, he told Steinhardt, that the Russians might be compelled to yield even to massive demands so long as they did not involve the ceding of territory or the demobilization of the Red Army. To prevent German gains Cripps thought it mandatory to obtain a frank statement from Molotov on the issue of future Soviet action. Eden was again urged to consider *de facto* recognition of the Soviet absorption of the Baltic and the obtaining of American approval.[49] Without waiting for instructions from London, Cripps handed Vyshinsky on the next day a long memorandum addressed to Molotov, who had declined to meet him. A lucid exposé of the dilemmas facing the Russians was followed by inducements and threats as a last resort to draw them into the Allied orbit. Read in conjunction with Churchill's famous warning, which Cripps was obliged to transmit a few days later, it achieved the opposite effect and had serious repercussions in intensifying the Soviet suspicion that in desperation Britain was striving to embroil Russia in war. In the preamble of the memorandum Cripps approved the Soviet defensive measures taken since the outbreak of war. These he now believed to be less effective as a result of the Germans' lightning campaign in the Balkans, which confirmed that Hitler had postponed his plans to invade Britain. Cripps pointed out to Molotov that to sustain their war effort the Germans were obliged to obtain their supplies of food and war materials either by forcing humiliating concessions from the Russians or by an occupation. The danger, he warned, was no longer 'a hypothesis at all', but a German plan 'for the spring of this year'. Cripps tried to convince Molotov that it was in Britain's own interest, once war broke out, to do the utmost to assist Russia in preventing Hitler from achieving his aim. An obvious shortcoming of the memorandum was the lack of any incentive to tempt the Russians in view of the retreat of British troops from south-east Europe and the Cabinet's procrastination on the Baltic issue. All he could do, therefore, was to make vague promises of economic assistance and other practical measures, such as the 'co-ordination of aerial activity', and gave hints of cooperation on post-war reconstruction and an unsubstantiated promise of American support for Soviet resistance. The overt threat was of a tightening of the economic blockade. However, of far more lasting effect was the implication, which had been made to Molotov and

faithfully reflected Cripps' own apprehensions, that although at present there was no question of a negotiated peace it was 'not outside the bounds of possibility if the war were protracted for a long period that there might be a temptation for Great Britain (and especially for certain circles in Great Britain) to come to some arrangement to end the war'. Cripps' impulsive approach, it should be stressed, was dictated by an urgent need to counteract Schulenburg's expected offer. This sense of urgency is evident in the avoidance of demands from the Russians which might entail prolonged deliberations and the request for a decision in principle. The Russians were called upon only to make an 'immediate exploration' of the various courses of action and state whether they were interested in bringing about an 'immediate' improvement of relations.[50]

The Soviet decision to avoid a conflict with Germany at all costs, even at the expense of worsening relations with Britain, must have been formally reached in mid April. The state of panic which had seized the Russians as a result of the fall of Yugoslavia was exemplified in the hasty conclusion of a neutrality pact with Japan on 13 April. The pact relieved the Russians of the nightmare of having to wage war on two fronts. Earlier negotiations when Yosuke Matsouka, the Japanese Foreign Minister, passed through Moscow *en route* to Berlin were courteous but betrayed little anxiety. All efforts were now directed to placating the Germans. Matsouka's departure from Moscow turned into an extraordinary scene when Stalin ostentatiously approached Schulenburg and loudly informed him of the need for Germany and Russia to remain friends. This took place the day before Schulenburg's departure for consultations in Berlin, just as news came in of Germany's occupation of Belgrade. Soviet concessions were also made in the economic sphere and in the settlement of boundary disputes in the Baltic.[51]

Vyshinsky, who had previously hardly ever expressed an independent opinion, did not feel the need to consult his government in turning down Cripps' memorandum on the grounds that the 'necessary prerequisites for discussing wide political problems did not exist', particularly as there was 'nothing new or material' in the memorandum on the Baltic issue. Vyshinsky had also prepared for Cripps a reply to his detailed personal letter of 11 April which comprised only four lines in much the same vein. Cripps now expressed the understated fear that the Russians had 'not turned at all in our direction as a result of recent

127

events'.[52] Despite the rebuff he had received from Vyshinsky, Cripps did not give up, pinning his hopes on the formal reply. In the meantime he continued to besiege Eden with demands for a definition of the Cabinet's policy. Although the Russians appeared to be 'short sighted', the solution of outstanding issues was essential for the inevitable further collaboration. If the British government were forthcoming he hoped to secure a secret Soviet undertaking to reduce supplies to Germany and a statement on non-aggression based on the Yugoslav model.[53]

Eden, as Cadogan grudgingly commented, had the 'usual itch to *do* something'. He seemed to have expected to divert criticism of his Middle Eastern policy by securing a success in Russia,[54] and accordingly instructed Halifax in Washington to sound out the Americans about Cripps' proposals, which he henceforth presented as his own. However, Eden, like Halifax before him, was fettered by his officials in the Office. In Halifax's case, this was a result of lack of interest and absence of motivation. Eden, on the other hand, was often driven to act against his convictions through weakness. The political concept cultivated at the Foreign Office had not been undermined by the dramatic events, the accumulating intelligence reports or Churchill's intervention. Collier perhaps expressed it best by warning that an approach was bound to be viewed by the Russians as a sign of vulnerability and 'reinforce the tendency at Moscow to compromise with the Germans'.[55] A marked 'strict reserve' attitude and a refusal to embark on fresh negotiations remained the declared policy of the government and were thus presented in Parliament on one of the rare occasions when Anglo-Soviet relations were discussed. Aware of the limitations imposed on him, Eden informed Cabinet on 21 April of his intention to try to open discussions, 'although he was not very sanguine of good results'. He did not intend 'to put the Soviets in good humour' with Britain in the hope that 'something might emerge'.[56]

In the Office it was agreed that because of his obsession with the Baltic issue Cripps was 'unsuited' to conduct the negotiations which, if resumed, would have to be carried out in London through Maisky. Churchill, as if oblivious of the motives which had prompted him to insist on the delivery of his warning to Stalin, was not in favour of proceeding with 'frantic efforts' to demonstrate 'love' but rather advocated 'sombre restraint'. His own addendum to a draft telegram to Cripps showed, however, that he was primarily reluctant to injure American

interests. It demonstrated Britain's growing economic and political dependence on the United States, especially after the introduction of Lend-Lease which saved her from bankruptcy. Eden hastened therefore to withdraw his instructions to Washington and to concur with the Prime Minister that there was 'nothing to be gained from further attempts with Russia now'. The Foreign Office was free once again to impress on Cripps that Russia's fundamental policy towards Germany had remained unaltered. It was up to the Russians, summed up Collier, to make the next approach, 'if any'.[57]

Cripps was not deterred by Churchill's adoption of the aloofness posture from seeking new avenues for improved relations. He adhered to his opinion that hostility in German–Soviet relations had not diminished but 'if anything increased by the approach of danger'. He correctly estimated that the Russian military were convinced that war was inevitable and were therefore anxious to postpone it. On the other hand, he did not expect the Russians to yield to German pressure if this would affect their war preparedness. Since British political proposals could no longer be considered attractive, the only effective, though obviously 'delicate', device was to play on Soviet fears of a separate peace. As events soon proved, Sargent was right in objecting to the use of this 'double-edged weapon', which might encourage Stalin to cling more tenaciously to his 'policy of appeasement'. Cripps' alternative suggestion of reopening negotiations in unison with the Americans had been ruled out in advance. The Americans' reluctance to negotiate had been only too often seized upon as an excuse for not following this course. Eden gave a warm reception only to the third and peripheral proposal of transforming the Turco-Soviet understanding into a firm commitment. This harmonized with the obsessive attempts to win over Turkey which had marred his Middle Eastern tour, while it did not demand any commitment towards Russia. He ignored Cripps' reservation that in the new circumstances Turkey could provide a further incentive only in combination with the other proposals.[58]

Thus by the beginning of May the British had resumed their aloofness in relations with Russia. For the Russians, however, the last week of April had introduced unprecedented anxiety, to a large extent a result of Cripps' alluded threats. The exploitation of differences among the western powers had been the cornerstone of their foreign policy since the Peace of Brest-Litovsk and the Genoa Conference of 1922 and

remained so until the German invasion. The logic of the policy, until the fall of Yugoslavia, was undoubtedly based on the establishment of a buffer zone in the wake of the failure to achieve security arrangements through diplomacy. It was assumed that while Germany and England were engaged in hostilities Russia would be able to improve her military preparedness. The fallacy of this assumption was first diagnosed when Poland was torn apart before the British had been able to mount their Expeditionary Force. The 'phoney war' was accompanied by constant fears of a separate peace. The collapse of France, followed by German encroachment in the Balkans, was even more alarming. Stalin, who had acquired ample evidence of German intentions and deployment, was equally aware of the weakness of his armed forces. Moreover, although the Soviet armaments industry had made vast strides, it was not ready to compete with that of Germany, which controlled most of Europe's industrial resources. By mid April Stalin must have realized that the overwhelming need for a 'breathing space' and the ultimate aim of exploiting the differences among his opponents could be achieved only through submission to Germany. This decision had hardly been taken when Cripps' memorandum landed like a bombshell in Molotov's office.[59] The Russians suffered from pathological suspicion based on past experience of the intervention and the Locarno Agreement of 1925 and the Munich Conference. Cripps' insinuations of a separate peace resuscitated their fears that Germany and Britain might close ranks and mount a crusade against Russia. These threats seemed real in view of the heavy defeats inflicted on Britain in Greece and North Africa and the unstable political atmosphere in London.

The return of Schulenburg empty-handed to Moscow at the end of April increased the suspicion that Hitler might be considering peace terms with Britain to avoid a war on two fronts. The Russians were placed in an unenviable position: they were determined to avoid a complete breakdown of relations with Britain while pursuing overtly conciliatory moves towards Germany. A typical display was the ostentatious placing of Dekanozov, the Soviet ambassador who was on leave from Berlin, next to Stalin in the review of the May Day Parade. On 9 May the Russians revoked their recognition of the Belgian and Norwegian governments in exile and expelled Gavrilovic, with whom they had signed a treaty of friendship only a month earlier. They further announced their recognition of the anti-British government in Iraq led

by Rashid Ali. The most outstanding demonstration was Stalin's resumption of the premiership on 6 May, a measure generally viewed as an assurance of closer collaboration with Germany.[60]

This side of Russian policy has been fully explored. What has passed unnoticed is the Russians' desperate attempts to keep the line open to Britain after the receipt of Cripps' memorandum. At the outbreak of war they had hoped to preserve neutrality through more or less open relations with both belligerents. After failing to do so, they had sought the services of emissaries like Cripps. When the war shifted to the Balkans, Cripps had been diverted to Vyshinsky in what could always be presented to the Germans as an uncommitted relationship. To assume the least provocative position the Russians now conducted their activities in London away from the scrutiny of the Germans in Moscow. Maisky was entrusted not only with saving relations from breakdown but also with keeping a vigilant watch on the so-called 'Cliveden' elements in the government and encouraging the anti-appeasers, notably Eden and Churchill. It was 'desirable' for England, as Maisky tried to impress on Monckton, that Russia 'should be a benevolent rather than a mistrustful neutral'.[61] The services of Cripps as a go-between had become tiresome. His independent, unpredictable and unorthodox methods could prove a source of embarrassment in the extremely delicate situation now developing. Cripps' memorandum, as Maisky intimated to the Webbs, had 'irritated' the Soviet government.[62] Inaugurating the new approach, Maisky complained to Butler that Cripps was a lawyer and that his proposals were couched in the 'wrong sort of terms'. That Maisky was seeking reassurance as a result of Cripps' threats was evident. The Russians, he readily admitted, were too scared to commit themselves to any negotiations in writing but were eager to receive a unilateral statement from Britain regarding German intentions in the east. The aim of this approach was presumably to dispel the rumours of peace feelers.[63] Russian hopes of effecting a change in London were also manifested at a party held by Oumansky in Washington. On this occasion he drew aside Neville Butler, the commercial attaché, and, obviously referring to Cripps' memorandum, complained of surviving hostility to Russia in 'British Government circles'. Cripps, he said, had a 'store of good will' but it was with Churchill in London that Russia wished to improve relations.[64]

The flight of Rudolf Hess, Hitler's deputy, to England on 12 May

preoccupies the Russians to this day. This preoccupation has always been regarded as essentially capricious. However, if examined in the light of the events described hitherto, the peace mission assumes a completely new dimension and emerges as a key to the understanding of the Soviet attitude to the approaching conflict. Hess had assisted Hitler in the drafting of the anti-Bolshevik elements of *Mein Kampf* and was well known for his pro-British sentiments and contacts. The Russians' suspicion was naturally aroused when the British government, taken aback by the unexpected arrival, maintained silence over the affair, at no time considering the impact this might have in Moscow.

The Germans were the first to break the silence on the evening of 12 May. Only then did Churchill confirm the news in Parliament, promising a subsequent full statement on 'the flight to this country of this very high and important Nazi leader'. The public was left gasping for news which, however, did not appear. Prompted by Cadogan, Eden carried with him the entire Cabinet in resisting Churchill's repeated attempts to make such a statement. The Foreign Office held the opinion that it was best to keep Germany guessing and draw out more from Hess 'by pretending to negotiate' and avoiding making a hero out of him.[65] The affair was further confused when a ban on reports was imposed, though after Duff Cooper, the Minister of Information, had supplied the BBC with inaccurate information regarding the Duke of Hamilton's previous contacts with Hess. Hess had parachuted into the vicinity of the Duke's estate hoping to use him as his liaison with the government. Speculations were rife and were never officially refuted, while the Cabinet had become engrossed in the evacuation of the British Expeditionary Force from Crete once the Germans had landed there on 20 May.

The Russians, though extremely disturbed, were wary not to make any commentary which might seem vexatious to the Germans. Maisky's memoirs, when read in conjunction with the archival material, give an illuminating insight into the impact of the affair in Moscow. Only a fortnight earlier Maisky had been instructed, as a result of Cripps' memorandum to Molotov which had unprecedentedly been transmitted to him *in toto*, to keep a vigilant watch for signs of a possible peace. It is not surprising that Maisky was dumbfounded by Hess' arrival, rushing to the Foreign Office to receive an explanation. Butler, faithful to the government's ban on publicity, was 'reticent', refusing to volunteer any

information; he 'spoke very well', was Eden's judgment the next day.[66] Maisky, as is revealed by his quoted diary entry of 1 June and confirmed by an earlier conversation with the Webbs, interpreted the blunder over the publicity issue to mean that the Cabinet was actually giving the peace offer serious consideration. The sole availability of distorted information and the initially enthusiastic reports in the press, combined with reports that the Duke of Hamilton, purported to have been formerly in touch with Hess, John Simon and I. Kirkpatrick, the former counsellor at the British embassy in Berlin, had been negotiating with the envoy, added force to his conclusion. Cripps' extempore warning suddenly seemed to be materializing. The gradual swing at the end of the month towards a more balanced and critical review of the mission and the announcement that Hess had been interned as a prisoner of war finally led Maisky to the following erroneous conclusion, the essence of which he undoubtedly cabled to Moscow:

A struggle began behind the scenes in British politics . . . Churchill, Eden, Bevin and all the Labour Ministers generally at once declared definitely against any negotiations . . . But among the Ministers there have been found men like Simon, who, supported by the former 'Clivedenites', have considered that the Government should make use of such an unexpected opportunity of sounding Hitler about possible peace terms.

Not until the beginning of June had it become obvious to Maisky that Churchill had emerged 'victorious' in this fictitious struggle.[67]

Even then suspicion in Moscow of a possible separate peace was not eradicated. The Hess incident was examined against the background of deep-seated suspicion of British motives. Neither Maisky, his contemporaries nor subsequent Soviet or western historiography have been able to establish beyond doubt the motives for the mission and whether it was carried out with Hitler's connivance.[68] At the time it only kindled Soviet apprehension, especially in view of the growing evidence of the German offensive deployment. That Maisky's views were indeed adopted in Moscow is evident from the fact that Stalin repeated this interpretation as early as October 1941 when the foundations for the Grand Alliance were being laid. When tension was introduced into the Alliance in 1942 on the issue of a second front and the Allies were encountering severe setbacks on the battlefield, Soviet fears of a separate peace surfaced once again. Hess was often referred to in Moscow

as being in close touch with the 'Cliveden set' and the 'Munichites' in the government.[69] Later, during Churchill's visit to Russia in 1944, he was astonished to find Stalin still convinced that Hess had been involved in organizing a joint British–German crusade against Russia which had 'miscarried'. Faced with Churchill's denial, Stalin was willing to concede that Churchill himself might have not been fully aware of the intrigues taking place behind the scenes; this seemed odd to Churchill but can be understood in connection with Cripps' warning and Maisky's report.[70] So deep-rooted is the belief in a well-coordinated German move that in the entry of 10 May in the chronological table of the official Soviet history of the war the two events mentioned are Hess' flight and the end of the massive bombing of London. The association between the events is striking because Churchill describes how he first heard of Hess' arrival on 11 May while news was received of an exceptionally heavy air raid on London.[71]

Maisky's impression was not the only vindication of Cripps' memorandum. Soviet Intelligence sources seemed to point in the same direction. Victor Sorge, the noted Soviet agent in Japan, conveyed reports originating from the German embassy in Tokyo that Hess' flight was a last-ditch attempt, sanctioned by Hitler, to negotiate a peace.[72] From Berlin Valentin Berezhkov, the Soviet First Secretary, reported that when visiting Wilhelmstrasse in early May he noticed with disbelief among the literature available in the waiting room the reappearance of pre-war pamphlets entitled 'German–British Friendship'.[73] Naturally the anxious Russians, like Cripps and his family, were to 'await the P.M.'s statement with eagerness' but in vain.[74]

At the peak of the thaw in Soviet historiography, Trukhanovsky, the distinguished Soviet historian, played down the conspiracy theory but hinted at the disastrous effect the affair had on the Soviet evaluation of British policy: 'For what reason did the British Government keep silent, in spite of the fact that certain circles in England and a number of other governments expressed anxiety in connection with the Hess mission, fearing that negotiations with him might prove conducive to a deal with Hitler's Germany?'[75]

Cripps had kept the Foreign Office informed of the interest displayed by the Russians in Hess. However, because of his complete isolation in Moscow and the Russians' efforts to belittle the affair, he mistakenly assumed that his threats had 'to all appearances been ignored'. Nor was

the Foreign Office hopeful that such threats were likely to disturb the Russians, who were in any case expected to be on the verge of concluding a second pact with Germany.[76] Unlike the Russians, Cripps did not believe Hess to have arrived in England as Hitler's envoy; he rather assumed he sought sanctuary from Nazi assassins as a result of a growing rift within the Nazi leadership. In presenting Hess as an Anglophile Cripps may have been influenced by Isobel who, strange as it may sound, had spent some memorable days with the Hess family in 1935.[77] Aware nonetheless of the explosive nature of the affair, Cripps proposed to exploit the information obtained from Hess to either play on Soviet fears or allay them. If exploited correctly, he explained, the information could discourage the Russians from speculating and convince them that 'they have something to dig their toes into now, but may have nothing that will hold them later on'. Both possibilities were, however, rejected, as they were likely to 'precipitate and complete [Stalin's] capitulation to Germany'. The genuine reason was that once the Cabinet had committed itself once more to aloofness, new initiatives received scant attention; the Russians were therefore left in the dark.[78]

The Soviet obsession with the affair does not result only from a lack of information. The reaction to Cripps' proposals underwent a sudden and dramatic change towards the end of May under circumstances which are still not absolutely clear. There may have been an urge 'to exploit H. [Hess] – mendaciously' after Simon's abortive interviews with him.[79] A 'whisper' was made to the Russians through 'covert channels' that Hess' flight indicated growing dissatisfaction in Germany over Hitler's policy of collaboration with the Russians. The Russians were expected to learn the lesson that if cooperation continued they would have 'lost potential friends and made vital concessions' and would be 'left to face Germany single-handed in a weakened state'.[80] Though not a well-thought-out policy, Cripps' threats, Hess' flight and the use made of it combined to deflect the Russians towards a faulty and tragic evaluation of German intentions.

### Cripps' recall

By the end of April Cripps was despondent about the crushing German victories, the abysmal British military performance and the stalemate in

relations with Russia. He felt 'physically sick' when news came on 27 April that the swastika was now flying also over the Acropolis.[81] This undermined his firm conviction that a German–Soviet clash was imminent. Having failed to effect a swift *coup* in relations, Cripps reached the logical though incorrect conclusion when Schulenburg returned to Moscow at the beginning of May that the Russians would now desperately seek a respite through extensive concessions. The clue to future German moves would be found in the progress of the expected negotiations. Both Schulenburg and the Russians kept their lips sealed. Moscow, under tight censorship, was swarming with conflicting rumours. Cripps himself had been deprived of direct contact with Soviet officials and his evaluations were formed on selective information repeated from London and checked against the current rumours. Fully conscious of his position, Cripps did not go further than examining the probability of negotiations. But the mere suggestion of a new phase of Soviet appeasement, possibly culminating in another Soviet–German pact, was readily accepted in Whitehall and hindered detached evaluation.

In Berlin Schulenburg had found Hitler outraged and implacable over Russia's treaty with Yugoslavia. Hitler would not listen to suggestions that the Russians were likely to concede on almost any issue if negotiations were resumed. He did not, however, divulge his definite plans to Schulenburg. Back in Moscow Schulenburg was disconcerted by the rumours of an imminent attack and sought Berlin's reaction. The rumours were denied but he was instructed on the desirability of 'quashing' them. Most misleading to foreign observers was the sudden appearance of Dekanozov in Moscow and his prominent placing next to Stalin in the review of the May Day Parade in Red Square.[82] Hilger, the Counsellor of the German embassy, stifled all suggestions of a German attack on Russia, but referred to further German requirements of economic assistance. It seemed to confirm Cripps' guess that a fresh rapprochement between Germany and Russia was under way. On the other hand, sources intimately associated with Schulenburg suggested that he had been depressed since his return; rumours originating in the embassy's 'domestic channel' disclosed that Schulenburg was in fact packing to 'leave for good'. There were further contradictory indications in Moscow. The talkative Italian ambassador divulged to a prominent Swiss banker visiting Moscow that German demands in the

forthcoming negotiations would be so 'acute' that he expected a 'show down' within a fortnight. This was confirmed by the sudden withdrawal of Italian correspondents and women on the embassy's staff. Perhaps more alarming was a visit by the Swiss guest accompanied by Isobel Cripps to the Commission Shop, set up for tourists and diplomats; they found out that in a matter of days the store had been denuded of jewellery, ranging in price from 10,000 to 35,000 roubles, by German residents presumably anxious to convert their large stocks of roubles into diamonds, necklaces and bracelets which were then transferred to Germany.[83]

The Foreign Office was fully aware of the conflicting evidence. The uncertainty was discernible in its weekly collation of intelligence reports. On the one hand the vital conversations 'probably in progress' were given prominence. However, attention was paid to the slogans calling for intense watchfulness against a possible surprise attack which dominated the May Day celebrations.[84] Evidence of the German build-up in the East was clouded by doubts of the economic advantages which Germany stood to gain by waging a war. The tempting conclusion that the concentration was only 'political', a prelude to an agreement, was offset by the realization of the risks Stalin would run by making vital concessions. The general tendency, however, was to gloss over the contradictions. The conclusions of an evasive memorandum presented to both Cripps and Churchill as embodying the Foreign Office's view were that it was impossible to establish 'whether and if so when' Germany would attack Russia.[85] Military Intelligence did not prove helpful at this stage. It continued to indicate German preparations for an 'eventual war' but wavered throughout May as to 'whether Russia would be attacked or merely persuaded by threats to comply with German wishes'. In the absence of clear-cut evidence on Hitler's intentions, the appreciation leaned heavily on the political concept, originating in the Foreign Office, that Germany and Russia shared a community of interests. This concept gained more credence as a German move against Russia seemed illogical from the military point of view.[86]

The suspended judgment accorded well with the 'reserve' attitude as it entailed no immediate reaction. The pattern established was to suppress any intelligence which did not tally with the preconceived ideas. When Cripps quoted various sources on Stalin's speech to Red Army officers as early as 5 May, in which he was purported to have warned of

the danger of a German invasion, the only comment made was the emphasizing of Cripps' casual question whether 'working reliance' could be placed on it. Corroborating information repeated later in the month from an independent source was ignored.[87] Likewise little attention was paid to detailed information from Switzerland, an inexhaustible source of intelligence on Germany, on the Wehrmacht's deployment on the Soviet borders after the occupation of Yugoslavia.[88] In the last week of May reports from Berlin through Eric Boheman, the General Secretary of the Swedish Foreign Office, that an offensive was scheduled for mid June shared the same fate. Boheman, Cripps informed the Foreign Office, was the person 'most able to form some sort of balanced judgement'. The special economic and strategic importance of Sweden to Germany ensured close contact between the two countries. Nevertheless the information was immediately dismissed as being 'mainly guess-work'. The Central Department, responsible for German affairs, had reached the conclusion that the final decision rested with Stalin's acceptance of the German demands, now assumed to have been made. It remained for Sargent to update the political concept which he had introduced by suggesting that Hitler was prepared to act at once 'in the improbable event' of Stalin's refusing his offer of a treaty 'involving close collaboration'.[89] Even the slight qualification that Germany might launch a war if negotiations did not proceed satisfactorily seems to have been inserted only at the insistence of the MEW. The Ministry, far better informed than the Northern Department, had been feeling uneasy about the prevailing views.[90]

Thus the belief in inevitable German–Soviet cooperation, which had been initially raised as a mere conjecture and gradually accepted as self-evident, was sustained by a 'negotiation theory'. By the third week of May rumours of an imminent German–Soviet understanding replaced those of an armed conflict.[91] When, for instance, Military Intelligence was informed by its attaché in Berne that German preparation to penetrate the Ukraine by successive 'concessions' had been completed and that the use of force would be 'unnecessary', Christopher Warner, the newly appointed Head of the Northern Department, was quick to comment that it was an 'extremely likely forecast of German tactics – & . . . of events'.[92]

The concept had come to dominate not only Whitehall but also the collators of diplomatic intelligence. The diplomatic intelligence net-

work possessed an integral drawback as a result of the routine practice of repeating telegrams. The embassies gradually became acquainted with and influenced by Whitehall's evaluation. This is well reflected in a substantial warning on German intentions sent by R. Craigie, British ambassador in Tokyo. He had learnt not only that Hitler was decided on war but that the hasty departure of the former German ambassador through the Trans-Siberian route was due to the imminence of hostilities. Although *inter alia* his source scouted the idea of a war of nerves, Craigie saw fit to add in his report that it seemed to be the 'more likely explanation'.[93]

It is an inherent weakness of intelligence in general that it not only produces evidence but is also invited to remark on it. The appreciation tends more often than not to correspond with the expectations of the superior political bodies. Such a feedback naturally only consolidates unsubstantiated concepts. The armed forces shared with the Foreign Office the prejudice against Russia. Moreover, the interdepartmental links dictated a measure of dependency. Cavendish-Bentinck, in charge of political intelligence at the Office, chaired the JIC. He had reviewed and often commented on all reports and minutes dealing with German intentions at the Office, as well as composing its weekly intelligence reports. The subjugation of the Intelligence is particularly striking if we consider the volume and quality of the raw material on the German deployment in the east at its disposal. From 3 May to 19 May a steady stream of deciphered signals from the German air force Enigma clearly indicated the German designs. Luftwaffe squadrons, together with their operational and ground auxiliaries, which had been engaged in the Greek campaign or associated with 'Operation Sea-Lion' had been transferred to the Russian front. Some of the units had even been recognized as having served as the spearhead in the battles of France, Greece and Crete. Moreover, the news that a prisoners-of-war cage had been ordered to Tarnow seriously challenged the theory that the German moves were only aimed at intimidating the Russians.[94] Air Intelligence had to concede, therefore, on 23 May that it possessed 'sufficient evidence' that the deployment of a substantial part of the German air force was 'well advanced'. Although their evidence and conclusions eventually left some impact, their main interest was to demonstrate that Germany's western defences would remain for a while 'considerably weakened'. In their overall evaluation they too were dominated by the

concept, assuming that by their painstaking preparations the Germans were staging a 'show of force' which would be needed to 'ensure complete Russian agreement to German demands'.[95]

In studying Enigma and supporting evidence, Military Intelligence had established already in mid-May that the concentration of German troops in the East could be 'probably regarded adequate' for an assault on Russia. They even estimated that a final offensive deployment could be effected within two to three weeks. However, they too resorted to an erroneous and highly speculative explanation which held fast until the very eve of the invasion. Whereas the German General Staff advocated war, they suggested, it was being restrained by political circles.[96] The appreciation rested, of course, on the assumption that negotiations would be conducted under the shadow of military threats. The JIC, whose first appreciation of German intentions was made only on 23 May, followed suit. In their opinion the Germans fully appreciated that to strike a bargain with Russia without resorting to force would be an unqualified gain; they therefore expected Germany would 'doubtless bring to bear every possible pressure to that end'. This appreciation assumed that negotiations would precede any hostilities. On the other hand the Committee had to reckon with the arguments put forward by Cripps and the MEW that Hitler's desires seemed unattainable and that therefore Germany might find herself with 'no alternative but to go to war'. To bridge between the differing interpretations the JIC argued that Germany, with her 'usual thoroughness', was making preparations for an attack so as 'to make the threat convincing'. The Soviet government was expected to go a long way to avoid a clash by 'yielding to German demands'. They concluded therefore that Germany would resort to force only if she failed to reach a swift and satisfactory agreement. In the final balance an agreement seemed the 'more likely event'.[97]

Although the Foreign Office had not altered its convictions, a feeling of uneasiness was nonetheless evident as a result of the absence of any tangible evidence that negotiations were under way. Cripps remained uncertain and puzzled, though he did not exclude the possibility of an agreement. In his observations he was influenced by the digested information transmitted from London and the expulsion from Moscow of the Greek and Yugoslav ambassadors, who had been his close friends in the last few months. He by no means shared Whitehall's confidence

that the outcome of the negotiations was a foregone conclusion; such an assumption was based, he complained, on 'straws in the wind'. On the contrary, even now he retained his views on the supposed collaboration: 'There is no "love" in it, we do not see how there ever can be a drawing together except for immediate expediency.'[98] Cripps drew the Office's attention to the fact that Schulenburg was involved in merely routine contacts, while negotiations held in Berlin were only on secondary matters. The Office in fact possessed corroborating evidence obtained from the Finnish Foreign Secretary, who had just returned from Berlin.[99] In a characteristically rational and detached analysis, by no means flattering to the Soviet leaders, Cripps argued that Stalin was not 'affected by any pro-German or pro-anything feeling except pro-Soviet and pro-Stalin'. Cripps expected Stalin to keep out of the war so long as he could do so without jeopardizing the régime, and to pay 'any price' short of the ceding of territory or demobilization. He regarded a settlement on the terms envisaged by Military Intelligence as totally unacceptable to the Russians. Personally Cripps doubted whether the Germans would be prepared to accept a 'lesser price'. He sustained his argument by quoting a sarcastic commentary by *Pravda*'s senior political commentator refuting rumours that Russia would agree to 'lease' the Ukraine to Germany. He went further than ever before in suggesting that Russia would resist rather than accept peace 'at any price'.[100]

Cripps' arguments were reinforced by the MEW. However, the axiomatic acceptance of the Russian–German alliance proved powerful enough to suppress any notion of inherent hostility between the two ideologies or obvious signs of the unpopularity of the cooperation in both countries. The received doctrine was that the outcome of the war could be decided simply through the exploitation of economic resources accompanied by stringent blockade measures. The remote possibility of Russia's entering the war would materialize only if she failed voluntarily to deliver goods to Germany. Postan, who was most competent to consider the prospects of possible negotiations, had become outspokenly sceptical not only of Russia's ability to satisfy German requirements but even of the feasibility of extracting such advantages through war. He dealt a devastating blow to the Foreign Office's economic premises by concluding that the concentration of forces might be 'almost entirely for military reasons, i.e., because it was desired to settle with the Soviets, and from a military standpoint the present campaigning season

was held to be a far more favourable occasion than in subsequent years'. Postan's *tour de force* was so overwhelming, and freshly accumulating evidence so confusing, that Cavendish-Bentinck seems for the first time to have given thought to this eventuality. Hitler, he admitted, tended to revert to the essential tenets of *Mein Kampf*: 'on revient toujours à ses premiers amours'. To avoid the practical implications, he produced a new psychological explanation placing Russia and Germany on the same degraded moral level; Hitler, 'revengeful and spiteful', he reflected, might be tempted to avenge the 'chicanery and double crossing' which Russia had perpetrated since August 1939.[101]

New circumstances developed at the end of May which encouraged Eden to pick up the gauntlet and seek Cripps' urgent recall to London. It is surprising that the decision had little to do with Russia but rather with buttressing the Mediterranean strategy, which remained the prime objective of both Churchill and Eden. In view of the economic, military and political reservations aired, the Intelligence had turned its energies towards guessing from fragmentary information the contents of the expected treaty and its repercussions on British strategy. The Intelligence's low-keyed weekly appreciation, following the lead of the JIC, produced an outline of an agreement on the delimitation of spheres of influence.[102] The German troops concentrated on the Polish and Romanian borders with Russia, which had intrigued the Intelligence, were now believed to be earmarked for Iran 'with Russian consent'. The suggestion was particularly inviting in view of Britain's vulnerability on that flank as a result of her recent involvement in Iraq and Syria.[103] This proved an elegant solution to the growing doubts expressed by the MEW that economic motives were strong enough to explain the German deployment. This highly speculative guesswork had in turn an immediate impact on policy-making towards Russia. It implied a German threat with Russian connivance to major British interests in the Middle East.

On 31 May the Sub-Committee of the JIC produced the first thorough paper on 'The Possible Outcome of German–Soviet Relations' including its effects on England. Except for a slight shift in emphasis it remained faithful to the previous conclusion that, although war could not be discounted, 'both evidence and arguments made an agreement for extended collaboration the most likely course'. An agreement seemed a 'poor return for the vast preparations', as was com-

mented in the War Office. The theory, however, emerged reinforced with the added explanation, based on sporadic unconfirmed reports, that there would 'almost certainly' be clauses in the treaty allowing German troops free passage to Iran.[104] The overwhelming significance attached to German designs in the Middle East was partly a result of an increase in deciphered Enigma reports from this area, while rigorous silence was imposed by the Germans at the end of May on wireless telegraphic communications concerning the final touches to the preparation of 'Barbarossa'.[105] This allowed Military Intelligence to be distracted by its fanciful interpretation until mid-June. The current hypothesis was accepted by Cripps, whose evaluation at that time was entirely dependent on information supplied by London.

More disturbing seemed to be the implications of direct pressure on Turkey to abandon her neutrality.[106] That Eden should still be seeking salvation from this quarter is remarkable, but he certainly displayed perseverance. After all, even when Cripps had produced his recent major proposals for rapprochement, Eden had opted only for the least significant option of cultivating Turco-Soviet relations. The approach had then been nipped in the bud when the Foreign Office acquiesced in Cripps' impression early in May that the Turks were deliberately 'doing nothing' to obtain help from Russia. The Turkish ambassador to Moscow was even prohibited by his government from approaching the Soviet government. Eventually, on 18 June, British hopes were shattered when the Turks signed a treaty of friendship with the Germans without 'saying anything to Moscow'.[107]

Even the COS, which had hitherto abstained from discussing the approaching conflict, was stimulated by the assumed Soviet complicity in a German offensive in the Near East. On 31 May it reconsidered the plans to bomb the Baku oilfields. The bomber capability was such, Eden was told by the Chief of the Air Staff, that there would be 'the biggest blaze ever' in the Russian oilfields. The Commander-in-Chief in the Middle East was instructed to take control of Mosul as a preliminary step.[108] Eden, however, was determined to produce a major diplomatic coup despite the resolute opposition in the Office bluntly expressed by Cadogan:

Fact is that with our military weakness and the sensational ineptitude of our commanders, diplomacy is completely hamstrung. For instance – Russia. You

can't do anything nowadays with any country unless you can (a) threaten (b) bribe it. Russia has (a) no fear of us *whatever* and (b) we have *nothing* to offer her. Then you can juggle with words and jiggle with drafts as much as you like, and you'll get nowhere.[109]

The stakes at risk in any negotiations were plainly seen by Butler:

The advantage of any positive move in the direction of the Soviet Union is that we recognise that Russia has been a great makeweight in the balance of power. If we make no move and pursue the present policy of negation, we have on the other hand the advantage that we have no bargain with the devil and can become his adversary later with a clear record.[110]

The new initiative was to be launched while Eden still adhered to the views held in the Office that the Russians had adopted an attitude of 'detachment' to the war and accepted their 'special relations' with Germany. It was agreed that sooner or later the Russians would 'give way and sign on the dotted line'. The approach aimed at forestalling those elements in the treaty which would allow a German advance into the Near East. Without even consulting the Turks it was hoped to persuade the Russians that the Turkish government was 'resolved to resist the pressure' exerted on her by the Germans, and that it was in their 'common interests' to resist such a threat through a coordinated policy.[111] The means of accomplishing this were not clarified. It was hoped that pointing out the threat to Russia and Britain in Iran could provide a common denominator. In desperation it was even proposed that the Russians could be activated by mendaciously intimating that the Germans had opened negotiations with Turkey. To create the appropriate atmosphere the Defence Committee accepted Eden's request to facilitate the release of one of the Baltic boats requisitioned in June 1940 and the repatriation of Soviet sailors, which had been a constant obstacle. As Cripps found all doors barred in Moscow, it was conveniently decided that negotiations would be carried out through Maisky in London.[112] Cripps, however, had been credited with the Turco-Soviet declaration resulting from his trip to Ankara in February. He was also known to be an intimate friend of Aktay, the Turkish ambassador in Moscow. Talk of his recall had been circulating for some months and his presence in London now finally seemed desirable.

The officials at the Foreign Office, throughout critical of Cripps' extraordinary position in Moscow, had been alert to check his

unpredictable initiatives. So long as Cripps concurred with them at the beginning of 1941 on the prospects of reaching an agreement with Russia his 'vagaries' of autonomous action, as noted by Sargent, could be overlooked. Cripps' resort to frenzied activities in reaction to the developments in the Balkans and the intelligence reports which were increasingly difficult to ignore created a different situation. In mid-April Sargent made an open bid to curtail Cripps' influence by demanding his immediate recall for 'consultations and instructions'. Sargent had adopted the idea from Henderson, Head of the Eastern Department at the State Department who, influenced by Steinhardt, had casually raised such a suggestion in conversations with Halifax.[113] Sargent's proposal was exceptionally well timed against the background of Churchill's rage over Cripps' handling of the message to Stalin, the Soviet refusal of Cripps' unauthorized proposals and the decision taken in Cabinet to refrain from further overtures. Sargent attributed the 'confusion' complicating the task of Churchill and Eden in conducting Anglo-Soviet relations entirely to Cripps' 'occasional unwillingness to carry out his instructions, combined with his tendency to take independent and unannounced action of his own'. In a memorandum which became a denunciation of Cripps' mission Sargent claimed that, while the government had a coherent policy towards Russia, its ambassador in Moscow was conducting a damaging and contradictory policy. The survey was in fact so biased that Butler, who had long ago recognized the odds against Cripps and ceased to shield him, sprang to his defence. There was no other objection to the recall, though the thought of bargaining with the Russians in London with nothing to offer and in Cripps' presence did not appeal to Cadogan. More influential, however, was Butler's final comment before the file reached Eden, bringing out a thought constantly at the back of the mind of those politicians involved in Cripps' mission. Butler had gleaned from Kingsley Martin, the famous left-wing publicist, that Cripps' friends were keen to get him back to British politics. He warned therefore that while it was reasonable to recall Cripps, he had a 'hunch that he would then be bitten by politics here and not wish to return'.[114] Indeed the leadership of the official Labour Party was, as emerges from Beatrice Webb's diary at that time, 'delighted' to have Cripps in Moscow 'and hoped he would remain there for good and all'.[115]

Butler had a good insight into Cripps' hopes. Were Russia to

associate herself with Germany he was indeed resolved to leave Moscow 'if he could by being in England build up anything constructive for the future'. Cripps was in fact thinking of major reshuffles in Cabinet. For the post of Prime Minister he was contemplating someone 'with at least a radical mind'. In that sense Eden was not a satisfactory choice; he simply was not 'big enough for the job'.[116] Eden first avoided a decision by raising a series of technical queries. Although he was duly assured that Lacy Baggallay, the Counsellor in Moscow, whose personality was not so 'forceful as that of Sir S. Cripps', was one of the Office's 'best men', and that Cripps could be flown to England within two days, Eden allowed the issue to lapse.

Cripps' recall, therefore, was ostensibly for consultations but was in fact a disciplinary step to call him to order. Only domestic political considerations militated against such a measure. On 20 May Eden reverted to the subject, seeking Butler's advice.[117] As Eden still continued to subscribe to the negotiations theory, his decision in favour of a recall at the beginning of June did not constitute a far-sighted attempt to co-ordinate British and Russian activities in case of war, as is often suggested; he rather sought the participation of Cripps in a limited agreement concerning Russia and Turkey. The impact a recall, even for consultations, might have on the Russians at such a crucial period was not given any consideration. Nor was Cripps provided with any explanation for the move. On the morning of 2 June he was simply informed in a short telegram that the development of Soviet policy in the 'immediate future' required consultations in London. Later in the day the Cabinet sanctioned the *fait accompli* without discussing the repercussions.[118]

Eden's overture towards a Turco-Soviet understanding and Cripps' recall now evoked a series of errors in judgment. In the evening Eden approached Maisky but neglected to tell him that Cripps had been recalled for consultations. Considering the Russians' state of suspense, this obviously had its consequences. Eden told Maisky of his hopes to obtain from the Russians an undertaking not to facilitate German infringement of British interests in the Middle East, especially in Iran. In what could be interpreted as a threat or an encouragement, depending on the Soviet attitude, Eden pointed to the build-up, with American assistance, of the British air force in that arena, which he believed could thwart a German advance. The incentive was a promise that if German concentrations turned out eventually to be aimed at Russia Britain

would be 'in a position to take useful offensive action to relieve pressure against Russia'. Eden's grave concern at German designs in the Middle East seemed to confirm Maisky's impression, formed a day earlier, that Hess' mission had met with difficulties. He was, however, still suspicious that the offer was a desperate attempt to embroil Russia in war and therefore volunteered his own evaluation that the German deployment was no more than a 'war of nerves'.[119]

In the course of May Cripps himself seems to have realized that his mission had in fact become temporarily superfluous. He spoke of Russia, recollected Sir Owen O'Malley, the British minister just withdrawn from Budapest via Moscow, with the 'kind of reticence to be expected from a politician still in doubt about the line he would take when he got back to the House of Commons'. The impression recorded by O'Malley, noted for his hostility towards Russia when employed in the Northern Department in the 1920s, that Cripps' disillusionment with Russia was already 'well at work', was however baseless.[120] Despite the present difficulties he encountered in communicating with the Kremlin, Cripps remained critical of his government's lack of vision. In approaching Russia he had expected them to put forward more attractive alternatives than an unfounded promise to 'smash Hitler' and a return to Europe of the 1930s. He was now resigned to the view that military events had 'almost completely taken charge in every direction'. More emphatically put to his foster-son: '1 million troops on a frontier are far more persuasive than any ambassador's tongue!!'

The 'frightful crop of rumours' had a personally depressing effect, especially in view of the expulsion of the Allied missions. The apprehension that the British embassy would fare similarily could not be excluded, as recorded in Isobel's diary: 'All our passports are in order & each day I do a little sorting & laying by of "essentials" should there be a great hurry. We *don't* anticipate this at the moment but on the other hand uncertainty is great all the time.'[121] At the end of the month Cripps was growing impatient and doubtful about staying on. It was 'astonishing', he confided, to be in Moscow with 'really little or nothing to do – that matters – and no chance of influencing events one way or the other'. The suspense and frustration combined to take their toll. Isobel was concerned about her husband being not 'too well', while Cripps himself admitted to feeling 'rather exhausted nervously by the strain and anxiety and inaction!' The temptation to return home either

for consultations or to resume his political activity was well-nigh irresistible. On the other hand there was still the hope 'that at any hour or day something may happen here which might make my presence essential and suddenly give me a chance to do something rapidly'. To provide a break Isobel was organizing a week away 'in the countryside by water' in Sweden.[122] Cripps' deliberations and Isobel's planning were resolved by Eden's unexpected invitation to return to London.

In view of the acute situation now developing and the absence of clarifications, Cripps seems to have assumed that the consultations would focus on evaluations of the likelihood of an agreement or an invasion. To discourage wild speculations, mostly in Germany, that his recall marked a crisis in Anglo-Soviet relations he announced Stockholm as his ultimate destination, ostensibly to see a throat specialist. The recall provided him with a last chance to influence Russian decision-making. In making his farewells to Vyshinsky Cripps revealed his true destination, adding that he would not return to Moscow if in his absence Russia concluded an agreement with Germany. There were sufficient indications that he meant business. His two younger daughters were shortly afterwards flown out as well, while arrangements were made for Isobel to accompany him to London. The Foreign Office was not fully briefed about Cripps' talk with Vyshinsky. To dispel the 'sense of great mystery' it was eventually decided to tell Maisky that the government had decided to take advantage of Cripps' presence in Stockholm to recall him for consultations. Maisky, who in the meantime had been informed by Vyshinsky about the new development, sought an urgent interview with Eden. To his amazement Eden produced a contradictory version and assurances that the consultations were only 'for a brief spell'.[123]

Eden, completely absorbed in his new initiative, hardly noticed the apprehension which the recall aroused. To the Russians it fitted in well with Cripps' earlier threats and the Hess affair. Only a few days earlier Maisky had assured the Kremlin that Churchill and Eden had the upper hand in the struggle against the 'appeasers' within the Cabinet. Given the extreme suspicion prevailing in Moscow, the recall of Cripps, combined with the disinformation spread by the Office just then on the nature of Hess' flight, seemed to lend force to the hypothesis that some kind of arrangement was nonetheless being worked out behind the scenes, allowing Hitler a free hand in the East. Maisky was so concerned

that on 2 June he hastened to ascertain from Monckton the reasons for Cripps' return. The prominence given to the Hess affair during their conversation leaves little doubt as to the repercussions it had on the interpretation of the recall. Moreover, in his conversations with both Eden and Monckton, Maisky displayed an exceptional interest in the British reaction to German involvement in Syria and Iraq, which had become a test case for the success of the supposed Anglo-German peace feelers. For the first time since September 1939, observed Monckton, Maisky was 'anxious' that Britain 'should get on with it vigorously and secure a success'.[124] An extraordinary situation thus evolved whereby Cripps' recall to prevent the intensification of German–Soviet collaboration was taken by the Russians to mean the final touch to an Anglo-German understanding. This was a reflection of the mutual suspicion, perhaps the outstanding feature of Anglo-Soviet relations since the revolution, from which only Germany stood to gain. However, Maisky's conviction that the peace offer was abortive carried some weight. The Russians were naturally concerned that the Germans would assume that the clandestine consultations in London represented an attempt to form a common strategy to forestall a German invasion. They hastily implied their lack of involvement by breaking the news of the recall. The result in London was wild speculations of either a sudden worsening of relations or a breakthrough; this depended on whether a particular newspaper subscribed to the concept of collaboration or imminent war. In these circumstances Eden was forced to issue a statement that the consultations were a matter of course and Cripps was expected shortly to resume his post in Moscow.[125] The evident contradictions in the different British statements did little to allay Soviet suspicion.

In the week that passed until Cripps' arrival in London the exaggerated stress laid on German designs in the Middle East enhanced the negotiations hypothesis, diverting attention from the real threat developing in the main arena. By 4 June the Foreign Office was clinging to an unverified supposition that negotiations, carried out through 'some medium or other', were nearing a satisfactory conclusion. Their rather crude explanation of the unbridgeable gap of Germany's presumed extreme demands backed by a massive build-up and Russia's determination not to yield ran as follows: 'The Director of the Kremlin may run things too fine in his efforts to avoid war and may make some

concessions, which will be found later to have sold the pass and to have let in such a flood of German control that the power will have slipped unnoticed from his hands.'[126] Eden likewise dismissed out of hand Maisky's assurances that if faced with a proposal for an extensive deal Russia would resist, telling the Cabinet that 'it did not follow from this that there had not been one'. The Russians, he more frankly noted in his diary, would give way 'unless the skin [was] asked of them'.[127] It was still possible to cling to this appraisal in face of the contradictory nature of the information during the first week of June, largely a result of the slackening of the Enigma intelligence. From Romania came detailed news that the Germans' operational activities were well advanced, only to be refuted by reports from Finland that the Russians had agreed to all demands without demur.[128] Naturally closer attention was given at the Office to those reports indicating that a German–Soviet agreement was 'in sight'. Thus information originating in Budapest of the actual move of German troop trains into Russia was accompanied by reports current 'everywhere' that an important agreement was to be announced 'very soon'. On the other hand suggestions of belligerent intentions were arbitrarily disregarded. Information from Stockholm, for example, that Goering had intimated to a Swedish businessman that Germany would invade Russia on 15 June was discounted because the date had been 'tipped so often that it [was] becoming suspicious'.[129]

The JIC, by now well informed of the extent and offensive nature of the German deployment, found it increasingly difficult to discount the possibility of an armed clash. If Germany wished to remove from her eastern frontier the 'potential threat of increasingly powerful Soviet forces' it was, they argued, 'hard to conceive how this could be achieved without war'. But in the absence of clear-cut evidence and in the current atmosphere of Whitehall they left open the question of whether war or an agreement was more likely.[130]

A shift in the appreciation occurred, however, shortly before Cripps' return to England, coinciding with new impressions he himself gained while in Stockholm. On 9 June fresh intelligence reports were presented to Eden indicating that important mechanized and air units were being transferred to the eastern front 'in great haste'. As the Russians had not responded to his diplomatic moves, Eden proposed to hinder the German moves, the aim of which had not yet been established, by increased air action over France and Belgium. The Chief of the Air Staff, presumably

convinced that Russia would still concede, preferred however to wait until she actually 'decided to resist'. Eden's performance in Cabinet did not mean that he had shed the collaboration concept, as emerges from his minute of the same day on a memorandum dealing with a possible German attack: 'But *if* Russia fights, a big *If* I will admit'.[131]

The Russians, presumably influenced by indications that Britain was contemplating bombing the Baku oilfields, the recall of Cripps and apprehension of a favourable response to the supposed German peace feelers, sent Maisky on the next day to deny rumours that a military alliance with Germany either existed or was even contemplated. No less significant was Maisky's revelation that no economic or political negotiations were in progress. He even suggested that the time might soon be propitious for improved relations.[132] It was perhaps, as presented by Cadogan, a 'cryptic, incomplete and wholly useless' answer to Eden's approach concerning the Middle East, but it rendered the pursuit of aloofness under the cloak of the negotiations theory increasingly difficult. The confusion resulting from the collapse of the political concept after 10 June is obvious from the varied explanations for what Cadogan defined as the 'incomprehensible phenomenon of German military action against Russia'. For the first time Sargent, the leading theoretician on the subject, resorted to a military–economic explanation. His argument, approved by Eden, was that it was worth while for Hitler to make a big effort to get rid of the 'incubus' of the Red Army breathing constantly down his neck. He could then demobilize and solve the acute labour shortage hampering German industry. The Foreign Office reluctantly admitted that despite the current report of the Kremlin's acquiescence in German demands, most signs pointed 'towards a final tuning-up of the preparations for an attack on the U.S.S.R. on the grand scale'.[133] More popular, however, was a last-ditch attempt to salvage the concept despite Maisky's assurances. It was now suggested that rather than negotiating the Germans intended to present the Russians with an ultimatum once their deployment had been completed. On 11 June Warner felt confident that 'an ultimatum has been or will v. shortly' be presented to the Russians.[134]

The reevaluation resulted not in a prediction of the course of events but in a rather more balanced examination of probabilities. This received an impetus when on 12 June, the day of Cripps' arrival in London, Military Intelligence produced a decrypt of a message from the

Japanese ambassador in Berlin on his talks with Hitler earlier in the month, in which he had disclosed his intention of eliminating Russia.[135] In conversation with the American chargé d'affaires in London Eden admitted that while previously he had expected the German concentrations to lead to some 'huge blackmail', he was now 'more inclined' to predict a military confrontation. Even Sargent conceded that the 'overwhelming evidence' proved beyond doubt that the German hostile intentions were not 'merely bluff'.[136] This manifest reversal was, however, partly connected with attempts to secure American assistance if war did break out. Eden took Maisky's message to mean that the build-up was a result of the Russians' 'refusal to negotiate', thereby leaving the door ajar for a political solution of the crisis; he did not exclude the possibility of the Russians' giving way when faced with an ultimatum.[137]

Cripps arrived in Stockholm on 7 June with the fatalistic outlook that only 'external forces' could 'sway the tide'. He expected, however, early developments 'for better or for worse'.[138] Assarasson, well acquainted with Cripps' views, witnesses that before leaving Moscow he remained almost isolated in his belief that a German attack was imminent. In contrast Boheman, who met him at a dinner given by Mallet, recalls in his memoirs that Cripps was determined to impress on the Cabinet that the German deployment was intended to extract major concessions from the Russians, whom he expected to yield.[139] Mallet's version in his unpublished memoirs is better suited to Cripps' balanced judgment. According to him, Cripps 'found it very hard' to predict the course of events. A similar impression was formed by the American minister in Stockholm who was also present.[140] Cripps may also have been impressed by Kollontay, who had told him earlier in the day that no political conversations were in progress while the economic talks were based on the old agreements.[141] All sources agree, however, that Boheman astounded those present with fresh information obtained from the German code, broken by the Swedes, saying: 'I can tell you exactly when Hitler is going to attack Russia. It will be on June 21st.'[142] The most accurate, though partial, contemporary information, however, is in Mallet's reporting to London. He did quote Boheman's conviction of a 'political show down', rating the chances at 'even money'. A follow-up telegram, however, informed that Prytz, the Swedish ambassador in London who was also invited to the dinner, implied that the 'show down' should be understood as an invasion and

8 Cripps is met by Sir Victor Mallet in Stockholm during a stopover *en route* to London, June 1941

impressed on Mallet and Cripps that he had never known Boheman to speak 'so positively' on anything.[143] The significant point is that his stay in Stockholm enabled Cripps to air his opinions and exchange information, which helped him to form a more balanced view upon reaching London. This he admitted in a letter to Boheman thanking him for the valuable information. Arriving in London on the night of 11 June, Cripps found himself close to the Cabinet in expecting an imminent conflict.

### A Tass communiqué

The origin of the pathological Soviet suspicion lay in fears of a renewed intervention. The major international events in the interwar period were examined in Moscow within this framework. Their terror of a separate peace undoubtedly severely hampered Russian judgment and contributed to the paralysis which became more pronounced as war drew nearer. With hindsight of Hitler's meticulous and unwavering preparation for 'Barbarossa', the intelligence available at the time and Churchill's immediate commitment to Russia, such suspicion can easily

be attributed to Stalin's sheer stupidity. The Russians' suspicion was fuelled by the series of diplomatic blunders and misunderstandings described earlier, which were partly a result of their compulsion to conduct such exceedingly subtle diplomacy that its meaning was often lost on their partners. Cripps, always confident of an ultimate German–Soviet clash, had come to regard the establishment of confidence before Russia's entry into the war as the ultimate aim of his mission. The prevailing political concept in the Office, their indifference bordering on hostility to Russia and Britain's worsening military position all militated against him.

The Russians increased their scrutiny of British politics when the deteriorating strategic position evoked mounting criticism and dissatisfaction in England. German military intentions were believed to be closely linked to the anticipated peace overtures. Ample evidence was in circulation that Hitler would not undertake a large-scale invasion, bearing in mind the precedent of 1812 and the dangers of waging a war on two fronts.[144] The really ominous event seemed therefore to be not so much the evidence of German deployment but Hess' flight, against the background of Cripps' insinuations of a separate peace and the sudden impetus of Eden's attempts to involve Russia in war. Hardly had Maisky reassured his superiors in Moscow at the beginning of June of the failure of Hess' mission when a succession of incidents raised new question-marks. Shortly after Cripps' hasty departure from Moscow in suspicious circumstances, Maisky learnt that John Simon, the apostle of 'appeasement', had been entrusted with Hess' debriefing. It was particularly disconcerting when taken in conjunction with the 'whispers' campaign deliberately initiated by the Foreign Office to alarm the Russians. When definite evidence on 9–10 June led Cabinet to recognize the likelihood of an invasion, the women and children of the British legation in Moscow, among them Cripps' two daughters, were evacuated to Teheran and Stockholm. This started an exodus from other embassies, a fact which was hushed up by the Soviet censorship.[145]

Indeed, circumstantial evidence implied that American pressure was being exerted on Churchill and Eden to sacrifice Russia in exchange for peace proposals. On almost the same day that Cripps left Moscow, John Winant, the recently appointed American ambassador to London, departed to Washington for consultations. This revitalized widely

publicized speculations, triggered by the Hess affair, that a separate peace was being discussed.[146] Hess' dramatic flight, to use Roosevelt's own words, had 'captured the American imagination'. The partial explanation provided by Churchill had started not only Stalin but also Roosevelt wondering what was 'really behind the story'. Although Roosevelt now publicly denied rumours of peace talks surrounding Winant's arrival, these persisted and emanated from creditable sources like ex-president Herbert Hoover.[147] Even after the invasion was launched, sources well informed on Russia still expected the 'resurgence of "appeasement" in Britain' in the light of Hess' presence there. What must have further alarmed the Russians was that Winant's arrival was followed by a marked worsening of American–Soviet relations. On 10 June two Soviet assistant military attachés were ordered to leave the United States.[148] This strengthened the feeling in Moscow that Germany was being encouraged to resolve her conflict with Russia by force. Maisky was forced therefore to review his rather intuitive conviction that Eden and Churchill rejected any idea of a separate peace.

In his memoirs Maisky misleadingly portrays his activities in those crucial days as being decisive. He dwells at particular length on his warnings to Stalin of the impending attack. As might have been expected of one of the few former Mensheviks to have miraculously survived the purges of the 1930s, Maisky was an extremely cautious politician.[149] He could not possibly afford to leave unexplained the chain of events starting with the British collapse on the Continent and in Greece, followed up by Hess' offer and Eden's sudden feelers, coupled with further vague warnings on 5 and 10 June, not to mention the bizarre circumstances surrounding Cripps' recall. There was always an outside possibility that even if the peace proposals were left unaccounted for Britain might signal to the Germans her non-involvement in case war broke out; more probably, the implication of the existence of close Anglo-Soviet collaboration and the imminence of war might provoke the Germans and divert them to the East. The memory of the punishment inflicted on Yugoslavia for her approach to Russia was still vivid. Maisky therefore deliberately deludes the reader into believing that on 10 June he transmitted to Moscow an 'urgent cypher cable' of specific information provided by Cadogan on the German intentions. Subsequently he claims to have received the Tass communiqué of 14 June, which dis-

counted the probability of war with Germany, with 'extreme amazement'.

Three times in his story, which otherwise glosses over this eventful period, Maisky directs the reader to the conclusion that 'the shaft in the direction of Britain with which the Tass communiqué began left no room for doubt that it was the reply to the warning given by Cadogan'.[150] The obvious discrepancy in Maisky's version is that the meeting with Cadogan, the records of which are still closed to research, took place not on 10 June, as is claimed by him, but on 16 June, after the publication of the communiqué. Maisky's brazen lie is connected with the historical controversy over Stalin's direct responsibility for the set-back resulting from the surprise attack. The critical reaction of Soviet historians and representatives of the armed forces to A. Nekrich's revisionist *22 June 1941* was based not on his revelation of the existence of warnings of the impending attack but on the fact that, like Khrushchev, he pinned all blame on Stalin. Nekrich was a disciple of Maisky. Maisky goes out of his way to confirm the conclusions of the revisionist school that overcoming the major reversals at the beginning of the war remained one of the cardinal problems of the war and was a direct result of Stalin's 'big blunder' in wrongly evaluating the situation on the eve of the war. Filip Golikov, the head of Soviet Military Intelligence, was specifically reprimanded by the revisionists for pro-viding Stalin with reassuring intelligence reports which 'might gratify him'. They called for a shared collective responsibility which was greater 'in proportion to one's place in the hierarchy'.[151] The analysis of the evidence in the intricate political situation was clearly an extremely complicated task which cannot be simply laid at Stalin's door. Maisky undoubtedly has much to answer for.

The clue to Maisky's distortion is to be found both in the communiqué's frame of reference and its extremely careful wording. The 'shaft' which supposedly puzzled Maisky read: 'Even before Cripps' arrival in London and *especially after he had arrived there*, [my italics] there have been more and more rumours of an "early war" between the Soviet Union and Germany . . . All this is nothing but clumsy propaganda by forces interested in an extension of the war.' Cripps had reached London only on the night of 11 June and the *démenti* referred to comments made in the press on 12 June. Though published on 14 June the communiqué

was submitted to the German ambassador on the night of 13 June.[152] Maisky could have been the only source for the compilation and evaluation of the British press's commentary. Indeed, in conversations with the *Times*'s foreign affairs correspondent on the evening of 12 June, Maisky bitterly deplored the 'Foreign Office stunt' in 'all' morning newspapers.[153] On the following day, still before the issue of the *démenti*,[154] Maisky expressed to Eden his concern over the 'type of reports' which were unlikely to be taken by his government to represent independent opinions.[155] That the Russians should attach such importance to newspaper reporting is not at all surprising considering the constant official leakages in both countries during the previous two years. Moreover, the Russians always expected the press to represent the government's views.

Speculation concerning Cripps' recall had not been defused by the Russians' calculated leakage nor by Eden's ensuing statement. The headlines of the British and German newspapers continued to imply that a 'certain sharpening' of German–Soviet relations was 'discernible'.[156] Under the headline 'Sir S. Cripps Returns; Possible Talks with Russia; Hope of Better Relations', *The Sunday Times* commented that Russia was striving to improve relations with Britain to thwart German aggression. Likewise the *New York Times*'s London correspondent stressed the coincidence between Cripps' arrival and the sudden release of the Baltic ships impounded in British ports.[157] The day after Cripps' return, noted the American military attaché in London in his diary, the press was 'full' of information on 'German pressure on Russia by the assembly of German divisions along the Russian frontier'.[158] The Foreign Office later admitted the unfortunate effect of the 'spate of activity' by the press immediately after Cripps' arrival and the impression gained by Maisky. The incredible fact is that, unknown to Cripps and possibly to Eden, the press had been briefed on the subject by the Foreign Office itself.[159] The motive for the release can only be surmised but Cadogan at least cherished the hidden hope, intimated in his diary, that the Russians would not sign the agreement: 'as I should love to see Germany expending her strength there'.[160]

Maisky's meeting with Cripps on the morning of his return did not dispel the impression gained earlier in the day from the morning papers. On the contrary, despite Maisky's assurances that he was 'persona grata

in Moscow – whether or not there was war', Cripps repeated the threat, denied by Eden, of his intention to resign his post were Russia to sign an agreement with Germany.[161]

Despite its declared destination the *démenti* was intended primarily for German eyes. It was hoped to elicit a German reaction to Soviet admissions that they were aware of the German concentrations. Just as significant was the attempt to prevent a German misinterpretation of Cripps' recall as a sign that negotiations were under way, as the British press was insinuating. Indeed, the Russians promptly complained through Rothstein that the *démenti* was not given sufficient prominence in the press, thereby again implying definite government inter-ference.[162] Maisky certainly condoned the action contemplated in Moscow which was based on his reports. There is nothing to show that before 15 June he was at odds with Moscow's appreciation of the German concentrations.[163] Maisky's hunch that Britain was indeed desperately trying to embroil Russia in war seemed to be confirmed in his first inter-view with Eden after Cripps' return on 13 June, just when the *démenti* was presented to Schulenburg in Moscow. Eden followed warnings of a general nature on the German deployment with a promise to send a military mission and economic assistance to Moscow once hostilities broke out. Maisky interrupted to point out that the message pre-supposed Anglo-Soviet 'intimate collaboration' which did not exist. Moreover, he clearly 'betrayed no personal reaction' to the warnings and professed 'not to believe in the possibility of a German attack'. In order to test assumptions once again before his government acted upon them, he urged Eden to provide him that very evening or over the weekend at the latest details of the intelligence reports.[164] The sense of urgency was completely lost on Eden and must have enhanced Maisky's suspicion of provocation. The decision to part with a body of evidence, partly provided by Enigma, was sanctioned by Churchill on Sunday 15 June but Maisky, who was thoroughly acclimatized to the British way of life, was spending the weekend in the country and could not be reached. He was therefore astounded when faced on Monday morning with Cadogan's detached and monotonous recital of 'precise and con-crete' evidence. What disturbed him was not that 'this avalanche, breathing fire and death, was at any moment to descend' upon Russia but rather the soothing content of his previous communications with Moscow. He therefore sent the urgent cable to Moscow after first

extracting from the information what he still thought was deliberately aimed to 'heighten the colours in order to have the biggest effect on the Soviet Government'.[165]

The exact nature of Maisky's telegram and the lengths to which he went in reversing his earlier appreciation remain unknown. According to Khrushchev's secret speech in 1956, Maisky supplemented his cable on 18 June with further details of the German deployment, quoting Cripps as 'deeply convinced' of the inevitability of an armed conflict. On 19 June Cripps observed that Maisky was deflated and depressed and seemed to have lost his overflowing confidence. The same impression was gained by Dawson, the editor of *The Times*, who found Maisky convinced of a German invasion.[166] On Saturday 21 June Maisky's weekend at Bovingdon, where he enjoyed 'rural peace, shaded garden, the perfumes of summer', was interrupted by a message from Cripps who implored him to return to London. Maisky hastily complied and was provided by Cripps with the essence of Enigma's latest information that war was expected the next day.[167]

The attitude of the British government to the developing crisis had been central to the Kremlin's own evaluation. Maisky's appraisals between 10 and 16 June played on Stalin's fear of provocation, as echoed in the famous communiqué, and lulled him to the real danger lurking in the military sphere. On the night of 13–14 June General F. I. Kuznetsov, the Baltic district commander, sought Stalin's permission to put the fleet on alert. He found that Stalin, who had just been briefed by Maisky about the reactions to Cripps' recall, did not exclude the possibility of an invasion but was concerned that Britain was plotting to involve Russia in the war. General G. Zhukov, the Chief of the General Staff, and Defence Commissar Marshal S. K. Timoshenko made a similar approach, which prompted a corresponding reaction: 'You propose carrying out mobilization, alerting the troops and moving them to the western borders? That means war!'[168]

The object of the subtle communiqué issued on 14 June was to forestall provocation. Its unequivocal message that no Soviet–British *entente* was in the making was at least expected to produce a German denial of belligerent intentions, if not to draw them to the negotiation table. It was not, however, even published in Berlin. Pondering with his advisers over the absence of reaction, Stalin was faced on 16 June with Maisky's revised appreciation after his talk with Cadogan. The reper-

cussions were immediate. On the evening of 16 June Baggallay made a courtesy call to the Kremlin, his first since Cripps' departure. Vyshinsky tried to minimize the effect of the communiqué which 'merely registered a fact and did so in careful words'. He even suggested that the recall of Cripps might have 'stimulated' the imagination of the reporters.[169] On 19 June, over lunch with Maisky, Cripps, with his characteristic political naivety, complained about the communiqué which he regarded as a personal attack and which rendered his service in Moscow 'quite useless'. A decision to return, he stressed, would be 'largely influenced' by the explanations made by the Soviet government. Maisky immediately assured him of the Russians' 'greatest personal regard' for him.[170] Within hours he addressed Eden with an explanation almost identical in wording to that made to Baggallay in Moscow.[171]

More revealing was the sudden frenzied activity in the Kremlin. While the fresh information did not eliminate the possibility of British provocation, it signalled the likelihood of war regardless of what was happening in London. Hitherto priority had been given to attempts to prevent provocation. On 18 and 19 June instructions were issued to both the air and ground forces to take precautionary measures. The commanders of the Baltic and Northern Fleet were ordered to put their crews on alert. On 19 June General Yeremenko was ordered to hand over his Far Eastern command and proceed to Moscow without delay. On 21 June Stalin clearly admitted the uncertainty of the situation. In similar fashion Molotov intimated to the Turkish ambassador that the situation had become 'confused and uncertain'. Zhukov remembers Stalin as being torn between anxiety and fear of triggering off an unwanted war. At the insistence of the General Staff he now issued Directive 1, pointing to the possibility of war and implementing essential defensive measures; it still warned the field commanders against 'any provocative action which may cause serious complications'.[172]

At long last the Russians had come to grips with the magnitude of the crisis on their threshold. The precautionary military moves were accompanied by desperate diplomatic efforts to impress on the Germans what the communiqué had failed to do. On Sunday 22 June Berezhkov was urgently instructed to register a personal complaint to Ribbentrop about the increase of German reconnaissance flights over

Soviet territory. He was ordered to follow it up with a warning that a 'military adventure might have dangerous repercussions'. More significant were instructions to express Soviet readiness to embark on negotiations. Several phone calls from the Kremlin insisted on the delivery of the message despite obdurate refusal in Wilhelmstrasse to respond. Weizsäcker finally consented to receive the note late in the evening but offered no commentary. Molotov next summoned Schulenburg but found him just as evasive. Berezhkov was again pressed to seek a meeting with Ribbentrop, but before this could be arranged he was informed by the Foreign Minister that German forces had invaded Russia.[173]

Well into the morning of 22 June the Kremlin did not exclude the possibility that Russia was not faced with a full-scale surprise attack but was rather being intimidated into political submission. As Molotov confessed to Cripps as early as 27 June, it was not anticipated that war 'would come without any discussion or ultimatum'. The earlier instructions to the front were to hold fire until the situation was grasped. There were even desperate attempts to seek the mediation of the Japanese.[174]

Extreme confusion prevailed as far as relations with Britain were concerned. There was still a slight chance of bringing the war to a halt, accompanied by the ever-present fear that Britain condoned the attack. There had been alarming signals in the days preceding the attack. The State Department continued its manifestly hostile attitude when on 14 June all assets of continental Europe deposited in the United States, including those of the Baltic states, were frozen. No less disconcerting was the unexpected announcement on 18 June of Turkey's treaty with Germany. In addition Cripps had asserted his determination to remain in England. To the chronically suspicious Russians it seemed as if a renewed intervention was materializing. 'All believed', recalled Litvinov later in Washington, 'that the British fleet was steaming up the North Sea for joint attack with Hitler on Leningrad and Kronstadt.'[175] Likewise the Politburo of the British Communist Party issued a statement on Sunday morning, before it had been briefed from Moscow and before hearing Churchill's pledge, that Hitler's attack was 'the sequel of the secret moves which have been taking place behind the curtain of the Hess mission'.[176] When Baggallay paid a visit to Vyshinsky on his own initiative and without specific instructions early on Sunday, he

found him not only, as might have been expected, 'exceedingly nervous' but also 'excessively cautious'. Even Maisky would not meet Eden until he had been assured by Molotov's famous speech at midday that the break with Germany was complete and that Russia was now bent on resisting.[177]

## 5

# AN ALLIANCE OF SORTS

### On the brink of war

Churchill's own description has left a misleading impression of the fateful weekend of 21–2 June at Chequers. Moreover, his overwhelming speech, cleverly weaving conflicting aspirations, swept public opinion and subsequently historians who still maintain that it launched Britain 'impulsively, even enthusiastically, on a policy of open-hearted partnership' with Russia.[1] Churchill's account, assisted by the reminiscences of his private secretary, places himself in the midst of the drama in harmony with the general mode of his memoirs. He portrays a leader struggling with a decision which would mark the 'turning point of the war'. A different version originated in Beaverbrook's later controversy with Cripps on championing aid to Russia. Cripps and Beaverbrook assume a central role in the deliberations culminating in Churchill's pledge of support to Russia.[2] Churchill, it has since been suggested, 'caught between the Scylla of a cautious Cripps and the Charybdis of an audacious Beaverbook made a bold decision: to announce ... all-out aid to the Russians'.[3] In November 1941, however, Beaverbrook still vividly recalled the 'momentous' occasion when in the library at Chequers Churchill divulged to him and Cripps the content of the speech. There is not the slightest hint of disagreement: 'Cripps and I sat listening to the Prime Minister's conclusions. We not only followed him but we agreed with him in all he said.'[4] Both versions, sustained by the exceptionally dramatic delivery of the speech on the air, enhance the myth of Churchill's instant discarding of his lifelong anti-Bolshevik prejudices when the interests of the nation so dictated.

In fact the weekend at Chequers was an anti-climax to the intense political activity which had started upon Cripps' return to London. In

163

the period preceding the German invasion Churchill, absorbed in the conduct of the stillborn campaign in Libya, allowed Eden a rather free hand in the conduct of relations with Russia, commenting only casually that 'either war or a show-down' were near.[5] However, it is apparent from off-the-record remarks made in an interview on 8 June that, unlike Cripps, Churchill expected Stalin to yield the Baku oil wells and the wheatfields of the Ukraine, and even to agree to demobilize the Russian army to avoid a conflict. Although before Cripps' return Churchill did not discount the possibility of cooperating with Russia, such prospects seemed too remote to be given any practical consideration. Churchill's unflattering metaphors for the Russians were not confined to the famous description of collaboration with the Russians as a partnership with the devil. In the past such expressions had included 'foul baboonery' and a 'plague-bearing' infection. A less well known phrase which, however, reveals the strength of his feelings on the very eve of the invasion is his comparison of the Russians to a 'formidable crocodile': 'If a crocodile came up on one side of our boat and helped to balance it, so much the better. But you never knew with Russia. You give the crocodile a hearty kick and he may be agreeable to you. You give him a pat and he may snap off your leg. We had tried both methods and gained nothing.'[6]

On the afternoon of 12 June, after only preliminary consultations with Cripps, Eden was not yet fully aware of the magnitude and implications of the forthcoming crisis. In Cabinet he was still obsessed by plans to effect a partial Turco-Soviet understanding which would prevent a German attempt to 'outflank Turkey'. However, he conceded that Cripps, who after all had been originally recalled to advise on this matter, was sceptical, inferring that 'a good deal of the blame . . . rested with Turkey'. For the first time the divergent appreciation was aired in the ensuing discussion that Germany 'might wish to destroy the U.S.S.R. military forces now, when they might hope to do so easily'.[7]

On the whole Churchill's detachment and Eden's misguided appreciation and peripheral interests, coupled with the Foreign Office's concept that Russia was a 'potential enemy rather than a potential ally',[8] precluded even a preliminary consideration of collaboration in case war did break out. It remained, therefore, for Cripps to galvanize the government into formulating a policy. As was widely

publicized, Cripps returned to London disappointed by his failure to establish close personal contacts with the Soviet leadership but in no way disillusioned. In fact he spoke 'ill' of the Foreign Office for having raised obstacles and was determined to exercise influence through direct persuasion, by-passing the Office.[9] Cripps' ability to influence policy-making was enhanced by the change in his political standing since his departure to Moscow. It is often argued that Cripps' meteoric rise from the fringes of British politics to high office was due to undeserved credit for having drawn Russia into the war. Signs of the change could however be detected even prior to the attack. To start with Cripps' bearing had changed as a result of the experience and prominence gained in Moscow. More significant was his reception by the press; a leader in *The Times* urged, for instance, the use of his 'exceptional capacities' nearer home. There was, it argued, a 'pressing need for all available talent; and nowhere more than in strengthening the quality of Labour Party representation in the supreme councils of the nation'.[10] It may well be that Cripps was, as is commonly argued, 'a goose politically',[11] but this was more than compensated by his integrity, drive, sense of purpose and analytical flair. Those qualities were brought to the fore in direct personal encounters. A case in point was the long and crucial meeting which took place on the night of 12 June, after the Cabinet session, between Cripps, Churchill and Eden. In spite of Churchill's rage over Cripps' handling of his warning to Stalin, earlier mutual recriminations and differences in temperament, the two got on together surprisingly well at that stage. Churchill with his superb political intuition was able to win Cripps over and prevent an undesirable confrontation by exercising his charm and giving him some latitude on the Russian issue. If at the beginning of the war Cripps had expressed doubts about his ability to work with Churchill, he was now ready to admit that he found him 'in first rate form: a splendid leader for the purpose'.[12]

The meeting took place just after fresh Enigma evidence had revealed the completion of the transfer of key formations of the German air force from France to the eastern front. The Luftwaffe's commanders, it was further learned, had been summoned to a conference at Goering's headquarters on 15 June. Meanwhile a ban was ordered on communications on operational matters by wireless telegraphy. There was nonetheless an increase in Enigma signals on German activities on Russia's

northern borders. Since his arrival Cripps had come to share un-
reservedly the conclusions drawn by the MEW that German economic
demands were likely to be so exacting that the Russians would be forced
to fight.[13] Assisted by the latest intelligence and the impression he had
gained in Stockholm, Cripps urged on Churchill and Eden the need to
inform the Russians of British preparedness to collaborate with her if
war broke out. Thus, the foundations for an alliance and the essence of
Churchill's public commitment in his speech were first considered, at
Cripps' prodding, a mere ten days before the outbreak of hostilities.
Maisky was promptly notified by Eden of the decision to send a military
mission and the readiness to discuss the question of Russia's
economic requirements.[14]

As a result the Cabinet, the military and Foreign Office experts, and
the Americans were faced with a *fait accompli* carried out by the triumvirate of Cripps, Churchill and Eden. It was now necessary to grapple
with the inevitable reservations. The Foreign Office, faced with
overwhelming intelligence indications that the German deployment
was in earnest, the powerful argumentations of the MEW and Cripps'
hold on Eden and Churchill, was finally forced to moderate its tone.
Sargent, backed by Cadogan, conceded that Germany's profits were
'not sufficient to outweigh the immediate military disadvantages'. An
explanation had to be sought elsewhere and it differed only in degree
from that reached in the Kremlin. By launching an offensive against
Russia, suggested Sargent, Hitler expected to rouse opposition to war in
the United States 'and indeed in other conservative minded countries,
not excluding our own'. Having failed to cross the Channel, Hitler was
now resorting to new tactics aimed at accomplishing a victory over
Britain by 'political methods synchronised and combined' with the
campaign on Russia. 'A crude peace offensive', he warned, 'may be
laughed at and brushed aside but there may well be a more subtle
approach, timed for the late summer of 1941.' A 'careful education' of
the home front 'especially as regards the Russian problem' seemed to
Sargent the order of the day. Failing this there would be a 'misguided
enthusiasm over Hitler's blunder' followed by 'disillusion' if Russia
collapsed and culminating in 'insinuation that the peoples of England
and the U.S.A. . . . can *get* out of it all and *stay* out of it all, with the
Empire intact . . . prosperous and inviolate, at the trifling cost of admitting that Germany has a free hand on her eastern front'. His thoughts

were hastily adopted by an interdepartmental meeting to form the basis of a new policy. From the outset propaganda was to substitute for real cooperation. The policy was to dispel suggestions of a separate peace but equally to resist the strong pressure expected from various circles in Britain 'to treat Russia as an ally'. The essence of the proposed policy, falling in line with the COS and essentially with Eden's and Churchill's views, was confined to an expression of 'sympathy with the new victims'.[15] In its last meeting before the German invasion the Cabinet failed to go beyond this outline. It in fact endorsed Churchill's intention based on those conclusions to present Germany as an 'insatiable tyrant, that had attacked Russia in order to obtain material for carrying on the war'.[16]

More significant at this stage was the military's self-imposed limitation in evaluating the situation and judging Soviet capabilities through preconceived ideas and emotional involvement. Dill regarded the Russians as 'so foul that he hated the idea of any close association with them'. In 1935 Dill had questioned the value of Russia as an ally and had even suggested that Germany should be allowed to 'expand eastwards' at her expense. Likewise General Ismay, who had intervened against Cripps' initiatives in 1940, now found the prospects of an alliance 'repugnant'.[17] The most up-to-date and accurate evidence of the disposition of the German forces continued to be interpreted in extremely sceptical fashion. The effects of a possible German–Soviet understanding were still being elaborated by the Intelligence when Eden made his first promise of help to Maisky.[18] The low-keyed military appreciation of 16 June continued to reflect the indecisiveness concerning the German deployment. That Germany was considering putting forward demands was taken for granted, though the nature of the demands was admittedly 'still obscure'. The suggestion that Germany might be anticipating 'the necessity of using force' was dampened, however, by the persistent wild conjecture that military and political circles in Germany were in confrontation while Hitler was still 'undecided'. The only certainty was that the Germans could complete their build-up by around 20 June. A similar appreciation was made by the Foreign Office in its last expression before the German invasion.[19]

The COS, faced with the triumvirate's *fait accompli*, examined on 14 June the implications of Russia's involvement in the war. Their negative conclusions were strikingly similar to those which had prevented

collaboration in 1939. In both cases they were based on an axiomatic appreciation of Soviet capabilities by General Wavell, made after he had attended the demonstrative manoeuvres in the autumn of 1936 and adopted shortly afterwards by Ismay, then in charge of military intelligence on Russia at the War Office. This perception was conveniently sustained by the purges and the Russians' performance in the Winter War. The astonishing Soviet successes against the Japanese in 1939 were ignored. The major premises were that although the Red Army was large it suffered from 'inherent failings', its equipment was 'obsolescent' and its value in offence was 'low'. Although the Russians were considered to be 'at their best in defence', a rapid Soviet collapse was anticipated. Therefore the timing of the campaign represented the 'only points of interest'. The JIC estimated that the occupation of the Ukraine and Moscow would take 'as little as 3 or 4 weeks, or as long as 6 weeks'. The relevance from the British point of view was the postponement by eight weeks of a possible invasion of Britain. Eden was naturally reproached for proposing a military mission to Moscow. The COS wished the Russians to understand that the step was a 'favour'. It was even suggested that the term 'mission' should be replaced by 'observers', whose main task, compatible with the expectations of a quick Russian collapse, would be to 'keep the "pot boiling" '.[20] The mission was expected to be a major source of intelligence. The reservation was made, however, that it was 'undesirable' to provide the Russians with reciprocal information. The military experience of the members of the mission was considered irrelevant as coordination of strategy was not called for unless Soviet resistance proved stiffer than expected. The more likely course was that the mission would split and stimulate resistance once the army was beaten and the Soviet government had disintegrated. The overall military expectations from the mission, to be known as the 'Liaison Mission' so as to 'avoid political complications', coincided with the Foreign Office's propagandistic objective: to 'demonstrate' that Britain was associated with Russia's struggle against a common enemy.[21] The only concrete proposal of assistance to Russia, also revealing the prognosis, was of collaboration in the destruction of the Caucasian oilfields in exchange for a promise of oil deliveries.[22]

From the outset, therefore, the legacy of the political concept was so powerful as to prevent a review of overall strategic planning as a result

of Russia's entry into the war. Such a contingency had never really been considered. There is no indication whatsoever that Churchill dissented from this stance. On 17 June he made only scanty inferences to the Defence Committee on the 'tendency' of the war to 'spread further eastwards'. He echoed the COS in rejecting a full alliance, preferring to 'take every advantage which such a conflict offered'. His mind was in any case entirely turned to Operation 'Battle-axe' raging in Libya.[23]

To keep in step with the Americans was the overriding problem facing Churchill in devising the degree of association with the Russians. In view of the British dependence on American aid, any assistance to Russia had to draw on American resources. More serious, however, were the possible repercussions on the American domestic scene. A German invasion, presented as a crusade against Bolshevism, was bound to invite pressure from influential conservative isolationists in the United States against a commitment to Russia and in favour of responding to the German peace feelers likely to follow. Indeed Eden's preliminary clarifications with the State Department, against the background of the rapid deterioration of American–Soviet relations, met a negative response. This reinforced the Foreign Office's and the army's case for qualified cooperation only. To ensure coordination Churchill personally addressed Roosevelt on 15 June, impressing on him the imminence of a German onslaught. In carefully chosen words Churchill did not advocate a firm alliance but rather an association based on the principle that Hitler was a common foe. More specifically he suggested that Britain would pledge 'encouragement' and such help as she could spare.[24] The American attitude remained a source of concern until the very weekend of the attack. Moreover, Halifax undid Churchill's carefully balanced message by intimating that Britain might sacrifice the Baltic states, to whose fate he showed a marked indifference. This outraged Sumner Welles, the Acting Secretary of State, and prompted Adolf Berle, one of Roosevelt's chief advisers on foreign affairs, to complain that the British were not showing 'even the remotest signs of statesmanship'.[25] Alarmed by the reservations in Washington, the Foreign Office reasserted their determination to adhere to the 'reserve' attitude and to deal with Russia only on the basis of reciprocity at least until the situation became 'more clear'. Eden was further informed that the aid promised to Maisky would have to be confined to material

which the British 'could agree should be diverted from themselves'. This was accompanied by an ominous reminder of Churchill's unauthorized commitment of American support to France a year earlier and a demand for 'parallel policies'.[26]

The State Department on 21 June finally arrived at a policy which went no further than relaxing restrictions on exports, and only on the basis of 'mutual advantage'.[27] The Americans undoubtedly anticipated a higher degree of British commitment. Churchill's attitude in the Defence Committee and his telegram to Roosevelt rested on the exploitation of the incidental convergence of interests with Russia. A German engagement in the East seemed to provide no more than an interregnum essential for the regrouping of forces. Eden expressed this bluntly when the probability of war increased: 'We shall surely not be idle meanwhile & we need a breathing space & could use it.' On 18 June he supplemented Churchill's message with a more outspoken one of his own, explaining to Hull that 'while we should not become allies of the Soviet Union, we should have a common enemy and a common interest'.[28]

Cripps' initial success in securing some commitment was therefore checked in the following days. The personal insult of the Tass communiqué did not help either. And yet, maintaining a detached and rational posture, he went on pursuing his objective, remaining the most outspoken champion of cooperation with Russia. On 16 June he was invited to state his case in Cabinet. His performance was tantamount to an open challenge to the long-standing political and military concept which had dominated relations with Russia. Fundamentally, he reiterated his conviction that Russia was hostile to both Britain and Germany. Britain, however, was regarded as the 'more stable of the two but Germany as the more dangerous from a short-term point of view'. As a result of recent events he expected the Russians to go to a 'considerable length . . . to appease Hitler'. However, he was critical of the Foreign Office, sharing the MEW's appraisal that Stalin would regard as a *casus belli* any demands which constrained his ability 'to stage a "come back"'. The probability of war seemed, therefore, very high. Cripps' conflict with the military was now only at its outset. He had no military expertise, while his military attachés had been deprived of any significant information. The categorical saying often attributed to Cripps that the Germans would cut through the Russians 'like a hot

knife through butter' had in fact been coined by Cavendish-Bentinck at the end of May, and reflected the views held by the COS.[29] In Cabinet, Cripps refrained from a definite assessment of the strength of the Red Army, as it was 'impossible for any foreigner' to estimate its military efficiency. He conveyed, but as mere information, the prevailing view in diplomatic circles in Moscow that Russia could not hold out for more than three or four weeks; this tallied with the estimates of the COS.

While not excluding the possibility that an ultimatum would be presented, Cripps now expressed a strikingly nonconformist opinion flowing naturally from his fundamental understanding of Soviet policy. In the Foreign Office there was a general belief that Stalin would capitulate. If war broke out none the less the army expected a speedy Soviet collapse but was interested in the respite that would be gained. Eden was still toying with the idea of a limited agreement to protect the British rear in the Middle East. Cripps' expectations reflect his rather paradoxical synthesis of logical and visionary thinking: his minute attention to detail and pragmatic solutions were accompanied by an idealistic perception. His idealism, it was observed in Moscow, was 'much more sensible and practical and realistic than so many of the "realistic" views which one hears about Russia'.[30] Although there was an obvious temptation to see Germany and Russia interlocked in war, Cripps believed Britain's interest was for Stalin 'to buy peace' temporarily. The signature under compulsion, he assured the Cabinet, would be 'worthless'. This view was not arrived at on the spur of the moment. Cripps had expounded the same idea to Beatrice Webb shortly after his arrival: 'If Stalin could secure peace by compromise he had better do so. Then the Red Army could be further fortified, while Germany would be exhausted by fighting Great Britain backed by the U.S.A.' Earlier in the day over lunch at the Savoy Cripps had told Eden and Dill that it was best for the Russians not to get involved in the war for a while and remain a 'potential enemy' of Germany.[31] Despite his ultimate wish, it was clear that his exposé leaned heavily towards the likelihood of an invasion. Here, as Attlee recounted,[32] he was more successful in swaying the Cabinet from its scepticism. In the course of the discussion which followed, Cripps dashed Eden's remaining hopes of a limited agreement. On the other hand, in sharp contrast to the views held by both the Foreign Office and the COS, he appealed for unreserved assistance to Russia once hos-

tilities did break out.[33] Beaverbrook followed up by launching the campaign in favour of all-out aid to Russia on the pages of his newspapers.

Churchill's famous broadcast, far from being a spontaneous expression of commitment, told the world 'after his own unrivalled fashion' of decisions which had been reached earlier, as Eden explained a few days later.[34] The motives for pledging aid to Russia, its form and particularly its limitations had all been worked out before Churchill left for Chequers on the afternoon of Friday, 20 June. However, the composition of the speech reveals political genius. The major difficulty facing Churchill that hot Sunday, restlessly pacing the garden and occasionally striding to his office to alter a phrase, was how to reconcile conflicting tendencies and satisfy anticipations at opposed political poles. The German turn eastwards brought immense relief to a worn-out nation which for an entire year had confronted the enemy practically on its own, exposed to demoralizing bombing, constantly in fear of invasion and lacking any foreseeable hope of salvation. To the government, which had been under increasing criticism for the heavy defeats in Europe and after 15–17 June for the collapse of 'Battle-axe' in Libya, the diversion was a godsend. Churchill had to ride with the enthusiasm sweeping the population without alienating those elements which deplored association with Russia; to sound decisive and yet not too committed considering the doubts of the Soviet ability to withstand the onslaught. Perhaps most exacting was the wish of a life-long warrior against communism to retain his integrity while exploiting the coincidental convergence of interests with the Russians.

Initially Churchill contemplated broadcasting to Russia on Saturday night. Assisted by knowledge of the response which his speech aroused, he claims in his memoirs to have postponed it to Sunday when he expected the situation to become 'clear' enough to utilize less 'guarded terms'. The Germans, who had hitherto maintained battle silence over their wireless telegraphic communications, were forced to resort to such means in communicating with Norway. Signals from Enigma on 15, 18 and 20 June revealed that final preparations were being made for a 'general crossing of the frontiers'.[35] This was the first unequivocal declaration of intent which prompted Cripps to alert Maisky. Churchill, however, could not know for certain the zero hour unless he counted, as Cripps did, on Hitler's strange habit of attacking on

Sundays.[36] As Roosevelt's reply to his personal message was expected over the weekend, it seems more likely that coordination with the Americans was uppermost in his thoughts. Neither Cripps nor Beaverbrook, who had already expressed their views earlier, but rather the diffident Winant assumes therefore the major role in helping Churchill to shape his speech. With American entry into the war still a remote possibility, it was realized in the White House, where serious reservations were aired about Churchill's Mediterranean strategy, that an association with Russia, even if precarious, promised the best returns. Unlike the State Department, Roosevelt was prepared to disregard his emotional and ideological differences with the Russians. He viewed his reply to Churchill as so urgent that Winant was flown over to England in a special bomber which did not turn back although one engine failed at the beginning of the journey. He was thus able to reach Chequers and confer with Churchill on Saturday evening. The verbal message he carried assured Churchill that once Germany struck at Russia Roosevelt would make an 'immediate supporting statement following any announcement the Prime Minister might make welcoming Russia as an *ally* [my italics]'. Churchill himself admits that he was greatly relieved by this 'important reassurance'.[37]

Early on Sunday morning Churchill's task was made still easier when news came in of the German invasion. Eden, who was spending the weekend at Chequers, was woken up by Churchill's valet bearing the message and a cigar on a silver salver. A short celebration took place in Churchill's bedroom, after which Eden was urged by Churchill to return to London and meet Maisky so that they could further discuss the broadcast in the light of his reaction.[38] Cripps and Beaverbrook, who came for lunch, had little to contribute beyond moral support. The speech after all was to announce the principles which had guided Cripps throughout and prompted him to activate the sluggish government after his recall. Maisky was familiar with the prevalent British opinion that Russia would either concede to German demands or be reduced to chaos in a short time. In the light of previous experience he postponed his audience with Eden until he had received specific instructions from Moscow. When finally Molotov's speech left little doubt about the state of affairs, Maisky could not respond to Eden's proposals for aid made in the previous week, since they had been condemned by the Russians as provocative. In composing his speech, therefore, Churchill

173

was greatly assisted by the fact that the issues of immediate help or alliance were not raised at all by Maisky. Maisky's immediate concern was to impress on Eden Russia's determination to resist. In return he sought assurances that the British government would not slacken its war effort and would not respond to the peace overtures which he expected Hitler to make. He was equally anxious about the position of the United States, where Hitler would 'hope to appeal to Wall Street as the opponent of bolshevism'. Maisky specifically requested Churchill to pledge unequivocally Britain's determination not to conclude 'in any case' a separate peace and firmly to support Russia. The Russians, still haunted by the spectacle of Britain's joining Germany in a crusade against communism, sought soothing words rather than concrete help. In that respect the speech more than fulfilled their expectations.[39]

On Sunday afternoon it had become easier for Churchill to achieve the right balance in composing his speech which, if reduced to its bare elements, reveals his main objectives. To allay Soviet suspicions Churchill reiterated his resolve 'to destroy Hitler and every vestige of the Nazi regime ... We will never parley, we will never negotiate, with Hitler or any of his gang.' On the home front the same passage was intended to discourage any thoughts in this direction and rally wavering political circles. Churchill's pledge might also have an encouraging propaganda value in occupied territories. On his personal instructions leaflets of the speech were to be dropped over France that night.[40] Having struck the right note Churchill gave vent to his sincere emotional feelings, thus ruling out accusations of an ideological sell-out. The Nazi régime, he stated, was 'indistinguishable from the worst features of Communism'; it was 'devoid of all theme and principle except appetite and racial domination'. Such a statement would uphold the British image in America, and paradoxically would also sound logical and reassuring to Soviet ears. Though confessing to being the 'most persistent opponent of Communism', Churchill admitted that the past was fading away before the spectacle now unfolding; everything was subjected to the purpose of defeating Germany. The closing of ranks in Cabinet and Parliament, while condemning the possibility of separate negotiations, necessitated a clear dissociation from communism. The day after the invasion Churchill was still concerned with the need to quell potential opposition. Much of the Cabinet meeting was devoted not to the implications of the major event on British strategy but to the need for

9  A warm reception for Cripps on his return to Moscow, 27 June 1941

Labour to maintain even in the new circumstances a clear demarcation line with communism in general and the Communist Party in particular. This was duly followed by Attlee in a broadcast on 24 June.[41]

On the really significant aspect of cooperation Churchill, who had been involved in the decision taken during the week, was exceedingly cautious. On the recommendation of the Foreign Office and the COS, he refrained from using the term 'ally' throughout the speech. Instead he described the aid in qualifying terms, which were not immediately apparent to listeners because of the exciting delivery: 'Any man who fights against Nazism will have our aid . . . It follows, therefore, that we shall give whatever help we can to Russia and the Russian people.' This was the limit to which Churchill was prepared to go in defining the future collaboration; he did not go further than what Cripps had advocated in Cabinet on 16 June. The myth of unreserved assistance has been inflated by the retrospective interpretations of key witnesses. John Colville, Churchill's secretary, recalled the instructions he was given not to disclose the content of the speech to Eden, who kept ringing up from Whitehall. His later interpretation was that Churchill wished to prevent Eden from toning down the speech.[42] It is more likely that the impulsive Eden, who had earlier given Maisky pledges of support, would have pressed for more definite commitments.

The irony is that although the United States would not gain any immediate benefit from the new front, Roosevelt was prepared to go much further than Churchill even at the risk of clashing with the State Department and isolationist public opinion. Churchill made no use of the latitude given him by Roosevelt to welcome Russia as an 'ally'. The supporting statement promised by the President was duly read in the White House on 23 June, following Churchill's lead. Although the Americans had not yet seen the transcript of Churchill's broadcast they were informed by Winant of its content on the phone directly from Chequers.[43]

Eden's summary statement in Parliament, conveying the essence of Churchill's speech with his usual dull delivery, was described by those not spellbound by Churchill's speech as 'almost as turgid as passages in *Mein Kampf*' and as having 'little meat on the bone'. In his memoirs Eden gives a more accurate and detached description of Anglo-Soviet

176

relations on Russia's entry into the war which 'could certainly not be described as friendly. They were eased but not transformed.'[44]

## Laying the foundations

The outbreak of hostilities in the East naturally meant that the COS and Defence Committee gradually replaced the Foreign Office and even Cabinet in handling relations with Russia. Despite the significant alteration in political and strategic circumstances there was no corresponding change in the widespread pre-war concepts and prejudices. This was well illustrated in the War Office's directive to field commanders that cooperation did not 'extend to military alliance'; nor were there 'any plans for despatch of military forces or supply of war material'.[45] The COS's initial plans were all short-term and aimed at exploiting to the utmost the 'temporary recession' of the invasion threat to Britain. Churchill's own suggestions of a major raid on the French coast, accompanied by the leakage of 'bogus plans' for operations on an even larger scale and massive air raids on occupied territories, were examined; they were expected to have 'considerable nuisance value' but would be primarily useful in raising morale at home. The intention, as Churchill explained, was to 'make hell while the sun shines'. The COS's Joint Planning Committee presented a multitude of reservations, opting instead for a much smaller raid.[46]

The lack of sufficient landing craft and other technical problems have often been quoted as the main reasons for the absence of diversionary action. At the time, however, neither a thorough examination of such measures nor a balanced reassessment of the new situation was attempted. The inherent reluctance to form an alliance was justified by the unfounded expectations of an imminent Soviet collapse. The opening of a second front seemed 'too hazardous'; it would result in the weakening of the British defences in face of renewed threats of invasion when the German war machine turned westwards once more.[47] The only steps taken which had a direct bearing on Russia were the infiltration of agents to organize sabotage in the Caucasus and the preparation of contingency plans to bomb the Baku oilfields and seize Soviet naval and merchant shipping before they could be handed over to Germany.[48] Maisky's first request for assistance on 23 June met a defiant Cabinet

resolved not to proceed beyond ostentatious gestures. The only minor departures from the course adopted before the war were the recommendation to the COS to select an 'outstanding personality' to head the military mission and a request for Cripps to resume his post.[49]

Cripps returned to Moscow with Churchill's speech as his only terms of reference on future collaboration. Aware of the limitations dictated by the army's perceptions, he conducted his initial contacts most cautiously. However, once again the vacuum allowed him to assert his own opinions and exert pressure on the Cabinet in matters of policy-making. In the past, when Cripps' manoeuvrability was limited by the circumstances in which he found himself, his interventions could be safely ignored. Now, however, all eyes were on Russia and his activities might lead to undesired commitments. The latent dissent gradually came into the open, hindering the successful completion of his mission. Paradoxically the rift and Cripps' popular association with aid to Russia eventually compelled Churchill to seek his inclusion in the Cabinet.

The main burden fell on the military mission. On 23 June Noel Mason-Macfarlane unwillingly agreed to head the mission with the acting rank of lieutenant-general. The choice of Mason-Macfarlane, who had previously served as military attaché in Berlin and Director of Military Intelligence with the British Expeditionary Force, corresponded only too well with the mission's primary task of gathering intelligence.[50] Mason-Macfarlane's instructions conformed with the reservations expressed on the eve of the war. In addition he was specifically warned against entering into any 'political commitment' or reaching independent decisions on assistance and supplies. Dill, seeing Mason-Macfarlane off, left him in no doubt that his duty was not to facilitate collaboration but to 'form centres of improvised resistance further east'. Once this proved hopeless his orders were to reach India over the Pamirs, which, Dill noted, 'would be a very long walk'.[51]

An unusually effusive reception awaited Cripps and the mission when on 26 June they disembarked from the Catalina sea-plane which had flown them from Scotland to Archangel. They were whisked off to a waiting yacht, given a 'terrific feast' and allowed to rest. A special bed had even been brought for Cripps from Moscow, though the others were allotted bunks. The next morning Marshal Timoshenko's luxurious personal Dakota flew them to Moscow, where they were met by senior officials. In the fortnight that had elapsed since his departure

the climate had changed so drastically that Cripps found it difficult to accept that it was the 'same place politically'. Nevertheless, embedded suspicion made the change too hard for both sides to digest. Although all doors were now opened for Cripps he felt that the atmosphere was still 'a bit sticky' and there was 'not as yet full mutual trust'.[52]

In an attempt to pin all the blame on Stalin Maisky presents himself in his memoirs as the champion of united resistance. He depicts in sombre colours the oppressive silence from Moscow in reply to his queries on future relations with Britain.[53] However, on reestablishing contact with the Soviet leadership on 27 June Cripps found the Russians in full control of the diplomatic situation. Maisky's activities mirrored those of his superiors. After establishing that the British were not involved in the German invasion, the Russians were mostly concerned about a slackening of the British war effort. Their primary objective was therefore to secure a formal and binding commitment rather than concrete assistance. On 24 June Maisky pressed for a 'diversion', which, however, was not a demand for a second front, as he claims, but rather a request for sporadic raids on the French coast and for evidence of an increase in RAF raids on Germany. Surely Maisky, who was an expert on military affairs, realized that these were of symbolic value only. In a similar way he prevailed on Eden during those critical days to promote cultural exchanges. Maisky's apprehension was not illogical considering that he was fully aware of the unanimous prognosis that the collapse of the Red Army was imminent. The lack of confidence might lead to the limitation of British assistance, as indeed was the case, and worse still a revival of talks of a separate peace. To counter this Maisky, like Molotov in his famous speech the day after the invasion, drew parallels to 1812, stressing the motive that despite the initial setback the Russians did not have the 'slightest doubt of the ultimate issue. Russia was unconquerable.'[54] Likewise Mason-Macfarlane was struck by Timoshenko's 'over-confidence and exaggerated optimism' during their first meeting and by a manifest lack of interest in even indirect help. That this was merely a smokescreen was evident in his first working session with General Zhukov, who appeared less optimistic and more businesslike. He too, however, refused to impart precise information on the course of the battle.[55]

After Cripps' two interviews with Molotov on 27 June, Steinhardt formed the correct impression that 'suspicion and mistrust' in Russia

continued, 'although somewhat diminished as a result of the exigencies of the situation'.[56] Molotov, like Maisky in London, was therefore pressing for a 'political agreement to define the basis of cooperation'. This was precisely the issue on which neither Churchill nor Cabinet had made up their minds; it was naturally outside Cripps' authority. Like most diplomats in Moscow, Cripps associated Molotov with the German orientation. With the Tass communiqué still ringing in his ears he assumed that Molotov was personally hostile to him. In spite of Cripps' superior analytical powers, as Gafencu observed, he had 'too straightforward a character, and too strict a code, to be able to understand or appreciate the turns and subtleties of Stalin's policy'.[57] Cripps had never been fully aware of the devious game played by the Russians in 1940–1. He erroneously interpreted Molotov's call for a political agreement as including post-war settlements which previously he had rejected outright. His reply was therefore unduly harsh, reminding Molotov that he had earlier warned him that a Russian failure to respond to the British offer would mean a postponement of political issues to the peace conference. After all, he concluded in an untypically vengeful mood, 'our new relations had only existed since last Sunday and it was better to wait till we had learnt to trust each other'.[58] This seeming procrastination, confirmed by commentary in the British press that despite Cripps' return to Moscow 'no formal alliance' was being contemplated, undoubtedly raised the alarm in Moscow. In New York the Russians could read reports from 'responsible sources' in London denying the existence of negotiations towards a 'commitment to refrain from a separate peace with Germany'.[59]

Maisky decided to outflank Churchill who, as he was fast learning, was reluctant to act upon the pledge made in his speech, and Eden, who was 'under too strong an influence' from Churchill. On 27 June he travelled to Beaverbrook's estate at Cherkley. Even Beaverbrook, committed to though not yet infatuated with the Russian cause, 'thunderstruck' him by posing a frank question: 'Will you really fight? Won't the same thing happen with you that happened in France?' Giving the obvious assurances, Maisky presented Beaverbrook with a three-point programme for assistance similar to that drawn up by Molotov in Moscow, which also formed the essence of Stalin's personal briefing to Golikov before he left for London. The most instructive point is that the Russians gave preference to naval action in Murmansk over air and

ground raids in Europe. It was not aimed at providing relief to the ground forces defending Leningrad, as the Defence Committee assumed in turning down the proposal. But bearing in mind the long-range aspects of cooperation, the Russians wished to secure the only available route for communications and supplies.[60] Eden too was urged by Maisky to promote a naval operation and a definition of the scope of collaboration. The British military mission, Maisky complained, lacked sufficient authority and had to refer to London on every small issue.[61]

There are obvious motives, apart from the existence of chronic suspicion, for the Soviet desire for a political agreement. The Russians understood that eventually the burden of supply was bound to fall on the Americans and were therefore already in the midst of negotiations in Washington.[62] On 29 June Zhukov submitted to Mason-Macfarlane his first massive shopping list, including *inter alia* a request for 3,000 fully equipped fighters, a similar number of bombers, 20,000 anti-aircraft guns and technical information on numerous secret devices. When Mason-Macfarlane expressed doubts about London's response, Zhukov suggested the list should be passed on to the Americans. The COS indeed showed no willingness to part with equipment designated for 'intensive operations in progress'. They were prepared to provide the Russians with a single specimen of a night fighter. Informing Mason-Macfarlane about the 'true position' regarding assistance, the COS suggested he should 'temporize' on the assumption that access to Archangel would before long be denied by the Germans.[63]

Supplies to Russia from the United States, however, were conditional on a political understanding with Britain which continued to be the aspiration of Soviet diplomacy. To this end Cripps' services once more became indispensable. At the beginning of July Cripps was assured by Molotov, whom he had now been seeing daily, that his outwardly hostile attitude had been dictated by a determination to postpone war and that relations could now be conducted 'frankly and without reserve'. Cripps was readily pacified; the approach was followed up by encouraging signs. A reception held by him at the embassy was for the first time attended by Russians, among them dignitaries like Vyshinsky and Golikov, accompanied by seven other generals who were '*very* nice, and friendly and cheerful'. The Soviet ambitions coincided with those of Cripps, who arrived in Moscow

resolved to lay the political foundations for collaboration and return home once the situation had stabilized within a 'month or so'.[64] The whole nature of his activity, which in the past had encompassed a large variety of issues, changed accordingly. The embassy was now bustling with the personnel of the large military and economic missions which handled all technical and routine business. 'The Big Boys of the Embassy', noted an observer, 'are working their hind legs off: it has become a very live place at the top.' Once he had become convinced that the Russians were determined to fight on, Cripps expected relations to 'slip gradually into an atmosphere of trust and friendship'. His role was confined to consolidating the alliance in the meantime, 'just keeping a general eye' upon the work of the experts.[65]

It would be naive to assume that Cripps' presence was not felt. The enclosed environment was suitable for the exercise of his natural persuasive qualities. Cripps had been one of the few to have envisaged a German conflict with Russia, though he had been swayed towards a more gloomy prognosis under the influence of the armed forces. His optimistic disposition led him to the conclusion shortly after his return that if the Russians lasted out until the winter this, rather than British military operations, would be the turning point of the war. Mason-Macfarlane had been converted to this overall assessment at an early stage. As he later recalled, he formed with Cripps 'a working partnership' of which he had the 'happiest recollections'.[66] Their association gradually proved a source of embarrassment in London. Despite a marked difference in personalities, life-style and background, they shared some distinctive traits. Independence and open-mindedness are not always associated with a career officer. Mason-Macfarlane, however, formed independent appreciations, acted upon them and was rarely deflected by opportunist considerations in reporting home. He matched Cripps in his almost blind commitment to a cause; he refused to act as an observer (the role assigned to him), and insisted on seeing his recommendations carried through. In fact his sour exchanges with the COS hindered his career. After being recalled in May 1942 he was formally promoted to the post of Governor of Gibralter, whose main task was to act as guide to Churchill's occasional tours of the Rock and to organize firework displays in his honour.[67] Under Cripps' guidance and through his encounters with the Soviet leaders and staff, Mason-Macfarlane too became convinced after only a week in Moscow that

Hitler's hopes of a lightning victory would be 'completely frustrated' by the Red Army.[68] The problem, as Cripps now saw it, was not dispelling the Russians' suspicion and ensuring their cooperation but rather making 'our people equally cooperative in London'. The government, he further complained in his diary, wanted 'all the advantages of co-operation without giving anything' in return. The waning of Churchill's spell was also evident in Cripps' reservations on the reconstruction of the War Cabinet; he had expected it to be 'something big and useful and not merely a reshuffle of a couple of posts'. Mason-Macfarlane reproached the COS in the same vein, expressing his conviction that the Red Army was looking forward to cooperation but the extent depended on 'reciprocal action' in London. He urged them at least to give the Russians the impression that Britain was 'trying to help'.[69]

The old dissonance with Whitehall, temporarily subdued during Cripps' presence in London, now reappeared. Instructions to Cripps to secure the presence of representatives of the military mission in the Russian Far Eastern Headquarters, presumably to ensure a British sanctuary after the fall of Moscow, were disregarded. With Mason-Macfarlane's support Cripps further objected to broaching with the Russians the proposal to demolish the Caucasian oil industry, which, as he explained, implied 'a degree of pessimism as to Soviet power of resistance'. For the same reason he deprecated the idea of establishing consulates in east-central Russia. Recalling past bickering with Cripps, Sargent suggested that all dealings concerning the different missions should be conducted through Maisky. Though Cadogan felt uneasy at acting behind Cripps' back, he consented to take appropriate steps if Cripps continued 'to kick'.[70] The Foreign Office, observed an insider, was in a frame of mind which paralysed action – maintaining the 'usual cautious mood, determined to see the worst and refusing to face the possibility that things might go right and anticipate them'.[71] Eden did display a moderating and even forthcoming attitude but he was promptly overruled by Churchill once relations with Russia assumed significance.

The armed forces became in fact the guardians of the reserved attitude. Any insinuation through Cripps and Mason-Macfarlane of the gravity of the situation was seized upon to enhance the gloomy predictions. The views held by the War Office, noted Harold Nicolson at the Ministry of Information, were 'coloured by political prejudices and

by the fact that Stalin murdered most of his senior officers'.[72] Revolted by the thought of a coordinated policy, they insisted that the war effort should be 'devoted to the accomplishment of a definite strategy for winning the war without having allowed for Russian aid'. The only avenue for victory seemed to be America's inevitable entry into the war and continued aid. They warned against being drawn into 'a false position' by undertaking a military action for political reasons. The Defence Committee and the COS therefore answered Molotov's urgent request for a major naval operation in the North with a minor one in the Norwegian fjords.[73] Neither Eden nor Beaverbrook succeeded during the first week of July in reversing the decision on assistance. The COS, adequately informed about the extent of the Soviet disasters through Enigma, entrenched themselves in their previous assessment that the Russian army was 'too inexperienced and Russian machine too clumsy'. They expected the imminent fall of Moscow and Leningrad, the self-demobilization of the army and the creation of a Nazi–Russian government.[74] It is no wonder that, in contrast with the hospitality that had been lavished on the British mission in Moscow, Golikov and the Soviet delegation were given a cool reception in their meetings with David Margesson, the War Secretary, and the COS.[75] The failure to draw up contingency plans to assist Russia in case of war was recognized by Cadogan, who commented on the Cabinet meeting at the end of the first week of fighting: 'We seem to have no plan for harrying Germans in West. Spoke to A. [Eden] about this, who also worried. "Daylight sweeps" no use, as the Germans ignore them! And we lost masses of bombers at night. No plan for raids. Nothing doing!'[76]

It was left for diplomacy to disguise the bare facts. In a retrospective attempt to play up his role in consolidating cooperation, Churchill claims that in the absence of a Soviet response to his speech he thought it his 'duty' to break the ice. He therefore addressed Stalin on 7 July pledging aid to Russia. Before Cripps' departure Churchill had in fact agreed to provide him with a personal letter to Stalin but apparently, thought Cripps, 'overlooked the matter'. Cripps reverted to the subject when the effusiveness of his welcome wore off and the difficulties in establishing contact seemed unsurmountable. He hoped the message would gain him direct access to Stalin. Typically Cripps also presented a draft which he expected Churchill to adopt. Cripps' draft, however, had gone beyond the limits set to cooperation in London in implying a

solid alliance. His main themes were the resolve of the British people to 'stand side by side with the peoples of the U.S.S.R.' and the need of 'devising ways and means whereby we can make our common action effective'.[77] Cripps naively assumed that the failure to hand him the letter was accidental. Eden rightly understood that a message was unlikely to impress Stalin unless it were accompanied by definite promises of military assistance, which he realized was 'difficult if not impossible'. He continued therefore to oppose the idea unless it became obvious that Molotov was deliberately undermining relations. For the same reason he discouraged Churchill from fraternizing with Maisky.[78]

Faced with these arguments, Cripps feared that the advantage gained by Russia's continued resistance might be forfeited. The key, therefore, lay in the United States' preparedness to act in unison with Britain. He wished Churchill to impress on Roosevelt that it might be too late if the Americans were to 'wait to see the issue of the German attack'. Various factors seem to have prevented Churchill from acting on this recommendation. He may have feared that he had already put the President in a difficult position by seeking a supporting statement considering the current aversion to communism and the opinions of the State Department. However, more telling was concern at the sacrifice Britain would have to make in competing with the Russians for American supplies. In his message to Roosevelt on 1 July Churchill preferred to omit any reference to the gravity of the situation, leaving Halifax to make casual appeals in the spirit of Cripps' proposal.[79] Churchill concurred with the COS that American supplies and eventual participation in the war were the only guarantor of victory. While his speech paid dividends in relations with Russia only for a short while, it had an immense success in the United States. Roosevelt told Halifax that he expected the 'whole thing would now boil up very quickly, and that there would very soon be shooting'. Though not as pessimistic as the British, he too was thinking about the new front in terms of a respite gained by Britain. Churchill's preservation of a cautious and reserved attitude was clearly calculated in the first place not to estrange the Americans.[80]

Meanwhile the initial difficulties in Moscow had been overcome and cooperation made swift progress. On 6 July Cripps addressed Churchill in an assertive and argumentative message which would become the guideline of the remaining period of his ambassadorship. The gist of it ran:

I think so far we have done quite well in overcoming the 20 years of distrust & suspicion . . . What is required now above all things is some *action* by us to demonstrate our desire to help even at some risk to ourselves if necessary . . . They realise what their fighting means to us and not unnaturally they look to us to do something practical to reciprocate the help they are giving. For this purpose speed – as you will fully realise – is of the essence of the matter . . . There is I think a liability in some quarters to regard this campaign as a matter of a few days and to over-emphasize difficulties that might occur if there was a collapse here. In order to avoid those difficulties we are in danger of encouraging the collapse if we do not fully and frankly give the Russians everything possible to help and strengthen their resistance . . . I would very much like you to see all those concerned and impress this point of view upon them so that there is no delay and no red-tapism stands on the way. Quick action in every field is vital in my belief and I am sure you will share that point of view.[81]

Churchill's vague promise of help and evasive definition of the association was also put to the test by Maisky. On 7 July he reminded Eden in his ironic manner that at long last Britain had 'an Ally who could fight and was determined to do so'. Maisky advocated combined operations and raids in France even if their psychological effect was in excess of their actual military value.[82] Although Cripps had meanwhile dropped his request for a personal message to Stalin, Churchill decided to seize the opportunity and exploit his reputation with the Russians to persuade Stalin that the government was determined to forward 'all aid in our power'. As this was practically nil he intended, as admitted elsewhere in his memoirs, 'to fill the void by civilities'. Indeed, as recorded by Cadogan, Eden realized after consultations with Churchill on 1 July: 'We are not prepared to take advantage of this Heaven-sent (and short) opportunity of the Germans being heavily engaged in Russia. We shall look awful fools! But there it is.'[83] Any hint of a direct commitment, such as figured prominently in Cripps' letter to Churchill and draft telegram to Stalin, were replaced with expressions of admiration for the 'strong and spirited' Soviet resistance and the 'bravery and tenacity of the Red Army'. Aid was now defined in even more qualified terms than in the famous speech as what 'time, geography, and our growing resources allow'.[84]

Cripps handed the letter to Stalin, whom he found friendly and frank. After his trying experiences with the Soviet government it was a

'relief to be able to talk to someone who can say what he thinks and whose word you know is the last word'. What impressed him most was Stalin's confession of the seriousness of the situation and yet confidence in an ultimate defeat of Germany. It is not surprising that, given the scornful appreciation of Soviet capabilities and the absence of a binding commitment in Churchill's message, Stalin was anxious to reach a formal understanding. To forestall unnecessary haggling he proposed an agreement of 'purely general nature' under two heads: mutual assistance 'without defining quantity and quality', and a mutual pledge against the conclusion of a separate peace. It was clear to Cripps that the fear of a separate peace was still uppermost in the Soviet mind. Curiously he was fully aware of his own contribution but lacked the slightest remorse: 'I don't blame them on being nervous on this score as we have tried to make them so in the past so as to prevent them going too far with Germany.' He was, however, determined to redress it by demanding from the Cabinet the prompt adoption of the proposal. Aware of the state of affairs in London[85] he took the precautionary measure of admitting to Stalin that there were still elements of public opinion which 'needed converting' to the thought of full alliance. He therefore suggested, as a possible alternative, an exchange of notes.[86]

The handling of relations with Russia, now that an adequate degree of confidence had been established by Cripps and the mission in Moscow, brought to the fore the latent strain in Eden's relations with Churchill. A previously unnoticed minor crisis concerning the agreement exposes Eden's weakness in this uneven competition and the precedent set by Churchill in asserting his predominance in formulating policy towards Russia. At the outset of the new war Eden's eastern policy lay in ruins. He naturally saw in Russia, particularly since relations with the United States were conducted almost exclusively by Churchill, an opportunity of enhancing his own political position. Impressed by Cripps' reporting on the change in the Soviet attitude and by Maisky's appeal, Eden had become impatient with Churchill's adherence to 'paper undertakings'.[87] Eden had also been alerted by an anomalous shrewd memorandum originating in the Information Department of the Office in which the possibility, hitherto dismissed as idle talk, was raised that Russia might before long be in the field to repulse the Germans. The memorandum agreed with Cripps that it was essential to anticipate such

a possibility by drawing a post-war map which could 'fire the imagination of Europe'. Eden therefore made an excursion into the military aspects of the cooperation by urging Churchill to consider mounting a major operation even if it entailed a substantial revision of the prevailing overall strategy.[88]

Russia's entry into the war had revived Churchill's somewhat waning popularity, especially after his stunning speech. He had no intention, however, of overruling the COS, where an uncompromising opposition to the idea of collaboration persisted. On the day that Churchill's message was dispatched to Stalin, the COS issued guidelines to its representatives in the forthcoming negotiations with the Soviet military mission. They were informed of the major objective of prolonging Russian resistance for 'as long as possible' but reminded that 'we are not allied with Russia nor do we entirely trust that country'.[89] Stalin's relatively modest request for an agreement presented Churchill with a comfortable chance to capitalize on the change of fortunes without conceding much in return. On receipt of Cripps' telegram at 2 a.m. on 9 July Churchill requested Eden to come over and discuss instant action, which he declined to do. When he arrived at the Office in the morning Eden found, to his manifest dismay, a draft of yet another personal message to Stalin which Churchill wished Cabinet to approve. It appeared that Churchill was adopting in relations with Russia the same type of personal relationship he had formed with Roosevelt, thereby bypassing Eden. Eden raised immediate objections, reprimanding Churchill for becoming 'involved in the day to day details of diplomacy'.[90]

Meanwhile the Cripps–Stalin proposal was undergoing the customary examination in the Foreign Office. Sargent observed that an exchange of notes would be binding and would consist of an agreement clothed in an 'inappropriate form'. On the other hand, a treaty of mutual assistance was going too far by opening the door to 'embarrassing discussions about the duration of the agreement, denunciation etc.'. The alternative, a 'constructive compromise', as Eden explained to Winant when seeking American approval, was a joint declaration which was both binding and honourable. To Cadogan it seemed more like 'one of our famous half measures'. The rather awkward precedent quoted was the similar form in which France and Britain had pledged to refrain from a separate peace in March 1940.[91] When Cabinet met in

the evening Eden found Churchill 'most arbitrary' in pressing for both the acceptance of Stalin's proposal and a personal message. Eden now exercised his mediatory talents. He preserved the Foreign Office's and his own reputation by quoting Winant's reservations about a treaty, to which he had in fact been manoeuvred by Eden earlier in the afternoon. Churchill, on the other hand, established his right against Eden's token protests to break the news to Stalin; 'the sheep', observed Cadogan 'baa'ed in chorus'.[92] Eden was so 'fed up' with Churchill's 'monopolistic tendencies' that in private he was even talking about resignation. Churchill, however, knew how to put Eden in his place and yet pacify him. Some days later he apologized for being so 'tiresome' over his telegram to Stalin.[93] A pattern had, however, been set for the future conduct of relations with Russia which was also to affect Cripps' standing in Moscow.

The message was delivered to Stalin by Cripps the next morning and the atmosphere was so encouraging that Cripps produced the draft agreement which he had been instructed to withhold pending American approval. Stalin's only request was for the title to read 'Agreement for Joint Action'; this presented no problem once it was established beyond doubt in London that 'joint action' in Russian had the distinct connotation of concerted action rather than alliance. Meanwhile Roosevelt, who so far had been at least one step ahead of the British, readily endorsed the agreement which, he was assured, did not constitute a treaty.[94] Cripps, who had become increasingly anxious about the Cabinet's attitude, was relieved and astonished to receive confirmation already in the morning of 12 July. Oblivious of the motives which had led Churchill to act promptly, he gave the government 'full marks' for their decision.[95]

The ceremony took place at 5 p.m. The text of the agreement, which in fact corresponded closely to the Cripps–Stalin earlier version, provided a commitment that the signatories would 'mutually undertake to render each other assistance and support of all kinds' in the war and would neither negotiate nor conclude a separate peace. At Cripps' explicit request the Kremlin's traditional festivities were modest. There was champagne and Soviet chocolates, which some jokingly suggested were an attempt to impress Laurence Cadbury, the chocolate manufacturer, who now headed the British economic mission to Moscow. Cripps 'definitely and ostentatiously' abandoned his teetotalism for the

10 The signing of the Anglo-Soviet agreement at the Kremlin, 12 July
1941

occasion. In the warm late afternoon Cripps then changed out of his
'glad rags' and joined the customary afternoon tea party at the
American dacha by the river out of Moscow. The announcement was
postponed for a day pending the approval of the Dominions, but observers
sensed the exceptional quality of the occasion, with Cripps himself
'natty in a costume of white trousers and blue coat . . . and the rest of
the staff of the embassy, all attired in their best suits. Their heads shone
from combing, their cheeks from shaving. They were obviously
excited.'

The far-reaching significance attached by Cripps to the agreement
stood in contrast to its interpretation in London as yet another means of
exploiting the breathing space. To Cripps, as is evident from his diary,
it signalled a crossroads: 'Well, so closes a chapter in the History of the
world and I believe that a far more hopeful chapter has opened in which
the sequels of this agreement will play a large and vitally important part
if the situation is handled aright.' The agreement comprised the foundations for a collaboration that would 'enable a post-war world to be

built on sounder and safer lines'. Henceforth he would maintain that unreserved association with Russia before the war ended was essential.[96]

The waning of Cripps' influence in London was further demonstrated in his attempts to participate actively in the negotiations leading to the Polish–Soviet agreement which followed the Anglo-Soviet accord. From the outset Eden showed unusual zeal to secure the agreement, and not only because of the British commitment to Poland in 1939. To pacify opposition to Russia in Catholic and Polish circles in the United States was an overriding necessity, as Eden told Churchill, in the attempt to 'carry the United States Government in what we are doing'.[97] Cripps was drawn into the negotiations only after it was learnt on 24 June that Maisky was reluctant to approach Moscow about the release of 300,000 Polish prisoners believed to be interned in Russia.[98] Cripps' services became obsolete when he found Molotov most forthcoming; he was prepared to arm Polish units and even reach an agreement on the establishment of an independent state whose frontiers would correspond with 'ethnographical Poland'.[99]

Further negotiations on the composition of the Polish delegation and the boundary issue could now be pursued between Sikorski and Maisky through Eden's eager mediation. The Poles, pressing for the annulment of the 1939 agreements, sought Soviet recognition of the pre-war borders.[100] The Russians, determined to achieve a political agreement with Britain and in the midst of direct negotiations with the Americans on aid, were anxious for a quick solution. On 11 July Maisky conveyed, to Eden's clear satisfaction, an agreement in principle. Eden's remaining problem was to reconcile Sikorski's territorial demand with the Soviet wish to defer the question to the peace conference.[101] In the meantime a new issue, which demanded Cripps' intervention, was that the number of Polish officers admitted to be held by the Russians fell below the figure specified by the Poles. It seemed to confirm the rumours circulating in London of a massacre performed by the retiring Russians. When the debate reopened in 1943 with the discovery of mass graves at Katyn, it led Stalin to revoke his recognition of the Sikorski government. Cripps urged Molotov on the eve of the signing of the Anglo-Soviet declaration to think of some 'practical and conclusive way of substantiating a denial so as to destroy at once the evil effect of this vicious propaganda'. Molotov followed his advice with a strongly worded denial accusing the

Germans of trying to 'cover up their crime and spread provocative fables'. To hasten negotiations the Russians also released high-ranking Polish officers and started organizing several Polish divisions.[102] Hard pressed on the battlefield and determined to secure American assistance, Molotov even agreed in conversation with Cripps to accept tacitly the Polish boundary definition. The British were to supplement the agreement with an undertaking reaffirming their commitment to Poland's 1939 borders. Cripps believed he could remove the last obstacle, which was a matter of *amour propre*, by careful drafting which did not imply Soviet aggression in the occupation of Poland.[103]

Once the Russians' objections were removed and the draft accepted by the Cabinet, the Poles were suddenly reluctant to proceed. They were showing, as was grudgingly remarked in the Foreign Office, the 'lack of political judgement, which [had] handicapped them throughout their history'.[104] To overcome the holdup in the negotiations Cripps decided on his own initiative to employ his legal skills and hammer out with Stalin a 'better' agreement based on the London draft. Stalin agreed to a compromise including the establishment of relations, the forming of an independent Polish army in Russia and the annulment of the German–Soviet agreement with regard to Poland. Cripps believed that the major Soviet concession was a separate public protocol declaring that all Polish citizens detained in Russia would be granted an immediate amnesty. In exchange Cripps suggested Sikorski should agree to postpone the discussion of the future borders. He did not expect this to prove a problem in view of the separate British undertaking.[105] Since it was more favourable to the Poles, Cripps' draft was recognized in London as 'definitely preferable' to the earlier one. However, Cripps' satisfaction over the 'excellent document' was premature. Maisky heard of it from Cadogan and immediately postponed the signature, which had been provisionally fixed for 28 July pending further communications with Moscow. He was particularly dissatisfied with the additional assurances to the Poles made by Eden and now sanctioned by Stalin. Cripps' typical interference therefore seemed to have achieved the reverse effect. It was a further proof of the necessity of conducting relations from London. In a 'desperate telegram' Cripps was instructed by Eden to hold his hand.[106] Indeed after Maisky's consultations, probably as a protest to Eden's assurances to the Poles, Cripps informed Eden that the Russians now proposed that

the agreement might be signed in London but that the release of prisoners would be regarded as a personal undertaking by Stalin. Eden, visualizing the failure of his long mediatory efforts, instructed Cripps to secure the acceptance of the London draft.[107] Eventually, probably in view of a visit by Hopkins to Moscow announced at short notice, the Russians gave way; so did the Poles under severe pressure from the British. The episode increased the strain marking Cripps' interchanges with London since his return to Moscow.

## New initiatives

The Anglo-Soviet declaration was the high-water mark of Cripps' achievement in Moscow. The test lying ahead was its conversion into an effective partnership. Early reactions on both sides seemed encouraging. The obviously relieved Soviet press printed photographs of the ceremony on its front pages, commenting rather prematurely that the failure of Hitler's peace overtures had now resulted in the 'mighty Anglo-Soviet coalition'.[108] In London, where Stalin's mysterious disappearance in the first two weeks of the war had led Dalton to wonder whether he was not preparing once more 'to sell out', fears of 'another Brest Litovsk' were dispelled by the signature. Cripps' own reputation was enhanced; Maisky now looked to him to lead the British left after the war because the present leaders were 'more reactionary than any liberals and tories'.[109] Eden congratulated him on the achievement of the 'Alliance, as we now dub it'. The closing lines of his telegram, however, contained ominous signs: 'We are doing our best not to complicate your task more than we can help.' Churchill was content merely to thank Cripps for the caviare he had sent to himself and Eden.[110] Cripps was misled, however, by Churchill's unambiguous definition of relations in Parliament the day after the signature: 'It is, of course, an alliance and the Russian people are now our allies.' Cripps expected that the Russians would be 'thrilled' by the statement; he was unaware that it was made in response to challenges in the House about the nature of the collaboration and of the army's persistent objection to a co-ordinated strategy. Eden, who knew better, was 'worried . . . at the lack of support of the Chiefs of Staff and even of the P.M. who, for all his brave words, is reluctant to agree to raids'.[111]

There were other alarming symptoms. The BBC customarily closed

its programmes with the playing of all allied national anthems. As early as 4 July Churchill issued instructions that the 'International' should '*on no account*' be included; it was noted at the Foreign Office that the 'Marseillaise', 'itself a revolutionary tune', was broadcast. Attempts to create cultural forums to popularize the bond with Russia were similarly vetoed. Cripps' own offer to record a regular 'Sunday postscript' for the BBC fared no better.[112]

The War Office viewed with misgivings even the minimal undertaking embodied in the agreement, expecting the Soviet government to be swiftly pushed beyond the Urals. A puppet Nazi government would then be installed in Moscow; by distributing land it would eventually gain the allegiance of most of the peasants now under the rule of the Bolsheviks. The agreement, they argued, precluded the possibility of supporting such elements which might be prepared to continue the struggle but no longer to recognize the sovereignty of the Soviet régime. A day after the conclusion of the agreement Mason-Macfarlane, who followed Cripps in criticizing the COS for denying help, was severely reprimanded. He was informed that neither combined operations nor the alteration of grand strategy were contemplated, as the Russians were fully responsible for Britain's desperate situation. The Russians were vindictively advised to 'save themselves just as we have saved ourselves in the Battle of Britain and in the Atlantic'. Mason-Macfarlane should be consoled by the fact that the increasing American aid to Britain would allow her to defeat Germany 'in time'.[113]

The agreement was timely for the Russians. It coincided with a temporary pause in the German advance after the exhaustion of their first thrust. However, in terms of loss of life, equipment and territory the Red Army had been devastated. The Germans had penetrated approximately 250 miles all along the front, reaching the outskirts of Smolensk in the centre and Kiev in the South. When the offensive was resumed in mid-July with the capture of Smolensk, Moscow came under a real threat. Stalin now matched his predominance in diplomatic affairs by assuming control over the armed forces, culminating in his appointment as Supreme Commander on 8 August.[114]

The upsurge of Soviet demands for action, which reached its peak in Stalin's personal message to Churchill on 19 July, ensued from the resumption of the offensive. Hardly had the ink dried on the agreement

when Maisky made the first appeal for a major diversion, thereby admitting the extent of the damage inflicted on the Russian air force in the early stages of the campaign. It was essential, he told Eden, to supply the Russians with new aircraft which the Americans were willing to provide from the British quota. He justified a diversion on land by claiming that the danger of an invasion of Britain was diminished by the Soviet engagement of the bulk of the German armoured divisions. Some days later he unwittingly echoed Eden's own feelings by complaining to him about the failure of the War Office to take account of Russia's entry into the war. The government, he reproached Eden, was giving Russia 'enormous assurances of help' but shrinking from 'giving effect to them'. Finally in a subsequent meeting he simply begged Eden not to 'underestimate the importance of providing Russia with some concrete military help'. The return to diplomatic channels reflected the failure of the military mission to establish a constructive relationship with the COS. Golikov was ordered back to Moscow on 12 July and shortly afterwards left for Washington.[115]

Having failed to extract any reply from Eden, Maisky initiated a direct appeal from Stalin, who also admitted, though in guarded terms, the 'tense situation' which he attributed to the 'unexpected . . . sudden attack'. Although Stalin understood the difficulties involved in a diversion, he believed the time was propitious for executing one in northern Europe or France while German troops were tied up in the East. The timing and mode of presentation of the note were well calculated. Maisky later claimed the situation at the front had become too grave to send the message through the usual diplomatic channels. He was also aware of Eden's helplessness and therefore further sidetracked him by adopting the habit of personally delivering to Churchill all Stalin's telegrams.

His journey to Chequers that Saturday must have been dictated, however, by weightier considerations. After failing to secure tangible results through London, Cripps or the mission in Moscow, the Russians had diverted their efforts to Washington. Their main objective was, as Golikov had been instructed, 'to supervise the placing of Soviet orders and to cooperate in the procurement of supplies and equipment'. At the beginning of August Golikov indeed succeeded in convincing the President that as Russia was bearing the full brunt of the war she was entitled to assistance. He also appeased the isolationist opposition by emphasizing

the abundant manpower at Russia's disposal with which she could engage Germany on her own if adequately equipped. The Americans showed ample goodwill: restrictions on trade with Russia were abolished and a five-year credit for the purchase of war materials was granted. Roosevelt had personally interfered in favour of expediting supplies; his close advisers had persuaded him, in contrast to the views held in London and the State and War Departments, that if massive help reached Russia before October she might be in a position to check the German advance. As a result of his intervention an interdepartmental committee was set up to supervise the organization of supplies.[116] Opposition from the State and War Departments none the less persisted. In Moscow, Major Ivan Yeaton, the military attaché, held fast to his predictions of an imminent collapse. He had great influence over Steinhardt who, as Cripps observed, was 'wholly concerned with trying to get away from Moscow'. Even within the White House there were dissenting voices: 'We cannot', warned Berle, 'bet our whole shirt on the continuance of relationship with Russia.'[117]

Shortly after the conclusion of the Anglo-Soviet agreement Harry Hopkins, Roosevelt's most intimate and trusted adviser, arrived in London to make preliminary arrangements for the first Churchill–Roosevelt summit scheduled for mid-August in Placentia Bay, Newfoundland. Aid to Russia figured prominently on the agenda. Hopkins was to impress on Churchill the need for a change of emphasis in the grand strategy consisting of a diminution of activity in the Middle East and a partial diversion of supplies destined for Britain under 'Lend–Lease' to Russia. Maisky was probably exploiting Hopkins' presence at Chequers over the weekend of 19–20 July to exert further pressure on Churchill. After reading Stalin's message Churchill drew a vivid picture of the massive fortifications on the French coast which the Germans had energetically constructed over the past year. He left Maisky in no doubt that a military diversion was out of the question. Back in the drawing room Maisky was introduced to Hopkins who, together with Winant, was predictably more sympathetic to the idea of aid. This acquaintance, whether coincidental or planned (the latter is more likely), paved the way to a series of rushed meetings ending in Hopkins' impetuous decision to visit Moscow to gain a first-hand impression and discuss details of assistance with Stalin before joining Churchill on the sea voyage to Placentia Bay.[118]

11 and 12 Maisky entertains Churchill and representatives of all Allied governments to lunch at the Soviet embassy, 29 August 1941

Churchill's reply to Stalin, drafted over the weekend in consultation with the COS, followed the line he had taken with Maisky. In his meeting with Eden on Monday Maisky launched the reoriented Soviet approach. It was based on the assumption that in the foreseeable future the Red Army would have to fight on its own. If the British regarded the difficulties of opening a second front as 'insuperable', Maisky complained, they could 'do more to assist Russia with supply'.[119] The main effort was now focused on securing American help; that depended to a large extent on British acquiescence in a diversion of supplies from America which she badly needed for pursuing her own aims in the Middle East. An open contest for limited American resources therefore ensued. The switch could also be detected on 23 July when Golikov met Eden on his way to the United States. Rather than advocating a second front, Golikov explored the possibility of occupying Spitzbergen and protecting the Greenland–Iceland supply route – Russia's lifeline to the West. Apart from this, he was interested only in meeting Hopkins and Averell Harriman, Roosevelt's roving ambassador, both of whom dealt directly with supply.[120]

The deflection of Soviet demands to material aid forced the Cabinet to coordinate its policies with the United States. Churchill was put in a delicate position. Unwilling to make sacrifices which would jeopardize any of his offensive plans, he was equally anxious to make a good impression on Roosevelt in their first meeting. The Cabinet therefore decided on 24 July to react more favourably to Soviet demands of material help in spite of a clash with the COS. For the first time Churchill instructed the COS to regard the issue of assistance as 'most urgent' and handle it in a 'sympathetic spirit'. When this did not bring about the desired results he overrode their objections to the dispatch of two squadrons of Hurricanes to Murmansk; 'We must give', he insisted, 'what help is possible.'[121]

The task of laying the foundations for the future Grand Alliance was now entrusted to Hopkins. Although predisposed to help Russia, Hopkins came to Moscow merely as an observer determined to resolve the controversy in Washington over the new association. In Moscow he could hardly expect to rely on Steinhardt, who was torn between his hostility to the idea of collaboration and his politician's instinct to please Hopkins. Steinhardt quickly sensed Hopkins' inclination. On reaching Moscow Hopkins was under the impression that the Wehrmacht would find it

difficult to penetrate the hundreds of miles of solid forests which he had seen during his long flight from Archangel. While briefing Hopkins, Steinhardt opted to remain noncommittal. He merely conveyed Yeaton's pessimistic appreciations countered by casual remarks on the historical lessons of Russia's magnificent resistance to invaders. Hopkins' biographer assures us that he was satisfied with this account, spending the rest of his first day in Moscow in leisurely sightseeing with Steinhardt.[122] This is based on the version which Hopkins published in 1941 where he adopted, as did many politicians before and after him, Cripps' ideas as his own. He was naturally unable to disclose the essence of his conversations with Cripps, which involved criticism of the American embassy.

Hopkins found his real encouragement and enthusiastic support at the British embassy. Shortly before Hopkins' arrival Cripps had abandoned hope that the Cabinet would proceed beyond the agreement he had secured. In the week preceding the visit Churchill, having overcome Eden's initial opposition, assumed direct charge of relations with Russia. A stream of personal communications at the end of July strove to win over Stalin by flattering references to the Russians' 'valiant fight', a clear attempt to revive the impact made by his memorable speech. The compliments amounted to a confession of Britain's unwillingness to comply with any of the Soviet requests apart from the gesture of releasing the Hurricanes. Churchill's third telegram to Stalin within a week was perhaps the most characteristic. After promising a delivery of scarce rubber, Churchill reverted to the main subject; he introduced Hopkins as a British as well as American representative, thus implying his share in the forthcoming American assistance.[123] This arrangement suited Cripps very well, enabling him to push through some of his own ideas. Cripps, like Eden, had been extremely critical of Churchill's intrusion and tried to curb the flow of 'rather emotional messages' which seemed to lose their effect through 'repetitiveness'. Eden was fully aware that the 'sentimental and florid' telegrams were liable to have an adverse impact on Stalin, who would 'think guff no substitute for guns'.[124] Cripps had, therefore, worked out short- and long-term plans for collaboration. These were conveyed to Eden in a personal letter, now missing from the archives, which was luckily copied by Cripps into his diary. With a typically pragmatic and yet visionary outlook Cripps advocated a preliminary discussion with the Russians on the post-war

structure of Europe before their victory. This was supplemented by demands for concrete help. Cripps further wished Eden to persuade Churchill to relieve him of his post, as he had been promised in London, and allow him later to return to Moscow not as an ambassador but as an emissary 'especially instructed to discuss with Stalin the post-war problems'. He believed he had established a degree of intimacy with Stalin which could enable him if he came back 'clothed with special authority' to reach such an agreement.[125]

Cripps' criticism and vigorous intervention were also a result of his sudden confrontation with the reality of war. Hitherto a rather sur-realistic calm had embraced Moscow interrupted only by false alarms, the filling of every open space in the city with dummy rooftops and buildings to confuse German pilots, and obvious internal security measures. The war was brought home to him with the first night air bombardment of Moscow on 23 July which thereafter became an almost nightly routine. In the very first wave three incendiaries had fallen on the roof of the embassy, causing severe damage to the building. The fire was finally brought under control by the combined efforts of the staff and the heads of the missions. Whereas other ambassadors fled to their dachas every evening, in the following three months Cripps stayed on at the embassy which was in a particularly vulnerable position just across the narrow river from the Kremlin.[126]

Not yet fully aware of the unbridgeable gap separating him from London, Cripps initiated his scheme through Hopkins, whom he had met before during his 1935 visit to Washington. Hopkins, accompanied by Steinhardt, visited Cripps on his first morning in Moscow. Sensing the strained atmosphere, he sent Steinhardt away on the pretext that he was carrying confidential reports from Churchill. Mason-Macfarlane and Admiral Miles, head of the naval mission, were then ushered in and impressed on Hopkins the need for and various ways of supplying the Russians. When left alone Hopkins admitted, in response to Cripps' criticism of the American representation in Moscow, that they had 'entirely failed to take any broad view of the situation'; Roosevelt was 'all out to help all he could even if the Army and Navy authorities in America did not like it'. There is little doubt that the conversation was most cordial and constructive. Cripps was delighted to find out that he saw with Hopkins 'very much eye to eye about the necessities of the situation'. He was all praise for Hopkins, whom he found: 'grown in

13 Harry Hopkins with Cripps and his Airedale Joe at the British embassy

stature as a statesman . . . He is a real democratic idealist and this is the sort of struggle that would bring out everything that man has in him, which is a very great deal. It was a great joy to have the opportunity of talking with him.'[127]

The first meeting with Stalin in the Kremlin confirmed Cripps' expectations. Hopkins was clearly enchanted by Stalin, who was friendly and open. He was particularly impressed by Stalin's confidence in his ability to 'fight for three or four years' provided he was granted long-term assistance, anti-aircraft guns and aluminium.[128] Cripps was briefed by Hopkins on the nature of the conversation over lunch at the British embassy on the next day. During their conversation, which lasted far longer than planned, Cripps produced some key ideas on the line which Hopkins should adopt in his concluding meeting with Stalin. These started a chain of developments with far-reaching consequences on the course of the Alliance. The two further discussed the attitude

which Churchill and Roosevelt should adopt in their imminent summit meeting.[129]

In the evening Stalin was again forthcoming, describing mostly the progress of the war and impressing on Hopkins that the 1942 spring offensive depended on the extent to which the Red Army was re-equipped. Hopkins now elaborated the scheme, which had originated with Cripps, for the three governments to convene a conference in Moscow at which 'the relative interests of each front as well as the interests of our several countries, was fully and jointly explored'. Such an association should form the basis for regulating supply problems. Cripps had convinced Hopkins of the need to hold the conference at ministerial level with Stalin's personal participation. This was based on his own experience, which Hopkins shared after meeting minor officials, that progress in relations could be achieved only through direct and authoritative dealings with Stalin. On the morning of 1 August, shortly before his departure, Hopkins held his last meeting with Cripps, who was delighted to see his plan materializing. They now agreed on the course of action at the summit which Hopkins should recommend to Churchill and Roosevelt. Cripps in fact brought with him a three-page joint message to Stalin which was eventually adopted by the two leaders.[130] He further transmitted through Hopkins a memorandum to be discussed in Placentia Bay in which he argued that the speediest victory against Germany could be achieved 'by way of Russia'. In veiled criticism of Churchill's communications with Stalin, he suggested that supplies to Russia should be considered not as 'merely sparing to a partner or ally what we feel we can spare but rather as the point upon which we should concentrate all the supplies that we can raise because that is at the moment the weakest point of the enemy and therefore our best chances of success'. It would be 'supreme folly', he warned, to deprive the Russians of material which 'might turn their retreat into a "rout"'.

Cripps thus found himself at odds with his own government on strategic priorities but in tune with the prevailing mood in the White House. To increase the chances of his scheme Cripps also addressed Roosevelt, whose guest he had been in 1935. The caviare he had sent to him conveyed the 'gratitude of those of us who appreciate the importance of the front here'. Hopkins' visit, he commented, was a 'real breath of fresh air' and he hoped that Roosevelt and Churchill would be

able 'to implement the suggestion which I know he is going to put forward'.[131] Hopkins' own resolute telegram impressing on Roosevelt the Russians' confidence about the front and their 'unbounded determination to win' was in many ways a victory for Cripps, who had found a way to communicate his plans to Stalin and to impress London and Washington.[132]

The principle of Cripps' plan was simple. As Hopkins told Stalin in their first meeting, his mission was originally confined to exploration. Cripps, however, had practically committed him, without seeking the authorization of the President, to a high-level coordination of effort with the Russians on a basis of equality. Cripps of course had a personal role in view. He now used Hopkins to convey another letter to Eden and asked him to prevail on Churchill to facilitate Cripps' return to England. If he were appointed a member of the War Cabinet he could then return to Moscow 'with the added authority not to stay but to settle up the future plan of help' in conjunction with an American representative. Some days later he told Steinhardt in confidence that a high-ranking member of the War Cabinet would soon reach Moscow to coordinate British aid and strategy. Although he mentioned Eden and Beaverbrook as the likely candidates, Cripps eventually confided to Steinhardt that he himself was expected shortly to be appointed as a member of the Cabinet. In his second letter to Eden, Cripps outlined the 'substantial agreement' he had reached with Hopkins which made it essential for him to return home if he were 'personally to handle the matter of the negotiations'.[133] An immediate result of the visit, which illustrates Cripps' influence on Hopkins, was a complete change in Steinhardt's attitude who, as Cripps noted, 'must have suspected that he might be in danger of being removed unless he changed his tune!'[134]

Churchill's involvement in Russian affairs intensified once the inroads on American supply threatened British strategy. The interference was bound to limit Cripps' independent moves and hasten the collapse of his mission in Moscow. Although the conference at Placentia Bay in mid-August hardly touched on Russia, it was carried out against the background of Hopkins' impressions of Russia which at least to some degree were formed by Cripps. The idea of an Atlantic Charter was Roosevelt's and was intended mostly for domestic consumption. It comprised a deliberately wide and general definition of war aims

reminiscent of President Woodrow Wilson's Fourteen Points during the First World War. Hitherto Churchill and the Foreign Office had on the whole deliberately deferred discussion of war aims, preferring statements on ultimate victory and a return to the pre-war political arrangements. The Charter was the inevitable price for a more active American commitment to the British war effort.[135] While the collapse of Russia was still regarded as imminent Cripps' advocacy of detailed and precise plans for post-war reconstruction, as conveyed by Hopkins and elaborated later in Cripps' telegrams, were ahead of their time. The significance attached by Cripps to the definition of war aims conformed with the American view but caused a delayed but unavoidable clash with Churchill.

The maintenance of the Middle Eastern arena, often criticized by Cripps, had now become tied up with assistance to Russia. Despite Churchill's staunch defence of his strategy during Hopkins' preliminary talks in London, the Americans continued to regard operations in the Middle East as a liability from which the British ought to withdraw. Hopkins' visit to Moscow only intensified Roosevelt's belief that Britain's sole hope lay in Russia's continued resistance, at least until the United States was drawn into the war. Roosevelt reached Placentia Bay with the conviction that aid to Russia was of such 'paramount importance for the safety and security of America' that he advocated 'substantial and comprehensive commitments'.[136]

When boarding the HMS *Prince of Wales* Churchill knew little about the extent and nature of the assistance designated for Russia. However, as is plain from his memoirs, he anticipated a 'painful splitting of supplies' now that Russia too was a 'welcome guest at a hungry table'. He dreaded the loss of what Britain expected and direly needed for the struggle in Libya and to forestall expected developments in the Far East. During the cruise to Newfoundland Churchill became acquainted with Hopkins' full conversion. Hopkins undoubtedly dwelt on Cripps' major role in the success of his mission; in any event he carried with him Cripps' memorandum to Churchill on the same lines as Hopkins' impression and the draft letter to Stalin, both devoted to the necessity of coordinating the war effort and mounting a conference. Churchill could not possibly have been pleased by the activities of his ambassador in Moscow. After all his immediate worries focused on the diversion of American supplies to Russia, on the pressure to abandon the Mediterranean

campaign and demands for a clear-cut definition of war aims. As there was no chance of deflecting the Americans, the method he adopted was to conduct only perfunctory talks on Russia on the very last day of the conference. Although Churchill claims together with Roosevelt the authorship of the message to Stalin, Cripps' draft was adopted almost verbatim. It committed the two countries to the assistance of Russia and the coordination of strategy in the forthcoming conference.[137]

If Cripps scored a success at Placentia Bay he also put the seal on his personal hopes of either returning to England or playing a role in the Moscow negotiations. His logical approach to the Russian issue overlooked the emotions it evoked and lacked a realistic appreciation of his ability to dictate an unacceptable political alternative. Never before had the absence of political support and the position of lone warrior been so frustrating. Although he had a strong feeling that Russia's entry into the war had created new opportunities for him at home, he could not find the appropriate means to exploit these opportunities. He was obliged to rely mostly on Isobel who had for the first time become involved in his politics, as a result of their common experience in Moscow, but lacked prior experience and despaired of propagating his ideas in London. Even Monckton, who had served as his main link with Halifax, now had little influence particularly after Brendan Bracken had replaced Duff Cooper at the Ministry of Information which he directed.[138] Cripps was aptly described by Beatrice Webb on the basis of his letters as lacking the political spark, as 'a singularly direct and honest-minded man – with no pretentiousness . . . not too optimistic – in short, a *business man*'.[139] Those qualities were, of course, no match for Churchill's political instincts.

In the wake of Hopkins' mission Cripps plunged into the preparation of the background for the conference. He persisted with his demands for the government to seize the chance presented by the Russian involvement in the war by tackling the substance of the outstanding difficulties and laying the foundations for post-war reconstruction. He criticized the short-sighted policy of trying to extract the utmost from the war in the East by alternately denying and conceding help regardless of the essential interests involved. Like most of his contemporaries, Cripps was haunted by the experience of appeasement and anxious therefore that conversations with Russia should be frank and encompass all the issues; as he remarked prophetically, 'sooner or later we should

have to take a stand and it would cause unpleasantness'. The delivery of supplies, combined with a solution of overall political difficulties within the framework of defined war aims was Cripps' general agenda for the Moscow conference.[140]

When London maintained silence Cripps' dismay at the substitution of comforting words for action was reinforced by the heads of the military mission. Mason-Macfarlane had been informed through the Russian liaison officer that although the 'strain was terrific' at the front, relations could not be smoothed so long as the British army was 'doing nothing on land' to help the Russians. The mission, witnessed Cripps, had become critical of the 'general running of the war'. On 14 August he was breakfasting with the chiefs of the military mission, as was his daily habit, when news came in of the major German assault in the South. It provoked vociferous 'concentrated criticism of H.M.G. for their defeatist attitude'. All those present were unanimous in that the government was 'still suffering from the result of Dunkirk and the general appeasement attitude of the Foreign Office as well as from the people who refuse to believe anything good of the Russians because they are so frightened of them in the future'.[141] In short, the reserve attitude was being maintained despite the altering circumstances. Cripps was not one to suppress frustration and therefore immediately after breakfast set out those opinions in blunt terms in yet another personal telegram to Eden. He criticized him and Churchill for their 'total war directive' which failed to account the 'enormous and absolutely vital importance' of the Russian front for Britain. He hit the nail on the head by insisting that the campaign in Russia was important as the home or the Middle Eastern fronts. The 'safety first' policy, based on the belief of an impending Soviet disaster, was short-sighted, unimaginative and endangered Britain in the 'most acute way'.[142]

Cripps' gradual recognition that he was being overlooked, the decrease in routine diplomatic activity and above all his expectations of a prompt return home caused a slackening of his communications with London. Eden now had often to rely on Isobel's occasional visits to the Foreign Office for a recital of selected paragraphs from her husband's letter–diary.[143] Instead Cripps now immersed himself in the subject of post-war reconstruction. This activity was boosted by the revival of the 'Club's' activity after the return to Moscow of Gavrilovic, who had been expelled in May. Cripps even prevailed on Gavrilovic to travel to

London and present their scheme regarding the Balkans. Cripps' intention, in the tradition of his rebellious past, was to present the programme to the public and 'get the discussion at least launched'. Such activities were apt to alarm the government. On 14 August Cripps in fact presented the Cabinet with a paper on the subject of war aims which he pressed them to discuss. Already during his recall Cripps had aired similar ideas in government as well as Labour circles. He had little doubt that Churchill's sole interest was in winning the war, leaving it for someone else to 'clear up the mess afterwards!' Although Cripps expected Eden to be more receptive, he was fully aware of his shortcomings and did not therefore reckon he would 'get very far beyond possibly giving it to someone in the F.O. to give him a critique on it which he will then adopt as his view!'[144]

Outwardly there was little to choose between Eden's and Cripps' dissatisfaction at Churchill's general handling of the war and relations with Russia in particular. Eden too was distressed by the 'woolly' Atlantic Charter and Churchill's conduct of the Defence Committee, which was acting 'by impulse – no proper planning'. To his intimates he expressed the fear that Churchill was 'deteriorating'. As he told Harvey, it was 'entirely due to [Churchill] that we cannot do more for Soviet Russia'. He even concurred with Cripps on the need to replace the 'present collection of amateur thoughts' in 10 Downing Street to give a 'proper lead to the military conduct of the war'.[145] Eden's complaints, however, were confined to his immediate entourage. His personal ambition and overall devotion and dependence on Churchill precluded any association with Cripps. Moreover, Eden was opposed to Cripps' general political leanings and disliked his political style, temperament and way of life. Their relations remained distant. Eden's interim reply to Cripps' stream of telegrams did not reveal any of his own misgivings, in fact repeating Churchill's arguments that Britain lacked 'ways and means of giving help effectively'. Eden was personally disposed to respond favourably to Cripps' request to return home on the assumption that his continued stay in Moscow was 'more of an obstacle than a help'. However, since he was aware that the Cabinet feared Cripps would be a 'thorn in their side' and was reluctant to take any drastic action in Churchill's absence, this decision was postponed.[146] The prospect of Cripps' presence in London, armed with what was regarded as revolutionary ideology and enjoying wide popularity from his associ-

ation with the heroic Soviet struggle, was indeed most unwelcome even in Labour circles. Dalton, for instance, made it clear that Cripps might constitute a 'damned nuisance' by inciting left-wing elements. It was essential that he should 'see the job through'.[147]

In the meantime Cripps had already invited Churchill's wrath in connection with his initiatives leading to the decision on Russia taken in Placentia Bay. Churchill did not have the slightest intention of responding to Cripps' personal appeals to lead the delegation to Moscow. On the eve of Churchill's departure the idea entertained was that Eden should proceed to Moscow at the beginning of September. While still in Placentia Bay Churchill hastily announced that Beaverbrook, whom he had flown over to assist him on supply matters, would be the British representative.[148] Cripps' assiduous and unselfish work behind the scenes in setting up the Moscow conference was lost on both contemporaries and historians but not on Beaverbrook:

Sir Stafford has been the driving force that prepared the situation in Moscow resulting in the agreement with Russia. On the way home [from Moscow] I sent him a telegram. I said: 'The corner-stone had been laid by you and the bricks were at hand when I reached Moscow.'[149]

On the day of his return to London Churchill reviewed Cripps' communications and plans for post-war reconstruction, which can only have reinforced his antagonism. Eden had a further talk with him and the two agreed that it was 'certainly time Cripps was changed'. Churchill, however, decided he should remain; unless he were included in the Cabinet Cripps was bound to be an 'infernal nuisance' and the Foreign Office would be accused of 'having jockeyed out Cripps'.[150]

Debarred from returning home, Cripps encouraged Mason-Macfarlane to make the journey instead. Mason-Macfarlane had in the meantime been allowed to visit the front for the first time and was greatly impressed by the organization of the headquarters he visited and even more by the discipline and courage of the ordinary population. Whereas he remembered that the roads in France and Belgium were crammed with refugees during the German blitzkrieg, in Russia agricultural work was being carried out meticulously a few miles behind the front. There was also evidence of the successful execution of a scorched-earth policy through the transfer of industrial machinery to the East. Dill reluctantly agreed to Mason-Macfarlane's return for con-

sultations. In the wake of the decision taken with regard to the furious Cripps, Churchill instructed Dill to retract on the pretext that Mason-Macfarlane should not leave Russia during those critical days.[151] Mason-Macfarlane now added his protest to Cripps', arguing that the alliance with Russia was 'fortuitous' and Britain could not hope to beat the Germans by 'fighting separate wars'. It was 'illogical' to coordinate munitions at the forthcoming conference when the United States would be dealing with two fronts 'fighting un-co-ordinated wars'.[152]

### Iranian diversion

The combined Anglo-Soviet operation in Iran in summer 1941 sheds light on the true nature of the evolving alliance as well as on the extent of Cripps' deepening rift with London. The proposal to expel the estimated 5000 German technicians from Teheran was first made by Stalin in conversation with Cripps on 8 July. Both Cripps and Reader Bullard, the British ambassador to Iran, were in favour of acceptance. Cripps warned the government against allowing the matter to be 'dragged out'; as relations with Iran had never been based on mutual confidence and friendship he suggested, rather ruthlessly, a diplomatic *démarche* reinforced by a military demonstration.[153] Although the Cabinet agreed on the desirability of eliminating German influence, it refrained from reaching any decision.[154] Surprisingly the COS welcomed the opportunity of improving the British position in Iran and the Far East but was less enthusiastic about concerted action, arguing that British and Russian interests were at variance. Indeed, the expulsion of the Germans was the least significant aspect to the British. General Wavell, for instance, who after the fiasco of the Libyan offensive was appointed Commander-in-Chief in India, joined in the call for action[155] because of his concern about British vulnerability in the area after the collapse of Russia. The main objective, of which Cripps did not have the slightest notion, was the Iranian oil. As Russia was expected either to be crushed or to come to terms with the Germans, the Joint Planning Committee of the COS warned that Britain might soon find a hostile power 'right on top' of the oil wells.

There was, however, marked apprehension about the operation. To start with, Britain would have to denude her own forces in the Middle East. Worse still, the government might be accused in the United States

of the 'carving up of a neutral country in a partnership with the Soviet Union', an inevitable comparison with Poland's partition in 1939. The COS finally overrode these scruples, opting for a 'firm action' as suggested by Cripps but making a strange revelation about the nature of the collaboration with Russia, particularly in view of the analogy to Poland in 1939. The Shah was to be threatened that unless he expelled the Germans Russia would intervene and Britain would 'feel obliged to safeguard [her] own interests in the southern part of the country'.[156] Although Eden liked to create the impression of impetuous advocacy of any action which might provide relief to the Russians, he suddenly attempted to call off the project, warning Churchill against moving 'diplomatically ahead of our military strength or we shall court disaster'.[157]

The initial hopes of avoiding a concerted action by inducing the Iranians to act through political and economic pressure were soon abandoned. Although Eden insisted on the exhaustion of all political alternatives, once military action seemed likely the COS did little to hide their genuine aspiration of occupying the oilfields and achieving a degree of control over the Iranian government. Such were the plans which were produced on 23 July for execution in mid-August.[158] While planning was in progress successive Soviet requests for military coordination were rejected by the COS, who insisted that British forces should 'retain the right of independent action'. Consequently only the ultimatum to Iran on 12 August, demanding the expulsion of the Germans, was discussed with the Russians. No combined operations or even coordination were embarked upon.[159] The securing of a supply route to Russia, usually considered a major aim of the operation, was low on the list of priorities at the time.

While the planning was already under way Churchill embarked for Placentia Bay leaving Eden in full control. Eden now attempted a show of strength by requesting the Defence Committee to abandon the whole plan, the only minor action which had been worked out in some association with Russia, because of the 'unfortunate repercussions' which it might have on Turkey. If launched none the less it would have to be conditional on Russia's delivery of assurances to Turkey that the Anglo-Soviet cooperation in Iran had no sinister intentions against her. Eden's real objective was to assure Turkey that Britain was not returning to the Anglo-Russian partition of 1907; the possible repercussions of

the declaration on the Russians were overlooked. Earlier on, as a special gesture, the Turks had been informed before signature of the Anglo-Soviet agreement.[160] Eden's continued obsession with seeing Turkey's 'political and military position strengthened' stood in sharp contrast to the attitude pursued towards Russia in 1939–41, although Turkey had by now adopted a distinct benevolent neutrality towards Germany. It shows Eden's consent to Churchill's overall strategy regarding the primacy of the Middle Eastern arena. However, while Churchill's efforts were directed to protecting the North African front, Eden's attention was turned to the Near East. To forestall the inevitable comparison Cripps was instructed to tell the Russians that although the Turks had 'treated us rather badly . . . in the present critical situation we should not allow our personal feelings to come in the way of our long-term policy'.[161]

Cripps quickly found himself isolated on the Turkish issue. His contribution to the Turco-Soviet rapprochement a few months earlier was forgotten, while the Foreign Office were not impressed with his protest that considering Turkey's thorough hostility to Russia and pro-German leanings the appeal might have a counter-productive effect in Moscow. Once it was decided to secure a Soviet declaration, Cripps did his utmost to assure that its wording would not imply a defeatist appreciation of Soviet capabilities.[162] The Turkish ambassador in Moscow, he warned Eden, had adopted a manifestly defeatist attitude which Cripps attributed to the Turkish wish to see Russia defeated. Eden merely thought it was a pity that Cripps' 'anti-Turkish prejudices' remained so strong. Cripps, however, had always been favourably disposed towards Aktay; the Turkish hostility towards Russia made both 'feel a reservation which rather spoiled the relationship' they had previously enjoyed. Eden would on no account allow the cooperation with Russia to impair relations with Turkey. Before launching the campaign in Iran he believed it imperative to smooth Turco-Soviet relations. In view of Cripps' objections this was carried out through Maisky in London.[163] Faced by a veiled ultimatum on which the mounting of the campaign in Iran depended, the Russians gave way. On 10 August Knatchbull-Hugessen and his Soviet counterpart in Ankara presented the Turks with a unilateral assurance of friendly intentions. Eden's aspirations of either improving British–Turkish relations or securing an effective Soviet–Turkish understanding were never fulfilled.[164]

Although the occupation of Iran, ostensibly to expel the German advisers, was the first military action to be undertaken in conjunction with the Russians, it was considered in London entirely in the framework of overall Middle Eastern strategy. Contacts with the Russians were minimized; there were in fact to be two separate fronts to be coordinated by liaison missions once the operation started.[165] Churchill's return from Placentia Bay gave the contemplated action a new significance. Hitherto the need to expel the German advisers, whose numbers were considered to have been highly exaggerated by the Russians, concealed the substantial and far-reaching objectives of the operation. The concern over the impact which a campaign of this nature might have on public opinion in the United States and in Turkey had deferred a decision on what otherwise seemed a most advantageous move. In Placentia Bay Churchill had become acquainted with the significance attached by the Americans after Hopkins' conversations with Stalin to the stiffening of Russian resistance. As Churchill even now had no intention of altering his strategic priorities in the light of the war in Russia, it seemed possible to achieve the genuine purpose of the campaign while presenting it as a move to secure the supply route to Russia. It would then be acceptable in the United States and would be presented to the Russians, as Churchill explained to the Defence Committee, as 'one of the few measures we could take to help a country which was making such a stupendous effort'.[166]

Anxious that the vacillating Iranians would accede to the British demands, Churchill now advocated great haste. Overruling the COS' haggling with the Russians over the position of the liaison mission, Churchill adopted Maisky's demand that the memorandum to the Shah be couched as an ultimatum, and abandoned preliminary steps that had earlier been considered vital for the successful completion of the operation. As he instructed the COS on the day of his arrival in London: 'The Persian reply must be followed by immediate action . . . Not an hour should be lost.'[167] The operation, however, had to be postponed for a few days at the insistence of the Russians, who had been taken by surprise, to allow the regrouping of their own forces.[168] Churchill's fears were indeed realized when on 23 August the Shah appeared willing to comply with the demands. His proposals, however, were dismissed as being 'fortunately, vague enough to be disregarded'.[169]

The new definition of the aim of the campaign, at Wavell's request,

as securing a supply route 'with Russian help' was odd as no political or military negotiations on such objectives had been discussed with the Russians. Stalin in fact, in his conversations with Hopkins, had dismissed that route because of the inadequate transport infrastructure. He still preferred the Murmansk route, which he believed could be kept ice-free through the use of ice-breakers. Moreover, it was admitted rather coyly by the COS that the establishment of the southern route depended on the 'attitude of the Persian Government when the oilbearing area has been occupied and whether they agree to the use of their railway'. It was estimated that the forces employed were barely 'sufficient to occupy the oil fields'.[170]

The 'brief and fruitful exercise of overwhelming force against a weak and ancient state', as later described by Churchill, ended on 27 August, barely three days after the opening of hostilities. Not for the first time in history, the progress of the battle introduced sharp variations in the definition of war aims. Once it was recognized that the Iranian opposition was crumbling faster than anticipated, Churchill impressed on the COS the need not to 'simply squat on the oil fields, but to get through communication with Russia'. By the beginning of September the ostensible motive for the war of expelling the Germans was referred to only as a propaganda device.[171] The rush to the North was dictated by the need to ensure that Teheran be left intact, now that the Shah had abandoned his resistance and 'friendly' relations had been established with the Persians. In view of the Germans' swing southwards in Russia, the foundation of a buffer zone had become a cornerstone in the defence of British interests in the Middle East. The aims of the operation were now defined, in order of priority, as the securing of the oilfields, the strategic position, a line of communication with the Russians and the naval interests in the Persian Gulf.[172]

The execution of the first joint Anglo-Soviet campaign provides a vivid example of Cripps' gradual exclusion from the conduct of relations with the Russians. Cripps was kept completely in the dark on the dynamic revision of the targets set earlier. He had learnt of the division into spheres of influence and the terms of the pending negotiations with the Iranians from none other than Molotov. Disconcerted by the 'elastic terms', which confirmed a drift from the declared purpose of expelling the Germans, Cripps vehemently opposed the Russian demands for extending their zones of influence in return for conforming with the

British plans for a settlement, warning that a continued Soviet occupation of northern Iran might lead to a similar move by the British 'without any honest justification'.[173] Cripps' sudden intervention was obviously resented by Eden and Churchill. Despite their assurances of respect for the integrity and independence of Iran, they could not conceal the embarrassing fact that this was Britain's 'first act of "naked aggression" '.[174] Cripps' criticism reflected his concern that a casual collaboration which was not consolidated in a political framework was fraught with danger. His prophetic and consistent warning henceforth was that a failure to reach understanding with the Russians and to check their progress beyond what had been agreed would mean 'infinite trouble in the future'; 'we are at present in a strong position', he explained, 'whereas later on theirs may be stronger than ours'. He was equally bitter that all arrangements were made in London while he could do 'very little'.[175] His comments were indeed unwelcome. It was now fully recognized in Whitehall that Britain together with Russia was 'drifting into a complete occupation' of Iran. Much as Britain would have liked to forestall further Soviet advances, it was clear that she too was 'trying to get away with gains outside of what had been agreed'. Cripps was therefore instructed to abstain from action and was given no further information on the progress of the campaign.[176]

Neither Cripps nor Bullard succeeded in swaying Churchill, whose strategic outlook tallied with that of the COS. He shared their gloomy prognosis of Soviet resistance particularly after the beginning of the new offensive. Of far more significance was his continued subjection of all military plans to the major campaign in North Africa. A possible German breakthrough into the Middle East through the northern back door would be bound to disturb the British deployment there. The 'grand prize', explained Churchill to the Defence Committee in advocation of the further expansion, was the establishment of a Trans-Iranian railway which would enable Britain to 'build up a front behind the natural barrier of the Caucasian Mountains'. This stands in sharp contrast to Churchill's later explanation of the operation as an attempt to 'establish more intimate and friendly relations with our new Ally'.[177]

Considering the prevailing pessimistic appreciation of Soviet capabilities, references to future collaboration with Russia were almost non-existent. Cripps' reservations were therefore completely ignored.

Thus the 'aloofness' which had reigned before the war was gradually assuming its wartime form. Control of the route from the Persian Gulf to the Caspian could always be safely presented as securing a supply link with Russia. Thus when Bullard complained on the extension of the war he was informed by Churchill that there was no apprehension of Soviet encroachment, as the 'supreme wish' was to ensure American supplies to the Russians via the new route.[178] The same façade was preserved in Cabinet, where both Eden and Beaverbrook had been reluctant to proceed to the Moscow conference empty-handed. A day after his exposé to the Defence Committee Churchill presented Cabinet with an entirely different justification for the decision to proceed beyond the original aims and control Iran for the duration of the war. It would, he said, help Beaverbrook to have something concrete to offer the Russians in the way of deliveries by railway.[179] The irony of the episode is that Churchill exploited the presumed success in establishing communications with Russia to secure substantial help from Roosevelt in return. This was to consist of shipping two British divisions, totalling 40,000 men, to North Africa to reinforce Auchinleck's troops in anticipation of an early offensive.[180]

# 6

# DISILLUSION

## *Drifting apart*

The Russians were disturbed by the lack of any evidence of preparations for the Moscow conference in the wake of the message from Placentia Bay. After Churchill's return to London, Maisky twice appealed to no avail for the conference to be convened at the end of August. Churchill's evasiveness reflected his desire to postpone the re-routing of supplies. In fact he was exploiting Cripps' suggestion, formed on the basis of a mistaken evaluation of the situation at the front, that the conference be held only at the end of September.[1] Hard pressed by the Germans, the Russians would not let the subject lapse. Maisky had detected through his contacts with Cabinet members the embarrassment over the failure to carry out a military diversion and some preparedness to compensate by material aid. In conversation with Eden he was therefore willing to recognize the obstacles to mounting a diversion but insisted that assistance was indispensable to sustain Soviet resistance and to 'avoid the danger of growing mistrust' which had marred the history of Anglo-Soviet relations. Moreover, like Cripps he brought up the need to discuss the general strategy of the war.[2] His requests were backed up by Cripps, who warned that the failure to convene the conference would negate the effect of Churchill's previous speeches and messages. Continuing the state of uncertainty seemed much worse than announcing a postponement considering the current disinformation that the meeting had been put off.[3]

Although the procrastination was conveniently attributed to the Americans, Churchill admitted to a 'strong element of uncertainty' as to the timing of the conference and 'major confusion' as to who would lead the British delegation. Meanwhile on 25 August Beaverbrook telephoned Hopkins in Washington and consented to fix an earlier date

for the conference.[4] Eden, impressed by the force of Maisky's and Cripps' reasoning, was carrying out similar lobbying with Winant. He had some harsh words for Churchill as well, a paraphrase of Cripps' arguments that 'despite all disadvantages' it was necessary to schedule the conference to avoid giving the Russians the impression that the British were not 'confident of their ability to hold and [were] waiting and watching to see their fate'. Churchill eventually bowed to the pressure. He agreed in Cabinet on 28 August that the delay was undesirable, but then manoeuvred them to the conclusion that the initiative should be left to the Americans.[5] To defuse any opposition he resorted to the familiar pattern of addressing Stalin with a reassuring message promising him a further 200 Tomahawk aircraft. In view of the overriding political considerations the COS waived their protest that the planes would pay a 'better dividend if sent to the Far East or the Middle East or Turkey'. Churchill further stressed the prospects held by the new route now opened in Persia for supplies to Russia, while references to the Moscow conference were conspicuous by their absence.[6]

Beaverbrook had been designated to lead the mission to Moscow even before he had joined the participants in Placentia Bay. On his return from the United States he attempted to step down. Meanwhile Churchill, who had earlier proposed that Eden should be his emissary, suggested that he should join Beaverbrook. By this measure Churchill probably hoped to demonstrate the British commitment, pacify Eden and appoint a watch-dog over Beaverbrook who, most likely as a result of his encounters with Hopkins in Washington, had turned out to be a more ardent champion of aid to Russia than he had appeared earlier. In view of Churchill's previous promise that he should go to Moscow, Eden himself was in two minds. In fact both he and Beaverbrook had become aware of the minor interest Churchill and the COS had in Russia. They knew that the conference was merely the price paid for continued American commitment to the British war effort and were therefore reluctant to face Stalin emptyhanded.[7] On 29 August Beaverbrook suggested to Churchill that as he had 'nothing to give or promise the Russians' Eden should proceed to Moscow; he would 'be able to make speeches and to encourage the martial and national spirit of the Russians'. Beaverbrook must have been aware that Churchill could not possibly dispense with his expertise on supply matters. He gave sufficient signs that he intended neither to proceed with nothing to offer

nor to divide the political spoils of the proposed mission.[8] Churchill indeed took some measures to put him at his ease. To start with he cleared the stage by informing Beaverbrook of his decision to withdraw the proposal to Eden. Beaverbrook, who realized this was another serious blow to Eden, exonerated himself from any accusation of plotting by immediately passing on the letter to Eden, who gave in without a murmur. Churchill next pledged to arrange 'long-term supply' of the Russian army, although admittedly 'almost entirely from American sources'. It was, he encouraged Beaverbrook, 'our duty and our interest to give the utmost possible aid to the Russians, even at a serious sacrifice by ourselves'. At the same time Churchill imposed some weighty restrictions. The real flow of supply was not designed to begin 'till the middle or end of 1942, and the main planning will relate to 1943'. The Russian front, it must be borne in mind, was expected to have ceased to exist by then. The promise was therefore no more than another morale-booster. Perhaps most revealing and significant was the instruction to Beaverbrook to watch the Americans and ensure that Britain was 'not bled white' in the conference.[9]

Beaverbrook could not be so easily won over by Churchillian eloquence. He attempted other avenues of escape which only widened the gap separating him and Churchill on the issues of a second front and the extent of assistance. It was not, however, until 3 September, when the Americans had appointed Harriman to replace the ailing Hopkins as the head of their delegation and as a result of further canvassing in Cabinet, that Churchill ordered the speeding-up of arrangements.[10]

Once his appointment was certain, the Russian issue provided Beaverbrook with an opportunity of placing himself 'on the high peak of reputation'; as his biographer explains, 'in his romantic schoolboy way, he saw himself as leader of the Radical Left, the hero of the masses'.[11] It was this personal ambition and lack of communication between Cripps, Eden and Beaverbrook which forestalled the formation of a powerful combination to deflect Churchill from the course he had adopted towards Russia. The attempt to exploit the spontaneous support of Russia for political advancement was not confined to Beaverbrook; the Labour members of the Cabinet also derived an undeserved popularity. There was a strong leaning towards Labour even in the high echelons of the Conservative Party. Eden recorded at that time complaints of such 'incompatibility with the right' that he visualized himself

working with Attlee and Bevin after the war. A subdued competition between him and Beaverbrook, whom he referred to as a 'scamp', was evidently taking place. Nor was Bevin satisfied with Beaverbrook's intrusion on Labour territory. Both he and Eden took advantage of Beaverbrook's departure to Moscow to raise charges against him in Cabinet and privately with Churchill.[12]

Stalin's reply to Churchill's evasive message was handed to Cripps on 4 September. Stalin pointed out the 'mortal menace' which Russia faced in the wake of the renewed German offensive in the second half of August. The demand for the opening of a second front in 1941 seems to have been still only secondary to the specific request for large amounts of aluminium, essential for aircraft production, and a 'monthly minimum' of 400 planes and 500 tanks.[13] Cripps was no longer properly briefed and had learnt from the wireless of the choice of Harriman and Beaverbrook, an indirect negative reply to his letter to Eden of a month earlier. The urgency of Stalin's appeal astounded Cripps and increased his alienation from the government, as he recorded in his diary:

Unless we can do something most immediately and effectively to help them the game is up at any rate for a long time if not all together . . . I can do little or nothing at this end and I only wish that I was in London to do my best there as I am sure that they have always underestimated the seriousness of this front and they have never looked upon it as our front and one for which we were responsible. If now it collapses we shall be left without the possibility of victory as you know I always thought this was the only front from which the Germans could be beaten.[14]

In transmitting the message he demanded that the Cabinet therefore treat it 'with great seriousness'; it was necessary to dispatch 'very large and immediate help, otherwise it is doubtful if it is much good doing anything at all'.

Maisky too was left under a strong impression by the dramatic message. Delivering it to 10 Downing Street on the night of 4 September, he chose similar words to those employed by Cripps. 'Heartily, excitedly, almost with inspiration' he impressed on Churchill the fatefulness of the moment: if Hitler were now victorious, 'there would descend on humanity a black night of the most monstrous reaction'. He too argued that, in spite of objective difficulties, there were occasions in war when

the 'political chiefs must be prepared to accept an overriding respon-sibility'. Maisky restated the need to broaden the scope of the con-ference to include questions of strategy as at present each country was 'pursuing its own plan'. His demands evoked a vindictive response when Churchill blamed the Russians for the burden which Britain had had to bear on her own until June 1941. More illuminating was his refusal to consider a landing in Europe while defining the British strategy as building up 'a position of strength from Persia to Libya, from which offensive action might later be possible'. The precedence given to the Middle East theatre was only too obvious. Supply remained therefore the only basis for cooperation. When Maisky left at around midnight, Dill joined Eden and Churchill in taking a 'grim view' of the Russian situation. A landing was unanimously ruled out, above all, as Eden somewhat critically witnessed, 'because of the power of the German air force, if [Air Chief Marshal] Portal had estimated it aright'.[15]

The COS had in fact maintained an absolutely uncompromising stand with regard to a second front. Although the time-limit originally estimated for the survival of the Red Army had elapsed, the war in the East continued to be regarded solely in terms of a respite and out of the context of overall British strategy. The only revision was the intro-duction of a new time-table at the end of July: the Russians were now expected to abandon Moscow and retreat beyond the Urals in mid-August, enabling the Germans to divert their forces to the West. However, it was already accepted that the burden of controlling the occupied Russian territories would mean a postponement until next spring of a German attempt to cross the Channel. The more likely course was for the Germans to use Turkey as a springboard for over-running the Middle East.[16] Throughout August, therefore, anticipation of an imminent collapse continued to prevent the rendering of even minor assistance such as cooperation in bombing Romanian oilfields, parachuting operations in Romania and the stationing of bomber squad-rons in southern Russia. These commitments, it was argued, would weaken Britain's ability to face a German advance into the Middle East.[17] Neither the summit meeting nor criticism at home prompted fresh attitudes. On 27 August the COS adopted the unequivocal con-clusion that a diversion would achieve 'no real valuable result and might have a seriously adverse effect'. For the first time the conclusions were

based on a thorough examination of landing sites, the strength of German fortifications, forces available and other strategic and tactical limitations. It is difficult none the less to establish to what extent the analysis was affected by the profound resentment of collaboration which was in evidence throughout the document. After all, the mere fact that Russia was again on the verge of collapse further hindered any serious thought of promoting the Alliance. Moreover, the examination was based on the assumption that, as Britain had been fighting the Germans single-handed for fourteen months, there was no need to alter the 'long term strategical and industrial plan' which for the time being did not allow for an intervention on the Continent. Nor were they enthusiastic about a mock invasion, which Churchill suggested might quieten the dissention at home.[18]

From Stalin's requests Churchill derived another objection to a diversion besides the obvious reluctance to redeploy forces destined for the Middle East. Both he and Eden had sensed, 'although there was nothing in the actual words which M. Maisky used to justify it', that the possibility of a separate peace could not be 'altogether excluded'. Even if a bridgehead could be successfully established in France it would fall into disarray once the Germans started transferring their forces to the West.[19] On balance it seemed essential not to discourage the Russians without, however, committing Britain too far. The day after receiving Stalin's message Churchill therefore subjected a 'dogged and worried' Maisky to a series of lectures by the heads of the different services on the insuperable technical difficulties involved in mounting a diversion; these included of course the overwhelming argument that it would weaken the British position in the Middle East. Once the COS had left, Eden was more forthcoming on the issue of supply, even suggesting the extension of 'Lend–Lease' to Russia.[20]

Churchill gives the impression that he promptly committed himself to supplying Russia already on 4 September after consulting Cabinet.[21] On the contrary, he had asked Maisky for time for reflection. In the meantime he expounded in Cabinet on the obstacles to British assistance to Russia, bringing with him Dudley Pound, the Admiral of the Fleet, to express the COS's objections to a diversion. The Cabinet had by then been informed of Cripps' outspoken telegram sustaining Maisky's appeal for superhuman efforts. To moderate its effect Churchill explained that, although he fully sympathized with Cripps, his views

'took no account of the hard facts of the situation'. Only then did Churchill present a draft reply to Stalin who, he believed, was 'worthy of being told the truth and was capable of facing the facts'. He did not wish Cabinet to make promises which it 'could not possibly fulfil'. The whole issue of supplies was absent from the draft. On behalf of Labour Bevin readily endorsed Churchill's draft. Beaverbrook, however, was most indignant about its 'too harsh and depressing' terms. He must have been seriously concerned about the repercussions it might have on his own welcome in Moscow and pressed therefore for a more forthcoming attitude. He further quoted from Cripps' telegram calling for the immediate dispatch of the delegation to the conference. Backed by Eden, Beaverbrook finally converted the Cabinet and later in the afternoon even the COS. The Labour ministers Bevin and Herbert Morrison realized that the promise of supplies could serve as a 'great incentive to increase production' at home as well as an inducement to Maisky to stop his involvement in the 'potential field of trouble in the activities of various bodies . . . trying to stir up a campaign against the Government on the issue of help to Russia'.[22] The reply to Stalin now represented an inconsistent compromise between Beaverbrook and Churchill. On the one hand a great deal was made of the decision to correspond to Stalin's demand for increased supplies. On the other hand there was a blank refusal to consider a second front followed by a clear statement that achieving British supremacy in the Middle East was the prerequisite for both future help to Russia and the defeat of Germany.[23]

While these communications were proceeding and the final touches being put to the Moscow conference, Cripps' exchanges with the Cabinet became sour in tone. It is inaccurate to suppose that Cripps was suddenly enjoying an undeserved reputation as a result of Russia's entry into the war. What was actually happening was a convergence of public opinion and sentiments with his own steadfast convictions.[24] However, Cripps' almost suicidal naivety deprived him of the immediate fruits of his success, although it later proved an important political springboard.

The confrontations in Cabinet and with Cripps had alerted Churchill to the need to mobilize the widespread spontaneous support of Russia rather than be overrun by it. He personally took pains to reconcile Sir Walter Citrine, the General Secretary of the TUC, who was obliged to postpone a visit to Moscow coinciding with Beaver-

brook's, by facilitating his expedition and giving it a semi-official cachet.[25] Churchill was less concerned about his Labour colleagues in Cabinet, who acquiesced with him partly from conviction and often because they lacked coherent overall information. He felt most threatened by Beaverbrook and Cripps. The popular pressure unexpectedly found its immediate outlet in Beaverbrook, whose power as Minister of Supply and as an influential publicist could not be overlooked.[26] Cripps, as Churchill and the Labour Ministers were aware, was a natural candidate to profit from the prevailing mood. He had also the reputation of an advocate of war aims, which were now being discussed.

For the time being Churchill remained on the defensive, protecting his priorities and those of the COS by employing rhetoric to muzzle the opposition in the absence of a real commitment to Russia. An outstanding example was his speech in Parliament on 9 September. While paying the customary tribute to the valiant Russian resistance, Churchill concealed the prevailing doubts about the prospects in store. Since the outbreak of war, he stated, Britain had 'cast about for every means of giving the most speedy help to [her] new Ally'; for security reasons he could not disclose the military projects studied. He glossed over the hesitation regarding the convening of the Moscow conference. On the other hand, referring to the limitations hindering the flow of aid to Russia, Churchill made an emotional appeal for the increase of productivity at home. He naturally made much of the ephemeral joint Anglo-Soviet interests and collaboration in the Iranian operation. With the Russian campaign already eighty days old, Churchill's spell had been somewhat fading. In the debate there were numerous criticisms of the withholding of support to the Russians and demands for more detailed information.[27]

Yet another example of Churchill's attempts to laud the cooperation, which called forth Cripps' indignation, was his reference to the limited naval operation carried out together with the Russians at the end of July to evacuate stranded Russian and Norwegian miners on the Arctic islands of Spitzbergen. The Foreign and War Offices had advised against publicizing 'yet another "glorious evacuation"' and disclosing operational information. With little in hand to display, Churchill depicted in Parliament the Allied front as running in an 'immense crescent from Spitzbergen in the Arctic Ocean to Tobruk in the Western

223

Desert'. Although he was later in his memoirs to condemn the exaggerated 'jubilation and publicity', Churchill himself favoured the lifting of the ban on reporting of the 'dangerous and important operation'. It occurred to Cripps immediately, as he complained to London, that the Russians would regard the publicity as an 'elaborate and stupid attempt to magnify a simple and safe operation into something large and important'.[28]

Meanwhile dramatic developments were taking place at the British embassy in Moscow. Cripps had become convinced that only his personal intervention would shift the Cabinet's policy and enable him to return to Moscow with the delegation to the conference. Reflecting on the grave situation after examining Stalin's telegram, Cripps made the impromptu decision on 5 September to return to London at once, taking along Mason-Macfarlane to maximize the effect. The latter was duly summoned from Tiflis, to which he had travelled only a day before to establish liaison with the Russians over the Iranian campaign. Cripps' political secretary was then ordered to fake a telegram from the Foreign Office recalling the two for consultations on the impending conference. Vyshinsky was next informed of the decision and Stalin and Shaposhnikov displayed eagerness to meet them before their departure. In the Kremlin the recall must have been received with satisfaction as a swift reaction to Stalin's message.[29] The fact that Cripps was on his way home landed like a bombshell on Churchill on the night of 5 September after a strenuous day in which he had to repel increasing demands to revise the attitude to Russia. Cadogan was just 'getting to sleep' at midnight when Churchill urgently instructed him over the phone to stop Cripps in view of important communications *en route* 'and other reasons'.[30]

It had become too risky simply to ignore Cripps' open challenge. Churchill therefore addressed him personally to forestall possible criticism of the reply to Stalin he enclosed, repeating at length the technical arguments against a diversion. He discouraged Cripps from pursuing bold initiatives, ridiculing his call for a superhuman effort which he took to mean 'an effort rising superior to space, time and geography. Unfortunately these attributes are denied us.' He also accused Russia, exactly as in his heated exchange with Maisky a day earlier, of indifference to Hitler's attempts to overrun Europe. The only conciliatory note was the promise of assistance which he had been

obliged to concede earlier in the day, though he clearly indicated that it was planned for the spring of 1942 and that the Russians would have to fight on their own for the time being.[31]

Churchill's command to remain at his post and the nature of the reply to Stalin irritated Cripps, as he was denied the right to 'carry on an argument'. His apprehensions were verified when he found Stalin 'very depressed and tired' and encountered the 'old attitude of suspicion and mistrust' which had been absent for some time. Stalin did not exclude the possibility of ceding the Donets Basin with its metallurgical works, and even Moscow and Leningrad with all their machine industries. Although he did not envisage a separate peace, he warned that he might be compelled to cease active fighting and 'dig in and wait on a defensive front, perhaps beyond the Volga'. In the absence of a second front the collaboration amounted to a question of supplies – and Stalin repeated his demands for aluminium, tanks and aircraft.[32] Although Cripps had not yet been officially informed of Churchill's rejection of the personal proposals conveyed by Hopkins, he was fast coming to terms with the fact that he was being deliberately pushed aside. This is evident from his diary entries:

One might have suspected that as we were out here and a very important decision had to be taken that we might have been consulted as to it. Indeed we might even have been able to help by our advice. But the P.M. thought otherwise . . . Last night I really felt very depressed at the outcome of events and the way we are being treated here, but there is nothing to be done about it and one must go on at least till the conference is held . . . Everyone here including all the heads of the mission are fed up with the treatment we are getting from the Government. We seem on most occasions just to be ignored.[33]

To prevent Eden from being 'taken by surprise and inconvenienced' Cripps reiterated on 10 September his determination to avoid another winter in Moscow. Unless the Cabinet adopted a more constructive attitude on the post-war settlement there was little for him to accomplish once the conference was over. The most alarming item from the government's point of view was a cryptic reference in the closing paragraph indicating that Cripps' wish to return had to do less with fear of a severe and solitary winter in Moscow than with being divorced from political life in England 'in view of the problems which remain to be solved'.[34] Hardly had the diplomatic bag left when Eden's long-due

answers to his earlier letters arrived. The first, dated 25 August, was in fact drafted in consultation with Churchill and was clearly designed to dampen Cripps' hopes. In a style characteristic of both it was simultaneously cheering and discouraging. It acknowledged Cripps' commitment to his mission, suggesting that his recall while Russia was engaged in a terrific struggle 'would be open to every kind of misconceptions'. The decision on his relief was indefinitely deferred while the possibility of a further mission was discounted:

You will not want to come back here and do nothing. There is not, Winston asked me to say to his regret, at the present time any vacancy in the Government nor any immediate prospect of there being one . . . Then as regards your proposal for later meetings with Stalin to discuss post-war problems, I truly think that this would be very difficult once you were back from Moscow and engaged here upon other work. Nothing is more embarrassing for a new Ambassador than for the shadow of his predecessor to fall across him at intervals, even if the predecessor is, as you would be, reluctant to interfere with his daily duties. There cannot be ever a king and ex-king on one throne with comfort.

To soften the blow Cripps was asked to regard the decision as a 'tribute' to the importance of his position in Moscow. To add insult to injury, the same bag contained a short and non-committal acknowledgement, dated 9 September, of the scheme of war aims to which Cripps had attached such great significance.[35]

Cripps' immediate reaction was uncompromising; he persevered in his intention of returning before long regardless of the situation at the front and the unmistakable tenor of the letters. His reply could not but increase apprehension in London:

I do not regard myself as in the least indispensable here! I have no expectation of being employed in the Government when I return home so that there is no need to bother about that aspect of the matter. I do not doubt that I shall find plenty to occupy me in the House of Commons and elsewhere. I quite appreciate what you say as to the new Ambassador and am glad that he has got as far as existing in your mind. I am quite prepared to cut all my connection with this country if that is thought to be the most helpful thing.

What I am not prepared to do is to put myself permanently out of British politics for the sake of a diplomatic career!

I feel that the time is approaching when I may want to play an active part in

that sphere, not at all necessarily as a member of any Government or in Government employ.

. . . I shall definitely stay here till after I have cleared up the results of the conference but after that I must be free to let you know if I feel that I ought to return home, and I shall not feel that I am letting you down by acting without warning.

Quite specifically you can tell Winston that I do not expect him to find me any job, that sort of attitude is not my form![36]

Cripps' relatively moderate earlier letter of 10 September 'showing restiveness' was sufficient to cause panic. 'Neither P.M. nor Cabinet want him back to play politics as leader of opposition', commented Harvey in his diary; Cripps was 'as much a menace to his friends (as Labour knows) as to his enemies'. Although he was now held to be a 'hopeless Ambassador . . . more of a liability than an asset', the necessity of keeping him in exile was unanimously recognized in Cabinet. On Churchill's advice a flattering reply was dispatched which dwelt on 'the greatest service' Cripps would render by remaining at his post until the situation cleared.[37]

Churchill's estrangement from Cripps on the eve of the Moscow conference was matched by a growing crisis with the Russians as a result of a marked worsening of the situation at the front. On 8–9 September the Germans resumed their thrust at the outskirts of Leningrad. In the critical situation which ensued Zhukov was rushed to Leningrad on 13 September to replace Voroshilov and ordered to hold the city at all costs. Meanwhile, against the opinion of his generals, Hitler had decided on 21 August to halt the advance on Moscow while making a dash southwards and maintaining the siege on Leningrad. After a fierce but swift armoured battle, Guderian succeeded on 7 September in ripping apart the Russian defences of the Bryansk and south-eastern fronts. On 11 September the legendary General Budenny found himself trapped in the Kiev salient; his request to withdraw resulted in his immediate relief from command and the appointment of Marshal Timoshenko in his place. A few days later Guderian and Field Marshal Edwin Kleist linked in a pincer movement some 100 miles east of Kiev, trapping Timoshenko's troops. Shaposhnikov cabled the General Staff on that day: 'This is the beginning as you know of catastrophe – a matter of a couple of days.' Kiev indeed fell on 18 September and the bulk of

the Soviet army was either annihilated or captured. The situation at the southern front seemed just as bleak, with German forces encircling Odessa and threatening the Crimea.[38]

These dramatic events almost entirely passed over Cripps and the military mission, who were living, as they had often pointed out, in a 'vacuum'. All they could rely on, as Cripps remarked, was 'an occasional piece of gossip through the Russian chauffeurs or dvorniks, or possibly through the foreign journalists'. The Russians' refusal to part with any significant military information did not reflect their attitude to the alliance, as the dejected Mason-Macfarlane was occasionally inclined to believe.[39] On the contrary, it must have reflected a fear that a disclosure of the disastrous situation might deter the British government from releasing substantial assistance. They tried therefore as far as was possible to mollify the embittered staff of the mission. Indeed, despite his resolve to obtain military information from Stalin, Cripps had little doubt that the Russians were protesting against the British refusal to be 'acting as full allies'.[40]

Stalin's request from Churchill on 13 September for the dispatch of twenty-five to thirty divisions to strengthen Russian resistance shows the despairing mood in Moscow. Stalin now entirely abandoned demands for a second front on the Continent. For the reasons given above his message did not divulge the actual extent of the crushing defeat. Stalin's message was backed up by Maisky's pleading in London for immediate intervention in the South, implying that a token force would be of no avail.[41] If he lacked the appropriate background intelligence, Churchill's judgment that it was 'almost incredible' that Stalin could commit himself to such 'absurdities' and that it was 'hopeless to argue with a man thinking in terms of unreality' would be understandable. However, unlike his representatives in Moscow, Churchill was in possession of Enigma decrypts which in those critical days often provided more accurate and detailed information on the progress of the war than was available to the Soviet leaders themselves.[42] This explains why, rather than dismissing the request as sheer lunacy, the COS considered means of at least a partial acceptance. Dill's inclination to turn it down on grounds of impracticability reflected in fact a distinct order of priorities in refusing to spare forces either from Britain or the Middle East. The shipping, including that obtained from the United States,[43] which would be required to fulfil Stalin's request

had been allocated to reinforcing the overseas garrisons. The technical difficulties outlined by Churchill were hardly mentioned in the discussion. The small-scale assistance contemplated took for granted a major German breakthrough in the South if not the entire collapse of the Red Army. Rather than contemplating full cooperation to forestall such an event, the COS was considering means to 'delay any German threat to Eastern Anatolia, Iraq and Persia'. A limited reinforcement could enable the evacuation of large Soviet formations from the Caucasus to be used later in the Middle East and the destruction of the Baku oilfields.[44] Still under pressure in Cabinet, Churchill apologized that his response might have been more favourable if the 'western flank in Libya was cleared'. Now that the Middle Eastern arena faced a new threat, Churchill revived the fanciful idea of mobilizing Turkey. He strongly warned against supplying Russia with aid designed for Turkey which 'might discourage the Turks from coming in on the British side'.[45] The pinning of hopes on the 'most awful brigands' was strongly resisted in the Foreign Office. It seemed unrealistic to expect Turkey in 'any circumstances or at any time' to come into the war, and it was doubtful whether the Russians would be convinced; they knew 'their Turks too well for that'.[46]

Churchill's reply to Stalin was thus entirely inappropriate. It avoided, as was realized in the Foreign Office, 'mentioning the Southern front suggested by Stalin and referred only to the importance of Turkey'. Churchill instead drew in advance on the expectations from the forthcoming conference.[47] In a typically wily move Maisky attempted to find out more from Eden by insinuating that Stalin would be 'much disheartened', regarding the message as a definite rejection. However, Eden was prevented by Churchill from conceding any further; there was 'no objection to study any plan', he instructed Eden, but the Russians should entertain no 'delusions that any large armies [could] be sent from Great Britain to fight in Russia'.[48] Maisky's only recourse was to impress on Eden that now that the Germans were overrunning the Donets Basin nothing prevented them from assuming control over the Caucasus. This was the key not only to the Soviet industrial resources but also to the fate of the whole war. He did not expect Turkey to abandon her neutrality once the Caucasus had fallen; the defence of the southern flank had therefore become the 'most urgent military problem for the Allies'.[49]

## The Moscow conference

Throughout the second half of August and the beginning of September Cripps was rancorous at not being sounded out on the conference which, he believed, could 'to some extent counteract the disappointment that now reigns'. Indeed, Cripps was only rarely approached by the Foreign Office and mostly regarding 'administrative arrangements, e.g., should any bedding be brought?'. 'Mere courtesy', he thought, demanded that the Russians, as hosts of the conference, should at least not be left in the dark. Churchill's prevention of his return home led Cripps to a mutinous reaction; in conversation with Stalin he raised doubts about the desirability of holding the conference at all in view of Churchill's discouraging messages. When Cripps, together with Steinhardt, was finally instructed on 10 September to inform Molotov of the expected arrival of the delegations on 1 October the conference seemed to hold little promise for him. Even now the embarrassing fact was that he could tell Molotov little beside the much-publicized fact that Beaverbrook had been nominated to lead the British delegation.[50]

Cripps was therefore fully aware that to all intents and purposes his presence in Moscow had become superfluous. However, he felt that his experience and the respect he commanded with the Russians were indispensable for bringing the conference, which he had been the first to contemplate, to a successful conclusion.[51] Together with the military mission Cripps was attempting to give the conference a different direction from that which was being worked out in London. However, the highest item on the agenda was that of supply, which was in the realm of the economic mission headed by Cadbury. Cadbury, it was observed in Moscow, did all he could to antagonize the Russians. His one object in life seemed 'not to integrate our joint strategy in the economic field, but to save dollars and to find out as much about [the Russians'] production as possible'. Cripps had found himself, therefore, increasingly involved in the economic negotiations with Mikoyan. To ensure control over the proceedings he persuaded Dalton to recall Cadbury in the earliest convoy and leave it to him to introduce the delegation to the Russians and give it his expert advice.[52]

In preliminary discussions in Moscow the military mission seconded Maisky's demand from Churchill to comply with what was actually a rather trifling promise to Stalin to broaden the scope of the conference

and include the coordination of strategy. This was fully backed by Cripps. The idea, however, appeared most objectionable to the COS. They opposed anything beyond the bare minimum of cooperation in Iran and the Murmansk region: such cooperation, they argued, could easily be handled by the military mission in Moscow. The inclusion of strategy on the agenda, they further objected, was bound to invite Soviet pressure for the establishment of a second front. The Cabinet eventually adopted a middle course, again symbolic in nature, based on a casual suggestion by Cripps that the inclusion in the delegation of an authoritative military figure would help to convince the Russians of the difficulties facing the British in mounting a diversionary action. Consequently Lt.-General G. N. Macready, Dill's assistant, and General Ismay were appointed, though they were constrained by the decision not to cooperate with the Russians on the battlefield.[53] While preparations for the conference were under way the War Office explained the advantages in continued Soviet resistance, insofar as it 'postpones the threat of invasion, affords us further time for preparing our forces and weakens the enemy by draining the resources at his disposal'. They vehemently opposed a deviation from the basic defensive strategy which might incur risks to the 'security of our base'. The priority in resources given to the securing of the 'life-line' across the Atlantic reflected reliance on the eventual appearance of the United States as a saviour. Even a successful landing, they insisted, might result not in relief to the East but a stabilization of the front, leaving Britain with inadequate forces to resist a subsequent invasion. The concession of supplies was accepted as indispensable for the extension of the breathing space on condition that it did not interfere with British strategic planning.[54]

On the very eve of Beaverbrook's departure the COS's grand strategy, fully adhered to by Churchill, was firmly reasserted. The unaltered conclusion was that all resources should be directed to the defence of the Middle East, which gave the 'greatest promise of good dividends'. Churchill was indeed pressing General Claude Auchinleck, who had relieved Wavell after the failure of the June offensive, to resume the initiative. He often referred to the desirability of exploiting the temporary respite to regain the initiative and even resorted to blackmail: Auchinleck was told that if action were not speedily taken forces would have to be diverted to 'sustain Russian left wing in the

Caucasus'.[55] As Anatolia rather than Russia was currently considered the 'key to the defence of the Northern Flank', any assistance contemplated had to take Turkey into account. Russia figured only insofar as she fitted into the Middle Eastern strategy; it was 'better to send equipment to Russian men than to send British men who have got to be maintained from long distances'.[56]

While Churchill and the services were resolute not to make any concessions on strategy, they were practically compelled by the Americans to divert supplies. The significance attached by Roosevelt to bolstering the eastern front, either to reduce the incessant British pressure for the Americans themselves to enter the war or because of misgivings about the Middle Eastern campaign, had become pronounced after Hopkins' return to Washington. A letter from Hopkins to Churchill preceded Harriman's arrival in London, stressing that 'substantial and comprehensive commitments' should be made to Russia on short- and long-term deliveries. The Americans were playing straight into Beaverbrook's hands. All Churchill could do was to appeal to Roosevelt's conscience and demand a rise in production to close the gap created by deliveries to Russia.[57] Roosevelt's enthusiastic response promising a substantial increase in production and deliveries is depicted in Churchill's memoirs in awkward proximity to another statement that the aid to Russia caused 'much derangement of our military plans, already hampered by the tormenting shortage of munitions'.[58] It was in fact admitted, after the quotas for Russia had been decided by the Defence Committee on 19 September, that 'commonly put, what we lose on the swings we will gain on the roundabouts'. In the Defence Committee Churchill emphatically stated that he would 'never agree to any agreement which would mean cutting down the size of our Army below its present level'. Diverting the pressure, he declared that America rather than Britain 'would have to be the arsenal for the Russian army'.[59] After the Moscow conference Harold Balfour, Parliamentary Under-Secretary for Air and one of Beaverbrook's young protégés who had accompanied him on the mission, underlined that the agreement was 'highly satisfactory from the British point of view . . . ensures Russian good will and effort in the air; it preserves our bomber position; it gives Russia no heavy bombers from the United States, thereby increasing our prospects of a bigger allotment; it preserves our Kittyhawk position in the Middle East'.[60] The motif of the sacrifice, frequently depicted in dramatic terms,

appeared all too often; to Ismay it was like 'having all one's eye-teeth drawn out at the same time, but there was nothing to do but grin and bear it'.[61] This was a safe device to quell domestic opposition as well as complaints in Moscow. But more significantly it proved a means of exerting pressure on the Americans to increase their own deliveries and taking the edge off their demands for a more definite coordination of strategy. Even from his sick-bed Hopkins telegraphed to Churchill on the day the conference opened in Moscow complaining that there was 'still an amazing number of people here who do not want to help Russia and who don't seem to be able to pound into their thick heads the strategic importance of that front'.[62]

Churchill's directive to Beaverbrook and the personal letter he was carrying to Stalin should be examined in this light. Both disappointed Beaverbrook, who told the Defence Committee right away that he could possibly show the directives to Harriman but certainly 'not to the Russians'. The documents were designed to restrain Beaverbrook from granting the Russians their pressing needs. The conference was expected above all to be a demonstration of cooperation while keeping to a minimum the loss of supplies called for by the Americans in return for sustaining the major theatre in the Middle East. Beaverbrook was therefore 'free to encourage the prolonged resistance' by presenting a hopeful view of the prospects of Anglo-American production as well as possible offensive diversions in 1942–3. The directive as a whole provided Beaverbrook with ample arguments to convince the Russians of the practical limitations to granting substantial assistance and the strain on manpower, which was 'engaged to the limit'. Churchill also equipped Beaverbrook with a stock of rhetoric which he was to employ when faced by the inevitable question: 'How do you propose to win the war?' The letter to Stalin was illustrative of how the delegation should act. It elaborated the difficulties in production and the element of sacrifice. There was only a passing reference to willingness to study plans for practical cooperation, while the need to complete the war in Libya before shifting forces to south Russia was taken for granted. As for the intermediate period, which for the Russians on the verge of catastrophe was of particular concern, Churchill suggested that the 'most speedy and effective help' would be if Turkey could be induced to resist the passage of German troops or even enter the war. It was tantamount in fact to a rejection of Stalin's personal message of 15 September.[63]

Beaverbrook's task might have been made easier if he had been accompanied by Hopkins. With Harriman, who hitherto was entrusted with fulfilling British needs, he clashed in the preliminary meetings in London. The differences were, as recorded by Harriman while cruising to Russia, that Beaverbrook 'now claims that the P.M. underestimates Russia. I can see no indication of this and, in fact, share the P.M.'s views regarding the importance of Turkey and the Middle East. I am personally also less ready to strip England than either of them.'[64] While he could exercise his dominating personality to tame Harriman, controlling Cripps was a different proposition.

Considering the fact that Cripps had fathered the idea of the conference and shared Beaverbrook's general attitude to Russia and overall strategic priorities, the two ought to have formed a combination which, if consolidated, would undoubtedly have proved a serious challenge to Churchill. Indeed, after Cripps' return to London, Churchill was quick to employ the principle of divide and rule to forestall such a development. Numerous factors prevented the cooperation. The dominant one seems to have been Beaverbrook's determination to champion the rising indignation on the left on the issue of help to Russia. Familiar as he was with the real objections to Cripps' return, he certainly recognized in him a challenge. Initially the subjection of Cripps was easy and was assisted by Cripps himself, who had successfully persuaded Hopkins of the desirability of keeping Steinhardt out of the talks. To Cripps' misfortune a message he had sent to London objecting to the inclusion in the delegation of Quentin Reynolds, who had been personally appointed by Harriman to handle press relations, was intercepted on board the cruiser carrying the delegation. It infuriated Harriman, who found it only too easy to convince Beaverbrook to dispense with the services of their respective ambassadors. Beaverbrook in turn told Harriman he was 'always ill at ease with teetotalers . . . particularly Socialist teetotalers who were candidates for sainthood'. Besides, he wanted to speak freely with Stalin and make his 'own' report to the War Cabinet 'without prompting or contradiction'.[65] Churchill's and Eden's manifest impatience with Cripps as a result of his demands to return to England made it easier for Beaverbrook to ignore him. Eden certainly did not encourage him to work closely with the ambassador in Moscow. On the contrary, he suggested that Beaverbrook leave behind in Moscow someone with 'sufficient status and personality to impress the Russians

who, in matters of this sort, [were] both touchy and snobbish', to carry on with the work he had started.[66]

After being informed of the composition of the delegation and the flow of discouraging letters from Eden, it dawned on Cripps that he was destined to play a minor role; when he had conceived the idea of a conference, he complained, it was of 'a very small group who could negotiate direct with Stalin but I am afraid that the thing has got on to quite a different plane'. Rather conceitedly, he expected that from the point of view of efficiency it would be preferable for him to 'stay outside and give any help' which was needed. He was probably contemplating working behind the scenes and counting on the persuasion which had proved so effective with Hopkins. He even attempted a *fait accompli* by reaching an agreement on military supplies with Mikoyan before Beaverbrook's arrival. Steinhardt, whose political senses were more acute, foresaw the threat. He almost pleaded with Cripps that they should 'help one another to protect [their] separate political interests against being jockeyed at the conference'. 'That sort of intrigue', was Cripps' typically self-righteous and contemptuous reaction, 'has no interest for me and I really dont care two pins about either his or my position if only we can get success out of the conference.'[67]

When HMS *London* dropped anchor at the mouth of the Dvina river on 27 September the delegation was transferred to a Soviet destroyer which shipped them to Archangel. On board were Molotov and John Russell, the third secretary, bearing a personal message from Cripps. It consisted of detailed guidance to Beaverbrook and the 'greenhorns', as Harriman resentfully noted, on how the conference should be run. It has been suggested that Cripps favoured bargaining with the Russians while Beaverbrook was unconditionally committed to helping them.[68] Cripps expected reciprocity but his views and priorities were essentially much like Beaverbrook's. In many ways Cripps' memorandum was more radical than the line Beaverbrook was compelled to pursue in view of the restrictions imposed on him by Churchill. Cripps aimed at the eventual establishment of an unreserved alliance and was prepared to tackle all contentious issues on the way. He suggested that Beaverbrook keep Hopkins' promise, the essence of which was the 'matching of the requirements and the available supplies upon the basis of the strategical needs of each country'. This would naturally entail thorough

political and strategical discussions on the basis of equality. Colonel Leslie Hollis, Senior Assistant Secretary to the War Cabinet, hit the nail on the head by commenting that Cripps 'wanted negotiations to take the place of utilization'.[69] Having decided to keep Cripps out of the conference, Beaverbrook did not even consult the memorandum, a précis of which was prepared for him on 6 October *en route* for home.[70] He would listen, complained Cripps, only to his friend E. Elliott, who had arrived with the American delegation two days earlier and now 'picked up some gossip from the journalists'.[71]

Beaverbrook's well-advertised *coup* in Moscow was no more than the fulfilment of Hopkins' modest but far more important visit. In many ways the protocol now signed to the sound of fanfares was a ceremonial delivery of supplies which, with insignificant exceptions, had been allocated to Russia earlier after bitter arguments with the Americans. 'There has not been any concession in excess of authority conferred on me', was Beaverbrook's assurance to Cabinet shortly after the protocol was signed.[72]

Beaverbrook was determined to avoid any controversial issue raised by Cripps, Harriman, the Polish government or the Russians themselves. He opted for a swift victory; 'It was to be', he later explained, 'a Christmas tree party, and there must be no excuse for the Russians thinking they were not getting a fair share of the gifts on the tree.'[73] Unlike Cripps, his devotion to the cause made Beaverbrook mute dissonances. Although the agreement gained stunning publicity, the proceedings reveal serious controversies which shortly burst into the open, casting a shadow on Russia's relations with her allies throughout the duration of the war. The most contentious issue, besides Cripps' demand for political discussion of post-war arrangements, were the coordination of strategy and the Polish problem. Beaverbrook left his military advisers in no doubt that he did not 'intend to allow any discussions involving military negatives to cut across and impede the supply negotiations'.[74] Cripps insisted on the need to lift the barrier of suspicion through exchanges on this subject. Throughout the conference, however, Beaverbrook 'would not allow' him to arrange for Mason-Macfarlane and Ismay to meet Stalin and Shaposhnikov, which he feared might spoil his declared intention of pleasing the Russians. Nor would he permit a thorough exposition of the difficulties facing the British in mounting a diversion.[75]

While Cripps' position and the strategic issues called for a simple and straightforward decision on Beaverbrook's part, the need to satisfy Sikorsky was tied in with pressure from Catholic public opinion in the United States. Harriman had been directed by Roosevelt to broach Stalin on the issues. In his memorandum Cripps too believed that the subject should be on the agenda. Beaverbrook, however, succeeded in preventing Harriman from going into the subject during the crucial meetings with Stalin. He consented to meet General Wladyslaw Anders, Commander-in-Chief of the Polish forces in Russia, and Stanislaw Kot, Sikorski's new representative in Moscow, only on 2 October, after the conclusion of the talks and at the American embassy. Mason-Macfarlane, also present, was the most outspoken; this undoubtedly contributed to his eventual downfall. A real discussion, as Kot discerned immediately, was made impossible by Beaverbrook, who was 'despotic by nature, knew everything better and had settled everything in advance'. Harriman, Kot disappointedly observed, acted 'far from independently, only noting desiderata of various kinds. Beaverbrook dominated everything.'[76] The avoidance of the Polish issue had troublesome consequences. Shortly after the conference had ended, the COS adopted Sikorsky's proposal that the Russians should arm the Polish divisions and dispatch them to the Caucasus. There they would reinforce the defence of the oilfields and from there, if things went wrong, they could 'escape more easily' and be a 'welcome addition to our Army in the Middle East, at no cost of shipping'.[77] Naturally such a proposition was most offensive to the Russians. The negotiations were entrusted to Cripps, whose authority had been seriously undermined as a result of the conference. After long months of haggling, the Poles were evacuated at the beginning of 1942.[78]

The arrival of Beaverbrook in Moscow was the first public display of the alliance. Clusters of flags consisting of the Union Jack, the Stars and Stripes and the Red Flag were bound together in terrific quantities and a guard of honour of some 500 soldiers, rushed from the front, performed an immaculate drill. Even Cripps, rarely inclined to sentiment, was moved by the event when after waiting for an hour at the airport in a bitterly cold dawn, the four Douglases carrying the delegation arrived 'in a formation . . . accompanied by fighters and looked extraordinarily nice as they came in from the opposite side of the aerodrome against background of heavy snow clouds with a glint of sun right in the centre'.

The entire staff of the two embassies was present and the sight of several scores of British, American and Soviet officers standing at the salute 'for the whole bag of tricks' was unique.[79] Beyond the excitement, informed observers at the British embassy shared a strong sense of scepticism and even contempt at Beaverbrook's publicity stunts. Beaverbrook ceaselessly made attempts to win over the press, making selected indiscreet revelations of his talks and throwing a party for the correspondents at his hotel suite 'complete with whisky and champagne and the orchestra of the Caucasian restaurant'. Already at the close of the first day sources intimate with Cripps noticed that 'a great many very angry men in Moscow are pretty sick of Beaverbrook's rudeness which is commonly mistaken for efficiency'. To the younger staff it was 'a real education to see a major political thug in action'.[80]

The most obvious omissions from Beaverbrook's selective and overdramatic reports are his numerous encounters with Cripps. From the moment his plane touched down Cripps, as he had planned, clung to Beaverbrook. He drove him to the National Hotel, the most luxurious in Moscow, which had been put exclusively at the disposal of the delegation. They lunched together and had tea at the embassy. Later in the evening Cripps and Steinhardt introduced the delegates to Stalin and retired, as had been requested. Beaverbrook, who had already divulged to Harriman his opinion of Cripps, certainly did not enjoy being managed. Cripps quickly sensed that this was not going to be a repeat of Hopkins' visit; Beaverbrook, he noted, must be a 'very difficult person to work with though alright to work under'. Beaverbrook, fully conscious of Cripps' integrity and aware that he was an adversary, tried to win him over. He and Eden, he told Cripps, were 'the only two Crippsites in the Cabinet!'; much as he would have liked to follow Cripps' advice and coordinate production with the Russians, he was held back by the Cabinet. Although Beaverbrook knew only too well that Churchill was determined to keep Cripps in Russia, he urged him to return, join the Cabinet and collaborate with him. To his dismay Cripps would not bend. He told Beaverbrook to his face that he would find it 'very hard to work with him' as their views on Labour and management questions differed widely. Cripps went even further, as is recorded in his diary:

He was a little upset I think the other evening when I told him he was thick skinned and little later that I was sure he would lie like a trooper for his country.

14 and 15 Moscow airport, 28 September 1941: top, l. to r.: Vyshinsky, Cripps, Beaverbrook, Steinhardt, Harriman and Oumansky at attention for the national anthems; bottom, l. to r.: Cripps, Steinhardt, Vyshinsky, Oumansky, Harriman and Beaverbrook inspect a Red Army guard of honour rushed from the front

He explained in a rather pained voice that he didnt regard it as being a bad thing to be like that and he would do anything however dishonest if he thought it could serve his country. And I believe him.[81]

Relations between Cripps and Beaverbrook shortly assumed an undisguised hostility. As an observer recorded, Beaverbrook's

conduct and attitude to staff here, and staff he brought over, was on a par with his conduct in everything else. Cripps asked him to dinner. Russell asked him if he was going. B. – 'No, I've seen enough of Cripps.' 'What excuse shall I give?' 'Don't give any – don't answer.' Nearer time Russell asked again if he should phone. 'No, let him wait if he wants to,' etc.

Nor could Beaverbrook resist the temptation to disparage Cripps in a 'half-jocular discussion' with Stalin which Harriman, unaware of Cripps' demands to return home, thought 'led to the early removal of Cripps and Steinhardt from Moscow'.[82] In their last meeting the conversation turned *inter alia* to a criticism by Stalin of Steinhardt which confirmed Cripps' earlier reservations. Beaverbrook, fully prepared to compromise Cripps' own position, hoped to elicit a similar reaction: 'What about our fellow?', he asked, 'barely concealing his personal distaste for Cripps', as Harriman observed. Stalin did not fall into the trap; he simply shrugged his shoulders and said: 'Oh, he's all right' without enthusiasm. Beaverbrook could not resist expressing his own opinion that Cripps was 'a bore'. In reporting to Cabinet he not only did not describe the way he had raised the subject but further attributed to Stalin his own opinion. Moreover, he told Cripps that Stalin was 'very complimentary' about him.[83] It should be added that Stalin's noncommittal attitude, besides being a result of Beaverbrook's provocation, might have been caused by a rather obscure but amusing episode. A current issue of *Life* which Oumansky brought along from Washington contained a large photograph of Hopkins, Cripps and his Airedale Joe, claimed to have been named after Stalin.[84]

Eden, recognized in Cabinet as the proponent of help to Russia, fared no better. Beaverbrook casually reported to Cabinet that Stalin was 'decidedly critical of British foreign policy'. His various attempts to interest Stalin in Eden had ended: 'without any success. He just failed to make any comment. I had the same result previously when Eden's name was mentioned by me through Litvinov.' On the other hand, Beaverbrook's scrappy reports of the conference referred time and again to the

immense interest displayed by Stalin in Churchill. The several records of participants in the conference depicting Beaverbrook's constant rather childish habit of engineering intrigues make it hard to assume the references were casual.[85]

Apart from Beaverbrook, most other leading members of the delegation developed a regard for Cripps. Balfour dined with him, discussed post-war reconstruction and believed he had 'done well' in Moscow. Unlike Beaverbrook, he even thanked Cripps and the staff for their efforts in a warm personal letter. Harriman bore no grudge against Cripps for the earlier incident and Beaverbrook's unflattering introduction. He developed a 'high regard for Cripps' intelligence' during a long intimate conversation on the night of 3 October. In contrast to Beaverbrook, Harriman found himself in agreement with Cripps on the importance of settling Russia's territorial demands during the war without delay. Moreover, it was through Harriman that Cripps received snippets of information on the progress of the negotiations.[86]

Beaverbrook was evidently wary of Cripps' reaction to the methods he had adopted and the results achieved. The day that the protocol was signed Cripps knew only that the conference was about to be wound up; 'on what basis I dont know as I have had little except scraps of information at mealtimes from Beaverbrook'. Beaverbrook finally departed without keeping his promise of revealing to Cripps the political topics which had been discussed with Stalin. Nor did he leave copies of his telegrams, which Cripps had not been shown in the first place. He did not even bother to pass on Stalin's information that the battle of Moscow had commenced. Cripps felt he was, as he told his daughter, 'merely ornamental and a host to our delegation'.[87] His reporting on the conference indeed confirms how little he knew of the proceedings. It caused dismay at the Foreign Office, where the conference was regarded as a 'complete newspaper stunt' and no credence was given to Beaverbrook's own account.[88] Beaverbrook also insured himself against Cripps' criticism by dispatching to Cabinet from HMS *London* a censored and tendentious report on the conference emphasizing the futility of Cripps' approach in contrast to his major success. He also presented Churchill on his return with a memorandum on his differences with Cripps. It was a masterpiece of cunning in that it conveyed the impression of thorough discussion and consultation between the two in Moscow. The complaints from Cripps that began filtering in, happily

seized on by Eden, became a source of embarrassment for Beaverbrook whose main battle was in London and not in Moscow. Rather belatedly he attempted to neutralize Cripps by flattering him, as is obvious in his letter of 13 October:

You may be sure that I am carrying out your policy of material aid to Russia to the full and that I am most anxious to co-operate with you in every way. There is much that I should like to discuss with you by cable or letter and I feel confident that our collaboration will have far-reaching results.[89]

To return to the conference: Stalin opened the first meeting with a sombre and frank review of the military situation. He described the initial setback and elaborated on the balance of manpower and munitions between the Russians and the Germans, specifying the army's needs which were beyond what Beaverbrook was authorized to part with. Beaverbrook's later report to Cabinet ended at that point; however Harriman, addressing the President, saw fit to add: 'There was considerable discussion all the way through the talk regarding British military cooperation with Russia.' Beaverbrook was clearly on the defensive, unable to conceal the fact that he could make no concrete proposals. He suggested instead exploratory discussions with Ismay, but would prefer that Stalin send a military mission to London to 'consider the British problem'. He alluded to the divisions Britain was 'building up' in Iran to link with Russia in the Caucasus; here he was interrupted by Stalin to the effect that there was 'no war in the Caucasus but there [was] in the Ukraine'. Stalin's brusque interjection revealed that he had grasped the pessimistic British appraisal that the Russians would withdraw deeply, and that the southern border should be reinforced to prevent a German breakthrough to the Middle East through the back door. Beaverbrook was resolved to avoid political arguments and therefore when the talks turned to war aims, a subject raised so often by Cripps in his talks with Molotov and Stalin, he 'dodged the answer with some generality about "we must win the war first"'. The other minefield Beaverbrook had to avoid was Harriman's occasional interposition on the need for information about Soviet military plans and production.[90]

Both Harriman and Beaverbrook considered the meeting to have been 'extremely friendly' and were 'more than pleased' with their reception. Beaverbrook rather prematurely opened the festivities in an extremely encouraging telegram read by Churchill to the War Cabinet

the next day.[91] Although Beaverbrook spent some two hours with Cripps after the meeting, he divulged little of what had transpired. He stressed the psychological rather than material value of the conference, again referring to it as a 'Father Christmas party' in which the United States and Britain were 'declaring' what they were prepared to do to 'help poor Russia'. There followed a discussion in which Cripps maintained that it was the 'wrong atmosphere altogether'. He expected Stalin to deduce that nothing else was 'possible at present' and to be 'unduly disappointed at the treatment that he gets'.[92]

The following morning the delegation woke up to find Moscow under a thin cover of the first, rather early, snow. It gave the city a mellow and romantic look; its military significance could not possibly be recognized at that point. In contrast the meeting with Stalin in the evening was 'very rough going'. Stalin, as Harriman recalled later, gave a clear indication that he was dissatisfied with the offers and appeared to question whether they were 'acting on good faith'.[93] Beaverbrook's hopes of an uneventful examination with Stalin of the supply list and perhaps even reaching an agreement on that very night were shattered. The hostile tenor of the meeting disconcerted him to the extent that the only reference he made in his notes was that Stalin was 'very restless, walking about and smoking continuously and seemed to be under an intense strain'. Beaverbrook was in fact so worried about the outcome of the negotiations that he was reduced to pleading with Stalin to adopt the following procedure: he would give an account of the help Britain was able to deliver and 'this recital should be entered into on the basis of M. Stalin's agreeing to accept the offers if he believes them to be sufficiently bountiful'.[94] In his account Beaverbrook skilfully concealed Stalin's great disappointment in order to inflate his own achievement. He preferred to present the protocol signed at the end of the conference as the execution of a precise plan laid down in advance. Thus in one of his rare telegrams from Moscow, announcing the successful conclusion of the talks, he described the plan in the following way: 'The eggs for the pudding were steadily increased from night to night culminating in scenes of complete happiness at the Kremlin.' This idealized description has been described by Harriman as 'sunshine after rain'.[95]

Beaverbrook had twice asked for information on the situation at the front but received evasive answers. In their last meeting Stalin revealed that the Germans had resumed the offensive with the clear intention of

taking Moscow.[96] It was convenient for Beaverbrook to attribute the change in Stalin's mood to this development, minimizing the substantial differences of opinion. This explanation is most unsatisfactory. The central front had stabilized in mid-August and was held mostly by reserve units while the battle raged in the South. In London Military Intelligence, assisted by Enigma, had been collecting information on German plans to resume the battle of Moscow. Nine warnings based on Enigma decrypts had been passed on to the Russians by the military mission between 20 and 24 September. Acting on the basis of this, and probably also their own intelligence, the Russians hastened to regroup their forces. On 30 September Guderian started a diversionary pincer movement in the southern sector, of which Stalin must have had previous knowledge. This happened on the night preceding the acrimonious meeting. In the early hours of 2 October the main German force under General von Bock started its advance at an alarming pace. Stalin was cheerful and betrayed no sign of anxiety at the seven-hour banquet he mounted in the Kremlin for the delegation while the crucial battle was raging.[97]

Stalin's change of heart must reflect a decision taken deliberately as a result of the proceedings of the first night. He perceived Beaverbrook's formalistic expectations and unwillingness to discuss the contentious issues which had been the implicit subject of his pressing communications with Churchill. It was clear that strategic issues were out of the scope of the conference and the commitment to supplies rested on a verbal undertaking. From the outset of the conference, therefore, the sub-committees set up to work out the details of supplies found themselves at 'loggerheads on one great matter of principle'.[98] Stalin certainly abhorred the idea of being at the mercy of British Christmas gifts. Considering the drastic change in his attitude on the second day, it is not impossible that many of Beaverbrook's exchanges with Cripps, which were conducted in public over dinner and tea at the embassy, were even passed on to Stalin. It was taken for granted that the majority of the staff at the embassy, who were Russians and some of whom were later exposed, worked for the secret police. Indeed, microphones had been discovered in the lodgings of the military mission.[99] What is obvious, however, is that Beaverbrook was suddenly faced with a fresh demand from Stalin for a public signature of a protocol on supply which he unsuccessfully resisted. Stalin's explanation that a written agreement

was necessary to counter Goebbels' propagandists, who were predicting the collapse of the talks, was rather flimsy.[100] Stalin did not conceal his desire to broaden the scope of the conference to include controversial issues and to give the alliance a more formal and permanent shape. In the last meeting and during the banquet he reverted to these topics, expressing a wish for the Anglo-Soviet agreement to be extended into a treaty, 'an alliance not only for war but for post-war as well'. He was extremely critical of the attempts to shift Turkey from her neutrality and further used a casual ten-minute encounter with Ismay to condemn British strategy, which he believed relied on a large navy and ignored the need to establish a standing army of any magnitude.[101] Those histories suggesting that Stalin's fluctuating attitude was a device which became a model for his future negotiations with western leaders follow Beaverbrook's censored version and underestimate the significant rift.[102]

Beaverbrook's account is inconsistent with his behaviour at the time. He returned to the British embassy after the second meeting in a state of 'deep depression'. He told Harriman of the 'damage to his political standing that would flow from the apparent failure of their mission'. In composing his reports Beaverbrook was 'constantly thinking of his own reputation with his colleagues in the British government'. To Cripps he disclosed nothing, on the pretext that he was 'too busy'.[103] Resolved to overcome the difficulties at all costs, Beaverbrook decided to dispense with the advice of his experts by virtually dismantling the committees. He proposed to work out a supply list to suit as far as possible the Russians' expectations and secure Stalin's acceptance. Using his undisputed authority he persuaded his various experts, who however noted that he was 'playing a bold and lone hand'.[104]

Beaverbrook approached the meeting on 30 September with grave apprehensions. The participants plodded through the detailed list of supplies. It should not have surprised Beaverbrook that Stalin appeared to be 'reasonable and not too exacting'; the supply commitment was now to be embodied in binding form though the thorny questions would remain outstanding. Beaverbrook, exultant and relieved, could not restrain himself from exclaiming: 'You are pleased?' Stalin, undoubtedly aware of Beaverbrook's anxieties, 'smiled and nodded indicating satisfaction'. To avoid a last-minute hitch Beaverbrook rather childishly kept adding unsolicited minor items to his offer. He

further promised a monthly increase of aircraft and tanks by 50% in 1942 and 100% in 1943. Beaverbrook returned in a jovial mood to the embassy, where with the help of the journalists he concocted a success story, minimizing the ominous signs which had emerged during the conference. Stalin and himself, he told those present at the embassy, were now 'great pals. The first day Stalin gave him tea; the second day nothing; to-day, tea and cakes!'[105]

In spite of his exclusion from the negotiations Cripps was not deluded by Beaverbrook's publicity campaign. The communiqué issued by Beaverbrook, he correctly observed, was: 'quite false in saying we satisfied the wishes of the Russians . . . after the spectacular success of the conference the time of disappointment will come when the things do not arrive'. Cripps therefore urged Churchill and Eden to maintain the momentum, as defaulting on deliveries would mean that the 'last state will be much worse than the first'.[106] Cripps was right in recognizing the Russians' severe misgivings about the exclusion of cardinal issues from the negotiations. He failed, however, to appreciate Beaverbrook's singlemindedness. Both Ismay and Balfour were instructed to draw up their recommendations in favour of fulfilling the undertakings while still on board the cruiser. The Cabinet was urged by both to 'endeavour to meet Russian particular needs so far as we are able and without a disposition to question every Russian basis of demand'.[107] In the short run Cripps' and Beaverbrook's pleas were unnecessary as the terms of the agreement had been worked out in advance. Churchill gained credit by making his first tangible offer to Stalin, informing him of the three convoys planned for October which fulfilled most of the quota as specified in the new protocol. Beaverbrook indeed saw to it that a large proportion of the deliveries promised under the first protocol, covering October 1941–June 1942, were made; however, it should be emphasized that deficiencies in the Middle East were avoided through the increase of production at home and in the United States.[108]

The Moscow conference and commitment to Russia crowned Beaverbrook with immediate popularity but had severe repercussions on his political career, leading to his exclusion from the War Cabinet in early 1942. At least part of it was due to Cripps. It is characteristic of Cripps, however, that despite the humiliating treatment he had suffered at the hands of Beaverbrook he bore no personal grudge against

him, as is evident from his diary: 'that is the Beaver and so I feel no resentment at all as he is what he is and his individuality has had some good points for the country though some very bad ones too'. In a personal letter to Eden he reported that, despite his misgivings, Beaverbrook had handled the proceedings 'extremely well' and had brought off a 'brilliant success'.[109] Politically Beaverbrook's presence in Moscow finally shattered Cripps' hopes of being entrusted with handling post-war planning in Cabinet. His encounters with Beaverbrook, whom he regarded as the closest 'friend and ally of the P.M.'s', confirmed his apprehension that the Cabinet was determined to win the war but reluctant to deal with its consequences. As he found Beaverbrook 'about the most reactionary person possible', he reached a firm decision not to serve with him in the same Cabinet as issues dear to him did not 'enter into [Beaverbrook's] sphere of comprehension'.[110]

The arguments against his continued stay in Moscow were now, therefore, less pressing than before. Eden had sent Cripps through Beaverbrook yet another placatory letter requesting him to remain at his post. Cripps' impression that the letter was a 'genuine expression of opinion' is a perfect example of his political naivety and failure to grasp that he was considered a political menace at home and was ostracized and charged with routine work. In a rather paradoxical way this weakness was also a source of Cripps' otherwise inexplicable strength. His attachment to his convictions was such that he was not discouraged by what seemed insurmountable difficulties and he sometimes insisted, almost to the point of eccentricity, on acting in a way which appeared to be political suicide. Thus, in replying to Eden, Cripps now confessed his doubts whether he could be 'of any use in the present Government set-up, even if others thought [he] might be'. The reasons Cripps gave for wishing to be recalled merely for consultations are an outstanding example of his failure to grasp the threat he posed at home: 'Assuming that all you say as to my utility here is strictly correct, I still feel that considerations as to the future may outweigh the importance of the present, not necessarily from the angle of Winston's view-point but from the direction in which my mind and a number of others are turning.'[111]

Finally, an episode which seemed trifling during the conference had later consequences and was entirely Cripps' doing. Oumansky had been appointed as interpreter in Beaverbrook's first meeting with

Stalin. He had a poor reputation with the Americans as being sly and untrustworthy. A month earlier Cripps had been rushed to the Kremlin's luxurious shelter during an air raid after a talk with Stalin. The really 'thrilling and interesting' experience, which he 'wouldnt have missed for anything', was the presence of Litvinov who, it transpired, was doing minor work for Narkomindel. Cripps now specifically requested Molotov to appoint Litvinov as a member of the Soviet delegation to the conference and then, to Beaverbrook's annoyance, almost forced Molotov to appoint him instead of Oumansky as the interpreter of the major meetings.[112] Litvinov at first sight was shabby and unlike his old self, but throughout the conference he gained American trust and confidence and this improved his standing with the Kremlin. Meanwhile Harriman had clearly signalled to Stalin that Oumansky was *persona non grata* in Washington. A month later the Russians informed the Americans of their decision to appoint Litvinov as the new ambassador. Cripps was justified in taking the credit for putting Litvinov 'right back on the political map'. To his unconcealed satisfaction Steinhardt was at the same time withdrawn from Russia.[113]

# FRUSTRATION

### *Retreat to Kuibyshev*

While in London the government was reasonably well informed on the extent of the German advance on Moscow, Cripps had to rely almost entirely on the BBC although the battle was raging only 150 miles away.[1] Within the first few days of 'Typhoon' the Germans broke the Soviet defences in a pincer movement, capturing Orel in the South and Torzhok in the North and encircling and destroying the main Soviet forces trapped in the pocket of Vyazma. The reserve forces on the 'Mozhaisk Defence Line' proved no match for the sweeping German armoured divisions: on 13 October Kaluga fell on the southern flank and two days later Kalinin, a key town in the approaches to Moscow from Leningrad. Out of a total of over half a million combatants the Russians were left with 90,000 under the command of Zhukov who was rushed from Leningrad. The Moscow defence zone now ran parallel to the previous Mozhaisk line, at places only 60 miles from the capital. It was no longer a distinct line but consisted of positions organized in depth along the main routes leading into Moscow, road junctions and railway stations. Anti-tank ditches were frenziedly dug by battalions of recruited civilians while barricades, road blocks and tank traps were mounted in the main city streets leading to the Kremlin. Discipline and morale now collapsed in Moscow and the hitherto insignificant flight of civilians became uncontrollable.[2]

The rapidly deteriorating situation had immediate repercussions on Cripps' fortunes. Beaverbrook had brought to London Cripps' new demands to be recalled for consultations, exposing his fundamental differences of opinion with the government. In view of the political unrest in Cabinet and the mounting enthusiastic support for the Soviet struggle in the wake of the conference, Churchill was 'determined to

16 and 17  Moscow under siege : Muscovites digging an anti-tank ditch in the city centre

keep him at his post'.[3] On 14 October Eden exploited the grave situation to persuade Cripps that his return would 'inevitably lead to the widest misunderstanding'. He promised to examine the subject 'if and when' the front stabilized. Cripps, still unaware of the motives for his cultivation, replied briefly: 'Of course I agree'.[4] Within a day a return to England became a physical impossibility.

The severe situation at the front brought to the fore the issue of evacuating government offices and foreign delegations. The Russians came up against the dilemma which had haunted them since the outbreak of war and which impeded collaboration: any display of weakness might encourage those expecting an early collapse and might damage the chance of further assistance. A decision was therefore deferred until the Germans established a bridgehead on the entrance to the Volga–Moscow canal on the night of 13–14 October. Considering the arguments against an evacuation and the fact that the major thrust in the centre had not yet begun, the extremely hasty decision to evacuate and Molotov's eventual strenuous efforts to justify the measure imply that it was taken as a result more of the breakdown of civil order and discipline than of the actual situation at the front. Evacuation, which had in any case been in the air since the early days of the German invasion, would be less damaging to the Russians than allowing the missions to witness the defeatist scenes and major disruption. This is borne out by the fact that as late as 11 October Cripps tactfully approached Vyshinsky on the desirability of sending most of the British subjects out of Moscow. Vyshinsky emphatically denied such a need. So as not to display a lack of confidence Cripps refrained from taking any precautionary measures while making it clear to Vyshinsky that if evacuation occurred he and a skeleton staff would stay behind.[5] Early on the morning of 15 October Cripps told Charlotte Haldane, a left-wing correspondent, that there was 'no cause for undue alarm or despondency, and that the sensational stories being spread by the Fifth Column could be contemptuously discarded'.[6] It was therefore with great surprise that Cripps and Steinhardt, summoned unexpectedly to Molotov at noon the same day, learnt about the military setback and were instructed to exploit the 'last opportunity' of evacuating their staff in a special train put at their disposal that very evening. Molotov, as Cripps witnessed, had never before looked 'so tired and ill . . . he was deadly pale and his collar all awry where he is generally very neat and tidy'. Troubled by the thought

of being permanently cut off from the Russian government, Cripps insisted that it was 'his duty' to remain in Moscow regardless of the risks involved. He was finally assured by Molotov that he and the General Staff would follow suit in a plane in which, unfortunately, there was no room for the ambassador.[7]

The evacuation was accomplished in great haste and carried with it a feeling of finality; 'Tomb closed', was the last dispatch sent by an American correspondent, convinced he was 'closing an epoch'.[8] Mason-Macfarlane was away in the South; his staff were interrupted at their lunch and rushed over to the embassy from their lodgings in the former premises of the Yugoslav embassy. A bonfire was lit on the tennis court and vast piles of correspondence, information and intelligence which had accumulated through the years were burned. Haldane left a candid impression of those last despairing hours at the embassy:

There was a grim moment when someone asked what should be done with the wireless. 'Smash it,' answered the Ambassador briefly. From the adjacent room came half a dozen hammer-blows. I listened to them with a sad heart. Then I went upstairs with the Ambassador, the Air Vice-Marshal, and the Admiral. The three of us ate cold chicken with our fingers; Sir Stafford, who is a vegetarian, had sour milk. His Airedale, Joe, was given something to eat, too. But he didn't show his usual enthusiasm for food. He knew that something very unusual was happening.[9]

The embassy's essential papers were hastily stored in cases while Cripps' devoted Greek butler packed tinned food and bottles of wine for the journey which in the confusion were eventually left behind.[10]

There was havoc at the restaurant of the Kazan railway station that evening where all the diplomatic corps sought refuge from the snow which was now falling heavily; 'baggage got mixed up on the floor with loose typewriters, a heap of embassy files and other odds and ends'. Some of the embassy documents, the military mission's radio equipment and other essentials were dispatched by car the following day with an armed escort. To a journalist the scene at the station looked like a 'cavern of damned souls . . . for whom this retreat meant, perhaps the end of all things'. Cripps sat alone at a table with Joe moving restlessly. 'The Old Man's heart is broken' was the opinion of Cripps' butler. Outwardly, however, he preserved the appearance of being 'reserved,

willing to be friendly, at peace' which had never left him in the enormous ups and downs he had been exposed to in the previous few months.[11] This latest episode, however, was making Cripps 'very heart sore' that the British help had been 'so delayed as to mean a great victory for the Germans'.[12]

After some hours' delay the party, as Cripps described it, had to push its way to the platform through the 'masses and masses of grey and patient bundles of humanity with their white and coloured bundles of belongings' also waiting to be evacuated. Outside a blizzard howled while they groped in the inky darkness, a result of the absolute blackout, only occasionally assisted by sudden flashes from some nearby guns.[13] The journey, which normally took twenty hours, lasted five days; the railways were jammed with trains carrying troops, hitherto kept in the East to forestall a possible Japanese attack and now rushed in the opposite direction to reinforce Zhukov's crumbling front. The decision was so hasty that the Russians were unable to provide the evacuees with food and facilities. There was a brisk trade in eggs and milk by peasants on the way. A group of enterprising journalists took pity on Cripps, who was 'obviously distressed', and prepared a vegetable stew for him. On the third day, arriving at the outskirts of Penza, they were at last provided with their first meal consisting of an 'unappetizing cabbage soup and chunks of black bread'. The precipitance of the evacuation certainly enhanced the feeling that the battle was lost. However, the endless journey through the Russian countryside, a 'landscape of pine forests, low hills covered in snow, frozen lakes and rivers, little villages and small towns' left a strong impression of Russia's 'vastness, monotony and inaccessibility'.

The evacuees finally reached Kuibyshev, a town with a population of half a million which doubled its size in the next few days. Although during the last two days of the journey they had scarcely enough drinking water and essential provisions, the state of affairs in Kuibyshev was much worse than on the train. It is quite possible that the slow pace of the journey was also dictated by the necessity of making minimal arrangements for accommodating the dignitaries at such short notice. The embassy and the mission were lodged at the 'Pioneers' Palace', which was like a barracks. It had about a hundred beds, two wardrobes, a few chairs and three small tables. The beds had only mattresses, most of them bug-infested, and pillows. There was a small kitchen with no

cooking utensils, no pantry and no blinds in the main hall. They had to take their meals at a hotel about a mile away, which was a trial once winter set in.[14] Before long, however, the Gastronome food store for foreigners was transferred from Gorky Street in Moscow to Kuibyshev Street. Even the tourists' antiques and souvenirs store turned up opposite the Grand Hotel. Within a few days Cripps himself improved his position by renting a tiny but tidy little bungalow which he shared with the heads of the missions and which, once provisional partitions were introduced, accommodated the main offices of the improvised embassy.[15]

Cripps' morale sank, however, when after the ordeals of the evacuation, the journey and the horrifying conditions encountered in Kuibyshev he found that Vyshinsky was the only government representative on the spot and had to refer to Moscow on any minor issue. He felt deceived in being dragged to that 'unattractive place more or less under false pretences and thereby deprived of any possibility of useful action to make [his] discomforts worth while'. In a fit of fury Cripps demanded to be returned instantly to Moscow. He just managed to control himself but he was inclined to tell the Russians that he would leave the country altogether if his request were turned down. Similar representations were made by Mason-Macfarlane. He had been forbidden to return to Moscow from Tiflis and soon found himself 'marooned on the eastern bank of the Volga and out of touch with everything and everybody'. On the next day Molotov was flown in from Moscow to quell the rebellion. He justified the hasty evacuation on the pretext that it was decided on only after Mozhaisk had fallen. Mozhaisk was indeed the last major obstacle in the German approach to Moscow but it was overrun only on 18 October. The same night Maloyaroslavets fell on the southern flank. It was therefore on 18 and not on 15 October that Stalin declared the existence of a state of siege in Moscow and introduced martial law there.[16]

### Enforced exile

With Russia's fate hanging in the balance the issue of direct British assistance, suppressed in the Moscow conference, came to the fore. It was inseparable from the direction assumed by the Iranian campaign. In mid-September Cripps proposed a military occupation of Teheran to

compel the Shah to conclude a triple alliance after securing Molotov's consent. He was, however, entirely ignorant of the government's real intentions and expected a settlement to guarantee a quick withdrawal of all troops from Iran.[17] Cripps' recommendations with regard to Teheran coincided with and reinforced a decision taken by the Defence Committee and approved by Eden, who, however, was resolved on deferring a final solution until the end of the war.[18] While defending in Parliament the military activities in Iran as joining hands with the Russians, Churchill now quite openly admitted, as he had told the Defence Committee earlier, that the occupation was 'presenting a shield which should bar the eastward advance of the German invader'.[19] The admission cancelled the earlier explanation in that it displayed little confidence in the Soviet ability to resist the German onslaught.

So far Churchill had refrained from responding to Stalin's request for the dispatch of troops to Russia. On 12 October, while the battle was raging at the gates of Moscow, he addressed Stalin, opening with the customary recital of material supplies on their way to Archangel. He then advised Stalin to withdraw five or six Russian divisions from Iran for 'use on the battle-front', while British troops would 'take over the whole responsibility of keeping order and maintaining the supply route'. This proposal did little to conceal his real preoccupation of maintaining sufficient British forces in Iran to 'ensure that the Caucasian barrier [was] held for the winter'. Churchill's repetitious praise for the Russians' 'heroic struggle' was unlikely to pacify Stalin.[20]

It immediately struck Cripps, while delivering Churchill's note to Stalin, that 'psychologically' it was a mistake which could have been avoided had Churchill troubled to 'consult the people on the spot before sending these messages!' Cripps indeed found Molotov embittered about Britain's failure to help with 'any armed forces'. Himself critical of the Cabinet, Cripps suggested to Molotov 'in a completely unofficial way' how the Russians should react to Churchill's message. On reporting home he credited Molotov with his own suggestion that Britain might send forces into the Caucasus, leaving Soviet troops in Iran.[21] Eden suggested to Maisky the compromise that the Russians should retire most of their troops from Iran, leaving a token force behind to guard their interests, while Britain demonstrated her solidarity by sending a nominal force into the Caucasus. That proposal

was far short of Cripps' but Eden doubted 'what, if anything' the army could do beyond this. Maisky then repeated his threat that if Hitler gained control of the Caucasian oil it would be 'very difficult for Russia to continue to fight'. Eden, complained Maisky, was perhaps the 'best of the lot' and understood that Britain's fate was tied up with that of Russia; however, he was submissive to Churchill, who was pursuing the wrong strategy of unwillingness to take risks and grant Russia substantial assistance.[22]

Maisky's conversations in London only increased Molotov's concern, caused by Churchill's message, that Britain aimed to take over all of Iran. 'The old suspicions', noted Cripps when Molotov revived the issue in Kuibyshev after the evacuation, 'are very near the surface and keep on cropping up.'[23] Shortly before returning to Moscow, Molotov summoned Cripps and Citrine, who with the TUC delegation had been stranded in Kuibyshev. He wished to impress on Citrine the need for both armies 'to be united on the common field of battle . . . somewhere and somehow'. When war scares had erupted in the twenties and thirties the solidarity movement had been formed to compensate for the failings of conventional diplomacy. Similarly an Anglo-Soviet Trade Union Committee had just been set up and the Russians were undoubtedly counting on popular support for Russia among the rank and file to bring pressure on the government. It further emerged in the conversation that because of the limitations imposed on Beaverbrook, Stalin's request for a major diversion in the Caucasus had never been acknowledged. Cripps, as Sargent admitted, 'manfully defended' the position of the government but the Russians had a 'certain amount of justification for asserting that it had never been definitely answered'.[24]

Even before Citrine took up the matter with Churchill, Cripps and Mason-Macfarlane outlined the futility of Beaverbrook's approach and pressed for action. Cripps felt that the Russians were obsessed with Britain's 'sitting back and watching them and nothing will dispel it except concrete action'. In his final verdict Russia's ability to survive the present crisis depended on the dispatch of at least a corps to either the North or the South. Eden, an expert in diverting embarrassing decisions, deferred to Churchill, who decided to put an end to the wave of criticism from Cripps, particularly now that Beaverbrook was pursuing a similar campaign from within.[25] On 25 October Churchill briefly but firmly turned down Cripps' arguments, insisting that it was up to the

Soviet divisions in Iran to 'defend their own country' and that the maintenance of British troops in the Caucasus was bound to choke the supply line to northern Iran. However, his confident words concealed a feeling of uneasiness. 'Considering the thin ice we are on in Russia while we are doing so little for them', he explained to Dill, it was necessary to check Mason-Macfarlane from reproaching the Russians about the maltreatment of the mission.[26]

Cripps was not mollified by the Prime Minister's letter. The opening paragraph of his immediate reply challenged Churchill's premises: 'A drop or two in a bucket or in a tumbler may make a great deal of difference where a stimulant is urgently required.' To repair the damage caused by Beaverbrook he called for the dispatch to Russia of an authoritative military figure with full information 'at his fingers' end' to explain the difficulties in carrying out a diversion. The only alternative was for him or Mason-Macfarlane to be briefed in London and then undertake to make the unpleasant explanations in Moscow. The letter ended in an unmistakable rebuke: 'If we are allies, as you have announced, surely they should not merely be told that we cannot send any troops to help them, but also should have the opportunity of discussing the matter.' The harsh tone of his telegram fully reflected Cripps' serious intention, if the reply was in the negative, 'of resigning and going home to make a nuisance' of himself.[27] Cripps' telegram coincided with a request by Maisky on 27 October for long-term coordination of strategy. Like Cripps he impressed on Eden that it was a matter of 'tremendous political importance' for British forces to fight 'side by side with Russia on their soil'.[28]

The pressure in Cabinet in favour of a diversionary action was now reaching its peak and was not devoid of power struggles. Churchill could always count on Eden by exercising his paternal authority – an intimate dinner, recollections of Eden's past glory at the War Office and a tap on the shoulder: 'I regard you as my son . . . I do not get in your way nor you in mine.' When Beaverbrook seemed to be undermining Eden's position, Churchill could win Eden over by ensuring a 'war to the knife against him'.[29] The neutralizing of Beaverbrook or Cripps demanded more sophistication. To preserve the integrity and reputation of the Cabinet Churchill resorted to reconciliation, exclusively entrusting Beaverbrook with the organization of supply and thus accepting his rather than Cripps' proposals in this sphere. He also

stood by most of the promises made by Beaverbrook in Moscow.[30] Beaverbrook, however, suffering from a false sense of security as a result of his talks in Moscow and spurred on by Cripps' provocative telegrams, mounted a public crusade including direct appeals to shop stewards in favour of a second front, which irritated Churchill. The challenge was further pursued in a memorandum discussed in the Defence Committee on 19 October which to Cadogan seemed 'simply a "Daily Express" Leader' but which in fact assailed the premises of Churchill's strategy. Beaverbrook challenged the COS to 'sacrifice' long-term projects which 'though cherished, became completely obsolete on the day when Russia was attacked'. Churchill vigorously repelled the attack until Beaverbrook 'blustered and growled and finally acquiesced'.[31] Consequently Beaverbrook composed but did not send a letter of resignation from the Cabinet on 23 October, replacing it two days later with a protest against the failure to establish a second front and a request to be relieved from the Defence Committee. Churchill, appealing to Beaverbrook's loyalty, refused to accept a move which would be seen as a 'mark of want of confidence'.[32]

Cripps' communications with Churchill were raised in Cabinet on 27 October; his unbridled criticism of Beaverbrook unintentionally damaged his own case. In his initial 'lively and entertaining' account of the conference, spiced with 'much gossip about Moscow', Beaverbrook had deliberately glossed over essential topics. Harriman felt obliged to intimate to Eden that Stalin had proposed 'an alliance after the war' and was undoubtedly expecting a response. Faced by the unpleasant choice described by Harvey as 'we mustn't snub them, but we mustn't compromise the future settlement', the Cabinet preferred to avoid the issue.[33] Beaverbrook, who had been zealously demanding military action, was placed in an awkward position. Pandora's box was now open and he was held responsible for the failure to make appropriate political and strategic clarifications in Moscow, to which it seemed the Russians had attached greater importance than his censored versions had suggested. Caught off balance, Beaverbrook tried unsuccessfully to divert the discussion to a review of the increase in deliveries with American help. The rather laconic conclusions of the meeting indicate that he was invited to provide the Cabinet with extracts from his and Harriman's records which 'bore on the question of sending military aid

18 Lord Beaverbrook returns from Moscow; on his right, Harold Macmillan

to Russia'. Nevertheless, Churchill succeeded in convincing Cabinet of the undesirability of sending troops to the Caucasus.[34]

More significant was Beaverbrook's absence from a meeting of the Defence Committee later in the evening where a thorough examination of Cripps' telegrams and the operation in the Caucasus was made. Churchill repeated his arguments against the dispatch of troops; his only problem was how to break the news to the Russians. He proposed to tell Roosevelt of Cripps' telegrams and ask him to explain to Stalin the impracticability of moving a division to the front. Churchill encountered unexpected opposition not on the issue of assistance to Russia as such but because of possible repercussions on the Middle Eastern arena.

Neither the Moscow conference nor the battle of Moscow had hitherto removed the COS's objections to any offensive diversions before spring 1942. They had dryly recorded that the 'impact of the Russian campaign had not altered [British] fundamental strategy' which

saw in the Middle East the only theatre of war in which an offensive offered any strategic advantage. Future raids on the Continent had been considered in this context only as a means to 'extend the enemy and so to add to his difficulties.'[35] However, introducing to the Defence Committee Maisky's renewed appeals for direct military assistance, Eden summed up rather neutrally that the Caucasus would be 'the best line on which to defend Russia'. Dill unexpectedly argued in favour of deploying two divisions presently in the Middle East, either deep in the Caucasus, if the Russians were still fighting there, or as a reinforcement of the defence line in northern Iran. He was backed by Portal, Chief of the Air Force, who proposed to station British squadrons there. Churchill's objections were overruled by the committee, while the COS embarked on preliminary planning. From his headquarters Auchinleck agreed to take the necessary measures to meet the rapid German advance in southern Russia. Churchill, however, had no intention of abiding by the decision. His pet operation 'Whipcord', the capture of Sicily, had also been turned down at the meeting of the Defence Committee. Apprehensive that the forces earmarked for 'Whipcord' might now be transferred to the Caucasus, he secured a force 'equivalent to two divisions and one armoured division with air proportionate' to stand ready for action in North Africa. He had reason to believe the Americans were enthusiastic. It was important to know 'at once what orders should be issued to convert WHIPCORD into GYMNAST', the code name of the new operation, thus ensuring the 'least possible inroads upon shipping'.[36]

In ignoring the decision of the Defence Committee Churchill was assisted by Eden, who then grumbled in private that Churchill was showing 'every evident sign of anti-Bolshevik sentiment. After his first enthusiasm, he is now getting bitter as the Russians become a liability and he says we can't afford the luxury of helping them with men, only with material.' Indeed, when a few days later the question of the form of the government's congratulations on the anniversary of the revolution was raised, Churchill stated demonstratively that 'nothing would tempt him to send a message'.[37] The day after the Defence Committee's meeting Eden repeated to Maisky Churchill's arguments that although the Soviet requests were sound from the political point of view it was 'surely foolish' to expect England to send even a small force into

Russia.[38] The explicit refusal to Maisky was also an indirect reply to Cripps' reservations about Churchill's message to Stalin.

Churchill, however, aware of the increasing threat posed by Cripps, sent a speedy reply to his defiant letters. The aim was not, as presented in his memoirs, 'to sustain our Ambassador in his many trials and hardships and his lonely, uphill task'. Churchill blamed the Russians' 'present agony' on their pact with Germany and their attitude to the West right up to the German invasion. To send troops into the heart of Russia, he reconfirmed, was 'silly', as they were bound to be 'cut to pieces as a symbolic sacrifice'. Churchill returned to his earlier suggestions of the relief of Soviet troops in Iran. Although he did not expect 'gratitude from men undergoing such frightful bludgeonings and fighting so bravely' he was not inclined to be 'disturbed by their reproaches'. The crux of his message was the appeal to Cripps' duty 'to remain with these people in their ordeal'.[39]

Churchill later justified the decision conveyed to Cripps on the grounds that 'winter now cast its shield before the Russian armies'.[40] Information obtained through Enigma and Cripps' meeting with Molotov in Kuibyshev indeed revealed that 'Typhoon' was exhausted by 20 October.[41] Before the meeting of the Defence Committee Churchill sought the Intelligence's views on when winter was expected to set in 'in earnest' in Russia. He was inclined to put 'even chances' on Moscow being taken before winter. The replies were not encouraging. Although it was recognized that the winter would play a major role in the next stage of the war, severe conditions were not expected to bring the offensive to a halt before mid-December. Meanwhile, as fierce battles were resumed, they rated the chances of Moscow's capture at '5 to 4'. The Germans indeed mounted their most determined offensive late in November, reaching the outskirts of Moscow in early December.[42]

Cripps had by now lost patience with Churchill. Churchill's telegram, he commented, was not 'the slightest help to anyone and really was not worthy of him'; it was 'petulant and irrelevant' and still worse reminiscent of the attitude adopted in the 1939 negotiations. He wrote to Isobel: 'If nothing comes of this last telegram I may be bringing this letter back with me.'[43] The telegram is worth examining in detail as it faithfully reflects Cripps' indignation, which had been on the increase

since the early stages of the war in the East. The letter also bears on his integrity and impeccable logic, particularly in comparison with the rhetoric used by Churchill at the time. His main criticism was that the government still seemed 'to be trying to carry on two relatively unrelated wars to the great benefit of Hitler instead of a single war upon the basis of a combined plan'. In spite of the new circumstances the Russians were still treated 'without trust and as inferiors rather than as trusted allies'. As for Churchill's historical references, Cripps reminded him that Russian suspicions dated from the still earlier intervention, in which Churchill had played a prominent role. It was impossible to secure vigorous Soviet resistance on the basis of Churchill's shallow explanations, which were apt to revive the legacy of the past. Cripps, who could not leave an argument unanswered, reminded Churchill that in spring 1941 Eden and Dill had spent considerable time organizing a Balkan defence, courting and concerting strategy with Turkey and Greece in approaches which had 'never been made to the Russians' although no one could deny that the Russians were now 'more important to us as Allies than the Greeks ever were'. The casual treatment of the Russians, in contrast with those intensive but frivolous activities, gave the appearance either that the government did not trust the Russians or that they did not think they were 'worthy to be consulted'. Cripps therefore reiterated the need for a high-level coordination of strategy, some form of assistance 'on land front' and the laying down of a common basis for 'European peace'. Once Cripps' telegram was deciphered Harvey, who undoubtedly under Eden's influence had hitherto tended to treat Cripps as a mere trouble-maker, admitted it was 'very closely reasoned with some bitterness'. Churchill thought likewise and deferred action pending consultations with Beaverbrook and Eden, who were away for the weekend.[44] Shortly after dispatching his telegram, Cripps was finally informed by the Foreign Office of the significance Stalin had attached in his talks with Beaverbrook to strategic and political issues. Cripps immediately added his protest 'against this method of being informed of what would appear to be discussions of first class importance taking place in Moscow nearly a month ago as to which I have so far been kept in complete ignorance. It is impossible for me to carry on my work in such circumstances.'[45]

Though Beaverbrook's misrepresentation of the conference had held up for a whole month, it was now fast collapsing. This aided Churchill

to curb Beaverbrook, who at the time was constantly threatening resignation over his working relationship with Bevin. When confronted with Cripps' letters, Churchill reproached Beaverbrook for having failed to make the proper explanations in Moscow of the British inability to carry out diversionary actions. What concerned Churchill more was that Beaverbrook's mishandling was to the advantage of Cripps, who was 'evidently preparing his case against us'. It was in the context of Cripps' political challenge that Beaverbrook recollected Stalin's complaints of not having been warned about 'Barbarossa'. Churchill now exploded in a denunciation of Cripps' 'effrontery' in withholding his message in April. Eventually these exchanges with Beaverbrook were incorporated almost verbatim, apart from Eden's defence of Cripps, in his war memoirs, thus unjustifiably making this episode the best-remembered aspect of Cripps' ambassadorship in Moscow. Churchill's confrontation with Beaverbrook was in fact a call for loyalty combined with blackmail; he was told he had better 'get the facts straightened out' because the issue was to be cleared up shortly in Cabinet. The day before Churchill had sent a personal letter which was 'designed to touch Beaverbrook's heart'. The threat of resignation and a common platform with Cripps was temporarily shelved.[46]

Churchill's fear of pushing Cripps into extreme action was justified. In an independent initiative to remedy the damage inflicted by Beaverbrook, Cripps prepared an extraordinary note to Stalin on 2 November. Assigning himself the role of unbiased intermediary, Cripps intended to urge Stalin to state his strategic demands despite the existing differences on active British participation, assuring him that he too had 'not hesitated to bring . . . constantly' to the government's notice his own misgivings. Although he referred to the desire of the government 'to do everything that they consider possible to assist the people of the Soviet Union', the letter was bound to aggravate Churchill as the 'very sincere desire' to overcome difficulties was attributed in mildly revolutionary terms to the 'two peoples'. The outstanding feature of the letter was Cripps' exploitation of the reputation he believed he enjoyed with Stalin in a last resort to achieve two purposes: opening the political and strategic dialogue avoided by Beaverbrook while convincing Stalin of the objective limitations of British policy. Once mutual confidence was restored, Cripps pointed to the need to discuss the 'mutual cooperation of the two countries after the war'. In the meantime he pledged the

fulfilment of the commitments undertaken by the government. Cripps' defiance was a deliberate move and connected with a further decision. Rather than resigning he preferred in fact to be dismissed 'as it would prevent Winston using my resignation against me which of course he will do if I have to resign on a difference with him'.[47]

What dissuaded Cripps from embarking on this road was the over-due arrival in Kuibyshev of Monckton, his bosom friend, who apart from Isobel was his major source of information on domestic political developments. Monckton, who was entrusted with the coordination of propaganda, was to convey to the Russians that they were not fighting alone and combat the 'impatience at scarcity and slow motion of British support'. Domestic considerations, however, dictated the principal objective of the Ministry of Information: to produce propaganda which would wipe out the remnants of opposition to collaboration with Russia following the lead set in Churchill's famous speech, while carrying out the more imperative task of curbing 'exuberant pro-Soviet propaganda from the left which might seriously embarrass H.M.G.'. Even Eden was in favour of curtailing public opinion in view of the limitations of British help. Monckton could both contribute to the cause and have a moderating influence on Cripps.[48] Nothing 'startling' came of Monckton's official talks, which in the circumstances were conducted with minor officials in Kuibyshev. The only agreement was on the need to appoint a press attaché at the embassy. Cripps' suggestion of Zilliacus, his former associate on *Tribune*, would certainly not appeal to London where Cripps' political challenge was at the back of everybody's mind.[49] Apparently Guy Burgess, who was later exposed as a Soviet 'mole', saw an opening here. He persuaded the Foreign Office to appoint Isaiah Berlin, with himself as an assistant. This arrangement, the possible consequences of which are incalculable, was foiled by Cripps' objection to the appointment.[50]

Monckton's more effective contribution was to temper Cripps and at last enlighten him as to the political reality at home. Cripps' fears were confirmed that while Beaverbrook and Churchill ran policy towards Russia between them, the Foreign Office and Eden had 'very little to do with it'. The prospect of joining Labour was dismissed by Cripps, as was witnessed by Arthur Greenwood's son, who accompanied Monckton and approached Cripps on the subject: 'He slammed the desk and said: "I shall never rejoin the Labour Party after the way they've treated

me." '[51] Cripps was led therefore to the gloomy conclusion that it was 'very difficult to spot the alternatives to the present Ministers bad though most of them are'. He was persuaded by Monckton to hold on to his letter to Stalin, and even to 'swallow all the inconveniences and impoliteness' to which he had been subjected, on condition that if he stayed in Russia he would be allowed to negotiate a treaty of post-war reconstruction. He showed Monckton an early draft of a booklet on the subject that he had been writing in the past months and with which he hoped to launch his public campaign if not allowed to pursue the subject officially.[52]

The pressure on Churchill was maintained as a result of the shelving of 'Whipcord' and the continued postponement of 'Crusader', the major offensive against Rommel in the Western Desert. Moreover, the Russians' insistent demand for a direct British commitment on the battlefield was fomenting public unrest, the echoes of which were distinctly heard in Cabinet. Since he had definitely to turn down the Soviet request, Churchill preferred not to be drawn into long discourses with Cripps, and certainly not to allow him a free hand in negotiations. Cripps soon realized that he was destined to become merely 'a post-office', while Churchill 'fired off the unwise' replies to Stalin.[53] Cripps indeed sent home a protest based on this impression and a modified version of his draft letter to Stalin demanding authority to embark on political negotiations. The letter only demonstrated the explosive repercussions his recall might have on domestic politics as it again assumed the government's agreement on the broad lines of a post-war settlement and collaboration with Russia. Such an agreement, he felt, was a prerequisite for smooth cooperation during the war. To exert pressure and emphasize the seriousness of his proposition he ended with an ultimatum: 'I have therefore come to a quite definite conclusion that, unless I can now be of some use . . . you will be better served by someone else in this post as I cannot remain long in the present unsatisfactory situation.'[54] Cripps had few hopes; by way of answer he expected to get a 'fair mixture of honey and explosive' if it came from Churchill or a 'reasoned appeal' if it came from Eden. It turned out to be, as defined in the Foreign Office, a 'mollifying reply' but 'wholly unsatisfactory and very vague and wishy-washy' from Cripps' point of view.[55]

Cripps' incessant criticism of Beaverbrook had meanwhile provided

Eden with a trump card to supersede Beaverbrook temporarily as the champion of aid to Russia and regain control in that sphere. Beaverbrook had been searching for new avenues to pursue the mission outside the Cabinet. On one occasion he had challenged Churchill: 'Why don't you send me as Ambassador to Moscow? I'll keep them in the war', while on another he had proposed that he should return to Moscow to complete his task by discussing war plans with Stalin. Resolved not to be passed over, Eden had proposed to Churchill 'over whiskies' that he should accompany Wavell to Moscow after the execution of 'Crusader' when he would be able to make concrete offers and prove that Britain was engaging the Germans in the field.[56] This tallied with Cripps' demands for high-level talks. Eden's reply to Cripps was composed of two separate but complementary telegrams. The first, a copy of which was ostentatiously sent to and discussed with Beaverbrook, was *inter alia* intended to put him off his guard by explaining to Cripps that he must have gained a 'false impression' of the extent of the political exchanges in the Moscow conference. With regard to his proposals, while the Cabinet was reluctant to formulate peace objectives beyond the Atlantic Charter, Eden welcomed the idea of examining post-war relations with Russia.[57] The subsequent telegram, which Eden did 'not propose to mention' to Beaverbrook, announced his projected visit. Eden had secured Churchill's consent by presenting it as a means of encouraging Cripps to stay at his post.[58]

The Cabinet was now talking in distinctly dissonant voices. Beaverbrook, Eden and Cripps were pressing, each in his own way, for a sincere incorporation of Russia in the Allied camp. They were sustained by the COS, whose main concern was to prevent a breakthrough in the Middle East's northern defences, and by public opinion.[59] Their policies, however, were uncoordinated and subordinate to the dissenting line adopted by Churchill. His views were implicitly expressed in the message to Stalin on 4 November. When he presented the draft in Cabinet it appeared that Churchill had selectively adopted some of Cripps' ideas. He exonerated Beaverbrook, with whom a temporary truce had been established, from having avoided strategic discussions. His proposal to send to Moscow General Wavell, who had been liaising with the Russians at Tiflis, was however intended virtually to end Soviet hopes by explaining the 'limited possibilities of sending a British force to Russia'. An indirect blow to Cripps was Churchill's suggestion to

Cabinet in that meeting, in response to complaints of the COS on the maltreatment of the military mission, to replace Mason-Macfarlane.[60] The Russians, now literally fighting for their lives, were left in no doubt about the purpose of the visit of the General, who was expected in Moscow only in 'about a fortnight'. Another issue was to bring further disappointment. Since June the Russians had been urging Britain to declare war on Hungary, Finland and Romania. Although Eden had advanced practical arguments against this, he now believed they should be overruled to avoid 'rebuffing and discouraging' the Russians. On 27 October, while the assistance to Russia was a subject of fierce debate, Eden told Maisky that a decision depended on American consent.[61] Maisky hoped that the government would be finally persuaded to declare war when on 31 October he provided Eden with information that Finnish units had been identified on the Moscow front. In his message to Stalin Churchill flatly rejected such a declaration. He further complained about the treatment of the military mission and misuse of British armaments sent to Russia.[62]

On the afternoon that the message was deposited with him, Maisky returned to the Foreign Office with enquiries certainly originating in Moscow. He wished to know the scope of the contemplated strategic negotiations and whether Wavell would for instance be empowered to discuss the dispatch of British troops to Rostov. Eden volunteered his impression, a repeat of Churchill's earlier statements, that the Russians would have to choose between supplies or troops. A few days later Eden, who had been left to 'mind the shop' while Churchill took a few days off, informed Maisky, probably in an attempt to pave his own way to Moscow, that Wavell would be authorized to discuss any topic.[63]

Before examining Stalin's reply, the background to Russia's desperate appeals for help, with which British Intelligence was well acquainted through its reading of the German order of battle, should be reviewed. Although the German offensive had been checked some 40–90 miles from Moscow, a war of attrition continued and both sides were regrouping their forces. By late October the Donets Basin was overrun after the fall of Kharkov. Timoshenko, now in charge of the southern command, carried out a tactical withdrawal to shorten his defensive line. It entailed the abandonment of extensive territories, even cutting off Sebastopol by the beginning of November. In the North the

Germans captured Tikhvin on 9 November, thus almost completely encircling Leningrad. On the same day Stalin, having lost hope of relief in the South by British forces, instructed Timoshenko to lead a counter-offensive against General Kleist in the Rostov area to stop a German swing towards the Soviet oilfields and the Caucasus. Both Kleist and Timoshenko chose 17 November for their campaigns, which was to coincide with the resumption of the battles in Moscow. The Russians therefore were unable to shift forces from one front to another; thus Maisky's judgment that the absence of active military help was 'felt with particular acuteness' can be taken at face value.[64] It was obvious to Stalin that the British were more sceptical than ever about the Soviet capacity to withstand the German onslaught. The communications with London had even revived Soviet suspicions that Britain might respond favourably to peace feelers from Hitler preceding his renewed assault on Moscow.[65]

Stalin's immediate reaction was a demonstration of confidence which, if studied carefully, divulges a growing disappointment with external help and a call for an extraordinary effort to win the 'patriotic war'. In a broadcast speech for the anniversary of the revolution Stalin attributed the Soviet military setbacks to the absence of a second front on the Continent; such a second front, he argued, 'ought unquestionably to be created within the shortest time'. After long discussions troops were withdrawn the following day from the front to the Red Square in the besieged capital to participate in the traditional military procession. That the parade was not only intended to boost the morale of the Muscovites was evident from the staging of a parallel one in Kuibyshev reviewed by Voroshilov. The display of some 16,000 troops and a fly-over of 200 planes had the desired effect, to judge from Cripps' evidence that the general feeling amongst diplomats was 'very much more optimistic than I have known it for ages'.[66] Although in his speech Stalin now declared himself grateful for the Allied material assistance his words could not altogether hide, as Cripps noted, 'the strong vein of disappointment and exasperation' which had marked the speech of the earlier day. Stalin further made an unprecedented appeal to national sentiments by reviving the spirit of Russian legends like Alexander Nevsky, Souvarov and Kutuzov. The reference to the second front, it was discerned in the Foreign Office, was an open appeal to

public opinion in Britain over the head of the government and therefore had a 'direct bearing on the reaction to Stalin's subsequent message'.[67]

On 11 November Maisky brought, to put it in Churchill's own words, Stalin's 'chilling and evasive' reply. However, after thorough examination the Foreign Office reached the conclusion that it was a protest at Churchill's own failure to proceed beyond elusive verbal communications.[68] The style, which seemed to irritate Churchill, was explained by Cripps as Stalin's habitual 'frank and blunt' approach, reflecting his lack of 'real contact with Western ways and diplomatic usages'. Even Eden defined it as 'sharp and critical, though . . . the presentation worse than the substance'.[69] Stalin criticized the British refusal to declare war on Finland and assured Churchill of the proper usage of supplies provided. What caused Churchill, however, to breathe 'fire and brimstone', as Maisky recalled, was Stalin's cynical admittance that it would not be 'worthwhile to intrude' upon Wavell, who clearly was not empowered to discuss definite understandings on 'war aims and on plans of the post-war organisation of peace', and in the shorter term 'mutual military assistance'. Only the intervention of Eden and Beaverbrook prevented an instant and perhaps irreversible confrontation with Stalin.[70] From Churchill's point of view the telegram was also ill-timed in that it revived the debate on the order of priorities on the eve of the offensive in Libya. The COS still advocated reinforcement of the Soviet defence by troops to sustain the northern defences. They were also attentive to the growing public indignation at the conduct of the war, warning of the repercussions to the government if Russia were allowed to collapse.[71]

Against this background Stalin's message seemed to presage the threat posed to Churchill if Cripps were to return; he would be the leader who would profit from the eruption of support to Russia. The 'whole business' was discussed by Beaverbrook, Churchill and Eden over dinner. Churchill's conclusion, as Eden entered in his diary, was that 'there will surely be more trouble with Cripps, whose one idea is to come home and play a part here'. Churchill was now adamant in ignoring Stalin's 'prickly message'.[72]

Meanwhile Eden's subdued confrontation with Beaverbrook had been resolved. Beaverbrook must have realized that his own cause

could be served even if a mission to Moscow were undertaken by some-one else. After his 'nerve storm' he was now behaving, as noted Harvey, in 'exemplary fashion', urging both Churchill and Maisky to allow Eden to go to Moscow to 'put it all right'.[73] Encouraged by Beaver-brook and the Foreign Office and resentful of Churchill's continued intrusions, Eden adopted a conciliatory approach in spite of Churchill's instructions to be 'fairly stiff' with Maisky. In an off-the-record con-versation he did all he could to allay Soviet suspicions and dispel the misunderstandings on military assistance.[74]

The anticipated wrath from Cripps was not long in coming and added fuel to the raging debate on the nature of the Anglo-Soviet alliance. When shown Stalin's telegram, Cripps thought it 'bears out everything that I have been telling the Government'. A succession of telegrams started with a refutation of all the explanations of Beaver-brook's bungling in Moscow. Eden was similarly berated for his failure to respond to the plans for consolidating future collaboration. Cripps simply refused to be kept waiting for the 'very off-chance' of Eden's visit taking place. He demanded that Eden and Dill, or alternatively he himself, initiate immediate negotiations in Moscow. 'I came here', he wrote, 'to do a special job and not as a professional diplomatist, and it was understood that when the job was at an end I should leave. Owing to the policy of His Majesty's Government, the job is now at an end and there is nothing more that I can do.'[75] As a commentary on Stalin's message Cripps reiterated that no measure was of 'any value' unless the government were prepared to modify their policy. Maisky had in the meanwhile approached Stalin about Eden's conciliatory move and the Russians, who had hitherto emphatically barred Cripps from returning to Moscow, suddenly urged him to visit the capital. He did not, as he told Eden, intend to do so unless he possessed 'some constructive policy to put forward'.[76]

Cripps had not been informed of Eden's personal efforts but was told that the Cabinet was taking a 'pause for reflection'. This resulted in two highly charged telegrams on 15 November, the essence of which was to convince the government that it could not avoid relating to the two issues of effective military help and post-war reconstruction raised by Stalin. An evasion, he explained, would prevent a true collaboration in the sense that Russia and Britain would 'continue to fight substantially

different wars'. Having given vent to his feelings Cripps had little to do but anxiously wait for the Cabinet's decision. His bitterness was expressed with unwonted cynicism; he expected them 'to take up the attitude that I must stay here and leave it to me to resign if I want to do so, and then they will raise difficulties about a successor and make me appear the most selfish and inconsiderate person!' However, he was determined not to be associated with a policy he disapproved of.[77]

Cripps' persistence was at long last having a softening effect. Both Sargent and Harvey were converted to the desirability of a 'Volga Charter' as a counterpart to the Atlantic Charter. It was felt that despite the Americans' intransigent refusal to discuss future settlements and boundaries, it was impossible to 'remain with vacant minds till the moment of the peace conference'. While such thoughts were developing in Whitehall, Eden was summoned to Churchill, who was 'indignant with Cripps and wanted him home at once to tell him so'. Beaverbrook, sensing an opportunity, immediately suggested that he should go and discuss post-war arrangements but was turned down. Eden viewed the need to restrain Cripps as a sufficient reason for going to Moscow himself. Churchill's outrage, as is suggested in Eden's memoirs, resulted primarily from a reluctance to consider post-war problems. Aware of Cripps' uncompromising views on the subject and of his strength of character in contrast to Eden's weakness, he disapproved of Eden's going to Moscow simply to 'keep Cripps quiet'. As Eden uncharacteristically held firm, the two departed for the weekend without reaching a decision on Cripp's recall and Eden's planned visit, which they deferred to Monday's Cabinet meeting.[78]

Considerable tension built up over the weekend which, complained Cadogan, provided ministers with time to reflect over long walks and 'lash themselves into a frenzy. Then on returning home, they seize the telephone receiver . . . and the whole place flares up . . . And the P.M. sits somewhere in the country like a spider in the middle of his webb, and tickles them all up.'[79] That weekend Churchill was contemplating a showdown with Cripps even at the risk of a confrontation in Cabinet, to end once and for all the incitement from the Moscow embassy which suddenly seemed to be falling on fertile ground. A draft telegram communicated to the Foreign Office on Saturday appealed to him, allegedly for his own good, to remember his duty. It was accompanied, however,

by numerous veiled threats and intimidations leading to the main message that no pressure would deflect the government from the course it was pursuing. And yet the letter betrayed in an unprecedented manner the domestic political advantages of keeping Cripps in Moscow:

I am sure it would be a mistake from your point of view to leave your post and abandon the Russians and the Soviet cause with which you are so closely associated while all hangs in the balance . . . Your own friends here would not understand it. I hope you will believe that I give you this advice not from any fear of political opposition which you might raise over here by making out we had not done enough, etc. I could face such opposition without any political embarrassment, though with much personal regret. The Soviet Government . . . could never support you in an agitation against us because that would mean that we should be forced to vindicate our action in public which would necessarily be detrimental to Soviet interests . . . You must not underrate the strength of the case I could deploy in the House of Commons and on the broadcast . . . You should weigh all this before engaging in a most unequal struggle which could only injure the interests to which you are attached.

Finally Cripps was told that once circumstances were conducive to his return, which might 'not be for some months yet', he would be informed. Churchill's confidence in his ability to handle both Cripps and the Russians was related to the offensive in Libya due to start on Tuesday of that week. He would then, as he assured Cabinet, no longer be in the position *vis à vis* the Russians that 'they were fighting and we were not'.[80]

Churchill's position therefore threatened both Eden's trip and future relations with Russia. Eden, however, had been intriguing with Maisky to secure a moderate telegram from Stalin to mollify Churchill and get collaboration started again. It was further held in the Office that to be 'unnecessarily argumentative' with Cripps would be injurious. On Sunday, therefore, Cadogan was assigned to prepare an alternative draft assuring Cripps of British readiness to cooperate with the Russians during and after the war while conveying the difficulties in producing a cut-and-dried scheme of war aims. A 'pure cock-shy', as Cadogan freely admitted, was the assurance that Eden's visit would convince Stalin that the cooperation was 'loyal and whole-hearted'. To forestall a diatribe and to avoid repeating Beaverbrook's mistakes, Eden noted the great value which he attached to Cripps' 'advice and co-operation' during the

forthcoming visit. This, rather than Churchill's draft, was adopted by Cabinet on Monday.[81]

The crisis, now reaching a solution, was an ominous sign none the less of the shaky foundations of the alliance. Maisky kept the Kremlin well informed of the encouraging outcome of the *coup* staged in Whitehall while the war was entering a dramatic chapter which did not allow the Russians to indulge in petty recriminations. The German order of battle for the final assault on Moscow before winter set in was drawn up in the Orsha conference on 13 November. It was based on a last pincer movement by which Guderian would capture Kolomna, south-east of Moscow, while a tank force in the North would sweep along the Volga Canal towards Moscow. The German Fourth Army, deployed opposite Moscow, was then to strike against the exposed salient at the centre and occupy Moscow. The offensive was launched on 16 November.[82] On 20 November Moscow was informed of the offensive in North Africa which was a welcome relief since it was expected to drain German resources. On that day a reconciliation was finally achieved in London; Maisky brought Stalin's excuses for the style of his message to Churchill, though even at this crucial moment he would not withdraw from his demand to reach an agreement on mutual military assistance and the organization of peace.[83] Churchill, now encouraged by misleading early reports from Auchinleck and absorbed in the conduct of the war, was pacified.

## Eden's visit

To ensure the success of his visit Eden had made up his mind to leave for Russia only if the outline of a political settlement and proposals or concrete assistance had been decided upon. On 20 November, however, Churchill, Attlee and Beaverbrook composed a reply to Stalin's recantation avoiding reference to his specific requests. The mere announcement of Eden's proposed visit was expected to remedy the deficiency. Superficially Churchill was more forthcoming in consenting to discuss the dispatch of troops to the Caucasus and even 'into the fighting line', but in fact Stalin was confronted with a Hobson's choice between 'troops and supplies'.[84]

Eden's temporary advantage was thus lost when he was committed to

a mission before any of the controversial issues had been clarified. In such circumstances the presence of Cripps in Moscow during the visit presaged a storm, especially since Cripps, failing to appreciate the delicate political balance in Cabinet, continued to react violently to Eden's communications. Cripps attributed the visit to his own efforts but noted Eden's failure to mention the post-war settlement. Having driven the Cabinet 'a little way' he now hoped to 'drive them a bit further'.[85] By doing so he unintentionally aggravated Eden's apprehensions. Cripps warned that Stalin was bound to be dissatisfied with another visit of 'good will'; unless Eden brought concrete political proposals which might offset the disappointment on the issue of military help the mission was doomed. Perhaps more disconcerting were Cripps' prophetic warnings on the consequences of the growing Soviet suspicion. Just when Moscow was closer than ever to capture, Cripps believed that as a result of Britain's manifest indifference, the Russians had elaborated concrete plans 'if not for decentralisation and partial dismemberment of post-war Germany . . . at least for the safeguarding of their western frontiers in the Baltic area and elsewhere'. He therefore believed the Russians to be at present 'far more tractable than they would be at a later stage when the German tide had been stemmed'. From Eden's point of view another source of embarrassment was Cripps' challenge that the Cabinet must decide on his immediate future, as he did not intend to betray his convictions in the conference.

Eden found himself in a straitjacket. Although in agreement with much of what Cripps was saying, he had been manoeuvred by Churchill into proceeding to Russia empty-handed. Moscow was now destined to become the arena of fierce collisions not only with the Russians but also with Cripps. Eden first drafted another mollifying reply but then suppressed it, apparently aware of the reprimands it was likely to recall, arguing that Cripps would be 'troublesome' wherever he was but more so as ambassador in Moscow than as a member of Parliament in London, where he would soon 'discredit himself'. But Churchill, as Harvey noted, 'won't have him back yet and he is to remain in Russia over the visit. A.E. very fed up as he thinks he will be a nuisance to him.'[86] Eden's retreat was barred when on 23 November Stalin welcomed his proposed visit. All he could do was to employ delaying tactics; he informed Cripps that although he was hopeful of following his advice he could not sanction preliminary negotiations in

Moscow before Cabinet had formulated its policy. Finally, he was counting on Cripps' 'advice and cooperation' while deferring until they met a decision on his recall.[87]

Eden's misgivings about the visit encouraged him to press Cabinet again to adopt a political platform for the negotiations. The Foreign Office had hitherto given little thought to the political aspects of collaboration because of the prevailing concept before the German invasion which had excluded such an eventuality, the reluctance to envisage a complete alliance once hostilities broke out and the direct handling of relations by Churchill and Eden. In the absence of any defined policy they opted for the conclusion of a tripartite treaty with Russia and the United States pledging the negotiation of the broad lines of a European settlement and mutual assistance before the peace conference. Such a proposition aroused some opposition on the grounds that no deviation should be made from the Atlantic Charter and that Eden should therefore conduct only 'exploratory' negotiations; the need to consult Washington could be exploited to 'stall upon Russian proposals that have awkward features'. Aware of the poor prospects of such an approach, Eden wished to guarantee success by consulting the Americans only after the memorandum had been submitted to the Russians.[88] The memorandum, a watered-down version of Cripps' proposals, was discussed in Cabinet on 27 November. Churchill, as Cadogan witnessed, 'opposed violently the paper – without having read a *word* of it'; he thought the issues too important to be discussed off-hand. The already amorphous document suffered further redrafting so that by the time it was raised again in Cabinet on 4 December it had become 'as thin as restaurant coffee'. The Cabinet further specifically inhibited Eden from committing himself to territorial changes, which were to be left to the peace conference.[89] Now the side-issues which Cripps wished to discuss with Stalin to pave the way for Eden had become 'ticklish'; if Cripps were to discuss them there was no point, commented Cadogan, in Eden's proceeding to Moscow.[90]

After a temporary relapse Churchill was fast recovering his firm grip on the COS. This came about partially through the replacement of Dill by Brooke but also because of the setbacks to 'Crusader'. In the first days of the offensive, launched on 18 November, Rommel had managed to regain the initiative and prevent the relief of Tobruk. Auchinleck was forced to replace his commander in the field and a war

of attrition continued for months, causing heavy losses on both sides but proving inconclusive. Whereas originally Eden had hoped that a quick decision would allow him to propose to the Russians assistance in the Caucasus as the 'best possible defensive position', Brooke reinstated the 'strategic defensive' concept, expecting the Germans to exhaust themselves in prolonged battles. In the absence of sufficient resources he opposed any diversion, ruling out active cooperation on the battlefield while giving clear priority to the African campaign. It was a return to the position held at the outbreak of war, as the assistance considered – to organize subversive and demolition activities which would postpone German penetration into the Middle East – took for granted the defeat of the Russians.[91]

Churchill scored a major victory on 3 December in the Defence Committee, attended by the Chiefs of Staff, Attlee, Beaverbrook and Eden. He explained that the 'evenly balanced' situation in Cyrenaica meant that no large force could go to Russia. He did not conceal that he had never been disposed to send even a token force. Dill, he claimed, had subscribed to the idea with the 'mental reservations that by the time these troops reached the Caucasus the Russian front would be back on the mountains and our troops would be well placed to deal with the Baku oil fields. Now the Chiefs of Staff were strongly in favour of keeping everything for the Libyan Battle.' The effect of the new appointment was felt when Brooke affirmed that Libya was the 'only offensive front' on which the Germans could be engaged. This was the 'second front' for which the Russians had been pressing; even if the situation deteriorated in the east it would be unwise to divert forces on 'such a doubtful mission'. Faced with such a resolute opposition Eden gave way. He was 'convinced in his own mind that this was sound military strategy'.[92] However, he was fully aware that as the dispatch of troops had not been excluded, Stalin was bound to 'take the disappointment badly'. He wished the new decision to be conveyed to Stalin before he embarked on his mission. As if oblivious of the harmful repercussions of Beaverbrook's mission, the committee followed his advice that Eden should 'arrive with the offer of a force in one hand and the offer of a further supply of tanks and aircraft in the other, and try and trade the latter for the former'. He expected Stalin to be satisfied by this decision, which Churchill easily carried in Cabinet the next day[93] and which was to lead Eden on the same abortive course which Beaver-

brook had followed earlier. However, all chiefs of the armed services objected to the proposed number of 500 tanks.[94] Eventually the number was reduced to 100 tanks while, bowing to the fierce opposition, Churchill agreed that the transfer of ten squadrons of fighters from Libya would be made at the 'earliest moment when success [had] been gained'. This was embodied in a short directive to Eden, drawn up by Churchill himself, which emphatically stated that the two divisions which had been earmarked for the Caucasus could 'not be considered available'. In his memoirs Churchill justified his decision in view of the diminishing threat to Moscow; however, this became known only a few days later. Eden's brief was therefore reduced to alleviating suspicion.[95]

Eden's sole success was in securing a British declaration of war on Finland on 5 December. Churchill had made extraordinary efforts to extricate Finland from the war, fully supported by Bevin and Greenwood. Eden prevailed by implying that his visit stood no chance of success unless the issue was settled. Churchill was obliged to sanction what he regarded as a 'historic mistake'.[96]

Shortly before Eden's arrival, Cripps was brought up to date on the situation in England. Sixty-four diplomatic bags which had gone astray for weeks reached Kuibyshev. They included illuminating letters from Isobel, who had been canvassing on his behalf in London. Her information was illustrated by press cuttings and Hansard reports which revealed the upsurge of popular views coinciding with his own. On the rivalries in Cabinet he was further briefed by Sikorski heading a Polish delegation to Russia and by Victor Cazalet, a member of Parliament and an old acquaintance, who was attached to it. The information hastened his disillusionment as regards both the government's perception of the emerging alliance and the potential of his own ambassadorship.

It became clear that Eden was repeating Beaverbrook's mistakes by reaching Moscow with no precise plans or offers; this was fraught with danger as Stalin had the 'most definite and fixed ideas'. In the absence of a coherent policy he had few expectations from Eden, who was 'a person who relies for his effect upon the personal charm element and nice phrases and friendly gestures, but these are just the things that will not only not do any good here but will be positively harmful as all the time Stalin thinks that they are intentionally used as substitutes for action of some kind'. After the inevitable failure of the talks Cripps saw no way

of effecting a rapprochement 'without a complete change of Government'. It also finally dawned on Cripps that 'Winston was more insistent on keeping me out here than I thought.' He now wondered whether the unexpected announcement of Monckton's appointment to Cairo during his stay in Kuibyshev was not 'an attempt to get him out of England, the technique that is becoming so common with Winston when anyone of any kind of independence is concerned'. It fortified his decision to return home despite the question-mark of his future political career:

My own view is that when I insist on coming back either Winston will feel obliged to try and get me into the Cabinet or else he will attack me for deserting my job so as to do all he can to destroy any influence I might have. I dont know which he will do it will depend on the exact circumstances at the time and how strong and how much threatened he feels his position.[97]

By the time Eden left Euston for Scotland on 7 December to embark on HMS *Kent*, both he and Cripps had few hopes for the visit. Two unrelated events of overwhelming importance inflicted a further blow. Eden was still on the train when news came in of the attack on Pearl Harbor, the joint declaration of war with the United States on Japan and Churchill's impetuous decision to proceed within days to Washington. Despite his occasional criticism of Churchill and somewhat different sentiments towards Russia, Eden shared Churchill's overall order of priorities. With Churchill he had anticipated the United States' involvement in the war through developments in the Far East. His instant and joyful reaction was therefore that while in the past he had 'believed in the end but never seen the means, now both were clear'.[98] His sense of relief conformed with the view held by the COS since the outbreak of war that the entry of the United States was essential for winning the war. No longer was despair a reason for clinging to the Russians, while the respite achieved through limited cooperation seemed justified. The Japanese attack on Malaya now meant that the two active fronts coincided with the defence of British imperial interests in the Middle East and the Pacific, while the establishment of a front on the Continent seemed further away than ever. Churchill's hasty departure for Washington stood in sharp contrast to his attitude to Russia. The repercussions on the future attitude towards Russia were all too obvious. The temptation for Eden to bale out at the last minute was

great, particularly as Churchill's departure was bound to 'take all the limelight off the Moscow visit'. Churchill and Maisky, who was accompanying the delegation to Russia, appealed to Eden that a postponement would confirm Stalin's worst suspicions. Churchill for his part, conscious of Eden's misgivings, tried to assuage him by stating that the war on the Continent 'must have priority in our minds', while making the admission, of singular importance since Pearl Harbor, that such a view did 'not bind the United States'.[99]

The less spectacular event, but as significant in its aftermath, was the Russian success in repelling the German assault on Moscow. The first stage of the renewed German offensive was swift and effective. On 16 November German troops crossed the River Lama, south of the artificial sea of Moscow, at the opening of the Volga–Moscow canal. Klin, a key point on the north-western approaches to Moscow, fell on 24 November. Four days later the Germans proceeded along the canal to a distance of only 20 miles from the Kremlin. Meanwhile Guderian was meticulously executing the pincer counter-move on a wide front in the South, pressing on Kashira beyond which there was not a single Soviet formation to prevent the capture of Moscow. The final German thrust was attempted on 1 December by Field-Marshal von Kluge who advanced on the Minsk–Moscow highway in fierce winter conditions. The next day, however, Zhukov made his bid and drove the Germans to positions they had held a few days earlier. Taking advantage of the parrying of the German offensive, Zhukov mounted a counter-stroke on 5 December with temperatures reaching −30°C and roads covered by heavy snow. By 9 December the Germans had been driven to positions held before the major assault, after which they were subjected to continued harassment in their rear and a second counter-offensive at the end of the month.[100]

Although the Russians delayed publicity on the successful repulse until the day after Eden's arrival, Churchill was acquainted with the German difficulties through Enigma decrypts of the 'Wheel-back' order of 6 December and Hitler's directive of 8 December bringing to a stop the major offensive operations for the winter. On board the HMS *Kent* Eden was informed by Churchill that in view of these successes, the war in the Far East and Auchinleck's inconclusive battle, he 'should not, repeat not, offer ten squadrons at present time'.[101]

The HMS *Kent* docked at Murmansk on 12 December. Rather than

flying to the capital in a few hours, the delegation started a tedious three-day train journey to Moscow. Although this was allegedly due to severe weather and the absence of proper air cover, it must have been connected to Stalin's preoccupation with the critical stage of the battle of Moscow. The threat in the North was removed when Kalinin was regained on the night of the delegation's arrival in the capital, while Guderian's formations in the salient south-west of Tula were fast disintegrating.[102] Stalin was therefore ready to embark on negotiations from a position of strength and a convincing claim to be treated as an equal. Eden consequently reached Moscow in a worse position than Beaverbrook and with inferior timing.

Eden's protracted polemics with Cripps, the experience of their encounter in Turkey and the influence of Beaverbrook's biased reports all prevented a constructive relationship. The Russians had earlier pressed Cripps to return to Moscow and conduct preliminary talks. When he finally arrived in Moscow on 12 December they did their utmost to please him and facilitate his conferring with Eden prior to the latter's arrival in Moscow. As the embassy had been plundered when panic seized the population in mid-October, he was lodged in the best suite of the National Hotel which had been allotted to the British delegation. Three days later he headed for Yaroslav, some 200 miles north of Moscow, where he joined Eden's train. As in his previous meeting with Eden, crucial consultations were conducted in haste in a dining car. Cripps, as might be anticipated, tried in vain to convince Eden of the necessity of drawing up 'something definite and concrete' to meet the Russians' distinct political expectations.[103] Eden, as Harvey observed, was 'very bored' with Cripps, a 'clever fool', whom he found 'most opinionated'. For the time being Cripps was assuaged by Eden's news that he would be allowed to return home once the conference was over. The potential danger of having a politician in Moscow was now fully recognized; Churchill and Eden agreed that he should be replaced by a '*diplomate de carrière*'.[104]

At midnight on 15 December the train pulled into Moscow station in a blizzard. Eden's failure to consider the political issues raised by both Cripps and Maisky and the successful defence of Moscow made the visit ill-omened from the outset. This was well expressed by Maisky's description of the scene at the station: the lamps were suddenly lit, ignoring for a minute the blackout, and exposed the delegates and the high

19 Eden, Molotov and Cripps at Moscow railway station, December 1941

arches above them cloaked in steam and smoke from the engine. Rather than reflecting the sense of the 'harsh reality' of the war it seemed 'a spectral picture out of some sinister fairy tale'.[105]

The apprehension in Eden's entourage that Cripps would be an 'infernal nuisance butting in everywhere' seemed to be justified early the next morning when he weighed in with a heavily corrected draft of the declaration which Eden had been forced to accept in London. Cripps warned that the Russians were likely to mistrust a vague document and therefore advocated its presentation in a form resembling a treaty. Cadogan conceded the logic of Cripps' approach and to the sounds of guns 'married' the two documents.[106]

In the first meeting[107] Stalin produced drafts of two short treaties, one on the military alliance during the war and the other on post-war collaboration, which were to replace the ephemeral July agreement. The drafts closely corresponded to the British document prepared in the morning. But, as Cripps had warned, Stalin strove for a more binding formula. Stalin had recourse to the popular Russian genre of metaphors to explain: 'A declaration I regard as algebra, but an agreement as practical arithmetic. I do not wish to decry algebra, but I prefer practical arithmetic.' Far more disconcerting was a secret protocol which Stalin insisted should be attached to the second treaty: 'already starkly definite' ideas of the post-war map of Europe, as Eden later noted.[108]

Influenced by the terrifying experience of the past six months and their recent successes, the Russians proposed arrangements which reflected their search for security since the early 1930s. These fell into two categories: Russia's western border and the future of Europe, including Germany. The resemblance to Cripps' predictions was astounding. Stalin clearly aimed at the dismembering of Germany and encouraged Britain to claim the right to bases on the coasts of Belgium and Holland. Stalin further raised precise ideas on the organization of peace and international military guarantees for its preservation. But he was inflexible on Russia's western borders. He called for the establishment of a powerful Poland but wished the Curzon Line to be the recognized frontier. In return Poland would be allowed to expand into East Prussia and up to the Oder river. While Stalin was prepared to defer discussion on the Polish borders to the peace conference, he demanded immediate recognition of the Soviet absorption of the Baltic states and Bessarabia and the right to bases in southern Finland. Since his arrival in Moscow Cripps, whose undoubted mental quality was the ability to identify the crux of a problem, had in vain pressed the Cabinet to reach a decision on this issue, which he believed was a prerequisite for winning over the Russians. The significance attached by Stalin to post-war reconstruction was evident in his steadfast judgment that the forming of a genuine alliance required a consensus on war aims.

Stalin's purely pragmatic approach clashed with Churchill's who, '*au fond* a diehard imperialist', as Harvey put it,[109] was not inclined to respond to Russia's claims. Churchill could conveniently invoke the principles of the Atlantic Charter, most of which had been drafted under his guidance partly as a barrier against such claims. Eden was thus placed in an unenviable position. Unlike Beaverbrook, he had little to offer the Russians in terms of supply or military assistance, as he frankly admitted to Stalin at an early stage. He was obliged to grapple with the contentious issues if he wished to avoid a fiasco. He followed the advice of his officials at the Office to shelter under the earlier British pledges to the Americans while postponing a decision until further consultations in London. Somewhat hypocritically he insisted throughout the talks that he had never encountered the Soviet territorial claims before he reached Moscow and that the Cabinet had not discussed the subject. However, to ensure success he left Stalin with the distinct impression that he personally was in accord with the Soviet ideas. He exposed him-

self to serious criticism at home by promising to prevail on the Cabinet to adopt his point of view.

The conversation was followed by a buffet dinner, champagne and, as Cripps attested, a 'good deal of laughter and chaffing'. Once again the lavish hospitality and cordiality misled the participants into assuming that full understanding had been reached. But Cripps, who had so lucidly foreseen the Soviet position, feared that Britain would have to 'pay the price' for failing to prepare for the visit and form concrete ideas on a post-war settlement. A definite policy would have at least allowed for free discussions before Soviet ideas 'crystallised too far as it will be difficult to shift them later'.[110]

Although during the next morning Eden succeeded in working out with Maisky[111] an acceptable formula as far as the treaties were concerned, Stalin had sensed Eden's lack of authority and reverted in the midnight meeting to a single subject – the recognition of the Soviet claim to the 1941 frontiers. Eden's attempts to break through the *impasse* by emphasizing the British prior commitment to Roosevelt to defer any discussion on future frontiers and the need to consult Cabinet and the Dominions were of no avail. Stalin insisted that the precedence given by the British to their pledges in the Atlantic Charter ignored, as had Chamberlain, the security requirements of the Soviet Union. At the end of an inconclusive and argumentative session Stalin finally made it absolutely clear that he had no intention of signing any agreement unless Russia's 1941 borders were recognized. As a last resort Eden, defying a contrary decision taken in London, revived in the next meeting the plan of a tripartite conference in which the borders would be discussed. For his part Stalin presented an amended draft of the second treaty whose meaning, though somewhat obscure, he soon clarified as involving the recognition of the 1941 frontiers. The diverging war aims that would eventually dominate the conduct of the war and shape post-war Europe were unmistakably surfacing. While the Russians were fighting for secure borders, Eden conveyed the apparent absence of a coherent British concept beyond the determination of 'fighting to beat Hitler'. The negotiations had reached a deadlock far more serious than in Beaverbrook's conference, as the Russians were now less concerned about military aid but were committed to a solution of the political issue. Cripps' judgment of the situation and perception of future developments were unequivocal:

The trouble is that they dont feel the need for our help to the same extent now and are much more confident in themselves and as I foretold long ago this has made them much more difficult to deal with . . . I am afraid now they will pay no attention to any arguments about their frontiers they will just insist on what they want and will feel capable of getting without any help from us. We shall fight two separate wars and we shall suffer as the result. It is all a muddle and a tragedy of another missed opportunity.[112]

Despite his gloomy and critical appraisal, Cripps' dissension was less apparent than in the Moscow conference two months earlier. Unlike Beaverbrook Eden handled Cripps well, confining his misgivings to his close associates. His decision to neutralize Cripps through patient and respectful consideration of his views and insistence on his participation in the actual negotiations[113] bore immediate fruit. Eden's determined bearing in the acrimonious meeting, which none the less displayed his commitment to the Russian cause in variance with the Cabinet, certainly appealed to Cripps. Eden, he admitted, was 'very good and kept his equanimity with great patience'; Eden recorded his impression that Cripps 'for the first time thought there might after all be something in this rather flotsam Tory'.[114] Cripps seemed to share a great deal with Harvey, who was the source for many of Eden's ideas, as is evident from Harvey's impressions of the situation:

I am worried because (a) we cannot win the war without Russia, (b) we cannot make peace without Russia (c) the 1941 frontiers of Russia (in Finland, Baltic States, Rumania) are not too bad in themselves. On the other hand Stalin is rejecting a golden opportunity. A. E. is the one man in England who is ready to put their case (P.M. anti-Russian, Cabinet contemptible, Labour leaders, Bevin, Attlee, Morrison violently anti-Soviet).[115]

Cripps attributed the difficulties to the Cabinet's continued negligence; Eden should not have come before the ground was properly prepared. Once absorbed in a problem Cripps, probably as a result of his legal training, always sought a pragmatic solution. Thus, although single-minded in pursuing his objectives, he was inclined to seek compromises in the intermediate stages. He brushed aside the temptation to speculate on 'the past . . . the might have been'. Instead he set out to help Eden to achieve his aims, though he was convinced that the real struggle would have to be conducted later in London. The result was a marked improvement in their relationship as the visit continued.[116]

20  Eden and Maisky visit the front at Klin

A pause in the negotiations occurred on 19 December when Stalin responded to a personal request made by Cripps to allow Eden to visit the front. Together with Maisky and the military mission he left for Klin, which had just been liberated, while Cripps 'volunteered to stay behind to give Molotov a lecture'.[117] Cripps brought along a concise statement which explained, in rather judicial terms, the limitations imposed on the British Cabinet by commitments undertaken prior to the German invasion of Russia. Perhaps more significant was the clear impression he conveyed, following in Eden's footsteps, that the impediments were of a formal nature and that Cabinet was disposed to assent to the Soviet demands. However, in his usual intimidating fashion, which was certainly more effective in court than in diplomacy, he warned Molotov that Eden's return empty-handed might provoke a disastrous reaction from forces hostile to the idea of collaboration. Molotov immediately rejected the statement, reiterating Stalin's earlier position. Many of the arguments he raised could have been attributed to

285

Cripps. He further disclosed Soviet mistrust by discounting Eden's claim that the frontiers were a new issue, citing the various Soviet approaches on the subject prior to the visit. The important conclusion was an appeal to recognize the changing circumstances; an alliance could not be 'built-up on a basis which existed one-and-a-half to two years ago'. Although Cripps had to greet Eden with news of the failure of his attempt, an element in his statement was later seized on by the two sides to prevent total collapse. Cripps proposed the issuing of a communiqué, after the signature of the two treaties, which recorded an agreement on the opening of immediate consultations on the question of the 'post-war European boundaries' in the hope of providing the signatories with 'greater security' in the future.[118]

Stalin's intention in calling a break in the negotiations, as well as demonstrating to Eden the turn of the tide, was to allow him to consult Cabinet and Churchill, then at sea on the way to Washington. Stalin, like Eden, must have been apprehensive about possible further commitments by Churchill and he was certainly ambivalent about the opening of the war in the Far East. He wished Churchill to be informed of Russia's determined position.[119] Eden, who could anticipate Churchill's reactions, had persisted in his refusal to do so in the first two meetings. When he did, it was purely a formality to prove his point to Stalin. Far from urging a revision of attitudes, his telegrams home only repeated what he had told Stalin: that he could not see how the government could 'here and now by Treaty agree to the post-war Soviet frontiers without American consent'. The Cabinet therefore had the easy task of rephrasing his telegram as a decision.[120]

With the Americans now embroiled in war Churchill was even less sympathetic to the Soviet demands. In retrospect he was to depict in ideological terms his reaction against 'Soviet territorial ambitions' and the need for the resurrection of those states which had been the 'outpost of Europe against Bolshevism'. At the time his attitude, though no doubt affected by emotional antagonism, was far more pragmatic. The Soviet demands were accepted at face value as a genuine aspiration for security enhanced by the experience of two world wars. The opposition to the annexations came mainly from Attlee, who later even threatened to resign his seat in the War Cabinet on this issue. Halifax himself, who was associated with the failure of the 1939 tripartite negotiations and who had rarely expressed strong views one way or another while in

21 On arrival in Scotland after their visit to Moscow, l. to r.: Maisky, Eden and Major General A. E. Nye

office, now felt the need to approach Churchill: 'I have a feeling, based on re-thinking over again our talks with the Russians in the summer of 1939, that Anthony is not exaggerating how important a place all those ideas of security are going to hold in Stalin's mind.'[121] Churchill quite clearly did not wish to start his visit in Washington by retracting his pledges to Roosevelt and probably courting a 'blank refusal'. The tightening alliance with the Americans greatly outweighed considerations of relations with Russia. The Russians, he explained to Eden and Attlee, had to 'go on fighting for their lives anyway' and depended upon British supplies. Eden should not therefore be downhearted if he had to 'leave Moscow without any flourish of trumpets'. The Russian demands, stated Churchill, lay 'in a future which is uncertain and probably remote. We have now to win the war by a hard and prolonged struggle.'[122]

The Cabinet's decision was read to Stalin at the opening of the last

session on 20 December. He could hardly have expected a different answer. For the reasons discerned by Churchill, he had no interest in ending the conference in a clash. After a few wry comments on Britain's loss of freedom through her dependence on the United States and on Eden's superfluous trip, he agreed to wait the three weeks in which Eden believed he could sway the Cabinet towards the desired result. Meanwhile, Stalin conceded that the 'progress of the war [compelled] the two countries to draw closer and closer'. To camouflage the serious dissensions the Russians turned to the communiqué which Cripps had earlier discussed with Molotov and which was further elaborated. At very short notice the whole delegation was hustled to Catherine the Great's throne room in the Kremlin for what Eden described as an 'embarrassingly sumptuous' banquet which outdid that staged for Beaverbrook. Eden left Russia on Christmas Eve. Stalin's frontier demands did not abate and varied little throughout the war. Eden's presentation of the conference to Churchill as 'worthwhile', having 'allayed some at least of the past suspicions', fell short of the expectations on both sides. Eden, who was only too well aware of his prime loyalties and sources of power, assured Churchill that the British and American position was 'completely safeguarded'.[123]

## 8

# AFTERMATH

Owing to a sudden recurrence of nettle rash and high fever, Cripps missed the final events of Eden's visit and the banquet which closed it on a note of undue optimism. On Christmas Day he reviewed the past six months and felt a sense 'not only of intense relief but also of triumph'. He was glad that he had not left earlier, as his presence in Moscow in those critical days was a 'symbol of closeness' to the 'heart of Russia'. In the Soviet victories Cripps recognized the fruition of his single-minded support of Russia in defiance of the overwhelmingly derisive opinions at home:

In England many people and especially the skilled professionals of war were almost wishing for the defeat of the Soviet Armies to prove the rightness of the forecasts which had been made of their easy defeat by Hitler. I have had as a result a straining anxiety to see these false prophets proved false and a lurking fear from time to time that after all perhaps they might prove not so wrong. Now whatever happens in the future they have been finally and conclusively proved to be absolutely wrong, and all the wishful thinking which lay behind their forecasts has been equally proved to be nothing but the reflection of their own biassed views.

The lesson he expected to be drawn in England was that the allegedly despised Soviet régime was able to rally the population, demand excessive sacrifices and maintain a front, which other western democracies had failed to achieve. He could now challenge the detractors who had proclaimed that the régime was 'rotten or that it has sapped the vitality of the country'. Were it not for the Russians, he mused, 'Hitler would now be the undoubted conqueror of the whole of Europe and our chance of ever being victorious would be precisely nil.' The inevitable conclusion was that the Soviet system 'with all its imperfections' had proved the 'triumphant saviour of all that we profess to uphold in democracy'.[1]

It was obvious to Cripps that Stalin could not be moved from his position on the frontier issue. He believed that the communiqué issued upon Eden's departure to all intents and purposes bound England to post-war collaboration. The main struggle would now take place in London, where Eden would have to fulfil his promise to carry Cabinet with him. From his knowledge of the political constellation Cripps feared that Churchill and the Americans would be 'stupid about the frontier question or perhaps it would be fairer to say unrealistic'. Indeed Eden, seconded by Beaverbrook, urged Cabinet to recognize Russia's 1941 frontiers shortly after Churchill's return from Washington. Faced by mounting discontent over the conduct of the war, Churchill deferred a decision by transferring it to the Americans. Communications with Washington dragged on for a month, in the course of which the Americans exerted pressure on Churchill to agree to a second front, presumably hoping to avoid a decision on the more controversial political issue. Meanwhile the Germans, recovering from the severe winter, unexpectedly resumed a vigorous offensive which pressed the Russians hard in the South. Fearful of a possible Allied desertion, Stalin temporarily abandoned his demand for a comprehensive treaty and authorized Molotov to sign in London in May a twenty-year treaty of mutual assistance. His opting for this course was also a response to an American pledge to carry out an early major operation on the Continent.[2]

Reluctant to abandon the projected joint Anglo-American landing in North Africa, Churchill was resolved to postpone a diversion in Europe to 1943 at the earliest. However, in view of the accusations levelled against him in public as well as within Cabinet about the meagre assistance granted to Russia, Churchill could not afford to neglect the implications of a Soviet defeat. In mid-August he therefore followed in Beaverbrook's and Eden's footsteps, seeking Stalin's consent to the postponement of the offensive promised for 1942. Having been let down on the issues of frontiers and the second front, the patently dismayed Stalin brought the talks to the verge of breakdown, as on previous occasions. A reconciliation, again glossing over the outstanding differences, was finally effected: Churchill was clearly negotiating in Moscow with a view to the home front, while Stalin could hardly afford a rift while the Germans were marching on Stalingrad.[3]

The discord which burst into the open in the famous conferences of

1943–5 and shaped the polarized world which emerged from the war had in fact marred Anglo-Soviet relations even before the formation of the Alliance. Cripps had accurately prophesied the consequences of the ominous signs but attempted in vain to goad the government into adopting a dynamic and revised attitude towards the Soviet Union.

Cripps' hopes of Soviet recognition of his efforts and his sympathy with their cause were never fulfilled. His buoyant feelings at Christmas were spoiled by Stalin's refusal to bid him farewell. On the contrary, the Russians were showing clear signs of dissatisfaction. The representatives of Narkomindel in Kuibyshev, who organized send-off dinners for even minor diplomats, did not do so in Cripps' case. On 10 January Cripps stopped overnight in Moscow on the way home and was again ignored by the Kremlin. No official was at the airport to see him off or to receive him at Archangel. On landing at Murmansk airport, some distance from the town, Cripps was driven in a blizzard to meet the local dignitaries in town rather than embarking on the cruiser lying close by. Once in Murmansk he was forced to spend the night there on the pretext of inclement weather conditions, while the Commissar of the district and the General in command were suddenly indisposed.[4]

The unceremonious farewell later enhanced the view that Cripps had been unwelcome in Moscow. Cripps' pragmatic approach to the Moscow talks undoubtedly drew him closer to Eden and must have been an unpleasant surprise to the Russians, who had been counting on his support. In addition, during his last days in Kuibyshev, Cripps' Cassandra-like prophecies, though essentially a criticism of the British government, had unflattering implications for Stalin. For instance, he told Assarasson during their leavetaking that a victorious Stalin would treat the Allies like 'pygmies'. He would strive to gain the utmost through power and deceit, following the motto 'mundus vult depici, decipiatur ergo' even if he had never heard of it.[5] Unpleasant as the personal experience may have been for Cripps, the Russians must have been registering a protest primarily at the failure of Eden's mission. It was a reminder that the cordial parting from him was based on a promise not yet fulfilled. The three weeks Eden had requested for winning over the Cabinet were just elapsing. Litvinov in Washington undoubtedly transmitted the information that Churchill was conducting daily strategic and political discussions at the White House from which the Russians were virtually excluded.[6] That the cavalier treatment of

Cripps was a demonstrative act is also borne out by the Russians' severance of communications with the military mission, which had earlier been encouraged to return to Moscow. Indeed, when on 27 December Cripps had made a last-minute effort to initiate a political compromise when parting from Molotov, he was told unequivocally that 'there would be nothing doing until [the Russians] got the agreement on frontiers'.[7]

Cripps could find consolation in the unprecedented wave of affection and esteem evoked by his departure both in the diplomatic colony and amongst the staff of his embassy. The heads of the military mission arranged an intimate farewell dinner in Moscow while he was still convalescing, at the end of which these undemonstrative military figures 'very shy and blushing murmured their thanks for all I have done . . . which made my throat feel quite lumpy'. To Kuibyshev they sent him further greetings signed 'Your three chiefs of staff': 'They so call themselves because we have often had jokes about the need for all of us to go home to take over and they always say that they will serve with me as the chiefs of staff if I want them when I get into the saddle of P.M.!'[88] Baggallay, left in charge, faithfully reflected the feelings at the embassy when reporting to Whitehall that he wished to place on record 'the regret that I and others who have served under [Cripps] feel at the departure of one to whom we are indebted for constant kindness and consideration, as well as the tribute to his qualities which I have received from all quarters in the diplomatic corps . . . Diplomatic worlds change quickly, but I think Sir Stafford's appointment will long be remembered at this post.' Indeed, Assarasson testifies how 'strongly Cripps' absence was felt' in the following year among the diplomats, while the whispers of criticism against him vanished as if they had never existed.[9]

When Cripps arrived in London on 23 January he had only a faint idea of what his next moves would be. Cripps had embarked on a diplomatic mission because of his shaky political position and the stifling atmosphere at the outbreak of war. At the time the mission seemed to be the optimum contribution to the war effort while advancing his own ideas on post-war reconstruction, at least on the international scene. The mission to Moscow, as Cripps had been careful to note, was no more than a respite before he plunged back into domestic politics. Though Cripps may be accused of pragmatism and altering tactics, he

religiously adhered to his essential philosophy. His advocation of a united front with communists and shortly afterwards his identification with a large body of progressive Conservatives did not lead him to sacrifice his tenets. It was this involvement with radical Conservatives which had gained him access to Russia in the first place and which now facilitated his meteoric rise, in addition to the esteem he enjoyed as a result of his association with the Russian resistance. The challenge he posed to Churchill should be examined in the light of the ideological discord with the government which had been steadily revealed during his ambassadorship.

Churchill's explanation of Cripps' rise to a prominent political position after Moscow is such as to warrant our investigation of his genuine motives in directing Cripps' career at the time. Churchill presents little evidence of his political controversies with Cripps, particularly during the eight months preceding his return. There is absolutely no reference to his manifest apprehension of the threat posed by Cripps' return if he were to launch a public crusade on the nature of the alliance with Russia or war aims in general. On the contrary, Churchill suggests that it was the austerity of life in Moscow and poor communications with home which led Cripps to seek his recall. Churchill then belittles Cripps' challenge, suggesting that as a result of the undeserved reputation of his mission there were 'some on the extreme left who appeared to regard him as worth running as an alternative Prime Minister'. He attributes the hasty inclusion of Cripps in the Cabinet to a much earlier appreciation of his capabilities as an assistant superintendent in one of Britain's largest munitions factories and to his 'liking him personally'.[10]

As has been shown, Churchill and the Cabinet were well aware of the danger lying ahead. Because of Churchill's account and the extraordinary reception Cripps received it is forgotten that Cripps had been tipped with Bevin as the likeliest candidates for premiership as early as spring 1941, before 'Barbarossa'.[11] The challenge was certainly not confined to the extreme left wing, as Churchill would like his readers to believe, but included his most trusted colleagues, notably Eden. In fact among Cripps' former associates on the left his position had perhaps even deteriorated as a result of his service in the government and realistic, at times even harsh, approach to Russia. To them he now appeared to embrace 'exactly the attitude of a more progressive type of Tory'. From their point of view his return constituted a danger. Once he joined the

Cabinet he would convince 'advanced' circles of its progressiveness, while if he stayed out he would 'lead ably a miscellaneous opposition' which would 'kid the progressives in much the same way'.[12]

The affinity of Cripps' ideas with those of progressive Conservatives outside and inside Cabinet posed Churchill with a most serious threat. This was accompanied by an unanticipated erosion in the Conservative attitude towards Russia. Thus Eden pressed for Cripps' inclusion in Cabinet even before his arrival in London, although the new arrival seriously undermined his position as the heir apparent. According to an April opinion poll 34% wished to see Cripps installed as Prime Minister were Churchill to be incapacitated as compared with 37% favouring Eden, while Attlee and Bevin trailed far behind with 2% each. In a typical though curious move Eden bowed to the pressure, accepting the 'assumption of equality'; he was, as he told Harvey, 'quite happy to see Cripps at No. 10 if he himself could be Minister of Defence and run the war side'.[13] Attlee naturally recognized in Cripps a challenge to his leadership of Labour in Cabinet but unsuccessfully attempted to bar his way into the War Cabinet.[14]

Perhaps most dramatic, however, was the effect of Cripps' return on Beaverbrook's career. Despite the sinking by the Japanese of the *Prince of Wales* and *Repulse* in December, the setbacks in Malaya and the depressed atmosphere at home, Churchill returned from Washington satisfied with the extent of collaboration he had achieved with Roosevelt. To forestall the fresh challenge he sought a foregone vote of confidence in Parliament. He also wasted little time in entertaining Cripps and Isobel at Chequers two days after Cripps' return to London and before the debate in Parliament, offering him the Ministry of Supply. The prompt proposal certainly seemed to pay off when Cripps, as Churchill noted with evident relief, refrained from participating in the debate.[15] The Ministry of Supply, however, did not carry with it a seat in the War Cabinet and was rendered even less significant by Churchill's intention of appointing Beaverbrook as overlord of production. Cripps' rejection of the offer should certainly be viewed in light of his encounter with Beaverbrook in Moscow and his vow never to serve with him.[16] In his judgment Beaverbrook's continued presence in Cabinet would jeopardize his intention 'to override private interests and make radical changes'. Beaverbrook vainly attempted over dinner to persuade Cripps to undertake the job, presenting himself again as a

'Crippsite' which partially at least must have been an attempt to ruffle Attlee.[17] Moreover, Cripps made his entry into Cabinet conditional on the exclusion of the remaining appeasers. Churchill, however, preferring 'a Cabinet of obedient mugwumps than of awkward freaks', as he told Eden, rejected the condition.[18]

Meanwhile the government's prestige reached a new low when the Japanese continued their thrust through the Malayan peninsula, capturing Singapore and some 60,000 British troops on 15 February. Auchinleck was unable to force a decision in the desert. An added embarrassment was the German battle cruisers *Scharnhorst, Gneisenau* and *Prinz Eugen* slipping unscathed through the Channel from the Atlantic to their bases. An opening was created for new and vigorous leadership, particularly on the home front, which would not recur during the war. Cripps was presented with an unprecedented opportunity of profiting from his gains in Moscow. A paradox became apparent: by encouraging Cripps to assume the post in Moscow, regarded as a dead end, and then by enforcing his prolonged exile, the Cabinet had achieved the opposite effect. The association of Cripps with the widely acclaimed Russian resistance, while the government had little to boast about, posed Churchill with the gravest challenge to his premiership during the whole war.

In a widely publicized speech to his constituents in Bristol on 6 February, Cripps criticized the government's attitude to Russia and overall conduct of the war. It was followed up two days later in an extremely popular 'Postscript' broadcast which appealed because of its dry and simple delivery, sincere survey of the situation and call for sacrifices – all trademarks of Cripps' credibility later on as the austere Chancellor of the Exchequer. It was in fact compared to Churchill's incandescent speeches after Dunkirk.[19] Churchill, Cripps later observed, feared two things: '(1) the Press, and (2) that someone should become a more popular broadcaster than himself'.[20] Churchill, whose popularity was waning fast, bowed to the pressure but in an extremely shrewd and well calculated move. On 23 February Cripps won the first round when he was invited to join the War Cabinet as Lord Privy Seal, while David Margesson and J.T.C. Moore-Brabazon were promptly dismissed as he had requested. Cripps' well-known antagonism to Beaverbrook undoubtedly contributed to Churchill's manoeuvring of Beaverbrook into resignation over the controversy with Attlee concerning the

22  Cripps gives a press conference at the Ministry of Information, February
1942, with Isobel and Brendan Bracken

demands made to Eden by Stalin. On the eve of the debate in Cabinet
on the Russian request Churchill might well have preferred to forestall
the formation of the powerful coalition of Beaverbrook, Cripps and
Eden. In his memoirs, however, Churchill preferred to attribute his
acceptance of the resignation to Beaverbrook's 'nervous breakdown'.[21]

Although Cripps was now openly spoken of as a future premier and
even accepted in Cabinet as such, he seemed to be the last to appreciate
the political avenue opened for him. Despite his gradual realization in
Kuibyshev of the growing confrontation and his increased popularity,
Cripps certainly did not appreciate the potential of the moment. Rather
than visualizing himself in the centre of the political scene, he was contemplating radical activity, wavering between assuming 'the great role
of referee of war aims' and his traditional back-bench role of an
'independent opposition'. In the latter case he would advocate the
introduction of planned production and the 'elimination of the profit

making principle'.[22] As has been shown, Cripps' confrontation with Churchill built up steadily throughout his ambassadorship. It was no secret that he was entertaining the idea of emerging as a national leader, clearing the debris of the war and laying the foundations of a reformed society. But at the same time he fully realized that Churchill could not be replaced as war leader. He therefore remained aloof from the widespread speculations and the various coups engineered inside and outside the Cabinet to oust Churchill. He was clearly not set on exploiting the favourable conditions at home.

It may well be argued that the opportunity had arrived too early. It took Cripps nearly another decade to reach a similar position but by then he was already mortally ill. His conduct throughout 1941 and 1942 demonstrates his typically detached and naive political appreciation of the opportunities at hand, aggravated by an obsessive absorption in the meticulous execution of the tasks imposed on him while constantly intervening in a multitude of issues outside his jurisdiction. Those characteristics, so pronounced in his mission to Moscow, were greatly to Churchill's advantage, enabling Cripps' removal from the political scene and depriving him at a stroke of the tremendous success he had gained in Moscow. On the other hand it is fair to say that Churchill's victory was a foregone conclusion. In the highly charged atmosphere of 1941 Cripps' attraction lay in his freshness, sincerity and dissociation from party politics. The most illustrative example of his lack of political judgment is the abandonment shortly after arrival of his trump card – the Russian issue. A temptingly simple answer would be to attribute it to Cripps' disappointment in Stalin's 'rude' and ungrateful farewell. But this does not tally with his forgiving nature. Moreover, Cripps was suffering from remorse for abandoning his post in Moscow in favour of domestic policies. He philosophically took Stalin's attitude to imply that he had exhausted his potential there. Besides, he correctly tended to explain the discourtesy of the leavetaking as a reflection of the attitude to Eden's visit.[23] From the outset Cripps had accepted the mission to Moscow as an interregnum, a temporary engagement enforced by political conditions at home. With Russia now fighting on the side of the Allies he felt the mission had been completed at a propitious moment for resuming his political activities. After all, even in Moscow his steadfast commitment and foremost interest was in introducing those political reforms to which he had always been devoted. Despite

his almost unrestrained interference with Churchill's daily conduct of the war, Cripps' main energy was still directed to the attainment of this aim. Oblivious of the advantage which his association with Russia supplied, Cripps surprised observers; he seemed to 'underestimate Churchill's loss of prestige, and hardly to contemplate his almost inevitable departure'. As late as August 1942 Cripps appeared to be 'entirely taken up with post-war reconstruction, not in so far as it affects current policy, but because he is confident he will be Prime Minister at that time and is thinking now what he will do then'.[24] Burning issues like the opening of a second front no longer fell within this category. Cripps did not abandon his commitment to Russia; in fact he continued to demonstrate his support in various public appearances in 1942. As late as 1945 the photo of his signing in the Kremlin of the Anglo-Soviet agreement of July 1942 was proudly displayed in his election manifesto.[25] However, he had never been infatuated with Russia like the fellow-travellers and other extreme left-wingers, nor had he supported Russia purely for political gain like Beaverbrook and at times Eden.

Churchill, who had been relentlessly criticized by Cripps, wasted no time in exploiting his weaknesses. An entirely unexpected move was Churchill's relinquishing his role as Leader of the House and appointing Cripps in his stead. He might well have remembered Eden's recent clairvoyant remark that Cripps would discredit himself in Parliament.[26] Furthermore, in his new role Cripps was required to represent the Cabinet in the House, which ensured a degree of allegiance and was a time-consuming task. Cripps' lack of political support was a serious impediment in this role, to succeed in which, noted Nicolson in his diary, it was not enough to be 'gifted or honest or wise, but "formidable". But to be formidable implies the capacity to bring votes in the lobby.' Cripps was certainly not cut out for the post. After a short honeymoon with the House, his handling of members with a 'schoolmaster's tone' and continued harassment for not attending to their tasks began to be an annoyance. Churchill, as Morrison testifies, 'found it convenient to change his duties'.[27]

The famous abortive mission to India in mid-March was entirely Cripps' initiative. It was an attempt to secure Indian support for the war in exchange for an interim arrangement for self-rule and a promise of independence after the war. The enthusiasm for Russia which had

rubbed off onto Cripps boosted his confidence in a mission which stood only scant chances of success. The mission, however, very nearly succeeded and was crushed, as Moore assures us, 'by the monolithic millstones of Churchillian Conservatism and Congress nationalism'. As Churchill did not instigate the mission he cannot be charged with plotting to weaken Cripps' standing. However, the alacrity with which he accepted Cripps' offer to go despite his reservations about his proposals, his undermining of Cripps' position while in India and the pressure he exerted on Cabinet to reconsider its attitude after Cripps' departure raise serious questions as to Churchill's good faith. Shrewd as he was, Churchill could not have been blind to the opposition building up in Cabinet. Eden had just made up his mind that once Cripps was back a 'frontal attack must be made'. The tactics used by Churchill are only too reminiscent of those used when Beaverbrook and Eden were launched on their abortive missions to Moscow. Moreover, it was certainly convenient to keep Cripps away and absorbed in such an intractable problem when Eden's proposals for the recognition of the Soviet absorption of the Baltic were being considered. Although Cripps' failure did not cause an immediate decline in his popularity, there was marked discontent in radical and left-wing quarters.[28]

It was, however, only after his return from India that Cripps started canvassing in earnest his plans for post-war reconstruction, which were regarded as 'uncompromisingly and radically socialist'[29] and incongruous with the wartime political truce. In fact their strength lay in their interparty appeal, with a remarkable following among progressive Conservatives. This direction was for Cripps the logical conclusion of a process which had started with his disillusionment with Labour after his expulsion in 1939 and was stimulated by the conditions created by the war. His success was furthered by his association with the Russian struggle but not initiated by it.

More alarming to Churchill than the ideas Cripps was preaching was his increasing interference in the conduct of the war. This was first discerned during Cripps' stopover in Cairo on his way to India. Churchill had hoped to use him to prod Auchinleck into renewing the desert offensive. Instead, to Churchill's fury, Cripps was persuaded by the General of the impediments to such an offensive.[30] Later in the summer Cripps strove to give the overall conduct of the war a more scientific and efficient direction, calling for the creation of a War Planning

Directorate to replace the omnipotent Defence Ministry through which Churchill was able to bypass the Cabinet and exercise almost unchallenged control of strategy. Cripps meddled in the appointment of commanders in the field and related matters.[31] His vociferous challenge carried particular weight after the fall of Tobruk on 20 June. But it was only when it seemed that the government was about to collapse that Cripps showed some interest in recruiting support, though he again expected Eden to precede him as Prime Minister.[32]

In the meantime Cripps' prolonged association with the government with little achievement to his credit caused erosion in his political standing, as was shrewdly noted by George Orwell at the time: 'I can't help feeling a strong impression that Cripps has already been got at. Not with money or anything of that kind of course, nor even by flattery and the sense of power, which in all probability he genuinely doesn't care about: but simply by responsibility, which automatically makes a man timid.'[33] This was not lost on Cripps, who in the autumn was bent on resigning. It was essential for him, explained Isobel, not to get 'so covered with tar' through his collaboration with the Cabinet that it would 'not melt off'.[34] Cripps' resignation in October might have seriously damaged Churchill. Playing on Cripps' patriotism, Eden persuaded him to postpone his resignation so as not to interfere with the planned Anglo-American landing in North Africa. After Montgomery's victory at El Alamein at the end of the month, Churchill's prestige was sufficiently enhanced to compel the now wavering Cripps to carry out his threat and resign. He was immediately offered the absorbing post of Minister of Aircraft Production, out of the War Cabinet. The considerations which led Churchill to manoeuvre Cripps into that Ministry are apparent from his own memoirs. For someone with such 'keen intellect' and 'exalted ideas', he explained, the task of a minister without departmental duties held a 'strong though dangerous appeal'. His energy therefore needed to be 'harnessed to a more practical task'. As Macmillan expressed it more bluntly, Cripps was 'safely encased in his demanding post for the rest of the war'.[35]

Though Cripps lacked much political influence during the remainder of the war, his reputation and impeccable work at the ministry assured his assumption of a key position in the Labour government after the war. In the 'unequal' confrontation between them, as Churchill had warned Cripps when still in Moscow,[36] Cripps was the obvious loser.

But his gospel was none the less the clearest and earliest harbinger of events yet to come. This was recognized and eloquently described at the time by Butler:

It is clear to all that the politics of Stafford Cripps and Winston Churchill are not alike, and they had some difficulty in running together. The P.M. is tending to turn more and more to the ancient ways and paths of tradition, and Cripps . . . is tending more and more towards a new world of rather undefined and unrestricted socialism.[37]

# NOTES

## Preface

1 See a representative article by R. C. Tucker, 'The Emergence of Stalin's Foreign Policy', and a symposium in *Slavic Review*, 4 (1977).

2 C. Cooke, *The Life of Richard Stafford Cripps* (London, 1957); E. Estorick, *Stafford Cripps, A Biography* (London, 1949); P. Strauss, *Cripps – Advocate and Rebel* (London, 1943).

3 H. Hanak, 'Sir Stafford Cripps as British Ambassador in Moscow, May 1940 to June 1941' and 'Sir Stafford Cripps as Ambassador in Moscow, June 1941 – January 1942', *English Historical Review*, 370 (1979) and 383 (1982).

4 See below, p. 37.


## 1 Origins of the mission

1 M. Gilbert, *Winston S. Churchill, 1922–1939* (London, 1976), pp. 1076, 1082–3.

2 Laski papers, DLA 15, exchange with Cripps, 14–28 Sept. See also Webb papers, diary, pp. 6745–6, 5 Oct. 1939, and T. D. Burridge, *British Labour and Hitler's War* (London, 1976), pp. 25–39.

3 Cripps was readmitted to the Labour Party only in 1945.

4 Cripps papers (Nuffield College), Box 586, 27 Sept. 1939.

5 An excellent survey is in B. Pimelott, *Labour and the Left in the 1930s* (Cambridge, 1977). See also W. D. Jones, *The Russia Complex: the British Labour Party and the Soviet Union* (Manchester, 1977).

6 For typical views see 'What Hope from the Churches', *Tribune*, 20 May 1938; Cripps papers (Nuffield), Box 664/24, Cripps' introduction to a pamphlet 'In His Faith We Live' and extracts from interview with Isobel, July 1949.

7 Cripps papers (Nuffield), draft of speech delivered in China in Feb. 1940.

8 *ibid.*, memo. of the UDC and Fabian Society on Russia, 29 Sept. 1939.

9 *ibid.*, Box 592–3, 7 Nove. 1939.

10 *Tribune*, 22 Sept. 1939.

11 H. S. Morrison, *Morrison: an Autobiography* (London, 1960), p. 158.

12 R. Jenkins, *Nine Men of Power* (London, 1974), p. 93.

13 The most up-to-date discussion of this contentious issue is in S. Aster, *1939: the Making of the Second World War* (London, 1973).
14 See below. On Maisky's extraordinary position in London see S. Aster, 'Ivan Maisky and Parliamentary Anti-Appeasement, 1938–39' in A. J. P. Taylor (ed.), *Lloyd George* (London, 1971).
15 *DGFP*, vol. 8, p. 76.
16 Dalton papers, Box II 5/2, memo. from Boothby, 17 Sept.; FO 371 23678 N5297/57/38, 5 Oct. 1941.
17 Dalton papers, Box II 3/2, letter from Strabolgi, 20 Sept.; Webb papers, diary, p. 6743, 2 Oct.; FO 800/328, Halifax to Gort, 8 Nov. 1939.
18 CAB 84/8 JP(39)49 and CAB 65/1 43(39)6,9, 6 and 10 Oct. 1939.
19 FO 371 23678 N5240/57/38, 12 Oct. For an impression of Seeds see Dalton papers, diary, 13 Feb. 1940.
20 FO 371 23678 N5240/57/38, 17 Oct. 1939.
21 FO 371 23678 N4571/57/38, min. by Lascelles, 18 Sept. 1939.
22 CAB 65/1, 31,32,38(39), 29 and 30 Sept. and 5 Oct. 1939.
23 FO 371 23678 N4571/57/38; Cripps papers (Nuffield), Box 586, letter to a *Tribune* reader, 23 Nov. 1939.
24 FO 371 23678 N4571, N4862/57/38, Cripps to Halifax, 16, 18 and 30 Sept., and mins. by Cadogan and Halifax, 18, 19 and 23 Sept.; N4807/57/38, min. by Vansittart and similar views by Chamberlain in CAB 65/1 30(39)6, 28 Sept. 1939.
25 Dalton papers, Box II 3/2, and Webb papers, diary, pp. 6736–9, 20 and 24 Sept. 1939.
26 J. Harvey (ed.), *The Diplomatic Diaries of Oliver Harvey, 1937–40* (London, 1970), p. 40; Earl of Birkenhead, *Halifax: the Life of Lord Halifax* (London, 1965), pp. 79, 112–13; Lord Butler, *The Art of the Possible* (London, 1971), pp. 76–7.
27 Birkenhead, *Halifax*, pp. 363, 417–20. See also D. Dilks (ed.), *The Diaries of Sir Alexander Cadogan, 1938–45* (London, 1971), pp. 75–80 and Harvey, *Diplomatic Diaries*, p. 294.
28 Ponsonby papers, MS. C6851, letter from Halifax, 6 July 1939. See also Earl of Halifax, *Fulness of Day* (London, 1957), p. 208 and Birkenhead, *Halifax*, pp. 368, 400–7, 419, 425–7.
29 A typical such thesis is in I. M. Maisky, *Memoirs of a Soviet Ambassador, the War, 1939–1943* (London, 1967).
30 Halifax, *Fulness of Day*, pp. 206–7.
31 FO 371 23678 N4571/57/38, min. by Halifax, 23 Sept.; FO 800/328, Halifax to Gort, 20 Oct. and 28 Nov. 1939. See also Aster, 'Maisky', pp. 338, 345–50.
32 CAB 65/1 19(39)8, 18 Sept.; Simon papers, diary, 18 and 21 Sept. 1939.
33 Butler, *Art of the Possible*, pp. 78–9, 84–5.
34 F. D. Volkov, *SSSR-Angliya 1929–1945gg: Anglo-Sovetskie otnosheniya nakanune i v period vtoroi mirovoi voiny* (Moscow, 1964), pp. 299–301.

35 W. Churchill, *The Second World War* (6 vols., London, 1948–54), vol. 2, p. 403.

36 Chamberlain papers, NC 18/1, exchanges with Hilda, Arthur and Ida Chamberlain, 25, 28 and 31 Oct. and 2 Nov. 1939.

37 Churchill, *Second World War*, vol. 2, pp. 399–403.

38 Maisky, *Memoirs*, pp. 31–4; G. Bilainkin, *Maisky: Ten Years' Ambassador* (London, 1964), p. 286.

39 Cripps' role in the negotiations is almost entirely ignored by both Soviet and western historiography, e.g. Hanak, 'Cripps as British Ambassador in Moscow' and Volkov, *SSSR-Angliya*. Maisky, *Memoirs*, p. 137 refers to it *en passant*, but at the time he told the Webbs that 'Cripps was working behind the scenes preparing memoranda for Ministers'; see Webb papers, diary, pp. 6751–5, 15 Oct. 1939.

40 *The Times*, 4 Oct.; Cripps papers (Nuffield), Box 521–3, draft of a speech, end of April 1941.

41 Birkenhead, *Halifax*, pp. 5, 190, 326, 560. After the war Cripps and Halifax were joint Patrons of 'Christian Action', an interdenominational movement aimed at stirring members of all churches to apply the ethics of Christianity to daily life. See also L. Fischer, *Men and Politics: an Autobiography* (London, 1941).

42 R. J. Moore, *Churchill, Cripps, and India, 1939–1945* (Oxford, 1979), pp. 6–10.

43 FO 371 23682 N5426/92/38, Eden to Halifax, 13 Oct. 1939.

44 Webb papers, diary, p. 6760, 25 Oct. 1939.

45 FO 371 23682 N5296/92/38, Cripps to Halifax and Halifax to Stanley, 13 and 14 Oct. 1939.

46 V. Tanner, *The Winter War: Finland against Russia, 1939–1940* (Stanford, 1957), pp. 27, 41; FO 371 23682 N5342/92/38 and 23697 N5343/1459/38, tels. to Seeds, 16 and 20 Oct. 1939.

47 FO 371 23683 N5598/92/38, memo., 21 Oct.; CAB 65/1 54(39)5, 58(39)9,13, 22 and 24 Oct. 1939.

48 FO 371 23701 N5717/5717/38, 25 Oct. 1939.

49 FO 371 23683 N5634/92/38, tel. to Seeds, 25 Oct. 1939.

50 *ibid.* N5773/92/38, memo. by Stanley; CAB 65/1 62(39)6,13.

51 Similar warnings to the Soviet military attaché are made by Butler in FO 371 23678 N6477/57/38.

52 CAB 65/2 67(39)9,10,11,13, 31 Oct.; CAB 79/2 COS(39)105, 1 Nov. 1939.

53 FO 371 23683 N6384/92/38, min. by Collier, 20 Nov. 1939.

54 *ibid.* N6477/57/38. W. Elliott, Minister of Health, conveyed a similar message from Maisky, N6574/57/38, 20 Nov. 1939.

55 CAB 65/2 84(39)10,11, 15 Nov. 1939.

56 *ibid.* 85(39)10, 16 Nov. 1939. See also Churchill, *Second World War*, vol. 2, pp. 415–16, 448–9.

57 FO 371 23693 N6717/991/38, memo. by Halifax, 27 Nov.; FO 800/328, Halifax to Gort, 28 Nov. 1939; *Diaries of Cadogan*, p. 21.

58 R. R. James (ed.), *Chips: the Diaries of Sir Henry Channon* (London, 1967), p. 225.

59 CAB 65/4 98(39)9, 29 Nov.; CAB 65/2 101(39)6, 2 Dec. 1939.

60 *Diaries of Cadogan*, p. 216; CAB 65/2 111(39)6, 11 Dec.; FO 371 23678 N7134/57/38, tel. from Seeds, 6 Dec.; 23667 N7752/5542/63, min. by Sargent, 20 Dec. 1939.

61 For a survey of Franco-Soviet relations see FO 371 24853 N3413/341/38, Halifax to Campbell (Paris), 18 Mar. 1940.

62 CAB 21/1051, Halifax to Campbell, 11 Dec. 1939.

63 CAB 21/1051, Butler to Halifax, 22 Dec.; CAB 65/2 105(39)7, 108(39)9,10, 112(39)10, 6, 8 and 12 Dec. 1939.

64 FO 371 23695 N7233/991/38, min. by Sargent, 10 Dec. 1939; *Diaries of Cadogan*, p. 243.

65 Webb papers, diary, pp. 6790–2, 19 Dec. 1939; Maisky, *Memoirs*, p. 40. See also *Daily Telegraph*, 24 Jan. 1940.

66 CAB 65/2 116(39)6,8, 15 Dec.; CAB 65/4 118(39)14, 18 Dec. 1939.

67 FO 371 24794 N3402/1/56, Noel Baker to FO, 13 Mar.; CAB 65/11 39(40)6,8, 12 Feb. 1940; Citrine quoted in *Daily Telegraph*, 4 Apr. 1940. See also Labour's condemnation in *The Times*, 8 Dec. 1939, and Morrison's in *Manchester Guardian*, 5 Jan. 1940.

68 CAB 80/8 COS(40)227, 31 Jan. 1940.

69 *ibid.* COS(40)24, 6 Feb.; CAB 84/2 JP(40)10, JP(40)12, 19 Feb. and 1 Mar. 1940.

70 CAB 65/5 26(40)7, 29 Jan.; CAB 65/11 35(40)1, 7 Feb; CAB 65/6 66(40)1, 12 Mar. 1940.

71 Chamberlain papers, NC 18/1/1144, letter to Ida, 23 Feb. 1940.

72 Cripps papers, diary, 17 Jan. and 4 Feb. 1940.

73 Maisky, *Memoirs*, pp. 34, 37–9; Webb papers, diary, pp. 6813–14, 29 Jan. 1940.

74 Steinhardt papers, Box 79, letter to Henderson, 2 Mar. 1940.

75 FO 371 24843 N1390/30/38, tel. to Le Rougetel, 30 Jan. 1940.

76 Cripps papers, diary, 16 and 17 Feb. 1940.

77 CAB 127/61, draft speech.

78 Cripps papers, diary, 15 Feb. 1940.

79 FO 371 24855 N5580/1523/38, Le Rougetel to Collier, 3 May 1940.

80 FO 371 24846 N2779/40/38.

81 CAB 65/11 35(40)8, 7 Feb.; FO 371 24855 N1523/1523/38, min. by Cadogan, 8 Feb. 1940.

82 WO 208/1754, 6 and 7 Mar.; FO 371 24846 N2779/40/38, mins., 8, 11 and 13 Mar. 1940.

83 CAB 65/6 61(40)4 and CAB 65/12 61(40)6, 6 Mar. 1940.

84 FO 371 24846 N2779(40)38, 6 Mar. 1940.

85 FO 371 24843 N1390/30/38, tel. to Le Rougetel; *DGFP*, vol. 9, p. 37.

86 FO 371 24793 N2329/1/56, 24 Feb. 1940.

87 Halifax papers, diary, A.7.8.3. and Simon papers, diary, 13 Mar. 1940. On the futile plans to bomb Baku see FO 371 24846 N3698/40/38 and C. O. Richardson, 'French Plans for Allied Attacks on the Caucasus Oil Fields, January–April 1940', *French Historical Studies*, 8 (1973).

88 FO 371 24846 N3485/40/38, tel. to Le Rougetel, 18 Mar. 1940.

89 CAB 84/11 JP(40)72, 25 Mar.; FO 371 24843 N3538/30/38 and 24846 N3485/40/38, mins. by Cadogan, Collier and Sargent, 13, 25 and 26 Mar. 1940; Leeper papers, diary, 7 Apr. 1940.

90 FO 371 24846 N3698/40/38, 23 and 25 Mar. 1940.

91 *ibid.* N3485/40/38, 18 and 29 Mar. 1940.

92 Dalton papers, diary, 15 Mar. 1940.

93 *DGFP*, vol. 8, p. 79.

94 FO 371 24839 N3706/5/38, tel. to Le Rougetel, and CAB 99/3 SWC(39/40)6, 28 Mar. 1940.

95 CAB 21/962, memo. by BOT, 8 Apr. 1940.

96 FO 371 24888 R4467/5/67.

97 Webb papers, diary, p. 6863, 12 Apr. 1940.

98 *Parl. Deb. HC*, vol. 359, cols. 541–2, 10 Apr.; vol. 360, cols. 181, 905–6, 1204, 24 Apr., 2 and 8 May 1940.

99 CAB 99/3 SWC(39/40)8, 22 Apr. 1940. See also CAB 65/6 93(40)11, 15 Apr. 1940.

100 FO 371 29480 N4652/5/38, 15 Apr. 1940.

101 CAB 65/6 97(40)11 and CAB 99/3 SWC(39/40)8, 19 and 22 Apr. 1940.

102 CAB 21/962, 30 Mar. 1940.

103 FO 371 29480 N4625/5/38, 15 Apr.; 24847 N4627, N4978/40/38, Halifax to Wedgwood and circular to Dominions, 16 and 24 Apr. 1940.

104 FO 837/1098, 25 Apr. 1940.

105 *DGFP*, vol. 9, pp. 108, 134, 222, 248.

106 FO 371 24840 N5273/5/38, tel. to Le Rougetel, 29 Apr. 1940.

107 FO 371 24847 N5129/40/38, min. by Collier, 29 Apr.; BT 11/1275, memo., 2 May 1940.

108 CAB 21/962, tel. to Le Rougetel, 8 May 1940.

109 *DGFP*, vol. 9, p. 316.

110 Webb papers, diary, pp. 6880–8, 20 May 1940.

111 Maisky, *Memoirs*, p. 137; National Archives, Department of State, 740.0011 EW 1939/3446, 1 June 1940.

112 Estorick, *Cripps*, p. 235.

113 *Parl. Deb. HC*, vol. 359, col. 1542, 10 Apr.; vol. 360, cols. 181, 905–6, 1203, 24 Apr., 2 and 8 May 1940.

114 CAB 65/7 121(40)7 and 123(40)13, 14 and 15 May 1940.

115 Churchill, *Second World War*, vol. 2, pp. 36–49; *Diaries of Cadogan*, pp. 284–5.

116 FO 371 24841 N5812/5/38, note by Butler, 16 May 1940.

117 *ibid.*, 17 May; Dalton papers, diary, 4 Apr. 1940.

118 Halifax papers, diary, A.7.8.4, 17 May 1940.

119 Webb papers, diary, p. 6863, 12 Apr.; Lansbury papers, Box 17, exchange of letters with Cripps, 22 and 24 Apr. 1940.

120 D. N. Pritt, *The Autobiography of D. N. Pritt* (2 vols., London, 1965–6), vol. 1, pp. 235–6.

121 Cripps papers, diary, 27 May 1940. See also Estorick, *Cripps*, p. 240.

122 CAB 126/61, Harvey to Cripps, 25 Apr. 1940.

123 FO 371 24846 N3698/40/38, min. by Butler, 11 Apr. 1940.

124 Cripps papers, diary, 13 July 1940.

125 FO 371 24841 N5812/5/38, 17 May 1940.

126 Halifax papers, diary, A.7.8.4, 17 May; FO 371 24847 N5689/40/38, Churchill to Cripps, 21 June 1940; Cooke, *Cripps*, p. 251.

127 CAB 65/7 127(40)13, 18 May 1940; H. Dalton, *The Fateful Years: Memoirs, 1931–1945* (London, 1957), p. 219. On Dalton's relationship with Cripps see M. Foot, *Aneurin Bevan* (2 vols., London, 1962–73), vol. 1, pp. 155, 248.

128 FO 837/1127, mins. by Dalton, 18 and 19 May 1940. On Postan see FO 371 24840 N5761/5/38.

129 FO 371 24840 N5499/5/38, tel. to Dormer, 23 May 1940.

130 FO 837/1127, min. by Dalton, 20 May 1940.

131 BT 11/127, memo. on meeting, 22 May 1940.

132 FO 837/1127, min. by Dalton, 25 May; Dalton papers, diary, 27 May 1940.

133 FO 371 24841 N5812/5/38, min. by Butler, 22 May; Halifax papers, diary, A.7.8.4, 20 May 1940.

134 Webb papers, diary, pp. 6880–8, 20 May 1940; Maisky, *Memoirs*, pp. 77–83.

135 FO 371 24847 N5648/40/38, tel. to Le Rougetel; CAB 65/7 132(40)38, 21 May 1940.

136 *ibid.*, 26 May 1940.

137 CAB 21/962, Halifax to Le Rougetel, and FO 371 24840 N5298/5/38, min. by Halifax, 23 May 1940.

138 G. Bilainkin, *Diary of a Diplomatic Correspondent* (London, 1942), p. 92.

139 FO 371 24841 N5812/5/38.

140 Cripps papers, diary, 25 May 1940.

141 *DGFP*, vol. 9, p. 470.

142 On the choice of Peterson see FO 371 24847 N5660/40/38, min. by Sargent, 24 May, and CAB 65/7 138(40)14, 25 May 1940.

143 Halifax papers, diary, A.7.8.4, and CAB 21/962, Halifax to Le Rougetel, 26 May; CAB 65/7 146(40)13, 29 May 1940.

144 Cripps papers, diary, 26 and 27 May 1940.

145 CAB 65/7 149(40)9.

146 FO 371 24847 N5689/40/38, tel. from Le Rougetel, 31 May 1940.

147 R. Manne, 'The Foreign Office and the Failure of Anglo-Soviet Rapprochement' and G. Ross, 'Foreign Office Attitudes to the Soviet Union, 1941–1945', *Journal of Contemporary History*, 16 (1981); D. Lammers, 'Fascism, Communism and the Foreign Office, 1937–39', *Journal of Contemporary History*, 6 (1971).

148 FO 371 24847 N5129/40/38, 25 May 1940.

149 *ibid*. N5648/40/38, 23 May 1940.

150 *ibid*. N5689/40/38, 2 June 1940.

151 *ibid*., 2 and 4 June; 29475 N941/29/38, mins. by Maclean and Collier, 10 Mar. 1940.

152 FO 371 24849 N5788/93/38, 13 June 1940.

153 Wedgwood papers, note by Wedgwood's daughter Helen on a letter from Cripps, 27 Feb. 1942.

154 Churchill, *Second World War*, vol. 2, p. 118. This misleading interpretation has frequently been repeated. Cripps himself subscribed to it in moments of despair, see V. Assarasson, *I Skuggan av Stalin* (Stockholm, 1963), pp. 18–19. The Russian attitude, as is shown, reflected Cripps' standing with the government at a given moment rather than following an ideological line.

155 Cripps papers, diary, 4 and 7 June 1940.

156 For evaluations of Soviet policy see FO 371 24839 N4114/5/38, tel. from Lothian, 8 Apr.; Harvey, *Diplomatic Diaries*, pp. 350–1; Cripps' interviews to the *New York Times* and *Daily Express*, 9 Apr. 1940.

157 *FRUS 1940*, I, p. 606.

158 G. W. Rendel, *The Sword and the Olive: Recollections of Diplomacy and the Foreign Service* (London, 1957), pp. 169–70.

### 2 The mission launched

1 Cripps papers, diary, 29 and 31 May, 4–7 June 1940.

2 FO 371 24849 N5729/93/38.

3 *ibid*., tel. to Cripps, 5 June 1940.

4 FO 800/322, Halifax to Johnson, 11 June 1940.

5 FO 371 24849 N5788/93/38.

6 On the embassy see M. D. Peterson, *Both Sides of the Curtain, an Autobiography* (London, 1950), pp. 255–6; H. Elvin, *A Cockney in Moscow* (London, 1958), pp. 9–10; Cripps papers, diary, 13–16 June, 3 and 17 July and letter to Diana, 24 Sept. 1940; Estorick, *Cripps*, pp. 253–6.

7 Cripps papers, diary, 15 Aug. 1940; FO 366 1094 X3156/230/305, Cripps to Butler, 22 Sept. and 28 Oct., and to Collier, 15 Oct. 1940; interviews with Sir John Russell, third secretary at the embassy, and Sir Geoffrey Wilson, Cripps' secretary.

8 *The Times* archives, letters from James Holburn, correspondent in Moscow, to editor, Feb. 1940.

9 Cripps papers, diary, 13 July and 25 Aug. 1940, Isobel's diary, 2 May 1941.

10 Cripps papers, diary, 2 and 3 July, 1 and 21 Aug. 1940.

11 FO 371 24844 N5808/30/38, exchange between Cripps and Halifax, 13 and 16 June 1940.

12 Cripps papers, diary, 20 Aug. 1940; Bilainkin, *Diary*, pp. 136–7; G. Gafencu, *Prelude to the Russian Campaign* (London, 1945), pp. 282–7. For background see E. Barker, *British Policy in South-East Europe in the Second World War* (London, 1976), pp. 71–2.

13 FO 371 24841 N5840/5/38, tel. from Cripps, 14 June 1940.

14 FO 371 24844 N5808/30/38, tel. to Lothian, 17 June 1940.

15 *ibid.*, tel. from Cripps.

16 *ibid.*, min. by Sargent, 18 June 1940; Churchill, *Second World War*, vol. 2, pp. 165–6.

17 Cripps papers, letter to Diana, 18 Sept. 1940.

18 J. E. O'Connor, 'Laurence A. Steinhardt and American Policy toward the Soviet Union, 1939–1941', unpublished Ph.D. thesis, University of Virginia (1968), pp. 21–2; C. Bohlen, *Witness to History, 1929–1963* (New York, 1973). For Steinhardt's anglophobia and isolationist attitudes see Steinhardt papers, Box 79, letter to Henderson, 2 Mar. 1940.

19 Hull papers, Box 61, memos., 2 Apr. and 12 June 1940; C. Hull, *The Memoirs of Cordell Hull* (2 vols., New York 1948), vol. 1, pp. 810–11; H. L. Ickes, *The Secret Diary of Harold L. Ickes* (3 vols., New York, 1953–4), vol. 3, pp. 200–1.

20 Harper papers, Box 22.f.7, letter from Henderson, 20 July 1940.

21 FO 371 24844 N5808/30/38, tel. from Lothian; State Dept. 740.0011 EW 1939 711.61/739, Lothian to Welles, 18 June; CAB 65/7 171(40)6.

22 *ibid.* N5853/30/38, min. by Risdale, 18 June 1940.

23 *ibid.*, tel. from Cripps, 18 June 1940. See also *DGFP*, vol. 9, p. 472; Ickes, *Diary*, vol. 3, p. 230.

24 *DGFP*, vol. 9, p. 566; Churchill, *Second World War*, vol. 2, pp. 118–19.

25 FO 371 24849 N5788/93/38, tel. to Cripps, 26 June 1940; *FRUS 1940*, I, p. 607. For background see G. L. Weinberg, *Germany and the Soviet Union, 1939–1941* (Leiden, 1972), pp. 101–4.

26 FO 371 24849 N5729/93/38; Maisky, *Memoirs*, pp. 37–9.

27 FO 371 24844 N5853/30/38, tel. from Cripps, 23 June, mins., 28 June, and draft tel. to Stalin by Maclean, 22 June 1940.

28 *ibid.*, tel. to Cripps, 25 June 1940.

29 FO 837/1127, exchange of notes between Dalton and Halifax, 24 and 26 June 1940.

30 H. Teske (ed.), *General Ernst Köstring* (Frankfurt, 1966), pp. 258–60; *DGFP*, vol. 10, p. 207.

31 FO 371 24844 N5937/30/38, tels. from Cripps, 1 and 2 July; Maisky's views conveyed to Halifax through Eden, FO 800/328, 12 July 1940.

32 Alexander papers, AVAR 5/4/36, letter to Halifax, 6 July 1940.

33 CAB 65/7 197(40)8, 200(40)14, 8 and 11 July 1940.

34 Harper papers, Box 22.f.7, memo. to Henderson on meeting with Oumansky, 17 and 18 July 1940.

35 FO 371 24850 N5967/96/38, tel. to Cripps, 6 July; *Parl. Deb. HC*, vol. 362, cols. 1358–9, 11 July 1940.

36 *Diaries of Channon*, p. 262.

37 FO 371 24844 N5937/30/38, 3 July 1940.

38 FO 371 24852 N6029/243/38, memo. by Sargent, 17 July, min. by Halifax, 18 July, and letter from MEW, 1 Aug.; FO 837/1130, mins. by Dalton, 27 July and 2 Aug. 1940.

39 Cripps papers, 9 July 1940.

40 CAB 127/64, 4 July 1940.

41 A. J. P. Taylor, *English History 1914–1945* (Harmondsworth, 1979), pp. 594–6.

42 Churchill, *Second World War*, vol. 2., pp. 229–32.

43 *FRUS 1940*, I, p. 608.

44 Cripps papers, diary, 20 and 23 July 1940.

45 Alexander papers, AVAR 5/4/31, memo. on meeting with Maisky, 28 June 1940.

46 CAB 65/7 178(40)5, 24 June; PREM 3/395/1, mins. by Sargent, Cadogan and Churchill, 3 and 7 June 1940; Bilainkin, *Maisky*, p. 318.

47 Webb papers, diary, pp. 6921–2.

48 Halifax papers, A.7.8.4, diary, 10 July 1940.

49 Dalton papers, diary, 26 July 1940.

50 *DGFP*, vol. 10, p. 321.

51 State Dept. 740.0011 EW39/4728, tel. from Wiley (Riga), 18 July 1940.

52 e.g. 'Soviet Now Seems Leaning to Allies', *New York Times*, 6 June; 'Premier Had Friendly Talk with M. Maisky', *News Chronicle*, 13 July; 'Improved Atmosphere', *The Times*, 18 July 1940.

53 See for this *The Times*, 18 and 19 July 1940.

54 Cripps papers, diary, 19 July 1940.

55 Weinberg, *Germany and the Soviet Union*, pp. 109–17; W. Warlimont, *Inside Hitler's Headquarters, 1939–45* (London, 1964), pp. 113–14.

56 FO 837 1127, MEW draft tel. to Cripps and mins., 4–7 June; FO 371 24841 N5799/5/38, mins. by Sargent and Collier, 5 June 1940.

57 FO 837 1127, 17 June 1940.

58 BT 11/1340, tel. from Cripps, 3 July 1940.

59 FO 837 1082, mins., 9, 10 and 12 July; BT 11/1340, tel. to Cripps, 16 July; Dalton papers, diary, 26 July 1940.

60 Cripps papers, diary, 2, 3, 6 and 10 July 1940.

61 *ibid.*, 26 July 1940.

62 FO 371 24844 N6072/30/38, 30 July 1940.

63 Cripps papers, diary, 1 and 2 Aug. 1940.

64 FO 371 24845 N6243/30/38, 2 Aug. 1940.

65 *ibid.*, mins. by Maclean and Collier, 1 Aug.; Dalton papers, diary, 31 July; CAB 65/8 217(4)2, 1 Aug.; *Diaries of Cadogan*, p. 318.

66 FO 371 24845 N6243/30/38, mins. by Sargent and Butler, 12 Sept. 1940.

67 FO 371 24844 N5853/30/38, 24 June; CAB 65/7 170(4)6, 17 June 1940.

68 CAB 66/10 WP(40)287 and CAB 65/8 214(40)6, 26 and 29 July 1940.

69 Cripps papers, diary, 18 July 1940.

70 FO 371 24761 N6081, N6241/1224/59, tel. and letter from Cripps, 7 and 16 Aug.; CAB 65/8 222(40)3, 8 Aug 1940.

71 FO 371 24761 N6081/1224/59, 8 Aug. 1940.

72 FO 837 1082, 6 and 7 Aug. 1940.

73 Dalton papers, diary, 26 July 1940.

74 Cripps papers, diary, 7 and 8 Aug.; Monckton papers, Box 3, pp. 71–2, 75–7, letters from Cripps, 31 Aug. and 2 Sept. 1940.

75 FO 371 24847 N6105/40/38, 8 Aug. 1940.

76 *ibid.* and FO 837 1082, Collier to Postan, 28 Sept. 1940.

77 CAB 65/8 223(40)2,3 and 225(40)2, 9 Aug. 1940; FO 371 24761 N6081/ 1224/59.

78 Weaver papers, letter from Cripps, 25 Aug.; Cripps papers, diary, 12 and 23 Aug. 1940.

79 FO 371 24848 N6263/40/38, tel. from Cripps, 14 Aug. 1940; *Diaries of Cadogan*, p. 321.

80 FO 837 1082, memos., 13 and 20 Aug. 1940.

81 *ibid.*, exchanges of notes between FO and MEW, 16–25 Aug. 1940.

82 Alexander papers, AVAR 5/4/48, 19 Aug. 1940.

83 FO 371 24852 N6458/283/38, 2 Sept. 1940.

84 FO 371 24761 N6250/1224/59, tel. to Cripps; Maisky, *Memoirs*, pp. 139–41.

85 BT 11/1340, tels. from Cripps, 22 and 26 Aug. 1940; Cripps papers, diary, 23 Aug. 1940.

86 FO 371 24761 N6454/2039/59, Collier to MEW; BT 11/1340, BOT mins., 5 and 6 Sept.; FO 837 1082, mins., 5–7 Sept. 1940.

87 *FRUS 1940*, I, p. 613.

88 FO 371 24841 N6488/5/38, mins. by Maclean and Collier, 5 and 6 Sept.; FO 837/1082, min. by Postan on meeting with Collier, 6 Sept.; Alexander papers, AVAR 5/4/57, letter from Halifax, 30 Sept. 1940.

89 CAB 65/9 245(40)5.

90 FO 418/86, tel. to Cripps, 14 Sept. 1940.

91 *NSR*, pp. 178–84, 190–4, 196–7. See also G. Hilger and A. G. Meyer, *The Incompatible Allies: a Memoir–History of German–Soviet Relations, 1918–1941* (New York, 1953), pp. 318–20.

92 A. Werth, *Russia at War, 1941–1945* (New York, 1964), pp. 114–15; Beaverbrook papers, D 338, letter to Halifax, 25 Sept. 1940.

93 Alexander papers, AVAR 5/4/53, letter to Halifax, 17 Sept. 1940.
94 FO 371 24845 N6783/30/38, note by Butler, 3 Oct. 1940.
95 Cripps papers, letter to Diana, 15 Sept. 1940.
96 FO 418/86, exchange of tels. between Cripps and Halifax, 14 and 19 Sept. 1940.
97 Monckton papers, Box 3, pp. 75–7, 115–18, 2 and 25 Sept. 1940, Box 4, p. 68, 13 Feb. 1941; Cripps papers, letters to Monckton, 5 and 20 January 1941.
98 Cripps papers, 1 Oct. 1940.
99 FO 800/322, Cripps to Halifax, 10 Oct.; Cripps papers, letters to Diana, 8 and 10 Oct. 1940.
100 *FRUS 1940*, I, pp. 610–12; FO 371 24841 N6681/5/38, tel. to Halifax, 21 Sept.; Weaver papers, letter from Cripps, 10 Sept. 1940.
101 Cripps papers, letter to Diana, 22 Sept. 1940; also Monckton papers, Box 3, p. 199, letter to Gwen Hill, 13 Nov. 1940.
102 FO 371 24852 N6822/283/38, tel. from Rendel (Sofia), 8 Oct., and tel. to Cripps, 13 Oct. 1940.
103 Cripps papers, Isobel's diary, 10 Oct. 1940.
104 FO 371 24851 N6675/176/38, tel. from Cripps, 13 Oct. 1940.
105 FO 800/322, Cripps to Halifax, 10 Oct. 1940.
106 CAB 65/9 270(40)3 and 271(40)4, 14 and 15 Oct. 1940; *Diaries of Cadogan*, p. 332.
107 FO 371 24845 N6875/30/38, 15 Oct. 1940.
108 *FRUS 1940*, I, p. 617; State Dept. 740.0011 EW 741/906, memo. by Welles, 18 Oct. 1940.
109 FO 371 24845 N6875, N7047/30/38, tels. from Cripps, 22, 23 and 31 Oct., min. by Collier, 24 Oct., and Halifax to Churchill, 26 Oct. 1940.
110 Cripps papers, letters to Diana, 28 and 30 Oct. 1940.
111 Cripps papers, 23 Oct. 1940.
112 *NSR*, pp. 207–13; Hilger and Meyer, *Incompatible Allies*, p. 321; Weinberg, *Germany and the Soviet Union*, pp. 140–1.
113 FO 371 24848 N6984, N7089/40/38, tels. from Cripps, 26 Oct. and 3 Nov. 1940.
114 *FRUS 1940*, I, p. 622.

### 3 Interregnum

1 Churchill, *Second World War*, vol. 2, pp. 519–24.
2 Weinberg, *Germany and the Soviet Union*, pp. 143–6; M. van Creveld, *Hitler's Strategy 1940–41: the Balkan Clue* (Cambridge, 1973), ch. 3 and pp. 179–81.
3 *FRUS 1940*, I, p. 573. Bohlen, *Witness*, p. 103, a typically anachronistic 'Cold War' approach.
4 FO 371 24852 N7164/283/38, tel. from Cripps, 11 Nov. 1940.

5 *ibid.* N7163/283/38, tel. from Cripps, 10 Nov.; Cripps papers, letters to Diana, 10 and 13 Nov. 1940.

6 FO 371 24848 N7173, N7165/40/38, tels. from Cripps, 11 and 12 Nov. 1940.

7 FO 371 24852 N7163/283/38, mins. by Collier, Sargent, Cadogan and Halifax, 11, 12 and 13 Nov.; CAB 65/10 288(40)3, 13 Nov. 1940.

8 FO 371 24848 N7165/40/38, 13 Nov.; see e.g. *Manchester Guardian*, 14 Nov. 1940.

9 FO 371 24848 N7233/40/38, mins. by Maclean and Sargent, 21 Nov. 1940.

10 E.g. on 16 Nov. 1940 'Soviet Ignores British Officers', *News Chronicle*; 'Still No Reply after Month', *Daily Mail*; 'Russia Snubs Britain', *Daily Mirror*; 'Moscow is Silent on British Proposals', *Daily Express*.

11 Cripps papers; FO 371 24848 N7200/40/38; CAB 65/10 290(40)5, 18 Nov. 1940.

12 A reference to the Zimmerman telegram during the First World War.

13 Bilainkin, *Maisky*, p. 257; Cripps papers, letter to Diana, 14 Nov. 1940.

14 Weaver papers, letters from Cripps, 24 Nov. and 7 Dec. 1940.

15 FO 371 24848 N7233/40/38, 13 Nov. 1940.

16 *ibid.*, mins. by Maclean, Sargent, Cadogan and Halifax, 21 and 22 Nov. 1940.

17 FO 837/1133, MEW mins., 22 and 27 Nov., and Dalton to FO, 23 and 28 Nov. 1940.

18 FO 371 24848 N7233/40/38, min. by Maclean, 22 Nov., and tel. to Cripps, 2 Dec. 1940.

19 WO 208/1757, 18 Nov.; FO 371 29484 N7348/40/38, 27 Nov. 1940.

20 CAB 65/10 295(40)3, 25 Nov.; FO 371 24853 N7279/283/38, memo., 24 Nov. 1940.

21 FO 371 29484 N7354/40/38, 3 Dec. 1940.

22 FO 800/322, 27 Nov. 1940.

23 *The Times* archives, 3 July 1941.

24 FO 371 24848 N7366, and 24849 N7387/40/38, tels. from Cripps, 3, 8 and 16 Dec., and mins. by Maclean, Sargent and Cadogan, 5, 9 and 11 Dec. 1940.

25 FO 837/1133, mins. from Dalton and MEW, 9 and 26 Dec., and BOT, 16 and 17 Dec. 1940.

26 E. Barker, *Churchill and Eden at War* (London, 1978), pp. 20–1.

27 Churchill, *Second World War*, vol. 2, p. 505.

28 Barker, *Churchill and Eden*, pp. 20–1.

29 S. Aster, *Anthony Eden* (London, 1976), pp. 57, 66; D. Carlton, *Anthony Eden: a Biography* (London, 1981), pp. 168–70; Taylor, *English History*, p. 661n.; A. Eden, *The Eden Memoirs: the Reckoning* (London, 1965), pp. 181–3.

30 J. Harvey (ed.), *The War Diaries of Oliver Harvey, 1941–45* (London, 1978), p. 50.

31 Harvey, *Diplomatic Diaries*, pp. 44, 128, 294; *Diaries of Cadogan*, pp. 54, 101.

32 Harvey papers, MS. 56397, diary, 15 Nov. 1940, 20 Feb. and 5 May 1941.

33 *Diaries of Cadogan*, p. 241; Barker, *Churchill and Eden*, pp. 23–5.

34 Aster, *Eden*, pp. 60–1, 73; Carlton, *Eden*, pp. 156–7, 164.

35 Cripps papers, letter to Monckton, 31 Aug. 1940; see also Monckton papers, Box 4, p. 50, letter from Cripps, 5 Feb. 1941.

36 *Daily Telegraph*, 29 Jan. 1941.

37 Carlton, *Eden*, p. 149 and see also pp. 16, 63 and 86–8.

38 FO 371 29500 N367/122/38, min. by Eden, 24 Jan. 1941; Eden, *Reckoning*, p. 54.

39 *Diaries of Cadogan*, pp. 345, 347, 372. See also W. P. Crozier, *Off the Record: Political Interviews, 1932–44*, ed. A. J. P. Taylor (London, 1973), p. 208.

40 Taylor, *English History*, pp. 514–15.

41 FO 371 24849 N7500/48/38, min. by Cadogan, and letter to Cripps, 27 and 28 Dec. 1940.

42 A concise but revealing survey of the expedition is in Carlton, *Eden*, pp. 170–82.

43 W. A. Harriman and E. Abel, *Special Envoy to Churchill and Stalin, 1941–1946* (New York, 1975), p. 95.

44 Cripps papers, letters to Diana, 7, 8, 10, 22 and 23 Jan. 1941.

45 Cripps papers, Isobel's diary, 26 Dec. 1940 and 25 Mar. 1941. For Cripps' involvement with the 'club' see her entries for May 1941. A journalist's lively description is in H. C. Cassidy, *Moscow Dateline, 1941–1943* (London, 1943), pp. 54–63.

46 FO 371 24848 N7323/40/38, 22 Jan. 1941.

47 Weaver papers, letters from Cripps, 30 Dec. 1940 and 27 Jan. 1941; Monckton papers, Box 4, letter from Cripps, 5 Feb. 1941.

48 Weaver papers, 22 Feb.; Webb papers, II 4 m7, Gwen Hill to Beatrice Webb, 18 Feb. 1941.

49 FO 371 29463 N373/3/38, tel. from Cripps, 29 Jan.; diary of Theresa Cripps (now Lady Ricketts), 29 Jan. 1941; *FRUS 1941*, I, p. 156.

50 Webb papers, II 4 m5, letter from Isobel, 12 Feb. 1941; *FRUS 1941*, I, p. 160.

51 Cripps papers, 3 Dec. 1940, and Isobel's diary, 1 Feb. 1941; Monckton papers, Boxes 3 and 4, pp. 204 and 50 respectively, 9 Dec. 1940 and 5 Feb. 1941.

52 FO 371 24849 N7548/40/38, 29 Dec. 1940.

53 FO 371 29463 N29/3/38, 31 Dec. 1940, and min. by Maclean, 3 Jan. 1941.

54 *ibid.* N54/3/38 and N355/3/38, mins. by Collier, 20 Jan., and Maclean, 23 Jan. 1941.

55 *ibid.* N103/3/38, 7 Jan. 1941.

56 Cripps papers, letters to Diana, 7 and 10 Jan. 1941.

57 For examples of disinformation see *FRUS 1941*, I, pp. 121–2.

58 FO 371 29497 N159/88/38, tel. from Cripps, 11 Jan.; Cripps papers, letter to Diana, 10 Jan. 1941.

59 Cripps papers, 1 Feb. 1941.

60 FO 371 29479 N159/88/38, mins. by Sargent, Cadogan, Eden and Butler, 15 and 16 Jan. 1941.

61 FO 371 29514 N290/290/38, 17 Jan. 1941.

62 FO 371 29527 N605/605/38, exchange between Churchill and Eden, 29 Jan. and 11 Feb. and min. by Collier, 7 Feb. 1941.

63 FO 371 29135 W53/53/50, 15 Jan. 1941.

64 FO 371 24849 N7548/40/38, tel. to Cripps, 27 Dec. 1940.

65 *NSR*, pp. 268–79.

66 FO 371 29500 N262/122/38, tel. to Cripps, 21 Jan., and 29463 N29/3/38, tel. from Mallet, 16 Jan.; State Dept. 740.0011 EW 39/7909, tel. from Sterling, 25 Jan. 1941.

67 E.g. FO 371 29463 N502/3/38, mins. by Maclean and Collier, 4 and 5 Feb. 1941.

68 FO 371 24829 N7484/40/38, mins. by Collier and Eden, 22 Jan. 1941.

69 Monckton papers, Box 4, p. 24, letter to Cripps, 27 Jan. 1941.

70 FO 371 29463 N382/3/38, tel. to Cripps, 30 Jan. 1941; Eden, *Reckoning*, p. 188.

71 FO 371 29463 N402,N411/3/38, 29473 N759/22/38, tels. from Cripps, 1, 2 and 20 Feb.; 29464 N829/3/38, verbatim report, 2 Feb. 1941.

72 FO 371 29463 N411/3/38, mins. by Sargent, Cadogan and Eden, 5, 6 and 7 Feb., and tel. to Cripps, 9 Feb.; FO 837/1098, Postan to FO, 15 Feb. 1941.

73 FO 371 29477 N492,N494/37/38, tels. from Cripps and Halifax, 8 Feb. 1941; *FRUS 1941*, I, pp. 157, 161.

74 FO 371 29477 N492/37/38, min. by Sargent, 12 Feb.; BT 11/1490, Dalton to Eden, 15 Feb. 1941.

75 FO 371 29473 N759/22/38.

76 Lady Ricketts' diary, 16 Feb.; FO 371 29464 N791/3/38, MI to FO, 25 Feb. 1941.

77 Webb papers, diary, pp. 7035–7, 3 Mar. 1941.

78 FO 371 29463 N675/3/38, tel. from Cripps, 22 Feb. and mins. by Maclean and Cadogan, 25 Feb. 1941.

79 Churchill, *Second World War*, vol. 3, pp. 62–3; *Diaries of Cadogan*, p. 363.

80 PREM 3/395/16, 22 Feb. 1941.

82 Weaver papers, letter from Cripps, 9 Mar.; see also Monckton papers, Box 4, pp. 106–10, letter from Isobel, 8 Mar. 1941.

83 Cripps papers, letters to Diana, 26 Feb. and 8 Mar.; FO 371 29463 N761/3/38, tel. to Cripps, 25 Feb. 1941.

84 Unless otherwise stated the account is based on a travel diary in Cripps'

papers; see also letters to Diana, 26 Feb. and 8 Mar. 1941.

85 Eden gives only a passing reference to the encounter in *Reckoning*, p. 208.

86 Creveld, *Hitler's Strategy*, pp. 109–14, 121–3; Carlton, *Eden*, pp. 170–9.

87 On the views of Dill and the COS see also A. Bryant, *The Turn of the Tide, 1939–1943* (London, 1957), pp. 245–55, and an unpublished paper by J. Herndon, 'British Perceptions of Soviet Military Capability, 1935–39'; Cripps' impression is mentioned in Lady Ricketts' diary, 6 Mar. 1941.

88 FO 371 29500 N1164/122/38, Cripps' summary of conversations, 9 Mar. 1941.

89 FO 371 29777 R700, and 29778 R1476/113/67, exchange of tels. with Cripps, 29 Jan. and 21 Feb. 1941.

90 FO 371 30067 R2129, R2248/112/44, tels. from Cripps, 7 and 10 Mar. 1941.

91 *ibid.* R1897/112/44 and 29778 R1476/113/67, mins. by Sargent, 6 Mar. and 25 Feb. 1941.

92 FO 371 29135 W918/53/50, 19 Feb. 1941.

93 FO 371 29780 R2392/113/67, tel. from Cripps, 12 Mar.; 30067 R2326,R2248,R2404/112/44, tel. to Cripps, 12 Mar.; min. by Sargent, 13 Mar.; min. by Churchill and tel. to Cripps, 14 Mar. 1941.

94 Barker, *British Policy in South-East Europe*, pp. 78–108.

95 Monckton papers, Box 4, p. 145, 25 Mar. 1941.

96 FO 371 29464 N1526,N1229/3/38, tel. from Cripps, 23 Mar., and mins. by Sargent and Cadogan, 28 and 29 Mar. 1941.

97 D. A. Stafford, 'SOE and British Involvement in the Belgrade Coup d'État of March 1941', *Slavic Review*, 3 (1977).

98 FO 371 30228 R2878, R2879/394/92, tels. from Cripps, 22 and 23 Mar. 1941.

99 Cripps papers, Isobel's diary, 26 and 27 Mar. 1941.

100 FO 371 29479 N1303/3/38, exchange of tels. with Cripps, 28 and 29 Mar. 1941.

101 FO 837/1098, 29 Mar. 1941.

102 See above, p. 116–18.

103 CAB 65/18 33(41)7, 31 Mar. 1941.

104 FO 371 29479 N1360/3/38, 2 Apr. 1941.

105 *ibid.*, mins. by Postan and Dalton, 2 and 7 Apr. 1941.

106 For more on this see above, pp. 119–20.

107 FO 371 29463 N1386/3/38, 4 and 10 Apr. 1941.

108 *ibid.*, mins. by Cadogan and Sargent, 10 and 16 Apr. 1941; Eden, *Reckoning*, p. 262.

109 FO 371 29463 N1386/3/38, tel. to Cripps, 17 Apr.; MEW's criticism, 16 Apr. 1941.

110 *Diaries of Channon*, pp. 299, 303; H. Nicolson, *Diaries and Letters, 1939–1945* (London, 1967), pp. 160–5; Carlton, *Eden*, pp. 182–3.

111 FO 371 29463 N1386/3/38, 15 Apr. 1941.

112 FO 371 29465 N1658/3/38, tel. to Cripps.

*4 The turn of the tide*

1 See the most revealing and authoritative study of F. H. Hinsley, *British Intelligence in the Second World War* (2 vols., London, 1979–81), vol. 1, pp. 237–41.

2 FO 371 29479 N255/78/38, Polish Minister for Foreign Affairs, 13 Jan.; N107/78/38, tels. from O'Malley (Budapest) and Kelly (Bern), 4 and 6 Jan., and mins. by Maclean, Collier, Cadogan and Eden, 10 and 18 Jan. 1941.

3 *ibid.* N286/78/38, 17 Jan. 1941.

4 FO 371 29528 N648/648/38, 20 Jan., and mins. by Maclean and Collier, 22 and 23 Feb. 1941.

5 FO 371 26518 C2317/19/18, 7 Mar. 1941.

6 *ibid.* C2222/19/18, tels. from O'Malley, Halifax and Mallet, 6 and 7 Mar., and mins. by Cavendish-Bentinck, Strang, Cadogan and Collier, 9, 10, 11 and 12 Mar. 1941.

7 FO 371 29135 W3205/53/50, 19 Mar. 1941.

8 FO 371 29500 N1164/122/38 and Cripps papers, letter to Diana, 9 Mar. 1941.

9 Elvin, *A Cockney in Moscow*, p. 54.

10 State Dept., 740.0011 EW/39/8919, tel. from Steinhardt, 7 Mar. 1941; Assarasson, *I Skuggan av Stalin*, p. 56; Gafencu, *Prelude to the Russian Campaign*, pp. 134–6; W. Duranty, *The Kremlin and the People* (New York, 1942), pp. 151–2; A. Werth, *Moscow '41* (London, 1942), p. 133.

11 FO 371 29500 N1164/122/38, 7 Mar. 1941.

12 State Dept. 740.0011 EW/39/8919, tel. from Steinhardt, 7 Mar. 1941.

13 On the accuracy of the information, B. Whaley, *Codeword Barbarossa* (Cambridge, Mass., 1973), pp. 50–1.

14 FO 371 26518 C2919, C2924, C2935/19/18, tels. from Cripps, 24 and 25 Mar., and mins., 26, 27 and 28 Mar. 1941.

15 Hinsley, *British Intelligence*, vol. 1, pp. 446–50.

16 Churchill, *Second World War*, vol. 3, pp. 316–19.

17 *Diaries of Cadogan*, p. 367.

18 Churchill, *Second World War*, vol. 3, pp. 151–319.

19 *Diaries of Cadogan*, p. 367.

20 Hinsley, *British Intelligence*, vol. 1, pp. 451–2; see above, p. 109.

21 FO 371 29479 N1316, N1324/78/38 and mins. 3 Apr. 1941. Whaley, *Barbarossa*, pp. 59–60, wrongly assumes the information was spread by the Germans to discourage anti-Nazi elements. At Eden's request the King of Greece received a personal confirmation from Paul.

22 WO 190/983; FO 371 29135 W3859/53/50.

23 PREM 3/395/16, tel. to Eden, 22 Feb. 1941.

24 Churchill, *Second World War*, vol. 3, pp. 320–1; PREM 3/403/7.

25 FO 371 29479 N1366/78/38, tel. to Cripps and min. by Cadogan, 4 Apr. 1941.

26 PREM 3/403/7.

27 Churchill, *Second World War*, vol. 3, p. 321.

28 FO 371 29479 N1397/78/38.

29 FO 371 29544 N1401/1392/38, tel. from Cripps, 6 Apr. and min., 7 Apr. 1941.

30 *ibid.* N1392/1392/38, tel. from Cripps, 6 Apr. 1941.

31 FO 371 29479 N1492/78/38, 6 Apr. 1941.

32 PREM 3/403/7.

33 FO 371 29479 N1364/78/38, 12, 15 and 19 Apr. 1941.

34 FO 371 29465 N1713/3/38, 12 Apr. 1941.

35 FO 371 29479 N1429/78/38, min. by Coote (who replaced Maclean in the Northern Dept.), endorsed by Cadogan, 8 Apr. 1941.

36 *ibid.* N1510/78/38.

37 *ibid.* N1534/78/38.

38 *ibid.* N1510/78/38, 11 Apr. 1941.

39 *FRUS 1941*, I, p. 163.

40 FO 371 29480 N1848/78/38, 11 Apr. 1941.

41 FO 371 29479 N1573/78/38, tel. from Cripps, 12 Apr. (also quoted in Churchill, *Second World War*, vol. 3, p. 321 with obvious omissions), mins. by Sargent, 13 and 16 Apr., and Eden to Churchill, 15 Apr. 1941.

42 On the effect of the news see *Diaries of Cadogan*, p. 371.

43 FO 371 29480 N1725/78/38, tel. from Cripps, 22 Apr. 1941; P. A. Zhilin, *Kak fashistskoi Germaniya gotovila napadenie na Sovetskii Soyuz* (Moscow, 1966), p. 219; V. Petrov (ed.), *'June 22, 1941': Soviet Historians and the German Invasion* (Chapel Hill, South Carolina, 1968), pp. 178–80; Whaley, *Barbarossa*, ch. 8.

44 Reported in *The Times*, 10 Apr. and commentary in *The Sunday Times*, 20 Apr. 1941.

45 FO 371 29465 N1658/3/38, tel. to Cripps, 16 Apr. 1941; *FRUS 1941*, I, p. 715.

46 Werth, *Russia at War*, p. 270.

47 *FRUS 1941*, I, pp. 702, 712–13, 715.

48 Monckton papers, Box 4, p. 201, 17 Apr.; Cripps papers, Isobel's diary, 16 and 20–4 Apr.; Weaver papers, letter from Cripps, 18 Apr. The sense of urgency is well reflected in Lady Ricketts' entry of 16 Apr. 1941 in her diary, which is otherwise almost devoid of political references.

49 FO 371 29465 N1667/3/38; *FRUS 1941*, I, p. 164; also Cripps papers, Isobel's diary, 28 Apr. 1941.

50 FO 371 29465 N1828/3/38.

51 *NSR*, ch. 8; Weinberg, *Germany and the Soviet Union*, pp. 159–63.

52 FO 371 29465 N1692/3/38, tel. from Cripps, 18 Apr. 1941.

53 *ibid.* N1725/3/38, 19 Apr. 1941.

54 *Diaries of Cadogan*, p. 372; Eden, *Reckoning*, p. 265.

55 FO 371 29465 N1667/3/38, 18 Apr. 1941.

56 FO 371 29473 N1889/22/38, min. by Sargent, 12 Apr.; CAB 65/18 42(41)3, 21 Apr. 1941.

57 FO 371 29465 N1725/3/38, Churchill to Eden and min. by Collier, 22 Apr.; draft tel. to Cripps, 26 Apr. 1941.

58 FO 371 29480 N1761, N1762/78/38, tels. from Cripps, 23 Apr., and mins. by Sargent and Eden, 25 Apr.; on American policy see 29465 N1806/3/38, tel. from Halifax, 25 Apr. 1941.

59 J. Erickson, *The Road to Stalingrad* (London, 1975), p. 77. On the significance attached to Cripps' threat see *Istoriya vtoroi mirovoi voiny, 1939–1945* (12 vols., Moscow, 1974–9), hereafter *IVMV*, vol. 3, pp. 142–3.

60 *NSR*, pp. 336–9; Weinberg, *Germany and the Soviet Union*, pp. 162–4.

61 Monckton papers, Box 5, p. 49, memo., 28 May 1941.

62 Webb papers, diary, p. 7079, 23 May; Pritt gained the same impression, see FO 371 29465 N2565/3/38, letter to Monckton, 21 May 1941.

63 FO 371 29465 N1801/3/38, 25 Apr. 1941. On the Soviet obsessions see Maisky, *Memoirs*, pp. 145–7.

64 FO 371 29465 N1999/3/38, 19 Apr. An indirect indication that Stalin might have been visualizing war with Germany on 24 Apr. 1941 is in I. Ehrenburg, *Eve of War, 1933–1941* (London, 1963), p. 505.

65 *Diaries of Cadogan*, pp. 378–80. References are based on J. Douglas-Hamilton, *Motive for a Mission: the Story behind Hess's Flight to Britain* (New York, 1971), J. B. Hutton, *Hess: the Man and his Mission* (London, 1970) and T. J. Leasor, *Rudolf Hess: the Uninvited Envoy* (London, 1962).

66 FO 371 29501 N227/122/38, memo. by Sargent and min. by Eden, 14 and 15 May 1946.

67 Maisky, *Memoirs*, pp. 144–7. The title significantly chosen by V. G. Trukhanovskii for the chapter dealing with Hess in *Vneshnyaya politika Anglii v period vtoroi mirovoi voiny, 1939–1945* (Moscow, 1965), is 'England Makes a Choice'.

68 *FRUS 1941*, I, p. 166; Whaley, *Barbarossa*, p. 79.

69 Werth, *Russia at War*, pp. 240–1, 453–5; *Diaries of Cadogan*, pp. 486–8.

70 Churchill, *Second World War*, vol. 3, p. 49.

71 *ibid.*, p. 43; *IVMV*, vol. 3, p. 472; a Stalinist version is in I. F. Ivashin, *Nachalo vtoroi mirovoi voiny i vneshnyaya politika SSSR* (Moscow, 1951), pp. 31–2.

72 F. D. Volkov, 'Neudavshiisya Pryzhok Rudolf Gessa', *Novaya i Noveishaya Istoriya*, 6 (1968), p. 116; see also F. W. Deakin and G. R. Storry, *The Case of Richard Sorge* (London, 1966), p. 229n.

73 V. M. Berezhkov, *Gody diplomaticheskoi sluzhby* (Moscow, 1972), p. 57.

74 Cripps papers, Isobel's diary, 15 May 1941.

75 V. G. Trukhanovskii, *Uinston Cherchil'* (Moscow, 1968), p. 333; also Volkov, *SSSR-Angliya*, pp. 335–8. A similar explanation was offered recently by V. Berezhkov, *History in the Making: Memoirs of World War II Diplomacy*

(Moscow, 1983), pp. 147–8.

76 FO 371 29481 N2466/78/38, 27 May; mins. by Strang and Sargent, 30 May 1941.

77 Cripps papers, Isobel's diary, and Lady Ricketts' diary, 13 May 1941.

78 FO 371 29481 N2171, N2466/78/38, 13 and 27 May; mins. by Sargent and Cadogan, 14 May 1941.

79 *Diaries of Cadogan*, pp. 386–7.

80 FO 371 29481 N2466 and 29482 N2728/78/38, tel. to Cripps, 10 June, and min. by Sargent, 30 May 1941.

81 Cripps papers, Isobel's diary, 27 Apr.; Weaver papers, letter from Cripps, 3 May 1941.

82 *NSR*, pp. 334–5, also 330–2; FO 371 29315 W5835/53/50, Political Intelligence Summary (PIS), 14 May 1941.

83 FO 371 29480 N1819, N1978, N2020/78/38, tels. from Cripps, 26 Apr., 2 and 5 May; Cripps papers, Isobel's diary, 27 Apr. 1941.

84 FO 371 29315 W5536, W6191/53/50, PIS, 8 and 21 May 1941.

85 FO 371 29481 N2234/78/38, memo. and min. by Warner, 12 and 16 May 1941.

86 WO 190/893, MI14, 22 Apr.; see also FO 371 29465 N2233/3/78, 12 May 1941.

87 FO 371 29481 N2130/78/38, 9 May, and min. by Coote, 11 May; N2393/78/ 38, tel. from Mallet, 23 May 1941.

88 FO 371 26520 C4791/19/18, 6 May 1941.

89 FO 371 29481 N2392/78/38, 23–5 May; FO 954/25, tels. from Cripps, 27 and 29 May 1941.

90 FO 371 29481 N2234, N2416/78/38, MEW memo. and letter to FO, 13 and 20 May 1941.

91 *ibid*. N2388/78/38, tel. from Halifax, 23 May 1941.

92 *ibid*. N2259/78/38, 17 and 19 May 1941.

93 *ibid*. N2260/78/38, 16 May 1941.

94 Hinsley, *British Intelligence*, vol. 1, pp. 460–1, 465–6; and also pp. 39–43 for interrelations between Military Intelligence and the FO.

95 WO 190/893.

96 *ibid*.

97 WO 208/1761 JIC(41)218.

98 Cripps papers, Isobel's diary, 10–17 May 1941; Gafencu, *Prelude to the Russian Campaign*, p. 189.

99 FO 371 29481 N2441/78/38, tel. from Verker (Helsinki), 24 May 1941.

100 *ibid*. N2380/78/38 and 29501 N2392, N2471/122/38, tels. from Cripps, 22 and 27 May. On Cripps' recognition of the limits to Stalin's ability to concede see also Lady Ricketts' diary, 3 May 1941.

101 FO 371 29481 N2500/78/38, 28 May and 2 June 1941.

102 WO 190/893 MI, 26 May 1941.

103 WO 193/644, comments, 11 June, on JIC of 9 June 1941.

104 FO 371 29483 N2906/78/38, JIC(41)234, 31 May, and final version, 9 June,

and comments by MI, WO 208/1761, 1 June 1941.
105 Hinsley, *British Intelligence*, vol. 1, p. 469.
106 FO 371 29481 N2380/78/38, tel. from Cripps and min. by Warner, 22 and 23 May 1941; State Dept., 740.0011 EW 39/11283, tel. from Steinhardt, 24 May 1941.
107 FO 371 30068 R4882 and R5558/112/44, tels. from Cripps and Knatchbull-Hugessen, 1 and 23 May 1941; *Diaries of Cadogan*, p. 623.
108 CAB 79/86 COS(41)197; CAB 84/31 JP(41)423; FO 954/24, min. by Sargent, 31 May 1941.
109 *Diaries of Cadogan*, p. 382.
110 FO 371 29465 N2565/3/38, 30 May 1941.
111 FO 371 N2566/3/38 and FO 954/24, mins. by Warner and Sargent, 28 and 31 May. See also Eden's conviction on 2 June 1941, FO 371 29481 N2538/78/38, that the Russians were about to 'give way'.
112 CAB 69/2 DO(41)35, 27 May; FO 954/24, min. by Sargent, 31 May 1941.
113 FO 371 29465 N1806/3/38, tel. from Halifax, 25 Apr. 1941.
114 FO 800/279, 26 and 29 Apr. 1941.
115 Webb papers, p. 7095, 6 June 1941.
116 Monckton papers, Box 5, pp. 40–2, 48, letters from Cripps and Isobel, 24 and 27 May 1941.
117 FO 800/279.
118 FO 371 29514 N2800/290/38; CAB 65/18 56(41)2.
119 FO 371 29465 N2570/3/38, tel. to Cripps.
120 O. O'Malley, *The Phantom Caravan* (London, 1954), pp. 213–14.
121 Weaver papers, 3 May; Cripps papers, 10 May. See also Lady Ricketts' diary, 19 May 1941.
122 See above, n. 116.
123 FO 371 29514 N2800/290/38, tel. from Cripps and min. by Butler, 3 and 5 June; 29466 N2628/3/38, tel. to Cripps, 5 June 1941. See also *FRUS 1941*, I, p. 167.
124 Monckton papers, Box 5, p. 96.
125 FO 371 29466 N2628, N2674/3/38, tel. to Cripps and FO min., 6 and 9 June 1941.
126 FO 371 29315 W6834/53/50, 4 June 1941.
127 CAB 65/18, 5 June 1941; Eden, *Reckoning*, p. 267.
128 FO 371 29482 N2624, N2666/78/38, tels. from Halifax and Verker, 5 and 6 June 1941.
129 *ibid.* N2667, N2668, N2673/78/38, tels. from Halifax and Mallet, 6 and 7 June, and min. by Coote endorsed by Eden, 8 and 9 June 1941.
130 FO 371 29483 N2893/78/38, JIC(41)218, 5 June. See also WO 190/893, weekly appreciation, 9 June 1941.
131 CAT 65/22 58(41)2; FO 371 26521 C6668/19/18; Eden, *Reckoning*, p. 267.
132 FO 371 29482 N2735/78/38, tel. to Baggallay, 10 June 1941; *Diaries of Cadogan*, p. 386.

133 FO 371 29483 N2893/78/38 and 29315 W7184/53/50, 11 and 13 June 1941.
134 FO 371 29482 N2707 and 29483 N2893/78/38, 10 and 11 June 1941.
135 Hinsley, *British Intelligence*, vol. 1, pp. 478–9; Whaley, *Barbarossa*, pp. 113–14.
136 *FRUS 1941*, I, p. 168; FO 371 29482 N2774/78/38, 12 June 1941.
137 *ibid.* N2735/78/38, 12 June 1941.
138 FO 837/1098, Cripps to Dalton, 3 June; Cripps papers, Isobel's diary, 24 May 1941.
139 Assarasson, *I Skuggan av Stalin*, p. 63; E. Boheman, *På Vakt* (2 vols., Stockholm, 1963–4), vol. 2, p. 194.
140 Mallet, 'Memoirs', p. 111; State Dept. 740.0011 EW 39/11787, tel. from Sterling, 8 June 1941.
141 FO 371 29482 N2678/78/38, tel. from Mallet, 7 June 1941.
142 Mallet, 'Memoirs', p. 112. See also Boheman, *På Vakt*, vol. 2, pp. 154–5; T. Barman, *Diplomatic Correspondent* (London, 1968), p. 26. Cripps quoted this date a few days later, Webb papers, diary, pp. 7103–7, 14 June 1941, and P. Strauss, *Cripps–Advocate and Rebel* (London, 1943), p. 159.
143 FO 371 29482 N2680, N2699/78/38, 8 and 9 June 1941.
144 Whaley, *Barbarossa*, pp. 210–13.
145 Webb papers, diary, pp. 7103–7, 14 June; FO 371 29483 N2982/78/38, tel. from Baggallay, 20 June 1941; *FRUS 1941*, I, p. 173.
146 J. G. Winant, *A Letter from Grosvenor Square: an Account of a Stewardship* (London, 1947), pp. 143–4.
147 J. P. Lash, *Roosevelt and Churchill, 1939–1941: the Partnership that Saved the West* (Norton, 1976).
148 Harper papers, H 22.f.21, Harper to Henderson, 22 June 1941; R. H. Dawson, *The Decision to Aid Russia, 1941: Foreign Policy and Domestic Politics* (Chapel Hill, 1959), pp. 60–1.
149 Maisky, *Memoirs*, pp. 147–51; A. Nekrich, 'Arrest and Trial of I. M. Maisky', *Survey*, 22 (1978), and 'Biografiya akademiki I. Maiskogo', *Voprosy Istorii*, 2 (1964).
150 Maisky, *Memoirs*, pp. 148–50, 165. A hint of a connection between Cripps' threats, the Hess episode and the communiqué is in Volkov, *SSSR-Angliya*, pp. 343–4.
151 Maisky, *Memoirs*, p. 150n. On Golikov see Marshal Zhukov, *The Memoirs* (New York, 1971), p. 215. For the ambiguous clues provided for the Russians by their own Intelligence see Whaley, *Barbarossa*, p. 98.
152 *NSR*, pp. 345–6.
153 FO 371 29483 N2862/78/38.
154 Eden, *Reckoning*, p. 288–9, is misleading.
155 FO 418/87, tel. to Baggallay, 13 June 1941.
156 'Cripps Visit Sets Berlin Wondering', *News Chronicle*, 9 June 1941.
157 9 and 8 June 1941.

158 J. Leutze (ed.), *The London Journal of General Raymond E. Lee, 1940–1941* (Boston, 1971), p. 308. See for example, 'Nazi Threat to Russia: New Evidence', *Manchester Guardian*; 'Nazi Armies on Soviet Frontiers: Crisis Expected in Week or Ten Days', *News Chronicle*; 'Nazis Gather near Russia: Big New Demands Forecast', *Daily Telegraph*; leader in *The Times*.

159 FO 371 29483 N2887/78/38, mins. by Cadogan and Sargent, 13 and 14 June; 29315 W7499/53/50, PIS, 18 June 1941.

160 *Diaries of Cadogan*, p. 382.

161 Webb papers, diary, pp. 7103–7, 14 June; FO 371 29483 N2862/78/38, memo. by McDonald (*The Times*), 13 June 1941.

162 FO 371 29483 N2873/78/38, min. by Coote, 14 June 1941.

163 FO 371 29483 N2862/78/38, memo. by McDonald. See also impressions of people close to Maisky: Pritt, *Autobiography*, vol. 1, pp. 260–7, and Bilainkin, *Maisky*, p. 332.

164 FO 371 29482 N2792/78/38, tel. to Baggallay. Eden, *Reckoning*, p. 269, is a tendentious and oversimplified version, reflecting his outlook at the time.

165 The main file in FO 371 is closed. Available information, FO 371 29484 N3047/78/38, min. by Cadogan, 15 June, *Diaries of Cadogan*, p. 388, and Maisky, *Memoirs*, p. 149. As a central piece of evidence on the warnings to the Russians, Maisky's version has led most historians to a faulty and condemnatory interpretation of the Tass communiqué, among them Whaley, *Barbarossa*, pp. 107–8, 114, whose account is otherwise exhaustive and reliable. He was misled by Cavendish-Bentinck's imperfect memory.

166 FO 371 29466 N3099/3/38; *The Times* archives, Dawson to Halifax, 22 June. On 24 June Gallacher revealed that a change in appreciation had occurred on 19 June, *Parl. Deb. HC*, vol. 372, col. 986.

167 Maisky, *Memoirs*, pp. 155–6.

168 Erickson, *The Road to Stalingrad*, p. 96; Zhukov, *Memoirs*, p. 230.

169 FO 371 29483 N2898/78/38.

170 FO 371 29466 N3099/3/38. For a similar erroneous British interpretation see FO 371 29482 N2842 and 29483 N2891/78/39, tel. from Baggallay and min. by Cadogan, 15 and 14 June 1941.

171 FO 371 29483 N2992/78/38.

172 Erickson, *The Road to Stalingrad*, pp. 94–7, 102, 108; Zhukov, *Memoirs*, p. 232; FO 29484 N3005, N3006/78/38, tels. from Baggallay, 21 June 1941.

173 Berezhkov, *Diplomaticheskoi sluzhby*, pp. 60–4; *NSR*, pp. 353–6.

174 FO 371 29466 N3231/3/38; A. Sella, ' "Barbarossa": Surprise Attack and Communication', *Journal of Contemporary History*, 13 (1978).

175 Davies papers, Box 11. See also Halifax papers, A.7.8.9, diary, 11 Dec. 1941.

176 *Daily Express*, 23 June 1941.

177 FO 371 29466 N3018/3/38; Maisky, *Memoirs*, pp. 156–7.

### 5 An alliance of sorts

1 Barker, *Churchill and Eden*, p. 227.
2 Churchill, *Second World War*, vol. 3, pp. 329–31; Butler, *Art of the Possible*, p. 89. Colville later admitted to discrepancies in his account; Beaverbrook papers, B 338, letter to Beaverbrook, 5 Aug. 1960; D 541, 'Second Front', part 1.
3 Leasor, *War at the Top*, p. 155, is based on the memoirs of General L. Hollis.
4 Beaverbrook papers, D 90.
5 CAB 120/681 and CAB 80/28 COS(41)350, mins., 3 June 1941.
6 Crozier, *Off the Record*, pp. 225–6; Lash, *Roosevelt and Churchill*, p. 343.
7 CAB 65/22 59(41)2. Criticism of Eden in *Diaries of Cadogan*, pp. 388–9, and defence by Churchill in *Parl. Deb. HC*, vol. 372, cols. 981–5.
8 See above, pp. 17–18, 22–5 and 54–5.
9 Dalton papers, diary, 12 June 1941.
10 Monckton papers, Box 5, pp. 40–2, letter from Isobel, 24 May 1941; *The Times*, 13 June 1941.
11 Leasor, *War at the Top*, p. 155, quotes Hollis.
12 F. H. Cripps, *Life's a Gamble* (London, 1957), p. 50; Strauss, *Cripps*, p. 155. See also Colville in J. Wheeler-Bennett (ed.), *Action This Day* (London, 1968), pp. 75, 105.
13 FO 371 29482 N2802/78/38, MEW to FO, 7 June; Dalton papers, diary, 12 June 1941; *Journal of General Lee*, pp. 309–10. See also Hinsley, *British Intelligence*, vol. 1, pp. 474–5.
14 *FRUS 1941*, I, p. 170; FO 371 29482 N2793/78/38, tel. to Baggallay, 13 June 1941.
15 FO 371 29483 N2904 and 29484 N3040/78/38, memos., 13 and 17 June; Harvey papers, Ms. 53697, diary, 18 June 1941.
16 CAB 65/22 61(41)7, 19 June 1941.
17 Herndon, 'Soviet Military Capability', p. 3; Leasor, *War at the Top*, p. 154; H. Ismay, *The Memoirs of General the Lord Ismay* (London, 1960), pp. 223–4.
18 FO 371 29484 N3046/78/38, JIC, 13 June 1941.
19 WO 190/893, MI14; FO 371 29315 W7499/53/50, PIS, 18 June 1941.
20 CAB 79/12 COS(41)210; JIC in FO 371 29484 N3047/78/38, min. by Cavendish-Bentinck, 15 June; CAB 84/31,32 JP(41)429,451, 13 and 14 June; CAB 84/3 JP(41)78, 16 June 1941.
21 CAB 84/32 JP(41)465 and CAB 79/12 COS(41)218, 19 June 1941.
22 FO 371 29590 N3295/3295/38, mins. by Coote, 19 and 21 June; 29560 N3092/3014/38, min. by Postan, 19 June 1941.
23 CAB 69/2 DO(41)42; R. Parkinson, *The Auk: Auchinleck, Victor at Alamein* (London, 1977), pp. 85–7.
24 Churchill, *Second World War*, vol. 3, p. 330.
25 *FRUS 1941*, I, p. 759; Berle papers, diary, vol. VII, pp. 123–6.

26 FO 371 29482 N2831/78/38 and 29507 N2909/211/38, tels. from Halifax, 15 and 17 June; 29483 N2969/78/38, min. by Sargent, 17 June 1941.
27 *FRUS 1941*, I, p. 766.
28 FO 371 26521 C6668/19/18, 9 June 1941; CAB 122/100.
29 FO 371 N2418/78/38; Ismay, *Memoirs*, p. 229.
30 Werth, *Moscow '41*, p. 61.
31 Webb papers, diary; Eden, *Reckoning*, p. 269.
32 *The Times* archives, Dawson to Halifax, 22 June 1941.
33 CAB 65/22 60(41)2,3; Sikorski's evidence of Cripps' commitment is in Erickson, *The Road to Stalingrad*, p. 93.
34 *Parl. Deb. HC*, vol. 372, col. 971.
35 Churchill, *Second World War*, vol. 3, pp. 329–30; Hinsley, *British Intelligence*, vol. 1, pp. 479–80.
36 Maisky, *Memoirs*, p. 156.
37 Winant, *Letter from Grosvenor Square*, p. 145; Leasor, *War at the Top*, p. 154; Churchill, *Second World War*, vol. 3, p. 330. See also Lash, *Churchill and Eden*, pp. 351–5.
38 Eden, *Reckoning*, pp. 269–71.
39 FO 371 29560 N3056/3014/38, tel. to Baggallay. For evidence from Oumansky and Korj on Maisky's reaction see 29466 N3081, N3180/3/38 and Maisky, *Memoirs*, p. 160.
40 Leeper papers, diary, 22 June 1941.
41 CAB 65/18 62(41)4,5,6; *The Times* and *Daily Herald*, 25 June 1941.
42 Wheeler-Bennett, *Action This Day*, p. 89; Beaverbrook papers, B 338, Colville to Beaverbrook, 5 Aug. 1960.
43 *FRUS 1941*, I, p. 767; Leasor, *War at the Top*, p. 156.
44 *Parl. Deb. HC*, vol. 372, cols. 992–4, 24 June 1941; Eden, *Reckoning*, p. 269.
45 WO 193/666, 29 June 1941.
46 CAB 84/32 JP(41)478,482,485,500, 23, 24, 25 and 30 June; CAB 79/12 COS(41)221,222, 23 and 24 June 1941; Churchill's note to Ismay in *Second World War*, vol. 3, p. 690.
47 FO 371 29486 N3718/78/38, memo. by Leeper, 7 July 1941.
48 CAB 66/17 WP(41)145, 30 June; CAB 84/32 JP(41)508, 1 July 1941.
49 CAB 65/18 62(41)4,5,6 and FO 371 29560 N3065/3014/38, tel. to Baggallay.
50 E. Butler, *Mason-Mac: the Life of Lieutenant-General Sir Noel Mason-Macfarlane* (London, 1972), pp. 131–4; Dalton papers, diary, 1 July 1941.
51 CAB 84/32 JP(41)482, 24 June 1941; Butler, *Mason-Mac*, pp. 133–4. Churchill misrepresents the mission in *Second World War*, vol. 3, pp. 340–1.
52 Butler, *Mason-Mac*, p. 132; Cripps papers, diary, 28 and 29 June 1941.
53 Maisky, *Memoirs*, pp. 160–1. The CPGB received instructions on 25 June at the latest to revise its policies: see e.g. *Daily Herald* 26 June, and *Manchester Guardian*, 27 June 1941.

54 FO 371 29466 N3204/3/38 and 29484 N3145/78/38, tels. to Baggallay, 24 and 26 June 1941.
55 WO 193/645, tels. from Cripps, 28 June 1941.
56 *FRUS 1941*, I, pp. 150–1.
57 Gafencu, *Prelude to the Russian Campaign*, p. 198.
58 FO 371 29466 N3231/3/38, tel. from Cripps.
59 *Daily Mail*, 23 June; *New York Times*, 27 June 1941.
60 Maisky, *Memoirs*, p. 162; CAB 69/2 DO(41)45, 3 July 1941; F. Golikov, 'Sovietskaya voennaya missiya v Anglii i SShA v 1941g', *Novaya i Noveishaya Istoriya*, 3 (1969), p. 102.
61 FO 371 29466 N3304/3/38, tel. to Cripps, 30 June 1941.
62 CAB 122/101, tel. from Halifax, 29 June 1941.
63 FO 371 29466 N3239/3/38, exchange of tels. between Cripps and WO, 29 June, 3 and 4 July; CAB 79/12 COS(41)229, 30 June 1941.
64 FO 371 29467 N3410/3/38 and 29485 N3389/78/38, tels. from Cripps, 2 July; Cripps papers, diary, 2 and 7 July 1941.
65 Elvin, *Cockney in Moscow*, p. 74; Cripps papers, diary, 1, 7 and 15 July 1941.
66 Assarasson, *I Skuggan av Stalin*, p. 69; Cripps papers, diary, 6 July 1941; Butler, *Mason-Mac*, p. 132.
67 Bryant, *The Turn of the Tide*, pp. 580–1, 632; Ismay, *Memoirs*, p. 291.
68 Butler, *Mason-Mac*, p. 134.
69 Cripps papers, diary, 30 June and 3 July; FO 371 29486 N3669/78/38, tel. from Cripps, 5 July; WO 193/645A, tel. from Macfarlane, 3 July 1941.
70 FO 371 29561 N3513, N 3449/3014/38, tels. from Cripps, 5 and 8 July, and mins. by Sargent and Cadogan, 5, 7 and 14 July. See also WO 193/644, tel. from Macfarlane, 10 July 1941.
71 Leeper papers, diary, 16 July 1941.
72 Nicolson, *Diaries*, p. 176.
73 WO 193/645A, 666, mins., 10 July; CAB 69/2 DO(41)45, 3 July; CAB 79/13 COS(41)234, 5 July 1941.
74 CAB 69/2 DO(41)50, 10 July; WO 193/644, tel. to Macfarlane, 11 July 1941.
75 CAB 79/12 COS(41)239, 10 July; Golikov, 'Missiya v Anglii', pp. 102–6; Dalton papers, diary, 18 Nov. 1941.
76 *Diaries of Cadogan*, pp. 390–1.
77 Churchill, *Second World War*, vol. 3, p. 340; FO 371 29466 N3302/3/38, tel. from Cripps, 29 June; Cripps papers, diary, 30 June 1941.
78 FO 371 29485 N3279/78/38, tel. to Cripps, 1 July 1941.
79 FO 371 29487 N3746/78/38, tel. from Cripps, 1 July, and mins. by Cadogan, 3 and 4 July 1941.
80 CAB 122/100, tels. from Halifax, 2 and 7 July 1941; FO 371 29486 N3540/78/38, mins. by Sargent and Cadogan, 9 and 10 July 1941.
81 PREM 3/395/16.

82 FO 371 29486 N3524/78/38, tel. to Cripps.

83 FO 371 29485 N3389/78/38, tel. from Cripps, 2 July 1941; Churchill, *Second World War*, vol. 3, pp. 340, 345; *Diaries of Cadogan*, pp. 390–1.

84 FO 371 29486 N3539/78/38, tel. to Cripps, 7 July 1941.

85 On this see *FRUS 1941*, I, p. 181.

86 FO 371 29467 N3529/3/38, tel. from Cripps, 8 July; Cripps papers, diary, 9 July 1941.

87 Harvey, *War Diaries*, p. 17. See also Carlton, *Eden*, pp. 201–2.

88 FO 371 29486 N3524/78/38, memo. by Leeper; Leeper papers, diary, 7 and 8 July; Beaverbrook papers, D 338, Eden to Churchill, 9 July 1941.

89 CAB 84/32 JP(41)523.

90 FO 371 29467 N3607/3/38, exchanges between Churchill and Eden, 9 July; Harvey, *War Diaries*, p. 17.

91 FO 371 29467 N3561/3/38, tel. to Cripps and min. by Sargent, 9 July; State Dept., 740.0011 EW 1939/12943, Winant to Hull, 9 July 1941; *Diaries of Cadogan*, p. 392.

92 CAB 65/19 67(41). On Eden's manoeuvring see tel. from Winant (ref. as in n. 91) and FO 371 29467 N3603/3/38, tel. to Halifax, 9 July 1941; *Diaries of Cadogan*, p. 392.

93 Harvey, *War Diaries*, pp. 18–19.

94 FO 371 29467 N3565/38, exchange between Cripps and Eden, 10 and 11 July 1941; 29564 N3613/3084/38, tel. from Halifax, 11 July 1941.

95 Cripps papers, diary, 13 July 1941.

96 FO 371 29467 N3660/3/38, tel. from Cripps, 12 July; Cassidy, *Moscow Dateline*, p. 52; Cripps papers, diary, 12–14 July 1941.

97 Eden, *Reckoning*, pp. 271–3; FO 371 26755 C7590/3226/55, Eden to Dormer, 9 July; 29467 N3607/3/38, Eden to Churchill, 9 July 1941.

98 FO 371 26755 C7016/3226/55, tel. to Cripps, 27 June 1941.

99 *ibid.* C7458, C7421, C7422/3226/55, exchange between Cripps and Eden, 3 and 4 July 1941.

100 *ibid.* C7591/3226/55, Eden to Dormer, 8 July 1941.

101 *ibid.* C7865/3226/55 and 26757 C8597/3226/55, Eden to Dormer and min. by Sargent, 15 July 1941.

102 FO 371 26757 C8191/3226/55, 11 and 13 July; 26755 C7890, C8027/3226/55, exchange between Cripps and Eden, 15 and 17 July 1941.

103 *ibid.* C8039, C8075/3226/55, tels. from Cripps, 18 and 20 July 1941.

104 *ibid.* C8306/3226/55, min. by Roberts, 26 July; CAB 65/19 74(41)2, 24 July 1941.

105 FO 371 26756 C8398, C8377/3226/55, tel. from Cripps and min. by Sargent, 27 and 24 July 1941; Cripps papers, diary, 27 July 1941.

106 FO 371 26756 C8484, C8404/3226/55, min. by Strang and tel. to Cripps, 27 July 1941; Cripps papers, diary, 25 and 28 July 1941.

107 FO 371 26756 C8448/3226/55, exchange between Cripps and Eden, 28 and 29 July 1941.

108 FO 371 29467 N3709/3/38, tel. from Cripps, 14 July 1941.

109 Dalton papers, diary, 1 July; Webb papers, diary, pp. 7119–23, 10 July 1941.

110 FO 371 26755 C7935/3226/55 and CAB 127/64, Eden and Churchill to Cripps, 15 and 22 July 1941.

111 *Parl. Deb. HC*, vol. 373, cols. 463–4, 1160–8; Cripps papers, diary, 16 July 1941; Harvey, *War Diaries*, p. 20.

112 FO 371 29602 N3605, N4065/3429/38, tel. from Cripps, 16 July, and mins. by Sargent, 4 and 12 July and 4 Aug. 1941.

113 WO 208/1777, MI13, and WO 193/644, COS to Macfarlane, 14 July 1941.

114 Erickson, *The Road to Stalingrad*, chs. 4 and 5.

115 FO 371 29487 N3795, N3933/78/38, tels. to Cripps, 16 and 18 July 1941. See also Harvey, *War Diaries*, pp. 20–1; Golikov, 'Missiya v Anglii', pp. 102–6.

116 *FRUS 1941*, I, pp. 768–95, 963, 971.

117 Berle papers, Box 213, diary, 30 July 1941.

118 Harriman and Abel, *Special Envoy*, p. 72; Ismay, *Memoirs*, p. 227; Maisky, *Memoirs*, pp. 148, 176–81.

119 CAB 79/13 COS(41)254, 21 July; FO 371 29487 N3955, N3956/78/38, tels. to Cripps, 21 July 1941.

120 FO 371 29488 N4025/78/38, tel. to Cripps; Golikov, 'Missiya v Anglii', pp. 106–7.

121 CAB 65/19 72(41)2,3,5 74(41)2, 21 and 24 July; CAB 79/13 COS(41)259, 264, 23 and 28 July 1941.

122 R. E. Sherwood, *Roosevelt and Hopkins: an Intimate History* (New York, 1950), pp. 326–7.

123 The text of telegrams on 25, 28 and 31 July is in Churchill, *Second World War*, vol. 3, pp. 345–6; significantly he omits most of the telegram concerning Hopkins, which is in PREM 3/170/1.

124 Cripps papers, letter to Diana, 29 July 1941; Harvey, *War Diaries*, p. 24.

125 Cripps papers, diary, 29 July 1941.

126 FO 371 29616 N4001/4001/38, tel. from Cripps; Cripps papers, diary, 22 July; Appiah papers, Cripps to Peggy Cripps (now Mrs Appiah), 24 July 1941. See also Elvin, *Cockney in Moscow*, pp. 63–98, and Cassidy, *Moscow Dateline*, pp. 100–4.

127 Cripps papers, diary, 30 July 1941.

128 An account of meetings with Stalin is in Hopkins papers, Box 306, memos., 30 and 31 July 1941.

129 Cripps papers, diary, 31 July, 1 and 22 Aug. 1941. See also M. Bourke-White, *Shooting the Russian War* (New York, 1942), p. 207. Sherwood, *Roosevelt and Hopkins*, p. 351, plays down Cripps' meetings with Hopkins, and reduces the three to one.

130 Hopkins papers, Box 306, memo. and note by Cripps; Cripps papers, diary, 1 Aug. 1941.

131 Roosevelt papers, Box 2987, Cripps to Roosevelt, 1 Aug., and reply, 21 Nov. 1941.

132 *FRUS 1941*, I, pp. 814–15. See also Cassidy, *Moscow Dateline*, pp. 93–4.

133 Cripps papers and FO 954/24, 1 Aug. 1941; *FRUS 1941*, I, pp. 817–18.

134 Cripps papers, diary, 2, 3, 4 and 9 Aug. 1941; *FRUS 1941*, I, pp. 634–5.

135 Based on T. A. Wilson, *The First Summit: Roosevelt and Churchill at Placentia Bay 1941* (Boston, 1969); L. Woodward, *British Foreign Policy in the Second World War* (3 vols., London, 1970–1), vol. 2, pp. 198–206; *FRUS 1941*, I, pp. 341–78; Sherwood, *Roosevelt and Hopkins*, pp. 349–65.

136 Churchill, *Second World War*, vol. 3, pp. 73–9; *FRUS 1941*, I, p. 826; Harriman and Abel, *Special Envoy*, pp. 76–7.

137 Churchill, *Second World War*, vol. 3, pp. 383, 394, 396–7, 402; Sherwood, *Roosevelt and Hopkins*, p. 350; Hopkins papers, Box 306, memo. by Cripps, 1 Aug.; FO 371 29571 N4744/3084/38, tel. to Cripps, 14 Aug. 1941.

138 Webb papers, Box II 4m, pp. 72–4, Isobel to Beatrice Webb, 17 Aug.; Monckton papers, Box 6, pp. 33–4, exchange between Isobel and Monckton, 24 and 27 Aug. 1941.

139 Webb papers, diary, pp. 7131–2, 30 July 1941.

140 Cripps papers, diary, 14 Aug. 1941.

141 *ibid.*; FO 371 29489 N4612/78/38, tel. from Macfarlane.

142 FO 371 29489 N4647/78/38.

143 FO 954/24, min. by Eden, 7 Aug. 1941, showing the extraordinary significance of the diary for the period after the invasion.

144 Cripps papers, diary, 25–8 July and 14 Aug. 1941.

145 Harvey, *War Diaries*, pp. 26, 31, 33.

146 FO 371 29489 N4647/78/38, 15 Aug. 1941; Harvey, *War Diaries*, pp. 29–30.

147 Dalton papers, diary, 25 Aug. 1941.

148 Harvey, *War Diaries*, p. 27; Churchill, *Second World War*, vol. 3, pp. 397, 763–4; Sherwood, *Roosevelt and Hopkins*, p. 359.

149 Beaverbrook papers, D 90, note, Nov. 1941.

150 Harvey, *War Diaries*, pp. 34–5.

151 WO 193/662, tels. from Macfarlane, 21, 22 and 27 Aug.; CAB 79/13 COS(41)295, 25 Aug.; CAB 120/683, exchange between Dill and Churchill, 27 and 28 Aug. 1941.

152 FO 371 29633 N5060/5060/38, Macfarlane to Dill, 31 Aug. 1941.

153 FO 371 29486 N3527/78/38 and 27230 E3707, E3844, E4056/3444/34, 8, 9, 14 and 17 July 1941.

154 CAB 65/19 68(41)2, 10 July 1941.

155 CAB 79/12 COS(41)241, 11 July; WO 193/644, tel. from Wavell, 18 July 1941.

156 JP(41)559 in CAB 79/13 COS(41)251 and CAB 80/29 COS(41)435, 18 July 1941.

157 CAB 69/2 DO(41)52, 21 July; CAB 80/29 COS(41)445, 20 July; FO 371 27230 E4141/3444/34, Eden to Churchill, 22 July 1941.

158 FO 371 N4198, N4141/3444/34, Dalton to Eden and min. by Eden, 21 and 28 July; CAB 69/2 DO(41)52 and CAB 80/29 COS(41)461, 21 and 28 July 1941.

159 CAB 79/13 COS(41)265, CAB 65/19 75(41)2,3,4 and CAB 65/23 76(41)5, 28 and 31 July 1941.

160 CAB 69/2 DO(41)55, 7 Aug.; FO 371 29467 N3719 /3/38, tel. to heads of missions, 13 July; 30068 R7312/112/44, tel. to Cripps, 3 Aug. 1941.

161 FO 371 30068 R7564/112/46, 23 July 1941.

162 *ibid.*, tel. from Cripps and mins. by Warner and Dixon, Southern Dept, endorsed by Eden, 20, 27 and 28 July 1941.

163 FO 371 29488 N4043/78/38 and 30068 R7564/112/46, tel. from Cripps, 24 July, and mins. by Eden, 27 July and 1 Aug.; Cripps papers, diary, 24 July 1941.

164 PREM 3/237/1, min. by Ismay, 9 Aug. 1941.

165 CAB 65/23 79(41)2, 11 Aug. 1941.

166 CAB 69/2 DO(41)59, 20 Aug. 1941.

167 CAB 65/23 84(41)1, 19 Aug.; FO 371 27231 E4662/4333/43, tel. to Cripps, 13 Aug., and min. by Churchill, 19 Aug.; CAB 79/13 COS(41)291, 20 Aug. 1941.

168 CAB 65/23 85(41)3 and CAB 79/13 COS(41)293, 21 and 22 Aug. 1941.

169 FO 371 27232 E4973/4333/43, tel. from Bullard, 23 Aug. 1941. It is no wonder that E4974, which deals with the subject, is closed indefinitely.

170 CAB 79/13 COS(41)294,295 and tel. to Wavell, 23 and 25 Aug. 1941.

171 Churchill, *Second World War*, vol. 3, p. 428; CAB 65/23 86(41)2 and CAB 79/13 COS(41)298, 25 and 27 Aug. 1941; PREM 3/237/2, Churchill to Cadogan, 2 Sept. 1941.

172 CAB 79/13 COS(41)298, 27 Aug.; WO 193/662, tels. to Wavell, military attaché in Teheran, and Macfarlane, 31 Aug. and 1 Sept. 1941.

173 FO 371 27233 E5192/3444/34, tel. from Cripps, 30 Aug.; Cripps papers, diary, 31 Aug. 1941.

174 Harvey, *War Diaries*, p. 36.

175 Cripps papers, diary, 31 Aug. 1941.

176 FO 371 27233 E5283/3444/34, exchange between Cripps and Eden, 2 and 4 Sept., and min. by Sargent, 4 Sept. 1941.

177 CAB 69/2 DO(41)60, 3 Sept. 1941; Churchill, *Second World War*, vol. 3, p. 428. Eden's retrospective presentation of the operation as securing supply to Russia is in *Reckoning*, pp. 273–4.

178 PREM 3/237/2, Churchill to Bullard, 3 Sept. 1941.

179 CAB 65/23 89(41)2, 4 Sept. 1941.

180 Sherwood, *Roosevelt and Hopkins*, pp. 574–5.

### 6 *Disillusion*

1 FO 371 29571 N4738, N4781/3084/38, min. by Cadogan, Eden to Churchill and tels. to Cripps, 20, 21 and 22 Aug. 1941.
2 FO 371 29489 N4840/78/38, tels. to Cripps, 26 Aug. 1941; Maisky, *Memoirs*, p. 187.
3 FO 371 29571 N4852/3084/38, tel. from Cripps, 27 Aug.; Appiah papers, letter from Cripps, 29 Aug. 1941.
4 FO 371 29571 N4852/3084/38, 28 Aug.; Hopkins papers, Box 306, memo., 25 Aug. 1941.
5 FO 371 29572 N4881/3084/38, Eden to Campbell (Washington) and Churchill, 28 Aug.; CAB 65/23 85(41)3.
6 CAB 79/55 COS(41)29 and FO 371 29572 N4880/3084/38, message to Stalin, 28 Aug. 1941.
7 Harvey, *War Diaries*, pp. 34, 38. On Beaverbrook's strong new commitment see Churchill, *Second World War*, vol. 3, p. 402.
8 Beaverbrook papers, D 94, Dew to Churchill , 29 July. See also A. J. P. Taylor, *Beaverbrook* (London, 1972), pp. 481–2. Significantly Churchill omits the whole episode in *Second World War*, vol. 3, pp. 402–3.
9 Beaverbrook papers, D 94.
10 FO 371 29573 N5159/3084/38.
11 Taylor, *Beaverbrook*, pp. 476, 477–84, 492. For Beaverbrook's initial hesitation see also Werth, *Moscow '41*, p. 149.
12 Harvey, *War Diaries*, pp. 47–8; *Diaries of Cadogan*, p. 232; CAB 65/19 95(41)8.
13 FP 371 29490 N5105/78/38; Maisky, *Memoirs*, pp. 187–8.
14 Cripps papers, 3 and 4 Sept. 1941.
15 Maisky, *Memoirs*, pp. 187–8; Churchill, *Second World War*, vol. 3, pp. 405–7; Eden, *Reckoning*, p. 275; FO 371 29490 N5096/78/38, tel. to Cripps, 4 Sept. 1941.
16 JIC(41)290 in CAB 79/13 COS(41)278, 31 July 1941.
17 e.g. CAB 79/13 COS(41)284,287 and CAB 80/29 COS(41)488, 12, 13 and 14 Aug.; WO 193/660, tel. to Macfarlane, 10 Aug.; FO 371 29489 N4704/78/38, Ismay to Sargent, 16 Aug. 1941.
18 CAB 84/34 JP(41)691, 23 Aug.; FO 371 29490 N4922/78/38, tel. from Macfarlane, 22 Aug.; CAB 79/14 COS(41)371, 8 Sept. 1941.
19 CAB 65/23 41(90), 5 Sept. 1941.
20 CAB 79/14 COS(41)312, 5 Sept. 1941; Eden, *Reckoning*, p. 275; Maisky, *Memoirs*, pp. 192–3.
21 Churchill, *Second World War*, vol. 3, p. 407.
22 CAB 65/23 41(90) and CAB 79/14 COS(41)313, 5 Sept. 1941.
23 Churchill, *Second World War*, vol. 3, pp. 407–9.
24 This convergence is reflected in the press, e.g. 'Soviet Aid Pledge by T.U.C.', *News Chronicle*, 11 July; leader in *The Times*, 14 July; 'Russia How Much and

How Soon', *Daily Herald*, 18 Aug.; 'Three Powers in Partnership', *Daily Telegraph*, 18 Aug. On WO recognition of pressure of public opinion, WO 208/1776, 12 Sept. On feelings on the left of Labour, Wedgwood papers, letter to Maisky, 29 Sept. 1941.

25 FO 371 29640 N5468/5379/38; PREM 4/21/4, Churchill to Citrine, and CAB 65/19 95(41)8, 22 Sept.

26 Taylor, *Beaverbrook*, pp. 482–6.

27 *Parl. Deb. HC*, vol. 374, cols. 72–83, 86–9, 105, 110–12, 138–47, 151–6, 9 Sept. 1941.

28 *ibid.*, col. 80; Churchill, *Second World War*, vol. 3, p. 461; FO 371 29490 N5169/78/38, tel. from Cripps, 9 Sept., and mins. by Warner, Sargent and Eden, 13 Sept. 1941.

29 Cripps papers, diary, 3, 4 and 5 Sept.; Appiah papers, letter from Cripps, 5 Sept. 1941.

30 CAB 120/678, min. by Churchill, 5 Sept.; *Diaries of Cadogan*, p. 405.

31 Churchill, *Second World War*, vol. 3, pp. 409–11, does not mention Cripps' wish to return; FO 371 29490 N5105/78/38, tel. to Cripps, 5 Sept. 1941.

32 FO 371 29490 N5113/78/38, tel. from Cripps, 7 Sept. 1941.

33 Cripps papers, diary, 7 Sept. 1941.

34 *ibid.*, Cripps to Eden, 10 Sept. 1941.

35 *ibid.*, Eden to Cripps, 25 Aug.; CAB 127/64, Eden to Cripps, 9 Sept. 1941.

36 CAB 127/64, Cripps to Eden, 14 Sept. See also Cripps papers, diary, 23 Sept. 1941.

37 Cripps papers, Eden to Cripps, 18 Sept. 1941; Harvey, *War Diaries*, p. 43.

38 Erickson, *The Road to Stalingrad*, pp. 196–210.

39 FO 371 29490 N5447/78/38, tel. from Cripps, 15 Sept.; Beaverbrook papers, D 90, excerpts from tels. from Macfarlane, Sept. 1941.

40 WO 193/664, tels. from Macfarlane, 16 and 18 Sept.; Cripps papers, diary, 19 Sept. 1941.

41 FO 371 29490 N5397, N5421/78/38, exchange between Cripps and Eden, 16 and 18 Sept. 1941. See also Churchill, *Second World War*, vol. 3, pp. 411–12.

42 Churchill, *Second World War*, vol. 3, p. 411; Hinsley, *British Intelligence*, vol. 2, pp. 67–73.

43 See above, p. 215.

44 CAB 79/14 COS (41)324 and CAB 84/35 JP(41)767, 16 and 19 Sept. 1941.

45 CAB 65/23 94(41)5, 18 Sept., and FO 371 29490 N5421/78/38, min. by Churchill, 19 Sept. 1941.

46 FO 371 29576 N5440/3084/38, mins. by Sargent and Eden, 20 Sept. 1941; *Diaries of Cadogan*, pp. 406–7.

47 Churchill, *Second World War*, vol. 3, pp. 412–13; FO 371 29490 N5501/78/ 38, 22 Sept. 1941.

48 FO 371 29490 N5421/78/38, exchange between Eden and Churchill, 18 and 19 Sept. 1941.

49 *ibid*. N5501/78/38, tel. to Cripps, 19 Sept. 1941.

50 *FRUS 1941*, I, p. 831; Cripps papers, diary, 10 and 11 Sept. 1941.

51 Appiah papers, letter from Cripps, 7 Sept. 1941.

52 FO 371 29563 N5186/3014/38, tel. from Cripps and min. by Sargent, 8 Sept., and P. Jordan of *News Chronicle* to editor, 25 July 1941.

53 Cripps papers, diary, 6 and 7 Sept.; FO 371 29633 N5115/5060/38, tel. from Cripps and mins. by Sargent and Eden, 7 and 9 Sept.; CAB 65/23 91(41)4 and CAB 79/14 COS(41)314, 8 Sept. 1941.

54 WO 193/664, instructions to Macready, 11 Sept. 1941.

55 Parkinson, *The Auk*, p. 163, also pp. 93, 97–8, 102, 107–8, 117–19, 179, 207.

56 CAB 84/35 JP(41)775, 22 Sept. 1941.

57 FO 371 29583 N7485/3084/38, 10 Sept. 1941; *FRUS 1941*, I, pp. 823–4.

58 Churchill, *Second World War*, vol. 3, p. 417; Roosevelt papers, Box 136, letter to Churchill, 1 Oct. 1941.

59 Balfour papers, diary, 26 Sept. 1941; CAB 69/2 DO(41)62.

60 CAB 66/19 WP(41)238, 6 Oct. 1941.

61 Ismay, *Memoirs*, p. 228; Hopkins papers, Box 306, memo. by Harriman, 28 Sept. 1941.

62 Hopkins papers, Box 136, 29 Sept. 1941. See also Roosevelt's message to Stalin in *FRUS 1941*, I, p. 836.

63 Churchill, *Second World War*, vol. 3, pp. 764–8; Beaverbrook papers, D 94.

64 Harriman and Abel, *Special Envoy*, p. 82.

65 *ibid*., pp. 84–5. A critical view of Beaverbrook's treatment of Cripps by the Moscow correspondent of the *News Chronicle* is in P. Jordan, *Russian Glory* (London, 1942), pp. 130–3.

66 Beaverbrook papers, D 338, 14 Sept. 1941.

67 Cripps papers, diary, 16, 19, 26 and 27 Sept. 1941.

68 e.g. J. Beaumont, *Comrades in Arms: British Aid to Russia, 1941–1945* (London, 1980), pp. 54–5; J. D. Langer, 'The Harriman–Beaverbrook Mission and the Debate over Unconditional Aid for the Soviet Union, 1941', in W. Laqueur (ed.), *The Second World War* (London, 1982); Taylor, *Beaverbrook*, p. 487.

69 Leasor, *War at the Top*, p. 159.

70 Beaverbrook papers, D 90, D99, 22 Sept. 1941.

71 Cripps papers, diary, 7 Dec. 1941.

72 CAB 120/36, 2 Oct., corroborated by Harriman, Hopkins papers, Box 306, 1 Oct. 1941.

73 Taylor, *Beaverbrook*, p. 487.

74 Quoted from Beaumont, *Comrades in Arms*, p. 56.
75 Cripps papers, diary, 28 Sept. and 4 Oct.; FO 371 29471 N6583/3/38, tel. from Cripps, 26 Oct. 1941.
76 Butler, *Mason-Mac*, p. 137; S. Kot, *Conversations in the Kremlin and Dispatches from Russia* (London, 1963), pp. 42–4.
77 CAB 79/14 COS(41)940, 2 Oct.; PREM 3 351/9, COS to Churchill, 5 Oct. 1941.
78 FO 371 26761.
79 Cripps papers, diary, 29 Sept.; G. Wilson to J. Cripps, 30 Sept.; Balfour papers, diary, 29 Sept. 1941. For a dismissal of Churchill's distorted version of the supposed hostile reception of the mission, see Beaumont, *Comrades in Arms*, p. 226, n. 59.
80 Cripps papers, Wilson to Cripps, 30 Sept.; Balfour papers, diary, 2–3 Oct. 1941. For Beaverbrook's public relations see e.g. 'Top-Speed Talks in Moscow', 'Midnight Announcement as Lightning Parley Ends' and 'Bountiful Supplies', *Daily Express*, 1 and 2 Oct. 1941.
81 Cripps papers, diary, 30 Sept.; see also *FRUS 1941*, I, p. 836, and Balfour papers, diary, 29 Sept. 1941.
82 R. R. James, *Victor Cazalet, a Portrait* (London, 1976), p. 269; Harriman, *Special Envoy*, p. 93.
83 Three versions should be read together: Beaverbrook papers, D 100, report, 1 Oct.; Hopkins papers, Box 306, Harriman's memo. on ambassadors, 30 Sept.; Harriman and Abel, *Special Envoy*, p. 94. See also Cripps papers, diary, 1 Oct. 1941.
84 Cripps papers, diary, 28 Sept. 1941; Bourke-White, *Russian War*, p. 207.
85 Beaverbrook papers, D 100, report, 1 Oct.; Harriman, *Special Envoy*, p. 83.
86 Balfour papers, diary, 3–6 Oct. 1941; Cripps papers, diary, 4 Oct. 1941; Harriman and Abel, *Special Envoy*, p. 95.
87 Appiah papers, 13 Oct.; Cripps papers, diary, 1, 4, 5 and 6 Oct. 1941.
88 FO 371 29578 N5883/3084/38, 3 Oct. 1941; Harvey, *War Diaries*, p. 49; *Diaries of Cadogan*, p. 408.
89 Beaverbrook papers, D 98.
90 Hopkins papers, Box 306, memo. by Harriman, 28 Sept. 1941.
91 CAB 65/19 98(41)5.
92 Cripps papers, diary, 29 Sept. 1941.
93 Balfour papers, diary, 29 Sept. 1941; Harriman and Abel, *Special Envoy*, p. 89.
94 Hopkins papers, Box 306, memo. by Harriman, 29 and 30 Sept. 1941.
95 CAB 120/36, tel. from Beaverbrook, 2 Oct.; FO 181/962, tel. from Cripps, 1 Nov. 1941. See also Harriman and Abel, *Special Envoy*, p. 92.
96 Beaverbrook papers, D 100, memo., 30 Sept. 1941.
97 Erickson, *The Road to Stalingrad*, pp. 213–15; Hinsley, *British Intelligence*, vol. 2, p. 73.

98 Balfour papers, diary, 29 and 30 Sept.; CAB 66/19 WP(41)238, memo. by Ismay, 6 Oct. 1941; Langer, 'Harriman–Beaverbrook Mission', pp. 308–9. Langer sheds light on the American point of view but uncritically repeats Churchill's account of his commitment, plays down his conflict with Beaverbrook in London and glosses over the tension in talks with Stalin, thus attaching undue significance to Cripps' wish to extract information from the Russians. See also W. H. Standley and A. A. Ageton, *Admiral Ambassador to Russia* (Chicago, 1955), pp. 67–8.

99 A. H. Birse, *Memoirs of an Interpreter* (London, 1967), pp. 61–2; Ismay, *Memoirs*, p. 230.

100 Harriman and Abel, *Special Envoy*, pp. 97–8; Sherwood, *Roosevelt and Hopkins*, p. 389.

101 Hopkins papers, Box 306, memo. by Harriman, 29 and 30 Sept.; CAB 66/19 WP(41)238, report by Ismay, 6 Oct. 1941.

102 Beaumont, *Comrades in Arms*, p. 83; Langer, 'Harriman–Beaverbrook Mission', pp. 308–9; Barker, *Churchill and Eden*, p. 235.

103 Harriman and Abel, *Special Envoy*, pp. 89–90, 230–1; Cripps papers, diary, 30 Sept. 1941.

104 Balfour papers, diary, 30 Sept. 1941.

105 *ibid.*; Hopkins papers, Box 306, memo. by Harriman, 30 Sept.

106 Cripps papers, diary, and FO 954/24, tel. from Cripps, 2 Oct. 1941.

107 CAB 66/19 WP(41)238. Harriman too appealed to Roosevelt, see Hopkins papers, Box 306, 3 Oct. 1941.

108 PREM 3/170/1, message to Stalin, 6 Oct. 1941; Beaumont, *Comrades in Arms*, chs. 3 and 4.

109 Cripps papers, diary, 4 Oct.; FO 954/24, 2 Oct. 1941.

110 Cripps papers, diary, 1 and 3 Oct. 1941.

111 CAB 127/64, 1 Oct. 1941.

112 Cripps papers, diary, 26 July, 26 Sept. and 2 Oct. 1941.

113 *ibid.*, 4–13 Nov. 1941; *FRUS 1941*, I, pp. 852–3. On the critical attitude to Steinhardt see a report on conversations with Oumansky in Harper papers, Box 22.f.13, 8 and 19 Nov. 1941.

7 Frustration

1 Cripps papers, diary, 5–16 Oct. 1941.

2 Erickson, *The Road to Stalingrad*, pp. 214–22.

3 Harvey, *War Diaries*, p. 51.

4 CAB 127/64.

5 FO 371 29558 N5922/2823/38, tel. from Cripps; Cripps papers, diary, 13 and 14 Oct. 1941. On the situation in Moscow see A. M. Samsonov, 'Moskva v Oktyabre 1941 goda', *Istoriya SSSR*, 5 (1981) and Cassidy, *Moscow Dateline*, p. 123.

6 C. Haldane, *Russian Newsreel: an Eye-Witness Account of the Soviet Union at War* (London, 1942), p. 168.
7 Cripps papers, diary, 16 Oct.; FO 371 29558 N6360/2823/38, tel. from Cripps, 22 Oct. 1941.
8 Cassidy, *Moscow Dateline*, p. 111.
9 Haldane, *Russian Newsreel*, p. 169.
10 Birse, *Memoirs*, p. 80.
11 *ibid.*, p. 81; Cassidy, *Moscow Dateline*, p. 112; Elvin, *Cockney in Moscow*, pp. 214–15; Jordan, *Russian Glory*, pp. 97–8.
12 Cripps papers, diary, 16 Oct. 1941.
13 *ibid.*, 16 and 17 Oct. 1941.
14 Birse, *Memoirs*, pp. 81–2; Jordan, *Russian Glory*, p. 102; Assarasson, *I Skuggan av Stalin*, p. 82; Appiah papers, letter from Cripps, 23 Oct. 1941.
15 Cassidy, *Moscow Dateline*, p. 115.
16 FO 371 29558 N6065/2823/38 and FO 181/962, tels. from Cripps and Macfarlane, and Cripps papers, diary, 21 and 22 Oct. 1941.
17 WO 193/662, tels. from Cripps, 8, 9 and 10 Sept.; Cripps papers, diary, 10 and 11 Oct. 1941.
18 CAB 69/2 DO(41)61 and CAB 79/14 COS(41)318, 8 and 9 Sept. 1941.
19 *Parl. Deb. HC*, vol. 374, col. 80, 9 Sept. 1941.
20 PREM 3/170/1.
21 Cripps papers, diary, and FO 371 29492 N6132/78/38, tel. from Cripps, 14 Oct. 1941.
22 FO 371 29492 N6029, N6040/78/38, tels. to Cripps, 16 and 17 Oct. 1941; Nicolson, *Diaries*, pp. 188–9.
23 FO 418/87, tel. from Cripps, and Cripps papers, diary, 22 Oct. 1941.
24 Citrine papers, Box 4/9, memo., Cripps papers, diary, and FO 371 29492 N6135/78/38, tel. from Cripps, 22 and 23 Oct. 1941.
25 FO 371 29471 N6548/3/38, tels. from Cripps and Macfarlane, 23 Oct., and min. by Eden, 26 Oct. 1941.
26 FO 371 29469 N5585/3/38; CAB 120/683.
27 FO 371 29471 N6583/3/38; Cripps papers, diary, 27 Oct. 1941.
28 FO 371 29492 N6230/78/38, tel. to Cripps.
29 Harvey, *War Diaries*, pp. 50, 55–6.
30 Beaverbrook papers, D 338, exchange with Eden and note by Dew, 14, 15 and 12 Oct.; FO 371 29471 N6583/3/38, 27 Oct. 1941.
31 CAB 69/3 DO(41)22; *Diaries of Cadogan*, p. 409; Harvey, *War Diaries*, pp. 54–5.
32 Taylor, *Beaverbrook*, pp. 497–8.
33 CAB 65/19 102(41)7,8; Eden, *Reckoning*, p. 278; Harvey, *War Diaries*, p. 50.
34 CAB 65/23 106(41)7,8. On Beaverbrook's concern about Cripps' telegrams see Beaverbrook papers, D 338, exchange with Eden, 25 and 28 Oct., and note to Harvey, 29 Oct. 1941, and also Harvey, *War Diaries*, pp. 58, 65–7.
35 CAB 79/55 COS(41)33, 7 Oct.; CAB 69/2 DO(41)65, 17 Oct. 1941.

36 CAB 69/2 DO(41)69, 27 Oct.; CAB 79/55 COS(41)34 and min. by Churchill, 28 Oct. 1941.
37 Harvey, *War Diaries*, p. 57; *Diaries of Cadogan*, p. 370.
38 FO 371 29492 N6231/78/38, tel. to Cripps.
39 Churchill, *Second World War*, vol. 3, p. 420, mentions neither the earlier correspondence nor the acrimonious exchanges with Stalin.
40 *ibid.*, p. 421.
41 Hinsley, *British Intelligence*, vol. 2, p. 73; *Diaries of Cadogan*, p. 410.
42 CAB 120/681, 24 Oct. 1941. On Churchill's appreciation see also Ismay, *Memoirs*, p. 235.
43 Cripps papers, diary, 30 Oct. 1941.
44 FO 371 29471 N6584/3/38, 30 Oct. 1941; Harvey, *War Diaries*, p. 59.
45 FO 371 29470 N6267/3/38 and FO 181/962, exchange between Cripps and Eden, 30 and 31 Oct. and 1 Nov. 1941.
46 PREM 3 403/7, Churchill to Beaverbrook and Eden to Churchill, 14 Oct.; Beaverbrook papers, D 93, Churchill to Eden and Beaverbrook, 1 Nov. 1941; Taylor, *Beaverbrook*, pp. 408–9.
47 FO 181/962, draft letter to Stalin, 2 Nov.; Cripps papers, diary, 3, 4 and 5 Nov. 1941.
48 FO 371 29526 N5594, N5878/552/38, Brendan Bracken to Cripps, and Ministry of Information memo., 24 and 25 Sept.; 29576 N5576/3084/38, Eden to Churchill, 23 Sept.; Leeper papers, diary, 29 Sept. 1941; Lord Birkenhead, *The Life of Viscount Monckton of Brenchley* (London, 1968), pp. 186–7.
49 FO 371 29526 N7009/552/38, tel. to Warner, 11 Nov.; Monckton papers, travel diary, 4, 5 and 6 Nov. 1941.
50 A. Boyle, *The Climate of Treason* (rev. edn, London, 1980), pp. 209–13.
51 Letter to author from Lord Greenwood of Rossendale, 18 Feb. 1980.
52 Cripps papers, diary, 3–12 Nov.; Monckton papers, travel diary, 9–11 Nov. 1941.
53 Cripps papers, diary, 5 Nov. 1941.
54 FO 181/962, 5 Nov. 1941.
55 Harvey, *War Diaries*, p. 62; Cripps papers, diary, 12 Nov. 1941.
56 Harvey, *War Diaries*, pp. 58, 60–1; Eden, *Reckoning*, p. 280.
57 FO 181/962, tel. to Cripps; Beaverbrook papers, D 90, copy of tel., 10 Nov. 1941.
58 FO 371 29493 N6544/78/38, Harvey and Eden to Churchill, 10 Nov. 1941; Harvey, *War Diaries*, p. 62.
59 CAB 84/36 JP(41)942, 8 Nov.; JP(41)955, tel. to Auchinleck, 12 Nov. 1941.
60 CAB 65/24 108(41)4; CAB 120/683, Hollis to Churchill, 3 Nov. 1941.
61 CAB 66/19 WP(41)245; FO 371 N6060, N6288/3/38, tels. to Cripps.
62 FO 418/87, tels. to Cripps, 31 Oct. and 4 Nov. 1941. See also Maisky, *Memoirs*, pp. 199–200.

63 FO 371 29493 N6373/78/38, tel. to Cripps, 4 Nov. 1941; Eden, *Reckoning*, p. 280.

64 Maisky, *Memoirs*, p. 199. He is wrong in suggesting that the issue was a second front on the Continent.

65 *Izvestiya*'s relief at Churchill's pledge in Parliament to continue to fight to the end in FO 371 29472 N7060/3/38, tel. from Cripps, 15 Nov. 1941.

66 FO 371 29558 N6438/2823/38 and 29449 N7008/114/38, tels. from Cripps, 8 Nov.; Cripps papers, diary, 7 and 8 Nov. 1941.

67 FO 371 29493 N6468/78/38 and 29494 N6631/78/38, 9 and 12 Nov. 1941.

68 Churchill's account of the crisis in *Second World War*, vol. 3, pp. 469–70, is incomplete and misleading; FO 371 29471 N6654/3/38, 18, 19 and 21 Nov. 1941.

69 FO 418/87, 15 Nov. 1941; Eden, *Reckoning*, p. 280.

70 Maisky, *Memoirs*, pp. 202–3; Eden, *Reckoning*, pp. 280–1; Harvey, *War Diaries*, pp. 62–3.

71 See n. 59 above. On the intensive public pressure see e.g., *Parl. Deb. HC*, vol. 374, cols. 1943–2010 and vol. 376, cols. 15–18, 75–78, 23 Oct. and 13 Nov.; 'Opinion', *Daily Express*, 7 Nov.; 'Salute to an Ally', *The Times*, 7 Nov.; 'Britain and Russia', leader in *The Times*, 7 Nov.; 'Co-operation with Russia', *The Times*, 14 Nov.; 'This Day', *Daily Herald*, 7 Nov. 1941.

72 Eden, *Reckoning*, pp. 280–1; *Diaries of Cadogan*, p. 412.

73 Harvey, *War Diaries*, pp. 62–3.

74 FO 371 29472 N6784/3/38, mins. by Eden, Sargent and Cadogan, 12, 18 and 19 Nov. 1941.

75 FO 371 29471 N6574/3/38, 13 Nov.; Cripps papers, diary, 15 Nov. 1941.

76 FO 371 29471 N6605/3/38, 13 Nov. 1941.

77 *ibid.*, 15 Nov.; Cripps papers, diary, 17 Nov. 1941.

78 Harvey, *War Diaries*, p. 63; Eden, *Reckoning*, pp. 82–3; *Diaries of Cadogan*, p. 412.

79 *Diaries of Cadogan*, pp. 412–13.

80 FO 371 29471 N6575/3/38, 15 Nov.; CAB 65/23 114(41)1,2, 17 Nov. 1941.

81 FO 371 29471 N6631, N6575/3/38, mins. by Eden and Cadogan, 13 and 16 Nov., and tel. to Cripps, 17 Nov. 1941; CAB 65/23 114(41)1,2; Harvey, *War Diaries*, p. 65.

82 Erickson, *The Road to Stalingrad*, pp. 251–2.

83 FO 954/24, tel. to Cripps, 20 Nov. 1941.

84 Eden, *Reckoning*, p. 283; FO 371 29472 N6799/3/38, tel. to Cripps, 21 Nov. 1941.

85 Cripps papers, diary, 19 and 20 Nov. 1941.

86 FO 371 29471 N6750/3/38, 20 and 21 Nov. 1941; Harvey, *War Diaries*, p. 65.

87  FO 371 29472 N6888/3/38, Stalin's message; FO 800/401, tel. to Cripps, 25 Nov. 1941.
88  FO 371 29472 N6835, N6839/3/38, draft memo. by Dew, mins. by Warner and N. Butler and final FO memo., 21, 24 and 26 Nov. 1941.
89  CAB 65/20,24 120(41)2,5 and 124(41)3; *Diaries of Cadogan*, p. 414.
90  FO 800/401, 4 Dec. 1941.
91  CAB 84/37, 79/16, 84/3 and 84/38, JP(41)1016, COS(41)404, JP(41)164, 1025, 29 Nov., 1 and 2 Dec. 1941.
92  Harvey, *War Diaries*, p. 69.
93  CAB 65/24 124(41)3.
94  CAB 84/38 JP(41)1037; a corrupt version in Eden, *Reckoning*, pp. 283–4; altered instructions to Eden, CAB 84/38 JP(41)1038,1066, 5 Dec. On opposition to assistance see CAB 79/86 COS(41)43, 4 Dec. 1941.
95  Churchill, *Second World War*, vol. 3, pp. 475–6; for his earlier directive and modifications introduced by Ismay see PREM 3/394/1, 5 Dec. 1941.
96  PREM 3/170/1; Woodward, *British Foreign Policy*, vol. 2, pp. 52–4.
97  Cripps papers, diary, 30 Nov.–7 Dec. 1941.
98  Carlton, *Eden*, pp. 189–90; Eden, *Reckoning*, p. 286.
99  Harvey, *War Diaries*, pp. 70–2; *Diaries of Cadogan*, p. 417; Eden, *Reckoning*, pp. 285–7, 217–23; FO 800/401, exchange between Eden and Churchill, 8 and 12 Dec. 1941.
100  Erickson, *The Road to Stalingrad*, pp. 255–77.
101  FO 371 29137 W14799/53/50, Churchill to Eden, 10 Dec. 1941.
102  The cover version in Maisky, *Memoirs*, pp. 225–9; *Diaries of Cadogan*, p. 418.
103  Cripps papers, diary, 13–16 Dec. 1941.
104  Harvey, *War Diaries*, p. 73; Eden's opinion of Cripps is deleted in the published version but is in Harvey papers, MS. 53697, diary, 15 Dec. 1941.
105  Maisky, *Memoirs*, p. 229.
106  FO 181/963, memo. by Eden, 16 Dec.; Cripps papers, diary, 7 Dec. 1941; Harvey, *War Diaries*, p. 74; *Diaries of Cadogan*, p. 421.
107  Unless stated otherwise all references to conversations are based on the detailed record in CAB 66/20 WP(42)8.
108  Eden, *Reckoning*, p. 289. In retrospect the Russians are rather reluctant to admit it; see e.g. *IVMV*, vol. 4, pp. 176–7 and Volkov, *SSSR-Angliya*, p. 379.
109  Harvey, *War Diaries*, p. 86.
110  Cripps papers, diary, 17 Dec. 1941.
111  Maisky, *Memoirs*, pp. 231–2.
112  Cripps papers, diary, 19 Dec. 1941.
113  *Diaries of Cadogan*, p. 421.
114  Eden, *Reckoning*, p. 296; Cripps papers, diary, 18 Dec. 1941.
115  Harvey, *War Diaries*, pp. 76–7.

116 Cripps papers, diary, 18 Dec. 1941.

117 Eden, *Reckoning*, p. 298,

118 FO 181/963, statement to Molotov and record of conversations, 19 Dec. 1941.

119 On Soviet reservations see Davies' impressions after meeting Litvinov in Roosevelt papers, Box 68, 12 Dec. 1941.

120 FO 181/963, tels. from Eden, 8 Dec. 1941; CAB 65/24 131(41)

121 PREM 4/27/9, Halifax to Churchill, 11 Jan. 1941. On Attlee's attitude see FO 954/25, Beaverbrook to Eden, 3 March 1942.

122 Churchill, *Second World War*, vol. 3, pp. 559–60, 615.

123 Eden, *Reckoning*, pp. 301–3; Harvey, *War Diaries*, p. 78; FO 800/401, Eden to Churchill, 22 Dec. 1941.

## 8 Aftermath

1 Cripps papers, diary, 22–3 Dec. 1941.

2 Barker, *Churchill and Eden*, ch. 17; Woodward, *British Foreign Policy*, vol. 2, pp. 236–44.

3 G. Ross, 'Operation Bracelet: Churchill in Moscow, 1942' in D. Dilks (ed.), *Retreat from Power* (2 vols., London, 1981). This is a representative revisionist approach, reaching similar conclusions to those of the present book. See also Woodward, *British Foreign Policy*, vol. 2, pp. 255–72.

4 Cripps papers, diary, 4, 5 and 11 Jan. 1942.

5 Assarasson, *I Skuggan av Stalin*, p. 98.

6 Sherwood, *Roosevelt and Hopkins*, ch. 20.

7 Cripps papers, diary, 27 Dec. 1941.

8 *ibid.*, 28 Dec. 1941 and 2 Jan. 1942.

9 FO 371 32941 N697/188/38, 3 Feb. 1942; Assarasson, *I Skuggan av Stalin*, p. 102.

10 Churchill, *Second World War*, vol. 4, pp. 55–6; this somewhat conflicts with his own account on p. 69.

11 S. Orwell and I. Angus (eds.), *The Collected Essays, Journalism and Letters of George Orwell*, vol. 2, *My Country Right or Left 1940–1943* (Harmondsworth, 1970), p. 143; Strauss, *Cripps*, pp. 159–60; an uncommon historical recognition of the challenge, P. Addison, *The Road to 1945: British Politics and the Second World War* (London, 1975), ch. 7.

12 Pritt papers, Box 1/3, diary, 15 Jan., and comment on Cripps' speech, 18 Feb. 1942.

13 Harvey, *War Diaries*, pp. 101–2; Addison, *The Road to 1945*, pp. 134–41, 200; Carlton, *Eden*, pp. 202–6.

14 K. Harris, *Attlee* (London, 1982). p. 206.

15 Churchill, *Second World War*, vol. 4, pp. 63–4.

16 See above, p. 247.

17 C. H. King, *With Malice toward None: a War Diary by Cecil H. King* (London, 1970), pp. 189–90; Webb papers, diary, pp. 530–1, 27 Jan. and 3 Feb. 1942;

Estorick, *Cripps*, p. 295. On attempts by Beaverbrook's press to undermine him see Orwell, *My Country Right or Left*, pp. 245, 248.

18 King, *A War Diary*, p. 176; Harvey, *War Diaries*, p. 87. Churchill, *Second World War*, vol. 4, pp. 71–2, does not mention this pressure.

19 Estorick, *Cripps*, pp. 290–9; Orwell, *My Country Right or Left*, pp. 240–1.

20 King, *A War Diary*, p. 190. On Churchill's furious reaction to the speech see *Second World War*, vol. 4, p. 69.

21 Taylor, *Beaverbrook*, pp. 508–18; Harvey, *War Diaries*, p. 97; Churchill, *Second World War*, vol. 4, p. 66.

22 Kot, *Dispatches from Russia*, p. 186; Webb papers, diary, p. 530, 26 Jan. 1942; Assarasson, *I Skuggan av Stalin*, p. 97. On Cripps' missed opportunity see Addison, *The Road to 1945*, pp. 190, 196.

23 Cripps papers, diary, 30 Dec. 1941.

24 King, *A War Diary*, pp. 176–7; Orwell, *My Country Right or Left*, p. 244.

25 Cripps papers.

26 See above, p. 274.

27 Nicolson, *Diaries*, p. 277; Morrison, *Autobiography*, pp. 216–17; H. Macmillan, *The Blast of War 1939–1945* (London, 1967), pp. 181–3; R. Jenkins, *Nine Men of Power*, p. 97.

28 R. J. Moore, *Churchill, Cripps and India, 1939–1945* (Oxford, 1979), pp. 63–83, 122–32; Nicolson, *Diaries*, p. 223; Harvey, *War Diaries*, pp. 106, 114.

29 Nicolson, *Diaries*, p. 225.

30 Parkinson, *The Auk*, pp. 175–6.

31 A revealing survey is in Addison, *The Road to 1945*, pp. 206–9.

32 King, *A War Diary*, p. 182.

33 Orwell, *My Country Right or Left*, p. 486.

34 King, *A War Diary*, p. 182.

35 Churchill, *Second World War*, vol. 4, pp. 202–3; Macmillan, *The Blast of War*, p. 183.

36 See above, p. 272.

37 Quoted from Moore, *Churchill, Cripps and India*, p. 137.

# BIBLIOGRAPHY

## I. UNPUBLISHED SOURCES

### 1. Public Record Office

ADM 199/1102 – British Naval Mission, Moscow, war diaries
BT 11 – Board of Trade, Commercial Department, correspondence and papers
CAB 65 – War Cabinet minutes
CAB 66 – War Cabinet memoranda
CAB 69 – War Cabinet, Defence Committee (operations)
CAB 79 – War Cabinet, Chiefs of Staff Committee, minutes of meetings
CAB 80 – War Cabinet, Chiefs of Staff Committee, memoranda
CAB 84 – War Cabinet, Joint Planning Committee
CAB 99 – War Cabinet, Commonwealth and International conferences
CAB 120 – Ministry of Defence Secretariat, files
CAB 122 – British Joint Staff Mission, Washington office files
CAB 127 – Private collections, ministers and officials
FO 181 – Embassy and consular archives, Russia correspondence
FO 366 – Chief Clerk's Department, archives
FO 371 – General correspondence, political
FO 418 – Confidential Print, the Soviet Union
FO 800 – Private collections of various ministers and officials
FO 954 – Eden's papers
FO 837 – Ministry of Economic Warfare
PREM – Prime Minister's Office:
   1/ Correspondence and papers
   2/ Operations papers
   3/ Confidential papers
WO 106 – War Office, Directorate of Military Operations and Intelligence
WO 178/25 and 26 – British Military Mission, Moscow, war diaries
WO 190 – War Office, appreciation files
WO 193 – War Office, Directorate of Military Operations
WO 208 – War Office, Directorate of Military Intelligence

# Bibliography

## 2. National Archives, Washington

General correspondence

## 3. Private papers

| | |
|---|---|
| Alexander, A. V. | Churchill College, Cambridge |
| Balfour, Harold | House of Lords Record Office |
| Beaverbrook, Lord | House of Lords Record Office |
| Berle, Adolf | Roosevelt Library, Hyde Park, N.Y. |
| Chamberlain, Neville | University of Birmingham |
| Citrine, Walter | London School of Economics and Political Science |
| Cripps, Peggy (now Mrs Appiah) | With Mrs Appiah |
| Cripps, Stafford | Deposited with Mr Maurice Shock or at Nuffield College, Oxford (unless otherwise stated, papers are those deposited with Mr Shock) |
| Cripps, Theresa (now Lady Ricketts) | With Lady Ricketts |
| Dalton, Hugh | London School of Economics and Political Science |
| Davies, J. E. | Library of Congress |
| Halifax, Lord | University of York |
| Harper, S. N. | University of Chicago |
| Harvey, Oliver | British Museum |
| Hopkins, Harry | Roosevelt Library, Hyde Park, N.Y. |
| Hull, Cordell | Library of Congress |
| Lansbury, George | London School of Economics and Political Science |
| Laski, Harold | University of Hull |
| Leeper, R. A. | With Lady Leeper |
| Mallet, Victor | Churchill College, Cambridge |
| Monckton, Walter | Bodleian Library, Oxford |
| Pritt, N. | London School of Economics and Political Science |
| Simon, Lord | Bodleian Library, Oxford |
| Steinhardt, Laurence | Library of Congress |
| *The Times* | *The Times*, London |
| Weaver, Tobias | With Sir Tobias Weaver |
| Webb, Beatrice | London School of Economics and Political Science |

## 4. Interviews

Conducted between Nov. 1979 and Apr. 1980
  The late Lord Butler of Saffron Walden

# Bibliography

Governor W. Averell Harriman
The late Professor Michael Postan
Lady Ricketts
Sir John Russell
Sir Geoffrey Wilson

## 5. Newspapers

Press cuttings, Royal Institute of International Affairs, Chatham House, London

## II. PRINTED MATERIAL

### 1. Documentary sources

Documents on German Foreign Policy, 1918–1945 (DGFP), Series D (1937–45), The War Years, vol. 8, September 4, 1939–March 18, 1940; vol. 9, March 19, 1940–June 22, 1940; vol. 10, June 23–August 31, 1940 (Washington, 1955–7)

Foreign Relations of the United States, Diplomatic Papers, 1940 (FRUS 1940), vol. I, General (Washington, 1959)

Foreign Relations of the United States, Diplomatic Papers, 1941 (FRUS 1941), vol. II, General, The Soviet Union (Washington, 1958)

Nazi-Soviet Relations 1939–41: Documents from the Archives of the German Foreign Office (NSR), ed. Sontag, R. J. and Beddie, J. S. (Washington, 1975)

### 2. Memoirs, diaries, collected works and biographies

Assarasson, V. I Skuggan av Stalin (Stockholm, 1963)
Aster, S. Anthony Eden (London, 1976)
Barman, T. Diplomatic Correspondent (London, 1968)
Berezhkov, V. Gody diplomaticheskoi sluzhby (Moscow, 1972)
  History in the Making: Memoirs of World War II Diplomacy (Moscow, 1983)
Bilainkin, G. Diary of a Political Correspondent (London, 1942)
  Maisky: Ten Years' Ambassador (London, 1944)
Birkenhead, Earl of Halifax: the Life of Lord Halifax (London, 1965)
  The Life of Viscount Monckton of Brenchley (London, 1968)
Birse, A. H. Memoirs of an Interpreter (London, 1967)
Boheman, E. På Vakt (2 vols., Stockholm, 1963–4)
Bohlen, C. Witness to History, 1929–1963 (New York, 1973)
Bourke-White, M. Shooting the Russian War (New York, 1942)
Bryant, A. The Turn of the Tide, 1939–43 (London, 1957)
Butler, E. Mason-Mac: the Life of Lieutenant-General Sir Noel Mason-Macfarlane (London, 1972)
Butler, Lord The Art of the Possible (London, 1971)
Carlton, D. Anthony Eden: a Biography (London, 1981)

# Bibliography

Cassidy, H. C. *Moscow Dateline, 1941–1943* (London, 1943)

Churchill, W. *The Second World War* (6 vols., London, 1948–54)

Citrine, W. *In Russia Now* (London, 1942)

*Two Careers* (London, 1967)

Cooke, C. *The Life of Richard Stafford Cripps* (London, 1957)

Cripps, F. H. *Life's a Gamble* (London, 1957)

Crozier, W. P. *Off the Record: Political Interviews, 1932–44*, ed. A. J. P. Taylor (London, 1973)

Dalton, H. *The Fateful Years: Memoirs, 1931–1945* (London, 1957)

Deakin, F. W. and Storry, G. R. *The Case of Richard Sorge* (New York, 1966)

Dilks, D. (ed.) *The Diaries of Sir Alexander Cadogan, 1938–45* (London, 1971)

Duranty, W. *The Kremlin and the People* (New York, 1942)

Eden, A. *The Eden Memoirs: the Reckoning* (London, 1965)

Ehrenburg, I. *Eve of the War, 1933–1941* (London, 1963)

Elvin, H. *A Cockney in Moscow* (London, 1958)

Estorick, E. *Stafford Cripps, a Biography* (London, 1949)

Fischer, L. *Men and Politics: an Autobiography* (London, 1941)

Foot, M. *Aneurin Bevan* (2 vols., London, 1962–73)

Gafencu, G. *Prelude to the Russian Campaign* (London, 1945)

Gilbert, M. *Winston S. Churchill, 1922–1939* (London, 1976)

Golikov, F. 'Sovetskaya voennaya missiya v Anglii i SShA v 1941g', *Novaya i Noveishaya Istoriya*, 3 (1969)

Haldane, C. *Russian Newsreel: an Eye-Witness Account of the Soviet Union at War* (London, 1942)

Halifax, Earl of *Fulness of Day* (London, 1957)

Harriman, W. A. and Abel, E. *Special Envoy to Churchill and Stalin, 1941–1946* (New York, 1975)

Harris, K. *Attlee* (London, 1982)

Harvey, J. (ed.) *The Diplomatic Diaries of Oliver Harvey, 1937–1940* (London, 1970)

*The War Diaries of Oliver Harvey, 1941–45* (London, 1978)

Hilger, G. and Meyer, A. G. *The Incompatible Allies: a Memoir–History of German–Soviet Relations, 1918–1941* (New York, 1953)

Hull, C. *The Memoirs of Cordell Hull* (2 vols., New York, 1948)

Ickes, H. L. *The Secret Diary of Harold L. Ickes* (3 vols., New York, 1953–4)

Ismay, H. *The Memoirs of General the Lord Ismay* (London, 1960)

James, R. R. (ed.) *Chips: the Diaries of Sir Henry Channon* (London, 1967)

*Victor Cazalet, a Portrait* (London, 1976)

Jordan, P. *Russian Glory* (London, 1942)

King, C. H. *With Malice toward None: a War Diary by Cecil H. King* (London, 1970)

Kot, S. *Conversations in the Kremlin and Dispatches from Russia* (London, 1963)

Leutze, J. (ed.) *The London Journal of General Raymond E. Lee, 1940–1941* (Boston, 1971)

Macmillan, H. *The Blast of War 1939–1945* (London, 1967)

Maisky, I. M. *Memoirs of a Soviet Ambassador, the War, 1939–1943* (London, 1967)

Morrison, H. S. *Morrison: an Autobiography* (London, 1960)

Nekrich, A. 'Biografiya akademiki I. Maiskogo', *Voprosy Istorii*, 2 (1964)

Nicolson, H. *Diaries and Letters, 1939–1945* (London, 1967)

O'Malley, O. *The Phantom Caravan* (London, 1954)

Orwell, S. and Angus, I. (eds.) *The Collected Essays, Journalism and Letters of George Orwell*, vol. 2, *My Country Right or Left 1940–1943* (Harmondsworth, 1970)

Parkinson, R. *The Auk: Auchinleck, Victor at Alamein* (London, 1977)

Peterson, M. D. *Both Sides of the Curtain, an Autobiography* (London, 1950)

Pritt, D. N. *The Autobiography of D. N. Pritt* (2 vols., London, 1965–6)

Rendel, G. W. *The Sword and the Olive: Recollections of Diplomacy and the Foreign Service* (London, 1957)

Scott, J. *Duel for Europe* (Boston, 1942)

Standley, W. H. and Ageton, A. A. *Admiral Ambassador to Russia* (Chicago, 1955)

Strauss, P. *Cripps – Advocate and Rebel* (London, 1943)

Tanner, V. *The Winter War: Finland against Russia, 1939–1940* (Stanford, 1957)

Taylor, A. J. P. *Beaverbrook* (London, 1972)

Trukhanovskii, V. G. *Uinston Cherchil'* (Moscow, 1968)
  *Antoni Iden* (Moscow, 1974)

Teske, H. (ed.) *General Ernst Köstring* (Frankfurt, 1966)

Warlimont, W. *Inside Hitler's Headquarters, 1939–45* (London, 1964)

Werth, A. *Moscow '41* (London, 1942)

Winant, J. G. *A Letter from Grosvenor Square: an Account of a Stewardship* (London, 1947)

Zhukov, Marshal. *The Memoirs* (New York, 1971)


### 3. Secondary sources

Addison, P. *The Road to 1945: British Politics and the Second World War* (London, 1975)

Aster, S. 'Ivan Maisky and Parliamentary Anti-Appeasement, 1938–1939', in A. J. P. Taylor (ed.), *Lloyd George* (London, 1971)
  *1939: the Making of the Second World War* (London, 1973)

Barker, E. *British Policy in South-East Europe in the Second World War* (London, 1976)
  *Churchill and Eden at War* (London, 1978)

Beaumont, J. *Comrades in Arms: British Aid to Russia, 1941–1945* (London, 1980)
  'A Question of Diplomacy: British Military Mission, 1941–1945', *Jour. of the Royal United Services Inst. for Defense Studies*, 118(3) (1973)

# Bibliography

'Great Britain and the Rights of Neutral Countries: The Case of Iran, 1941', *Journal of Contemporary History*, 16 (1981)

Beitzell, R. *The Uneasy Alliance: America, Britain and Russia, 1941–1943* (New York, 1972)

Beloff, M. *The Foreign Policy of Soviet Russia, 1929–1941* (2 vols. Oxford, 1947–9)

Bialer, S. *Stalin and his Generals: Soviet Military Memoirs of World War II* (New York, 1969)

Boyle, A. *The Climate of Treason* (rev. edn, London, 1980)

Burridge, T. D. *British Labour and Hitler's War* (London, 1976)

Butler, J. R. M. *Grand Strategy: September 1939–June 1941* (London, 1957)

Cecil, R. *Hitler's Decision to Invade Russia, 1941* (London, 1975)

Colvin, I. *The Chamberlain Cabinet* (London, 1971)

Creveld, M. van *Hitler's Strategy 1940–41: the Balkan Clue* (Cambridge, 1973)

Dallin, D. J. *Soviet Russia's Foreign Policy, 1939–1942* (Yale, 1942)

Dawson, R. H. *The Decision to Aid Russia, 1941: Foreign Policy and Domestic Politics* (Chapel Hill, S. Carolina, 1959)

Douglas, R. *The Advent of War 1939–1940* (London, 1979)

Douglas-Hamilton, J. *Motive for a Mission: the Story Behind Hess's Flight to Britain* (New York, 1971)

Erickson, J. *The Road to Stalingrad* (London, 1975)

Gus, M. ' "Taina" missiya Gessa', *Voienno-ist. Zhurnal*, 9 (1960)

Gwyer, J. M. A. and Butler, J. R. M. *Grand Strategy: June 1941–August 1942* (London, 1964)

Hanak, H. 'Sir Stafford Cripps as British Ambassador in Moscow, May 1940 to June 1941', and 'Sir Stafford Cripps as Ambassador in Moscow, June 1941–January 1942', *English Historical Review*, 370 (1979) and 383 (1982)

Herndon, J. 'British Perceptions of Soviet Military Capability, 1935–39', unpublished paper

Herring, G. C. *Aid to Russia, 1940–1946: Strategy, Diplomacy, the Origins of the Cold War* (New York, 1973)

Higgins, T. *Hitler and Russia: the Third Reich in a Two Front War, 1937–1943* (New York, 1966)

Hinsley, F. H. *British Intelligence in the Second World War* (2 vols., London, 1979–81)

Hutton, J. B. *Hess: the Man and his Mission* (London, 1970)

*Istoriya vtoroi mirovoi voiny, 1939–1945* (12 vols., Moscow, 1974–9)

Ivashin, I. F. *Nachalo vtoroi mirovoi voiny i vneshnyaya politika SSSR* (Moscow, 1951)

Jenkins, R. *Nine Men of Power* (London, 1974)

Jones, W. D. *The Russian Complex: the British Labour Party and the Soviet Union* (Manchester, 1977)

Lammers, D. 'Fascism, Communism and the Foreign Office, 1937–39', *Journal of Contemporary History*, 6 (1971)

# Bibliography

Langer, J. D. 'The Harriman–Beaverbrook Mission and the Debate over Unconditional Aid for the Soviet Union, 1941' in W. Laqueur, (ed.), *The Second World War* (London, 1982)

Lash, J. P. *Roosevelt and Churchill, 1939–1941: the Partnership that Saved the World* (Norton, 1976)

Leach, B. A. *German Strategy against Russia, 1939–1941* (Oxford, 1973)

Leasor, T. J. *War at the Top* (London, 1961)
  *Rudolf Hess: the Uninvited Envoy* (London, 1962)

Lewin, R. *Ultra Goes to War: the Secret Story* (London, 1978)

Manne, R. 'The Foreign Office and the Failure of Anglo-Soviet Rapprochement', *Journal of Contemporary History*, 16 (1981)

Moore, R. J. *Churchill, Cripps and India, 1939–1945* (Oxford, 1979)

Nekrich, A. 'Arrest and Trial of I. M. Maisky', *Survey*, 22 (1978)
  'Politika Anglii v period "strannoi voiny" ', *Novaya i Noveishaya Istoriya*, 3 (1960)
  'Politika angliiskogo pravitel'stva na severo-zapade Evropy (sentyabr' 1939g.–aprel' 1940g.)', *Novaya i Noveishaya Istoriya*, 5 (1962)
  *Vneshnyaya Politika Anglii, 1939–1941gg* (Moscow, 1963)

Niedhardt, G. *Grossbritannien und die Sowjetunion, 1939–1943* (Munich, 1972)

O'Connor, J. E. 'Laurence A. Steinhardt and American Policy toward the Soviet Union, 1939–1941', Ph.D. thesis (University of Virginia, 1968)

Petrov, V. (ed.) *'June 22, 1941': Soviet Historians and the German Invasion* (Chapel Hill, S. Carolina, 1968)

Pimelott, B. *Labour and the Left in the 1930s* (Cambridge, 1977)

Richardson, C. O. 'French Plans for Allied Attacks on the Caucasus Oil Fields, January–April 1940', *French Historical Studies*, 8 (1973)

Ross, G. 'Foreign Office Attitudes to the Soviet Union 1941–1945', *Journal of Contemporary History*, 16 (1981)
  'Operation Bracelet: Churchill in Moscow, 1942' in D. Dilks (ed.), *Retreat from Power* (2 vols., London, 1981)

Samsonov, A. M. 'Moskva v Oktyabre 1941 goda', *Istoriya SSSR*, 5 (1981)

Seaton, A. *The Russo-German War, 1941–5* (London, 1971)

Sella, A. ' "Barbarossa": Surprise Attack and Communication', *Journal of Contemporary History*, 13 (1978)

Sherwood, R. E. *Roosevelt and Hopkins: an Intimate History* (New York, 1950)

Stafford, D. A. 'SOE and British Involvement in the Belgrade Coup d'État of March 1941, *Slavic Review*, 3 (1977)

Taylor, A. J. P. *English History 1914–1945* (Harmondsworth, 1979)

Trukhanovskii, V. G. *Vneshnyaya politika Anglii v period vtoroi mirovoi voiny 1939–1945* (Moscow, 1965)

Tucker, R. C. 'The Emergence of Stalin's Foreign Policy', *Slavic Review*, 4 (1977)

Volkov, F. D. *SSSR-Angliya 1929–1945gg: Anglo-Sovetskie otnosheniya nakanune i v period vtoroi mirovoi voiny* (Moscow, 1964)

# Bibliography

'Neudavshiisya Pryzhok Rudol'f Gessa', *Novaya i Noveishaya Istoriya*, 6 (1968)

Weinberg, G. L. *Germany and the Soviet Union, 1939–1941* (Leiden, 1972)

Werth, A. *Russia at War, 1941–1945* (New York, 1964)

Whaley, B. *Codeword Barbarossa* (Cambridge, Mass., 1973)

Wheeler-Bennett, J. (ed.) *Action This Day* (London, 1968)

Wilson, T. A. *The First Summit: Roosevelt and Churchill at Placentia Bay 1941* (Boston, 1969)

Winterbotham, F. W. *The Ultra Secret* (London, 1974)

Woodward, L. *British Foreign Policy in the Second World War* (3 vols., London, 1970–1)

Zhilin, P. A. *Kak fashistskoi Germaniya gotovila napadenie na Sovetskii Soyuz* (Moscow, 1966)

# INDEX

Index

Bullard, Sir Reader, 209, 214, 215
Burgess, Guy, 264
Butler, R. A., 29, 31, 38, 97, 102, 131; and
Cripps' appointment in Moscow, 30, 31,
32, 34–5; and Cripps' recall, 145, 146;
and German–Soviet conflict, 115, 144;
on Halifax, 9; and Hess, 132; mediator
in Soviet–Finnish war, 15, 16, 18, 23,
24–5; protagonist of Cripps, 23, 31, 50,
63, 73, 95, 145, 301; position in FO, 11,
37, 101, 109
Butler, Neville, 131

Cabinet, British, 78, 128, 174, 176, 187,
188, 192, 238, 249, 265, 300; and
attitude to Soviet Union, xiii, 6, 83,
109, 112, 135, 145; and policy towards
Soviet Union after outbreak of war, 6–
7; during Winter War, 17–18, 23; and
bombing of Baku, 24; and Cripps'
appointment as ambassador, 32, 33, 35,
50; and Cripps in Moscow, 53–4, 60;
and FO's concept on relations with
Russia, 55, 81, 85, 109; and Soviet
annexation of Baltic, 63, 64, 65, 67–9,
71, 79, 109, 126, 282; and trade negotiations, 66; and Molotov's visit to
Berlin, 81, 82, 85; and Eden's Middle
East tour, 101; and Hess, 132; and
Cripps' recall, 146; and German intentions towards Russia, 150, 154, 164;
and aid to Russia, 167, 170–1, 177–8,
180, 184, 198, 216, 219, 221, 225, 257;
and Moscow Conference, 217, 218, 222,
231, 234, 236, 240–2, 246, 258; and
Eden's visit to Moscow, 274–6, 282,
285–7, 288; and recognition of Russia's
1941 frontiers, 190; and Cripps' return
to England, 207, 208, 227, 278, 293–5,
299
Cadbury, Laurence, 189, 230
Cadogan, Sir Alexander, 9, 38, 224, 258;
and Cripps, 8, 95–6; and Eden as
Foreign Secretary, 88–90, 95–6, 101;
influence in FO, 11, 88; opposed to
rapprochement with Russia, 8, 36;
opposed to Cripps' appointment to
Moscow, 37; and Cripps' early difficulties, 63; and Soviet annexation of

Baltic, 68; and Cripps' offer (Sept.
1940), 87, 89–90; and Moltov's visit to
Berlin, 82; and Eden's response to
Cripps' overtures, 109–10, 143–4; and
appreciation of German intentions, 113,
115, 117–18, 151, 155–6, 157–9, 168;
and Churchill's warning to Stalin, 118–
19, 122; and Hess, 132; and Cripps'
recall, 145; and aid to Russia, 183–4,
186, 188–9, 271–2; and the Polish problem, 192; with Eden in Moscow, 281
Carol, King, 46, 75
Caucasus, 124; projected British–French
bombing of Baku oilfields, 24, 26, 55,
104, 142, 151; oilfields threatened by
Germany, 164, 168, 177, 256, 268; proposed British bombing of oilfields (1941),
183, 229, 237, 276; as barrier to
German advance, 214, 229, 242, 255,
259, 260, 273, 277
Cavendish-Bentinck, Victor, 121, 139, 142,
171, 323n.
Cazalet, Victor, 277
Chamberlain, Neville, 1, 66, 88; and
bombing of Baku, 25, 26; in Churchill's
Cabinet, 57; and fall of France, 25–6;
and guarantees to Poland, 28; and
handling of foreign affairs, 9, 10; and
hostility to Russia, 8, 10, 11, 18–19, 25;
mistrusted by Russians, 6, 283
Channon, Henry, 16, 54
Chiang Kai-shek, 19
Chiang Kai-shek, Mme, 20
Chiefs of Staff Committee, 83, 176, 182,
233, 275; preconceived ideas on Russia,
xii, 6, 139, 221; and assistance to
Finland, 15, 18, 22; and appreciations of
German intentions, 143, 167, 171; and
aid to Russia, 167, 177–8, 181, 183, 185,
193–5, 198, 213, 217, 220–2, 229, 260,
269, 276–8; and Soviet resistance, 214,
220; and Moscow Conference, 222, 231;
and Polish issue, 237; and Mason-
Macfarlane, 266–7; and Eden's visit to
Moscow, 276
China, 19, 20, 102
Churchill, Sir Winston, 1, 55, 56, 100,
115, 131, 137, 182, 200; and *The Second
World War*, xi, 38, 49, 51, 81, 116, 118,

# Index

Hopkins, Harry, 193; and visit to Moscow, 198–202, 204–6, 213, 225, 234–6, 238, 240; and Moscow Conference, 216–18, 232–3
Hull, Cordell, 48, 71, 124–5, 170
Hungary, 71, 267

India, 81, 209, 238–9
Iran, 76, 81, 242, 256, 257, 260, 261; threatened by Germany, 142–3, 146, 229; Soviet–British invasion of, 209–15, 223–4, 231, 254
Ismay, Major-General Hastings, 26, 167–8, 231, 236, 242, 245–6
Italy, 8, 29, 75, 80
*Izvestiya*, 120

Japan, 75, 80, 81, 127, 161
Jodl, General A., 59
Johnson, Hewlett, 30
Joint Intelligence Committee, *see* Military Intelligence

Keitel, Field-Marshal W., 59
Kennedy, Joseph, 27
*Kent*, HMS, 278, 279
Khrushchev, N., 156, 159
Kiev, 194, 227
Kipling, R., 26
Kirkpatrick, I., 133
Kleist, Field-Marshal E., 227, 268
Kluge, Field-Marshal von, 279
Knatchbull-Hugessen, Sir Hugh, 79, 102, 105–6, 211
Kollontay, Alexandra, 97, 152
Korj, 100
Köstring, Ernst, 52, 58
Kot, Stanislaw, 237
Kuibyshev, 253–4, 256, 261, 268, 277–8, 291–2, 296
Kuznetsov, General F. I., 159

Labonne, M., 44, 46–7, 49, 50, 55
Labour Party, 207; policies towards Russia, xiii, 1, 26, 29, 284; and Winter War, xiii, 18, 26; Cripps' standing in, 1, 3, 31, 32, 73, 145, 165, 208, 223, 264, 294, 299, 300; and German invasion of Russia, 176, 218–19, 222; and post-war

government, xiii
Lansbury, George, 30
Lascelles, Dan, 32
Law, Richard, 73
League of Nations, 17
Libya, *see* Middle East
*Life*, 240
List, Field Marshal von, 115
Litvinov, Maxim, 42, 161, 240, 248, 291
Lloyd George, David, 33
Locarno Agreement (1925), 130
*London*, HMS, 235, 241
Lothian, Lord, 48, 70, 87

MacDonald, Ramsay, 3
Maclean, Fitzroy, 66
Macmillan, Harold, 259, 300
Macready, Lt.-General G. N., 231
'Maginot Line', 112
Maisky, Ivan, 49, 61, 68, 94, 96, 104, 115, 125, 183, 185, 269, 303n.; and Cripps, 9, 13, 30, 34–5, 62, 100, 131, 193; and Halifax, 11, 28, 58, 65; asserts Russia's neutrality, 5, 6; and Soviet invasion of Poland, 5; initiates trade negotiations, 11–14, 304n.; and Winter War, 15, 16, 17, 19–20, 23–4, 26; resumes trade negotiations, 25, 27–8; and Churchill's Cabinet, 28, 57–8; and Cripps' appointment to Moscow, 30, 34–5; seeks closer relations (May 1940), 49, 50; and Soviet annexation of Baltic, 70–1; and appreciation of British resistance, 72; and leaks to press, 82–3; and Molotov's visit to Berlin, 85, 94; and Eden as Foreign Secretary, 97–8; and appreciation of German intentions, 97, 119, 121, 124, 155–6; attempts improved relations (Nov. 1940–June 1941), 98, 100, 102, 111, 131, 144, 151; and Hess affair, 132–4, 147, 154; and Cripps' recall, 146, 148–9, 157–8; and Tass communiqué (14 June 1941), 155–60, 323n.; and German invasion, 162, 172–3; and aid to Russia, 166, 169, 171–2, 177–81, 186–7, 195, 198, 219–22, 224, 228–9, 255–6, 260, 267; and the Polish problem, 191, 192; and Hopkins' mission, 196, 198; and invasion of Iran, 211–12; and Moscow

357